THE SLOW DEATH OF THE DEATH PENALTY

The Slow Death of the Death Penalty

Toward a Postmortem

Edited by Todd C. Peppers, Mary Welek Atwell, and Jamie Almallen

NEW YORK UNIVERSITY PRESS
New York

NEW YORK UNIVERSITY PRESS
New York
www.nyupress.org

Library of Congress Cataloging-in-Publication Data

Names: Peppers, Todd C., editor. | Atwell, Mary Welek, 1943– editor. |
    Almallen, Jamie, editor.
Title: The slow death of the death penalty : toward a postmortem / edited
    by Todd C. Peppers, Mary Welek Atwell, and Jamie Almallen.
Description: New York : New York University Press, [2025] |
    Includes bibliographical references and index.
Identifiers: LCCN 2024039909 (print) | LCCN 2024039910 (ebook) |
    ISBN 9781479819638 (hardcover ; alk. paper) | ISBN 9781479819645
    (paperback ; alk. paper) | ISBN 9781479819669 (ebook) | ISBN 9781479819690
    (ebook other)
Subjects: LCSH: Capital punishment—United States. | Punishment—United States. |
    Criminal justice, Administration of—United States.
Classification: LCC HV8699.U5 S476 2025 (print) | LCC HV8699.U5 (ebook) |
    DDC 364.660973—dc23/eng20250207
LC record available at https://lccn.loc.gov/2024039909
LC ebook record available at https://lccn.loc.gov/2024039910

This book is printed on acid-free paper, and its binding materials are chosen for strength and durability. We strive to use environmentally responsible suppliers and materials to the greatest extent possible in publishing our books.

The manufacturer's authorized representative in the EU for product safety is Mare Nostrum Group B.V., Mauritskade 21D, 1091 GC Amsterdam, The Netherlands. Email: gpsr@mare-nostrum.co.uk.

Manufactured in the United States of America

10 9 8 7 6 5 4 3 2 1

Also available as an ebook

CONTENTS

Foreword   vii
Sister Helen Prejean

Introduction   1
Todd C. Peppers, Mary Welek Atwell, and Jamie Almallen

PART I: SYSTEMIC ISSUES WITH
THE DEATH PENALTY

1. Innocence and the Death Penalty: Transforming
   the National Debate   7
   Frank R. Baumgartner

2. The Hidden Costs of Capital Punishment: Beyond
   the Monetary   26
   Richard C. Dieter

PART II: THE CONDEMNED AND THEIR STORIES
3. Juveniles and the Death Penalty: A Failure of Law
   and Morality   45
   Bharat Malkani

4. Capital Sentencing and Mental Illness: Proportionality
   and Procedural Fairness   73
   Richard J. Bonnie

5. Gender Matters: The Execution of "Unwomanly" Women   93
   Mary Welek Atwell

6. Discrimination and Capital Punishment: Will Persistent
   Racism Seal the Fate of the U.S. Death Penalty?   120
   Ngozi Ndulue

PART III: ACTORS AND DECISION-MAKERS

7. Conflicted Justices and a Divided Court: The U.S. Supreme
   Court's Death Penalty Jurisprudence   139
   John D. Bessler

8. Leveling the Playing Field: Quality Representation
   in the Capital Defense Community   179
   Maya Pagni Barak and Jon B. Gould

9. Mitigation and the Death Penalty: Successes, Obstacles,
   and Forced Constraints   191
   Russell Stetler

10. The Capital Jury as the Community's Conscience:
    From Illusion to Reality (and Back Again?)   213
    Scott E. Sundby

11. The Death and Life of Clemency: Mercy versus Finality   233
    Laura Schaefer

PART IV: METHODS OF EXECUTION AND RATIONALE

12. The Fate of Lethal Injection: Decomposition of the
    Paradigm and Its Consequences   257
    *Austin Sarat, Mattea Denney, Nicolas Graber-Mitchell,
    Greene Ko, Rose Mroczka, and Lauren Pelosi*

13. Deterrence and the Death Penalty: A False Promise   290
    Michael L. Radelet

Acknowledgments   309

About the Contributors   311

About the Editors   315

Index   317

FOREWORD

SISTER HELEN PREJEAN

My introduction to the death penalty came in 1982, when I walked into the Angola State Prison to visit a death row inmate named Elmo Patrick Sonnier. At the time, I had no idea that my first meeting would lead to me serving as a spiritual adviser to both Sonnier and fellow inmate Robert Lee Willie. Nor did I have an inkling that the next four decades of my life would be dedicated to fighting capital punishment.

Over the last forty years, I have witnessed the horrifying rise of the death penalty as well as its slow decline. Through the 1980s and 1990s, prosecutors raced to see how many men and women they could sentence to death and execute. These defendants were disproportionately poor minorities who were assigned mediocre defense counsel and lacked the resources to file appeals challenging the fundamental procedural errors committed during their trials. Once on the row, they languished in an environment of violence and despair until the day they were marched to the death chamber and killed by electrocution or poison. And why didn't people care? Because it's easy to kill a prisoner whose humanity is overshadowed by their monstrous acts.

I am thankful that the battle waged against what Justice Harry Blackmun called "the machinery of death" has witnessed important victories. The United States Supreme Court has held that it is unconstitutional to execute the intellectually disabled and offenders who committed their crimes as juveniles. The Court has also held that the death penalty cannot be applied to offenses not involving murder. In the face of studies that show that the death penalty does not deter others from committing crimes and is more expensive than imposing life sentences, as well as media reports about the exoneration of almost two hundred death row inmates, public support for the death penalty has declined and almost half of states have abandoned the death penalty. As a result, new death penalty convictions have plunged from a high of 315 in 1996 to 20 in 2022; executions have followed a similar dramatic decline. Tragically, a handful of traditional pro–death penalty states have doubled down on their commitment to killing their citizens by embracing largely abandoned methods of execution (such as the firing squad) and threatening to expand the death penalty to a larger range of offenses.

The authors of the essays contained in this book explore why capital punishment is slowly dying. They hypothesize that the death penalty contains the seeds of its own destruction, as the many flaws found in the criminal justice system have led to injustices and abuses that our society can no longer stomach. These include the undeniable racism that has led to death rows filled with minorities. Poorly trained defense attorneys who lack the skills to mount a proper defense. The executions of the mentally ill. Botched executions. Clemency hearings driven by politics, not justice. The damning impact of gender in capital murder cases. The lack of funding for the effective presentation of mitigation evidence. The past prosecutions and executions of inmates who committed their crimes when they were still children. And the lack of any evidence that killing people reduces murder rates.

I pray for a time when it is no longer necessary for me to write introductions such as this one, because the death penalty has been abolished in every state in our country. Until then, I will lend my voice to the arguments presented in this book and continue to urge you, the reader, to consider the violence and futility of killing to show that killing is wrong.

Introduction

TODD C. PEPPERS, MARY WELEK ATWELL,
AND JAMIE ALMALLEN

On March 24, 2021, a historic event occurred at the Greensville Correctional Center, location of Virginia's death house and the site of over one hundred executions. After taking a tour of the death chamber and seeing firsthand the electric chair and lethal injection gurney, Governor Ralph Northam stepped outside, sat at a small table, and signed legislation ending Virginia's four-hundred-year practice of putting its citizens to death. Since the execution by firing squad of Captain George Kendall at Jamestown in 1608, Virginia has executed approximately 1,400 men, women, and children—more than any other state. Now, to the surprise of many, it became the first former Confederate state to abolish capital punishment.

At the signing ceremony, Governor Northam told the assembled crowd that "there is no place today for the death penalty in the commonwealth, in the South, or in this nation."[1] Specifically, Northam pointed to the racism and false convictions that plagued the "fundamentally flawed" system of capital punishment. "We can't give out the ultimate punishment without being 100% sure that we're right and we can't sentence people to that ultimate punishment knowing that the system doesn't work the same for everyone,"[2] said Northam. In support of his argument that Virginia judicial system had convicted and sentenced to death the innocent, Northam pointed to the case of Earl Washington Jr.—a mentally disabled Black man who was wrongly convicted for the sexual assault and murder of a young white mother. What Northam didn't add, however, was that Washington did not have an attorney when he was transferred to the death house and that his execution was stayed, and his case reinvestigated, because of the efforts of fellow death row inmate Joe Giarratano and a small team of death penalty activists.

While Virginia's decision to abolish the death penalty was out of step with other southern states, it was in keeping with a growing national trend; in the last two decades, ten states have outlawed capital punishment (Colorado, Connecticut, Delaware, Illinois, Maryland, New Hampshire, New Jersey, New Mexico, New York, and Washington) and another four states have adopted moratoriums ending executions (Arizona, California, Oregon, and Pennsylvania).[3] The abolition movement is driven by a number of factors, from the racially biased application of the ultimate punishment and the rising numbers of false convictions to concerns about the high litigation costs surrounding capital murder trials and appeals.

In states that have retained the death penalty, prosecutions, convictions, and executions have fallen dramatically over the last two decades. State attorneys seeking the death penalty now face talented and well-trained defense attorneys, which makes death sentences harder to obtain and appeals of convictions more likely to be successful. Juries now have the opportunity at sentencing hearings to hear from mitigation specialists, who offer compelling reasons why a death sentence is not just. The Supreme Court has outlawed the death penalty in cases involving minors or the intellectually disabled, thereby shrinking the pool of potential capital murder cases. And the population of death row is declining, in part due to an alarming number of exonerations.

Outside of the criminal justice system, public support for capital punishment continues to decline, as scholars, journalists, and death penalty activists share studies and stories about the high costs of capital cases, the lack of evidence of its deterrent effect, and the brutality of state-sanctioned death. A recent Gallup poll reported that public support for the death penalty is at a fifty-year low,[4] and for the first time since polling began twenty years prior, a slim majority of Americans expressed concerns that the death penalty is not fairly administered.[5]

We do not want to create the impression, however, that the death penalty has disappeared. Capital murder trials and executions continue across the United States, albeit in substantially reduced numbers. In 2023, twenty-one defendants were sentenced to death in courtrooms across seven states. And in the same year, only twenty-four executions were carried out in Alabama, Florida, Missouri, Oklahoma, and Texas. These numbers are dwarfed by the killing sprees of previous decades, where in

1999 alone, 279 defendants were sentenced to death and another ninety-eight were executed.[6] Nevertheless, the executions continue.

In those states that cling to the death penalty, a renewed and aggressive embrace of capital punishment has emerged. New (gas) and old (firing squad) methods of execution have been adopted. Basic rights of condemned men have been cruelly challenged, as in the efforts by Alabama and Texas to deny inmates access to clergy during the final days and hours of their lives; Texas even unsuccessfully tried to prevent ministers from saying prayers in the death house in the moments before an execution. Florida recently passed legislation extending the death penalty for the rape (not murder) of a child, notwithstanding clear Supreme Court precedent to the contrary. And the United States Department of Justice is pursuing the death penalty in the murder trial of self-avowed white supremist Peyton Gendron, despite President Joseph Biden's campaign pledge to end capital punishment in federal prosecutions. In short, it would be premature to pronounce that the death penalty is dead across all states and jurisdictions. But its power and destructive impact is waning.

The idea for this book project was sparked by a gruesome post-execution ritual. Under Virginia law, an inmate's body was not released to the family until an autopsy was performed and the cause of death determined. So after the condemned had two thousand volts of electricity run through his body or a fatal cocktail of medications injected into his veins, his corpse was sent to the state medical examiner's office. Organs were weighed. Fluids were tested. Stomach contents analyzed. And, finally, the cause of death was determined and the box on the form next to "homicide" was checked. Having confirmed what every participant in the execution already knew, this final indignity concluded, and the mutilated remains were given to the decedent's loved ones for burial. For those inmates who wanted to be organ donors, the autopsy meant that their wish to give back to society could not be granted—the procedure ruined all viable organic materials.

Taking our cue from Virginia, we decided to put together a collection of essays that would constitute, in effect, an autopsy of capital publishment; our authors have done a postmortem on the death penalty to determine the pathologies that have caused its illness and death. Racism. Sexism. Mediocre defense counsel. Conviction-prone juries. Botched executions. Poorly presented mitigation evidence. The lack of a deterrent effect. Inconsistency in case law. Cost. A politicized clemency process. The thread that runs through these essays is that the death penalty as a public policy carries the seeds of its own destruction—pathologies that drive the push toward abolition.

Unlike the autopsies performed on Virginia's dead, our dissection of the death penalty has a rational purpose. The findings presented in this postmortem confirm the systemic and fatal flaws in a criminal justice system that has taken sixteen thousand lives since colonial times, flaws that persist despite reform efforts. We hope that these essays convince current lawmakers in states with the death penalty to push for abolition and persuade future lawmakers that the capital punishment corpse cannot be revived and repaired.

Notes

1 Amy Friedenberger, "Va. Ends Death Penalty," *Roanoke Times*, March 25, 2021.
2 Frank Green, "'It's the Moral Thing to Do': Virginia's Death Penalty Abolished in Historic Signing," *Richmond Times-Dispatch*, March 25, 2021.
3 "States with and without the Death Penalty—2024," Death Penalty Information Center, https://deathpenaltyinfo.org/.
4 Jeffrey M. Jones, "Death Penalty Support Holding at Five-Decade Low," Gallup, November 18, 2021, https://news.gallup.com/.
5 Megan Brenan, "New 47% Low Say Death Penalty Is Fairly Applied in U.S.," Gallup, November 6, 2023, https://news.gallup.com/.
6 Death Penalty Information Center, *Facts about the Death Penalty* (Washington, DC: Death Penalty Information Center, August 30, 2024), https://deathpenaltyinfo.org/.

PART I

Systemic Issues with the Death Penalty

1

Innocence and the Death Penalty

Transforming the National Debate

FRANK R. BAUMGARTNER

In the "modern" period of the death penalty since the *Furman v. Georgia*[1] decision in 1972, over nine thousand individuals have been sentenced to death. Almost 1,600 have been executed, and about 2,400 remain on the various death rows in those states that still have capital punishment. That means that fewer than 20 percent of all those condemned to die have been put to death, and about 30 percent remain on death row today. Where are the other five thousand individuals, and how can it be that they represent a majority of all those sentenced to death since *Furman*? These individuals have seen their sentences overturned on appeal or they have died while on death row. Among those whose sentences were overturned, some were resentenced to long prison terms or to life, some received a governor's commutation (removing them from death row, but not from prison), and some were released from prison entirely. The number of individuals exonerated after having been convicted and then sentenced to death stands at 188, as of the close of 2023.[2]

Sentencing an individual to die in a formal legal proceeding, and later removing the threat of death, often after years of legal appeals, is the single most likely outcome of a death sentence in the modern system. Readers should consider what that means: a solemn pronouncement that one shall die for one's crimes, only later to be reversed. Many times, the successful appeal is followed by a second death sentence, and in some cases that second death sentence is in turn reversed, and the cycle repeats. Sister Helen Prejean has referred to this as a system of state torture.[3] One form of torture is to impose a harm, remove the person from the harm, and repeat the cycle. Sometimes, Sister Helen writes, individuals come to seek out the punishment that they fear so much. The anticipation of the harm can grow to be worse than the harm itself. The United States death penalty system does this routinely.

Most people are not aware of the inefficiency of the death penalty. People expect and assume that a death sentence, once handed down so solemnly by the judge, will be carried out. In fact, about 70 percent are later overturned. And there has been one full exoneration, with the individual walking away with their liberty restored, for every eight people executed. As the public becomes more informed, the fact that there is such a high error rate has shaken people's confidence in the death penalty and contributed mightily to its long-term decline. This chapter focuses on these surprising inefficiencies and their effects on public opinion and on the decline of the death penalty.

Previous reviews have explored the "discovery of innocence,"[4] the most common causes of wrongful convictions,[5] the growth of the innocence movement,[6] and the impact of wrongful convictions on public opinion.[7] Similarly, various reviews have explored the reasons for the decline of death penalty usage nationally.[8] This chapter makes use of some of the information contained in these histories but does not repeat all the information there. Rather, this overview explores the process by which the innocence argument transformed the debate about the death penalty away from an abstract one focused on whether or not there is a moral justification for capital punishment. By moving the conversation to the practical realities, on the ground, associated with the actual administration of the death penalty system, the innocence movement opened a line of questioning that has ballooned into a wholesale critique of the death penalty, not as a moral construct, but as a practical matter. Of course, many of those involved in developing various arguments against the death penalty are morally convinced that the death penalty is wrong, and they may be motivated by these moral concerns. The focus here is not the motivations of the actors within the system, but rather the impact on the development of the national debate about capital punishment of this shift from the abstract to the practical. It has been profound.

Moving from an abstract to a practical frame of reference is closely related to assessing the "Marshall hypothesis."[9] In his concurring opinion in *Furman*, Justice Thurgood Marshall famously stated that public opinion on the death penalty is less interesting than what it would be if people were fully informed about the facts of the death penalty. Marshall wrote, "In other words, the question with which we must deal is not whether a substantial proportion of American citizens would today, if polled, opine that capital punishment is barbarously cruel, but whether they would find it to be so in the light of all information presently available."[10] That is, Marshall was not very concerned with public opinion because he assumed that most members of the public did not know much about how the death penalty system actually functions—a set of facts with which he was acutely familiar. If they knew more, they would not like what they saw. If they knew little about it, they might have false assumptions about how it works. Marshall knew very well that most individuals had little knowledge about the death penalty; this is important to keep in mind today as well. By moving toward an evaluation of the practical administration of the system, rather than its value in the abstract, the debate moved in a direction suggested by Marshall's insights.

This chapter reviews many elements that may surprise. Bringing attention to these surprising practical shortcomings of the death penalty system has had the impact that Justice Marshall would have expected.

A System Prone to Errors and Reversals

One might think that a death sentence would be handed down only after the most careful processes to guarantee accuracy. Such a thought or assumption would be strongly at odds with the facts. Capital trials often take place in a highly charged emotional atmosphere. After all, they have in common that there has been a terrible crime. To be sure, these are not always the worst crimes, as many scholars have documented.[11] Still, the prosecutor decided that the crime merited a capital prosecution, and a judge or a jury agreed. Emotions, particularly anger and revulsion, can be strong. Many trials involve a significant focus on the details of the crime and how the victim may have suffered. After listening to these details, there can be no wonder that many jurors are angry, upset, and want to do something to "send a signal" that such crimes will not be tolerated.

It is not the place here to dissect any possible errors in any particular trials. Rather, the point is to have in mind that capital murder trials are murder trials first and foremost. To convince a jury to put the defendant to death as a punishment for the crime, a prosecutor must lay out evidence that the crime was truly awful. This requires emotional appeals. So capital trials are emotional, not sterile, affairs. They have to be. However, our collective emotional desire to "do something" may have an effect on the high rates of error that we see in capital trials. Note that a finding of innocence requires a discovery of error in the finding of guilt. But when a death penalty is reversed on appeal to a lesser sentence, that is also an acknowledgement of a significant error in the process, even if a lesser one than when an innocent person is sentenced to death. When a guilty person is sentenced to death and, on review, courts determine that they deserve a lesser punishment, that is also an important finding of error. And it is very common.

Figure 1.1 lays out the outcomes of capital sentences across the United States since 1972. It shows the outcomes of 9,011 death sentences from the *Furman* decision (June 1972) to the end of 2023.

The single most likely outcome of a death sentence, affecting 4,047 individuals, is that the sentence was overturned. Generally, this means a sentence of life in prison, but it could mean a lesser sentence, and it includes the 188 individuals mentioned earlier who were fully exonerated. Although it may sometimes take decades to see this reversal, it is the most

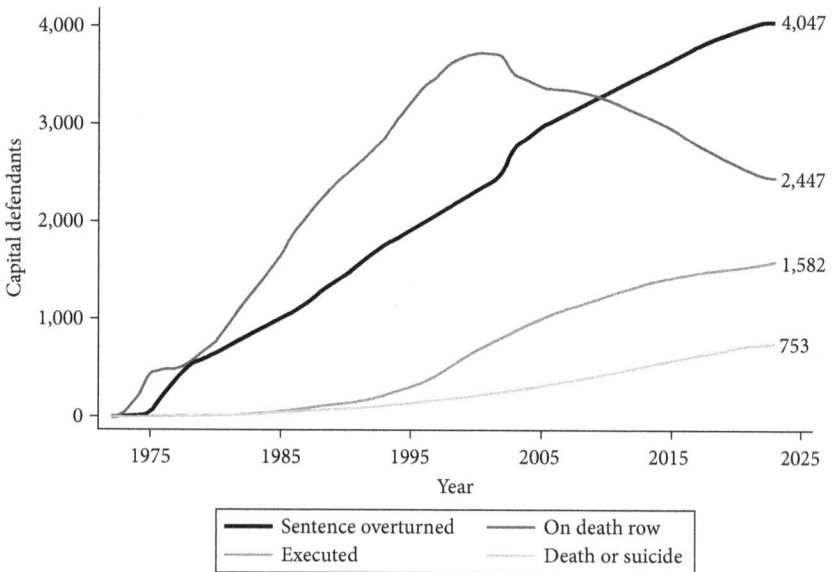

Figure 1.1: Death Sentence Outcomes, 1972–2023

likely outcome. The second most common outcome of a death sentence is nothing at all: 2,447 individuals have been moved to death row, and there they remain today. Many have been there for decades. The state has not carried out the execution, and the sentence has not been changed.

This "warehousing" outcome is particularly common in California, which has sentenced almost 1,100 individuals to death, executed only thirteen of them, and retains almost seven hundred individuals on death row as of 2023. The federal government had also executed very few inmates (just three) until thirteen executions were carried out in the period of July 2020 through January 2021, the last months of the Trump administration. Pennsylvania is a third example, with just three executions from more than four hundred death sentences. Some states, in other words, have many death sentences but almost no executions. Individuals either remain on death row for decades under a hypothetical sentence of death or they see their sentences eventually reversed to terms of years or life.

With approximately 9,011 death sentences and 1,582 executions, fewer than 20 percent of the condemned are executed. The number who have died in prison, whether by suicide, violence, or disease, is 753, or about 8 percent of those condemned. We should also note that the Death Penalty Information Center (DPIC) lists 150 of those executed as being "volunteers": individuals who have effectively committed suicide by government by instructing their attorneys to drop all appeals. Leaving aside the morality of this issue and the use of the term *volunteer* to refer to a prisoner who might be acting under a severe mental illness, this suggests that about 10 percent of the executions actually carried out were based on a truncated appeals process that might well have led to the reversal of the sentence.

This overview of death sentence outcomes makes clear that executions eventually follow from only about 20 percent of all death sentences. Other outcomes are much more likely: languishing for decades with no action, or reversal. Reversals, of course, can come in many stripes. The next section explores those further.

Exonerations and Other Types of Reversals

Figure 1.2 shows the breakdown of the 4,047 reversals from figure 1.1, distinguishing among those resentenced to a sentence of life, those

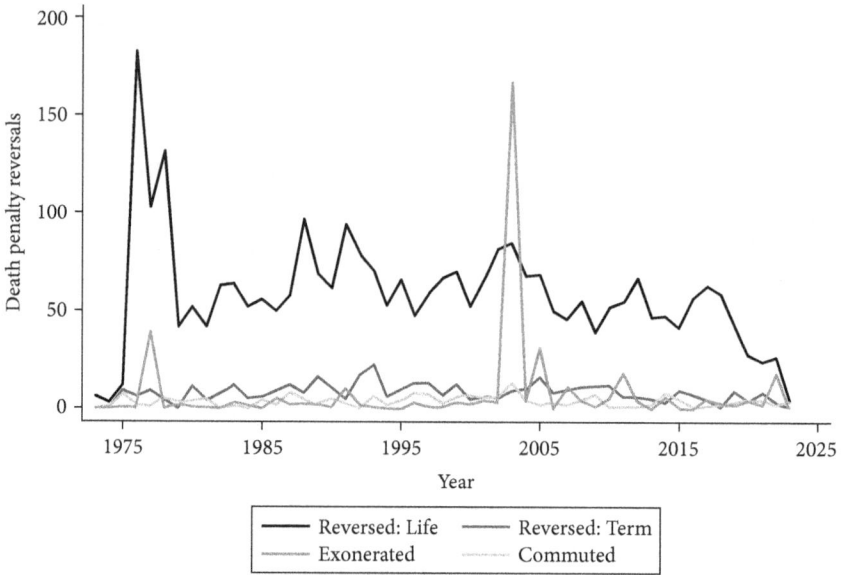

Figure 1.2: Various Forms of Death Sentence Reversals

resentenced to a sentence with a term of years, those whose sentences were commuted, and those who were exonerated.

By far the most common outcome of a death sentence reversal is that the individual is resentenced to a term of life in prison. In the earliest years of the modern period, this sometimes happened to entire groups of death row inhabitants as state laws were ruled unconstitutional in *Gregg v. Georgia*[12] and other decisions. For example, at the same time as *Gregg*, the Court ruled in *Woodson v. North Carolina*[13] and *Roberts v. Louisiana*[14] that those states' sentencing systems, which mandated death for everyone convicted of a capital-eligible crime, were unconstitutional. The Court ruled that every death sentence must be an individual determination, not an automatic one. These decisions were handed down at the same time that the Court accepted the Georgia, Florida, and Texas systems, which were different from each other but which all allowed some form of individualized assessment not only of the crime, but also of the offender.[15] These decisions invalidated the mandatory death sentence schemes from North Carolina and Louisiana, requiring over one hundred inmates to be resentenced to a life term in prison. At the time, this was a sentence that allowed for parole (most states adopted "life without the possibility of parole").[16] Overall, 3,102 condemned individuals have been resentenced to terms of life.

The next most common form of death sentence reversal is to see the sentence reduced to a term of years; 408 individuals have seen this outcome. Commutations by state governors have occurred in 381 cases, making this the third most common form of reversal. Finally, there are the 188 exonerations. Before we move to the exonerations, figure 1.3 reviews the commutations, because these have some peculiar and troubling characteristics.

Commutations were once a common feature of death penalty jurisprudence. Before World War II, it was not uncommon for states to have mandatory death sentence systems and for judges to petition the governors recommending commutations, even as they transmitted the required death notices. Governors granted these requests in large numbers, and this was considered a regular part of the system, with the governor acting as a "safety valve" or fail-safe to ensure individuals who did not deserve the ultimate punishment were spared from it.[17]

In the modern period, however, governors are loath to use this power, though they all retain it in some form. In fact, no year has seen more

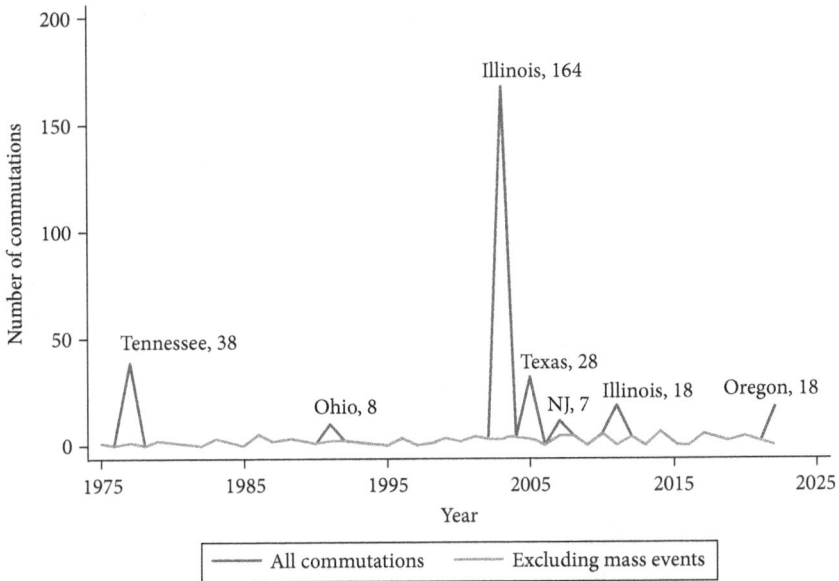

Figure 1.3: Commutations

than six commutations nationwide, other than what I refer to here as "mass events." Mass events are ones where governors commute the sentences of entire groups of individuals. Generally, this has come on the heels of troubling information about the reliability of the convictions for large numbers of condemned individuals. The most notable of these events was the time that Illinois governor George Ryan pardoned four individuals he found to be innocent and commuted the sentences of the remaining 164 individuals under sentence of death in his state.[18] Such events, as the figure shows, have occurred in Tennessee (1977), Ohio (1991), Texas (2005), New Jersey (2007, associated with the abolition of the state's death penalty law), Illinois (2011, again associated with abolition), and Oregon (2022, associated with a near abolition consisting of a severe restriction in the number of death-eligible crimes, such that no individual then on death row in the state would have qualified under the new statute). These incidents seem to accelerate the movement toward abolition. Fellow essayist Laura Schaefer provides more context on clemency in chapter 11 of this volume.

Exonerations, numbering 188 in the modern time, have slowly accumulated. Figure 1.4 shows the cumulative number of exonerations over time, based on the date of the exoneration.

Exonerations have come in a steady stream, generally a handful in each year, with more in the late 1990s and early 2000s, but no single time showed a surge, and no single period lacked exonerations; they are a steady part of the system, year in and year out. Generally, the reasons for capital exonerations are similar to those for other exonerations. Official misconduct is the single most common contributing factor (82% of cases studied in a recent DPIC report included official misconduct).[19] Every single case studied there had either official misconduct, perjury or false accusation, or false or misleading forensic evidence, and more than three quarters of the cases studied had at least two of these factors simultaneously. An individual cannot be released from a sentence of death and fully exonerated on the basis of a rumor or innuendo (nor can their sentence be overturned to a lesser sentence). There must be powerful evidence of a major flaw in the conviction, trial, or sentencing phase. For exoneration cases, the guilt phase of the trial must be undermined by demonstrable and serious errors. Perjured testimony, false or misleading forensics, and exculpatory evidence withheld from

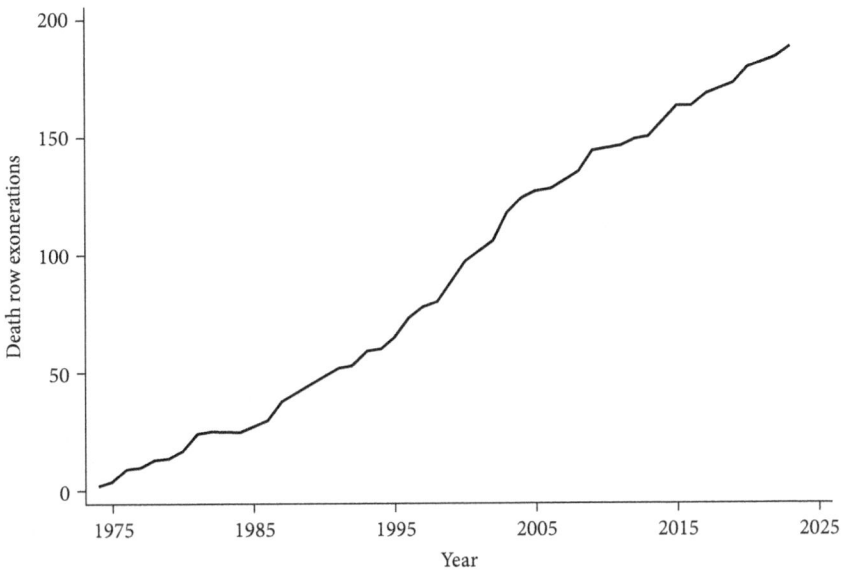

Figure 1.4: Cumulative Death Row Exonerations

the defense are common problems in these cases. The National Registry of Exonerations, which included over 3,400 cases (not limited to capital crimes) as of the end of 2023, also lists perjury or false accusation and official misconduct as leading contributing factors.[20]

Media Discovery of Death Row Innocence

Figure 1.4 showed that there was no particular spike in the number of death row exonerations. A few occur each and every year. Media attention to the issue, however, is a different story. Even though the United States has had wrongfully convicted individuals in its prisons, on death rows, and at the gallows since at least the Salem witch trials, the concern about making a mistake and convicting an innocent person was not a large part of the debate. Specialists knew of it; Edward Borchard published a book about it in 1932, aptly titled *Convicting the Innocent*.[21] Borchard told chilling stories of individuals coming to watch persons being executed for the crime of having killed them, when they had simply fled from the state, and he provided other examples that made clear that judicial errors in capital cases were not only possible but had indeed occurred. Michael Radelet, Hugo Bedau, and Constance Putnam published a similar book, *In Spite of Innocence*, in 1992.[22] There is no doubt that some people were paying attention.

However, the "innocence frame" was not a major part of the debate. Media coverage of capital punishment rarely focused on innocence until there was a surge of attention to the concept in the late 1990s and early 2000s. Baumgartner, De Boef, and Boydstun documented the shift in media frames in great detail, showing a dramatic shift in anti–death penalty news stories around the year 2000 and a spike in attention to issues related to innocence.[23]

The detailed analysis of media frames associated with the death penalty from Baumgartner, De Boef, and Boydstun makes clear several things. First, the "discovery of innocence" was abrupt; there had been very little attention to the issue before the mid-1990s, and there was no particular spike in exonerations that caused the change. Second, this shift drove a downward movement in the "tone" of media coverage of the death penalty: it became more critical. Third, the shift from positive/neutral coverage to negative stories about capital punishment had a demonstrable effect on public opinion. Over time, as opinion was affected by these shifting terms of debate, it moved toward greater opposition to the death penalty. The next section focuses on these trends.

Public Response to the Multiple False Convictions of the Death Penalty System

Hundreds of public opinion surveys have been conducted since the 1930s regarding Americans' views on the death penalty. And while Justice Marshall said he was not interested in public opinion because the public was not well informed on the matter, others disagree. The state of public opinion correlates very closely with the number of death sentences imposed nationwide. When the public turned more punitive in the 1970s and through the mid-1990s, death sentences rose, as did other harsh criminal justice policies. As opinion has moved back from those punitive positions, critiques of mass incarceration have become more common among our political leaders, and death sentences have declined. Figure 1.5 updates an overall index of public opinion on the death penalty

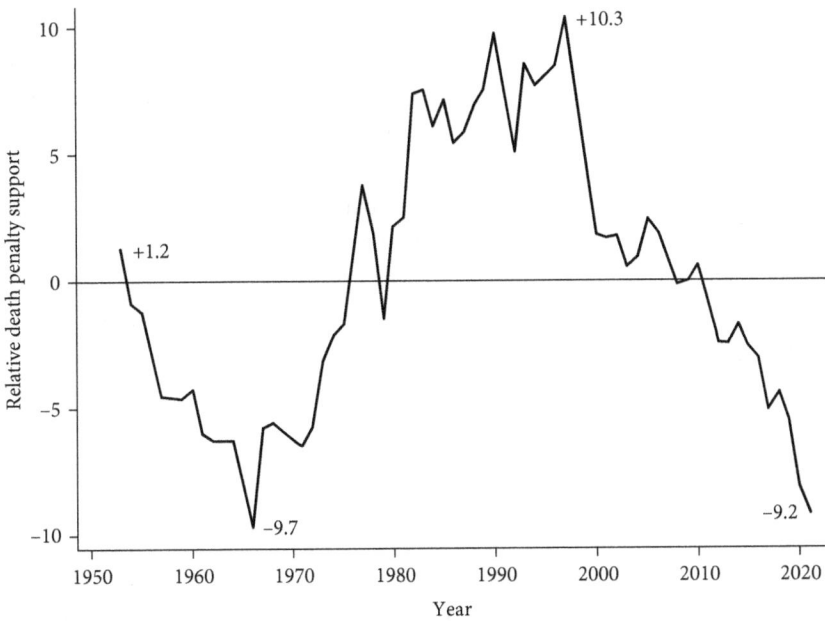

Figure 1.5: Index of Public Opinion Concerning the Death Penalty

first presented by Baumgartner, De Boef, and Boydstun in 2008[24] and later updated by Baumgartner et al.[25] This version is based on 448 polls about the death penalty asking questions with identical wording by the same survey organization at least twice in the period from 1953 to 2021. The most common was the familiar Gallup poll question, posed fifty-seven times: "Do you favor or oppose the death penalty for persons convicted of murder?" In total, there were sixty-five different questions. A methodology developed by the political scientist James Stimson[26] allows the inclusion of these diverse questions into a single index, making use of the maximum amount of information. Because the questions differ, we cannot interpret the resulting index score as supportive of or opposed to the death penalty. Rather, we can assess whether it is moving in the direction of more support or less support, and we can assess how it compares with previous periods in time. Figure 1.5 shows that public opinion support started declining sharply just at the time when the innocence argument began its rapid surge, and that opinion today stands at its lowest point since 1966.

U.S. public opinion on the death penalty has varied dramatically over time, and these changes have corresponded with public policy. The last execution of the pre-*Furman* period took place in 1965, just as support for the death penalty was reaching its low point. The response to *Furman* and the rise in crime during the 1970s saw a sharp and long-lasting increase in public support for capital punishment (and harsh criminal justice policies in general) that peaked in the mid-1990s, a full generation later. Since that time, with the discovery of innocence, an even sharper decline in support has occurred, leading the series to end at a point similar to its historical minimum.

The Public Policy Response to the Crisis of Confidence in Capital Punishment

As public opinion began to shift away from ever-increasing support for punitive criminal justice policies in general[27] and capital punishment in particular, concerns about innocence was likely the single most important contributor to that shift. But as the shift has accelerated, several other factors have come into play. Whether we look at public opinion or the arguments used in legislative debates, it is clear that the anti–death penalty movement has been ascendant since the early 2000s. Common arguments about the death penalty now focus on whether it costs too much; whether states are capable of procuring the relevant lethal injection drugs they need; whether their staffs are properly trained to carry out these protocols without inflicting needless suffering; and whether the death penalty is racially biased in its application, particularly with regard to the race of the victim of a capital crime.

The simple point is that the innocence movement began a shift in the conversation, in the nature of the public debate about capital punishment. By moving the debate from centering on the abstract morality of the death penalty to focusing on its logistics and whether the government can be counted on to administer such a system without error, the innocence argument spawned many other troublesome discussions about the practical value of capital punishment. Looking closely at the system itself as it actually operates (as opposed to an abstraction of how it should operate in principle), it is clear that it has many failings.

The previous sections touched on a few of those failings, but there are many others. For example, many on death row suffer from severe mental illnesses. Many were young when they committed their crimes, although after *Roper* they had to have passed their eighteenth birthday. Many were under the profound influence of drugs or alcohol at the time of their crimes. The system has been shown to be arbitrary with respect to both geography (e.g., the same crime may be many times more likely to lead to a death sentence if it occurs in one location rather than another) and time (e.g., the same crime was more likely to lead to a death sentence and possible execution in 1995 than in 2015). Currently, executions often occur after the inmate has already served decades on death row, sometimes more than thirty years. row. In sum, no one would design a death penalty system like the one that operates today. As we shift our collective attention away from the abstract question of whether we would support a hypothetical death penalty system to evaluate whether we support the one we actually have, opinions have turned much more negative. And public policy has followed this shift in opinion.

Declining Use of the Death Penalty

The death penalty has never been used much, in the context of the vast numbers of homicides the United States experiences every year. It has not been uncommon in the modern period to see over twenty thousand homicides per year, according to FBI statistics. And yet, no year has seen even 320 death sentences, and we have never seen more than ninety-eight executions in one year. Death sentences are given to a very small share of homicide offenders, and executions (as discussed above) are imposed on fewer than 20 percent of the condemned. Since 1976, there has been a cumulative total of approximately one million homicides and exactly 1,583 executions (through 2023). This equates to 0.15 percent of homicides. So it is wrong to think that the death penalty ever has been a statistically large part of the criminal justice system. Small as it always has been, though, it is vanishing before our eyes.

Several indicators illustrate this movement away from capital punishment. One is the number of states or other jurisdictions that have a capital punishment statute. Figure 1.6 shows these numbers.

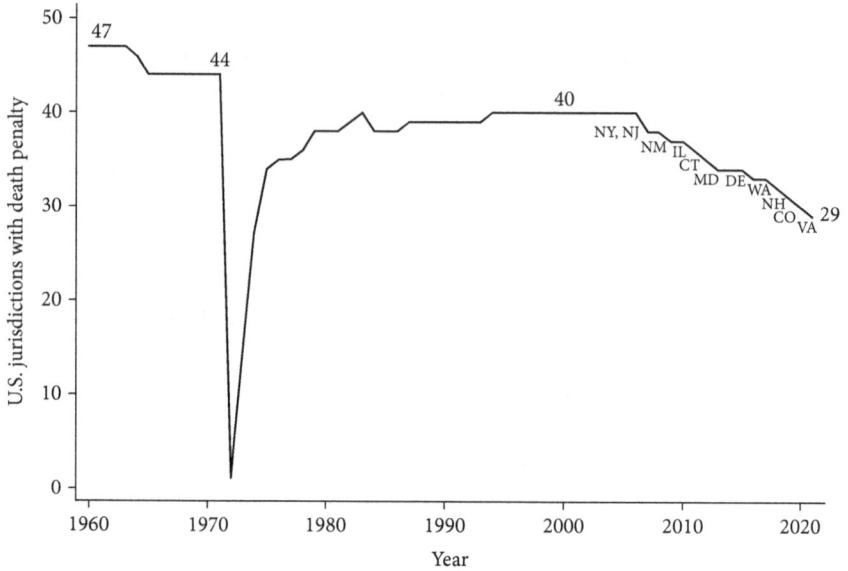

Figure 1.6: Number of U.S. Jurisdictions with Capital Punishment

Counting the fifty states, the District of Columbia, the federal government, and the United States military, there are fifty-three jurisdictions of
interest. As of 1960, forty-seven of these had a valid death penalty law on
the books. These were all invalidated by the *Furman* decision in 1972. By
the end of that year, only Florida had restored its death penalty statute.
By about 1980, the number of jurisdictions had risen to forty, where it
stayed for over two decades with little movement in one direction or
the other. Beginning in 2006, however, eleven jurisdictions eliminated
the death penalty: New York, New Jersey, New Mexico, Illinois, Connecticut, Maryland, Delaware, Washington, New Hampshire, Colorado, and,
in 2021, Virginia. Three states—Pennsylvania, Oregon, and California—
have moratoria on executions, though they have not eliminated death
sentencing processes. Oregon has virtually abolished it by adopting a
statute that severely restricts the applicability of the death penalty to only
a small set of possible crimes and removing all the people from death
row who were convicted under the previous statute. No state has reinstituted the death penalty, or adopted it for the first time, since Kansas
adopted it in 1994. Eleven states have abolished since 2006. So the trend
is clear.

Another way to assess trends is to look not at the statute books but at patterns of actual use of the punishment. Figures 1.7 and 1.8 report the total numbers of death sentences and executions as well as the numbers of counties and the numbers of states from which they came.

Figure 1.7 focuses on death sentences. These peaked in 1986 and 1996 with 326 and 313 death sentences; respectively; after this period of high usage (shown in the thick black line), the annual numbers declined sharply and steadily. In the period from 2016 to 2023, there was an average of just 28.5, a decline of over 90 percent.

The dotted line in figure 1.7 shows the numbers of counties from which the death sentences derived. The United States has over 3,100 counties, but the maximum value on this measure of death penalty usage was 205, in 1986. In no other year was the number as high as 200, and by 2004 it had declined to below 100. This sharp decline has continued as well, with an average of just twenty-five in the period from 2016 through 2023. The gap between these two figures represents individual counties that sentenced multiple individuals to death in the same year. The counties surrounding the cities of Los Angeles, Philadelphia, Chicago, and Houston sometimes sentenced more than ten individuals to death in

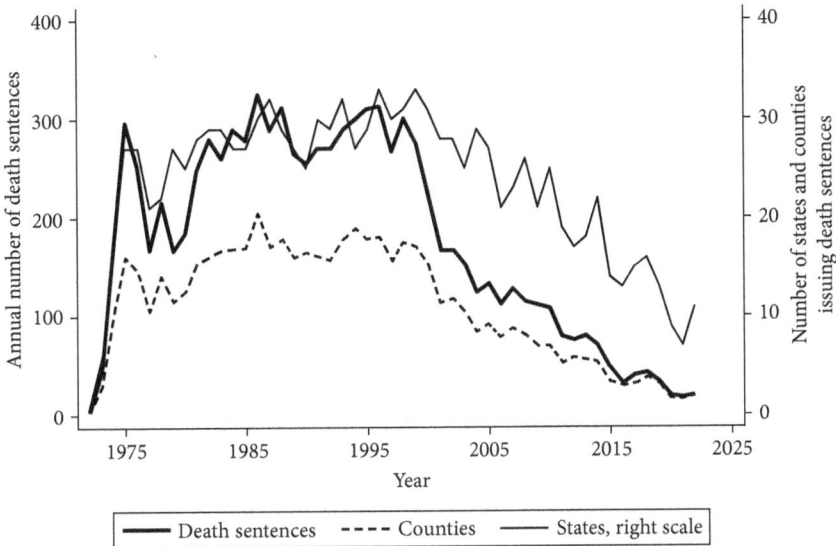

Figure 1.7: Annual Number of Death Sentences and the Number of States and Counties Issuing Them

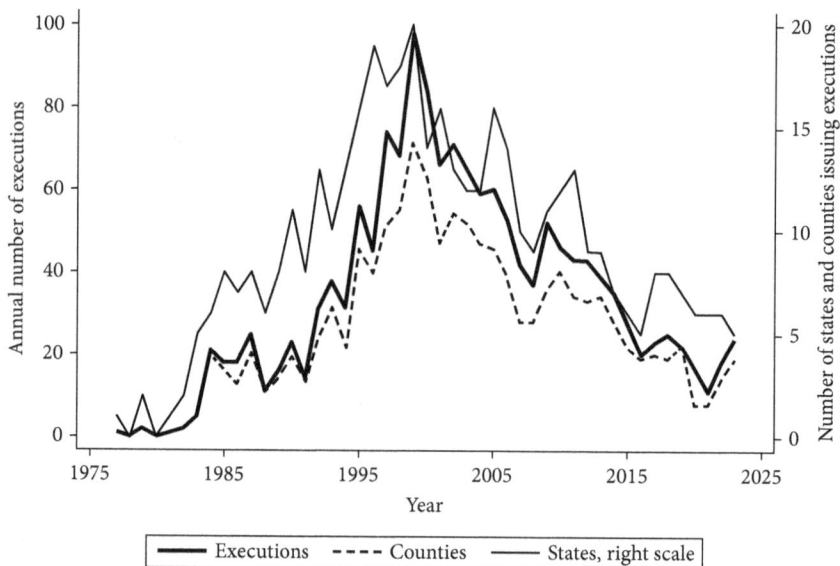

Figure 1.8: Annual Number of Executions and the Number of States and Counties Issuing Them

a single year during the period of peak death penalty usage, generally from the mid-1980s through about 2000. Since 2015, the number of death sentences and the number of counties imposing them is almost the same; this means that almost no counties are imposing more than one death sentence per year. And of course, with about twenty or fewer counties imposing death sentences from a total of over 3,100 counties, it is an extremely rare event. Finally, the thinner solid line in the figure shows how many states imposed at least one death sentence; this value reaches a peak of thirty-three states in 1996 and declines to a value of just seven states in 2021.

Just as figure 1.7 showed with regard to death sentences, figure 1.8 shows that executions rose from the early period through the late 1990s, reaching a peak of ninety-eight executions stemming from seventy-one counties and twenty states in 1999. Since then, these numbers have declined to just eleven executions (2021), five states (2016, 2023), and eight counties (2020, 2021). The number of distinct states carrying out an execution may be a singularly important indicator of "evolving standards of decency" for the Court, and if that number were to be reduced much further from the five or six that we have seen in recent years (no year since 2011 has seen more than ten states carry out an execution), the argument that such a punishment was "cruel and unusual" might gain greater empirical weight. If only a few states carry it out, at what point is it "unusual"? This is a question that the Court will decide, but the data trends reviewed here suggest that the question may soon be posed.

Conclusion

This chapter has reviewed a number of troubling facts about the death penalty. If we look at the system in detail to examine how it actually works, we see that it does not work very well. A focus on innocence is, of course, a partial but important element of the debate about the death penalty, but no matter what the number of innocents may be, most of those sentenced to death are guilty of the underlying crime. Yet, the innocence argument generated an important change in the death penalty debate that goes well beyond an assessment of whether the United States or any particular state has executed innocent individuals, and whether such a thing is acceptable. The innocence debate shifted the focus of debate away from abstract principles about whether the death penalty is morally acceptable or whether it deters crime, elements of the debate that previously dominated. Since the mid-1990s, attention has focused on the practical realities of the death penalty system—that is, how it really works and what its empirical flaws may be. Does it in fact target the worst of the worst? Is it applied fairly across geographic locations? Is it racially biased? Is it acceptable to have a death penalty where 70 percent of the cases are later overturned? Are lethal injection protocols designed to prevent suffering? Do corrections officials have the training to follow these protocols? The questions continue. The shift from abstract to practical considerations in evaluating the death penalty has been a sea change. And this all stemmed from the "discovery of innocence."

As attention moved from the abstract to the practical, public opinion turned against the death penalty. Looking at the practicalities, few like what they see. As opinion shifted, so did usage. Eleven states have abolished the death penalty in the past fifteen years, and none has established or reestablished it in thirty years. Death sentences and executions have declined by very large percentages since their peaks in the mid-1990s, and the number of states and counties carrying them out suggest that the U.S. Supreme Court may one day be faced with the question of whether a punishment is constitutionally acceptable if it is applied only in a few states or counties.

Notes

1 *Furman v. Georgia*, 408 U.S. 238 (1972).
2 The "innocence list" compiled by the Death Penalty Information Center includes 196 death row exonerations. Eight of these relate to death sentences imposed before *Furman*, and for consistency I exclude them from this analysis.
3 Helen Prejean, *The Death of Innocents: An Eyewitness Account of Wrongful Executions* (New York: Random House, 2005).
4 Frank R. Baumgartner, Suzanna L. De Boef, and Amber E. Boydstun, *The Decline of the Death Penalty and the Discovery of Innocence* (New York: Cambridge University Press, 2008).
5 Brandon L. Garrett, *Convicting the Innocent: Where Criminal Prosecutions Go Wrong* (Cambridge, MA: Harvard University Press, 2011).
6 Robert J. Norris, *Exonerated: A History of the Innocence Movement* (New York: New York University Press, 2017).
7 Robert J. Norris, William D. Hicks, and Kevin J. Mullinix, *The Politics of Innocence: Wrongful Convictions, State Policy, and Public Opinion in the United States* (New York: New York University Press, 2023).
8 Frank R. Baumgartner, Marty Davidson, Kaneesha R. Johnson, Arvind Krishnamurthy, and Colin P. Wilson, *Deadly Justice: A Statistical Portrait of the Death Penalty* (New York: Oxford University Press, 2018); Brandon L. Garrett, *End of Its Rope: How Killing the Death Penalty Can Revive Criminal Justice* (Cambridge, MA: Harvard University Press, 2017).
9 For more information on the Marshall hypothesis, see Robert M. Bohm, Louise J. Clark, and Adrian F. Aveni, "Knowledge and Death Penalty Opinion: A Test of the Marshall Hypothesis," *Journal of Research in Crime and Delinquency* 28, no. 3 (1991): 360–87.
10 *Furman*, 408 U.S. at 362.
11 David C. Baldus, George G. Woodworth, and Charles A. Pulaski Jr., *Equal Justice and the Death Penalty: A Legal and Empirical Analysis* (Boston: Northeastern University Press, 1990).
12 *Gregg v. Georgia*, 28 U.S. 153 (1976).
13 *Woodson v. North Carolina*, 428 U.S. 280 (1976).
14 *Roberts v. Louisiana*, 428 U.S. 325 (1976).

15 For more details, see Baumgartner et al., *Deadly Justice*; Carol S. Steiker and Jordan M. Steiker, *Courting Death: The Supreme Court and Capital Punishment* (Cambridge, MA: Harvard University Press, 2016); Evan J. Mandery, *A Wild Justice: The Death and Resurrection of Capital Punishment in America* (New York: Norton, 2013).

16 Frank R. Baumgartner, Tamira Daniely, Kalley Huang, Sydney Johnson, Alexander Love, Lyle May, Patrice McGloin, Allison Swagert, Niharika Vattikonda, and Kamryn Washington, "Throwing Away the Key: The Unintended Consequences of 'Tough-on-Crime' Laws," *Perspectives on Politics* 19, no. 4 (2021): fig. 2.

17 Seth Kotch, *Lethal State: A History of the Death Penalty in North Carolina* (Chapel Hill: University of North Carolina Press, 2019); Stuart Banner, *The Death Penalty: An American History* (Cambridge, MA: Harvard University Press, 2002).

18 Jodi Wilgoren, "Citing Issue of Fairness, Governor Clears Out Death Row in Illinois," *New York Times*, January 12, 2003.

19 See Robert Dunham, *DPIC Analysis: Causes of Wrongful Convictions* (Washington, DC: Death Penalty Information Center, May 31, 2017).

20 "% Exonerations by Contributing Factor" and "% Exonerations by Type of Crime," National Registry of Exonerations, updated September 13, 2024, www.law.umich .edu/.

21 Edward M. Borchard, *Convicting the Innocent* (New Haven, CT: Yale University Press, 1932).

22 Michael L. Radelet, Hugo Adam Bedau, and Constance E. Putnam, *In Spite of Innocence* (Boston: Northeastern University Press, 1992).

23 Baumgartner, De Boef, and Boydstun, *Decline of the Death Penalty*, 116–20.

24 Baumgartner, De Boef, and Boydstun, 178.

25 Baumgartner et al., *Deadly Justice*, 274.

26 James A. Stimson, *Public Opinion in America: Moods, Cycles, and Swings*, 2nd ed. (Boulder, CO: Westview, 1999).

27 Peter K. Enns, "The Public's Increasing Punitiveness and Its Influence on Mass Incarceration in the United States," *American Journal of Political Science* 58, no. 4 (2014): 857–72.

2

The Hidden Costs of Capital Punishment

Beyond the Monetary

RICHARD C. DIETER

Of all the arguments about the wisdom of keeping the death penalty, its cost might seem the least important. The death penalty is about fundamental principles—it is imposed for the taking of life, and it ends with an execution of another human being. How much money taxpayers must spend to make this happen seems to pale in the face of greater moral questions.

If the costs of the death penalty were miniscule, they might indeed be ignored in favor of more weighty issues. However, the expenses involved in capital punishment are far from negligible—states and the federal government must pay hundreds of millions of dollars to pursue a relatively small number of executions each year. The costs per defendant render it probably the most exorbitant part of the criminal justice system. In recent years, as states have relied less and less on the death penalty, the costs per case have risen even higher.

Every government program should be put to a cost-benefit analysis. There is only a limited pool of money available for state initiatives. Money spent in one area is then not available for other programs that might do more to protect society. Finding the costs of many government programs is not a simple process, because expenses are spread over many areas of the budget. Benefits are likewise hard to analyze because they cannot generally be measured in dollars and cents.

All of this is particularly true of the death penalty. Superficially, one might argue that capital punishment is a bargain because executions are inexpensive, and afterward the government is freed from incarcerating an individual for the rest of his or her life. However, the true financial burden of the death penalty is found in the myriad of legal costs necessary to get to that execution: expensive investigations, lengthy trials and appeals, and the involvement of prosecutors, defense lawyers, and judges over many years. Every step of the process leading up to an execution is far more expensive than the same steps for other criminal cases, and those extra costs overwhelm any savings from avoiding further imprisonment afterward.

Potential Benefits

The two main justifications for the death penalty are that it saves lives by deterring other murders and it provides orderly retribution for those affected by heinous crimes. Other chapters in this book will address whether capital punishment achieves those goals. Suffice it here to note that the prestigious National Research Council of the National Academies reviewed three decades of deterrence studies and concluded that claims of any deterrent effect on murder rates from the death penalty were fundamentally flawed.[1]

The benefit of retribution that involves the taking of another life to aid the families of murder victims has also been sharply challenged by many who have been through this process.[2] As the length of time between sentencing and execution has stretched out to almost twenty years[3] and the likelihood of a murder resulting in an execution has shrunk to less than two in one thousand murders,[4] almost all families of murder victims will never see this promised retribution.

There is one other claimed benefit of the death penalty: it gives prosecutors a tool to induce plea bargains in exchange for lesser sentences, thereby saving the government the time and money of an expensive trial. This would be an odd benefit, if true, because it depends on *not* using the death penalty as the preferred outcome. It is also constitutionally and ethically suspect because it can interfere with a defendant's right to a trial ("take the deal or we will kill you"). It risks convicting innocent defendants who plead guilty solely to avoid the possibility of a death sentence, which has occurred on numerous occasions.[5] Whether this practice actually saves money will be addressed later when the actual costs of the death penalty are discussed.

Even if these benefits of the death penalty were realized, it is very hard to put a monetary value on them. Perhaps it might be argued that these benefits are worth any costs that might accrue. However, just as these benefits are intangible, so too are many of the hidden costs of capital punishment, and these must be put on the opposite side of the scale.

Hidden Costs: The Problem of Innocence

The United States has an embarrassing record when it comes to accuracy in the use of the death penalty. About two thirds of death sentences are overturned because of serious errors in the trial process. When those cases are retried, almost all of them result in life sentences.[6] The most serious mistakes occur when the entire conviction of a capital defendant is thrown out and, on further review, the defendant is either acquitted or has all charges dismissed. In other words, someone whom the state deemed unworthy to even live another day is not just resentenced, they are completely exonerated and returned to society.

Since 1973, 186 defendants who were sentenced to death were later exonerated, often decades after their convictions and typically because of fortuitous circumstances that enabled the mistakes to be caught.[7] Compared to the number of executions during this time, one person is exonerated and freed from death row for every eight executions carried out. In addition to the years these people have lost because of their wrongful convictions, there is also a clear risk that many cases of innocence were never discovered and the defendant was executed. That is surely a cost that should be considered in any cost-benefit analysis.

Moreover, these mistakes, including likely wrongful executions, are directly related to the costs of the death penalty. For many years after the death penalty was reinstated in 1976, states refused to pay what was necessary to prevent mistaken sentences, convictions, and executions. The death penalty on the cheap is no bargain at all. It risks innocent lives—precisely the opposite of the key rationale proffered for its existence.

Reading through the capital cases overturned by the courts reveals numerous examples of defense lawyers who were drunk during trial, asleep during trial, or totally inept in the practice of criminal law.[8] Good lawyers are more expensive; poor lawyers will offer to take a capital case for $1,000, and the resultant quality of representation is predictable. As Justice Ruth Bader Ginsburg remarked, "People who are well represented at trial do not get the death penalty. I have yet to see a death case among the dozens coming to the Supreme Court on eve-of-execution stay applications in which the defendant was well represented at trial."[9] Underpaid public defenders with impossible caseloads were assigned to death penalty cases, while higher paid prosecutors could call on the resources of the state and even the federal government to pursue the death penalty. In addition to the many capital cases that suffered from of ineffective assistance of counsel, there are many other capital cases overturned because of prosecutors improperly withholding critical evidence that good defense lawyers might have obtained.[10]

The issues of innocence and effective representation are intricately entwined with the issue of costs. Many of the death row exonerations were attributable, at least in part, to inadequate representation.[11] One of the key reasons why death sentences and executions have plummeted in the past twenty years is that states have been shamed and cajoled into providing better representation in capital cases.[12] Once special defense offices were established to deal with capital trials and appeals, the expertise of the seasoned and dedicated practitioners raised the quality of representation and greatly limited death sentences. And many prosecutors, once they realized they would face high-level challenges at every step, elected not to pursue a death sentence, contributing to the dramatic decline in the use of the death penalty. Of course, these reforms in the capital defense system come at a significant—but necessary— cost. It is *that* death penalty system that reveals the true costs of capital punishment.

Hidden Costs: Racism

The problem of racism in the United States permeates all aspects of our society and has been especially evident in the criminal justice system. Racial impact in capital cases has been clearly demonstrated in the prosecutorial decision to pursue death (cases involving Black defendants and white victims being most prevalent)[13] and in jury composition (often nearly all-white juries).[14] It is not clear that racism has been worse in the capital realm than in other areas of criminal justice, but the consequences are far more devastating. The decision on who lives and who dies has often been influenced by race, prompting the critique of the death penalty as an extension of lynching and Jim Crow law.[15]

It is impossible to put a cost on the damages inflicted by racism, and the remedies to this injustice can only be found deep within our culture and societal structures. But because the impact of bias in the death penalty is so searing and often cannot be undone, the effects of racism should be counted as a death penalty cost. The unfair use of a process that determines life and death produces distrust in the whole justice system. It may take many more decades to uproot the impact of racism in our country, but the ongoing divisiveness and terror of the death penalty can be stopped in one stroke. Just as the dismantling of statues honoring protectors of slavery does not rewrite history, abolishing capital punishment would only be a step, but it would be a step in the right direction that can be taken immediately.

A larger problem related to racism is the overall arbitrariness of the death penalty. Whether you will be punished with death depends heavily on geography, the quality of counsel you can afford, and the ebb and flow of election years.[16] As with racism in particular, the capricious application of our most consequential laws generally creates a distrust of the entire system. While our legal process cannot come to a halt as we wait for the blindfold of justice to be more securely fixed, alternatives to the death penalty exist now and are being used by close to half of our states.

Measuring the Financial Burden

There are many other intangible costs associated with the death penalty, such as the damage done to innocent family members of the accused, the country's loss of credibility in its pursuit of international human rights, and the risk of justifying mass incarceration because it is viewed as a lesser punishment than death. All these and more should be weighed against any purported benefits from capital punishment. However, it is also important to examine the real financial costs of this practice.

State budgets do not have an expense line for all death penalty costs. The expenses crop up in many areas such as the district attorney's office, indigent defense, the judicial system, the correctional system, and the attorney general's office. Moreover, the costs may not be counted as expenses at all. Many of the costs are what are called "opportunity costs." Prosecutors, judges, and public defenders are usually salaried

Table 2.1: The Additional Costs of Capital Cases

Steps in the Criminal Justice System	Death Penalty Cases	Other Criminal Cases	Notes
Pretrial investigation	Two parts: Guilt/innocence evidence Life/death factors	One part: Guilt/innocence evidence	Death cases require complete examination of defendant's life
Appointment of counsel	Two experienced defense attorneys plus other experts	One attorney	Similar additional resources needed for the prosecution
Trial	Longer trials and two phases: conviction and sentence. Longer jury selection process.	Shorter trial with only conviction phase	95% of criminal cases result in plea bargains— no trial
Appeals	Two appealable issues: conviction and sentence. Appellate attorneys often paid throughout appeals process.	One issue: conviction, and none if guilty plea. Minimal funds for appeals beyond the first stage.	Sentence generally within statutory limits in noncapital cases, so little to appeal
Application of sentence	Executions delayed 10–20 years, if they ever occur. Many death sentences are overturned.	Incarceration begins immediately	In death cases, resentencing to life is common
Incarceration	Death row: heightened security; single-celled	Double-celled or dorms; fewer officers per inmate	Death row inmates rarely work in prison
Final years	Expensive execution of small minority after inmate has served much of a life sentence	Longer total incarceration, but significantly less cost per year	Only 17% of those sentenced to death have been executed

employees, who will be paid the same amount whether assigned to death penalty cases or other work. But when calculating costs, it would be inaccurate not to include the extra time these salaried participants spend involved with death penalty cases compared to involvement in typical criminal cases. Table 2.1 summarizes these costs.

If it takes one thousand hours of state-salaried work to arrive at a death sentence and only one hundred hours to have the same person sentenced to life without parole (LWOP), the nine hundred hours difference represents an opportunity the state has to save money. If the death penalty is eliminated, the county or the state can decide whether to direct those employee hours to other work that had been left undone or to save money by keeping fewer employees. There is a financial dimension to all aspects of death penalty cases, and the better cost studies take these "opportunity costs" into account.[17]

It should be noted that lower expenditures on LWOP sentences might be evidence of inadequate representation and resources for this problematic alternative to capital punishment. If so, the money saved from ending the death penalty could be directed to more resources in LWOP cases, which affect many more defendants than the death penalty.

Under current law, a death penalty case is considerably more expensive to litigate than an LWOP case due to structural differences in the procedures in each area. Because of the Supreme Court's decision in *Gregg v. Georgia*[18] and subsequent cases, capital prosecutions require two trials—one to determine guilt, the other to determine the sentence. The penalty phase can take weeks of court and jury time, preceded by in-depth investigations into the defendant's full history. The right to representation is guaranteed at this stage, resulting in the likelihood that at least two defense attorneys will be assigned to a case and mitigation experts will be needed. Appeals in death penalty cases will examine both phases of a capital case. Although it is conceivable that similar structures could be put in place in LWOP cases, courts have consistently held that death as a punishment is categorically different than any other sentence.

Taking a Systemic Approach

One approach to the cost question is to add up the expenses of each step in a typical capital case, such as the investigation, trial, appeals, and execution. However, this calculation focuses only on the distinct minority of cases that go through the whole system. The vast majority of capital cases end before execution, but because those initial stages cost more than a typical case, the "failed" cases add to the death penalty's expense. Only about 17 percent of death sentences have proceeded all the way to execution,[19] and many capital cases end with lesser sentences.

A more comprehensive and accurate approach involves assessing the *extra* costs to the state for maintaining its death penalty system over a system in which life in prison is the maximum sentence. Every state study is dependent on that state's laws, pay scales, and the extent to which it uses the death penalty. Studies have been conducted by research organizations, public defender offices, legislative committees, and the media. Researchers have employed different approaches, using different assumptions. However, the studies have consistently concluded the death penalty *system* is far more expensive than an alternative system in which the maximum sentence is life in prison.[20]

One of the most comprehensive cost studies was conducted by the Urban Institute, measuring the expenses of Maryland's death penalty (including the extra costs incurred in capital cases resulting in less-than-death sentences), as compared to the comparable costs in obtaining and carrying out life sentences. The study concluded that each death sentence incurs a cost of $3 million over the entire course of the case, while a comparable life sentence case cost $1.1 million.[21] However, because only few death sentences result in an execution, the cost *per execution* is much higher. Since each death sentence costs $3 million and only one in twelve of Maryland's death sentences resulted in an execution, the cost to the state *per execution* is $36 million. Cost estimates like these are causing state officials to rethink the wisdom of such expenditures.

A cost of over $30 million per execution may even be a conservative estimate in most states, where few executions have been carried out compared to the number of death sentences imposed.

The California Commission on the Fair Administration of Justice conducted an exhaustive investigation into the state's capital punishment system and reported that the state was spending $137 million per year on the death penalty. They estimated that a comparable system that sentenced the same inmates to a maximum punishment of life without parole would cost only $11.5 million per year.[22] Since the number of executions in California has averaged less than one every two years since the death penalty was reinstated in 1977, the cost *per execution* is over $250 million.[23]

New York and New Jersey have both abandoned the death penalty, with the high costs of capital punishment being one factor in each state making that decision. New York spent about $170 million over the nine years that the law was in effect and had no executions. New Jersey spent $253 million on its death penalty over a twenty-three-year period and also had no executions.[24] In states with no executions, the cost per execution obviously cannot be calculated, but even assuming they eventually reached one execution every other year, and continued the annual expenditures indicated in their studies, the cost per execution would be in the $20-to-$40 million range, not counting the money spent leading up to this period.

The Maryland study described above estimated the extra costs to taxpayers for death penalty cases prosecuted between 1978 and 1999 to be $186 million.[25] Based on a total of five executions (resulting from sixty death sentences) carried out from the state's reinstatement to abolition in 2013, this translates to a cost of $37 million per execution.

Death Penalty Costs Are Rising

The costs of the death penalty measured per execution are increasing. Since 2000, executions and death sentences have both declined over 80 percent, but the size of death row has declined only about 27 percent. As a result, while the nation's total expense for capital punishment may be going down with fewer cases, the resources required for each case are growing substantially. In 1988, a media study estimated the costs of the death penalty in Florida at $3.2 million per execution, based on the costs and rate of executions at the time.[26] A later study by the *Palm Beach Post* found a much higher cost per execution than in 1988: with a rising death row population and higher costs, it estimated that Florida's costs were $51 million a year over what it would spend to punish all first-degree murderers with life in prison without parole. Based on the forty-four executions Florida carried out from 1976 to 2000, that amounts to a cost of $24 million for each execution, a significant rise from earlier projections.[27]

A comparable increase has occurred in California. In 1988, the *Sacramento Bee* found that the death penalty cost California $90 million annually beyond the ordinary expenses of the justice system, mostly at the trial level.[28] Although executions had not yet begun in the state, the newspaper projected a cost of $15 million per execution. But the costs have increased sharply since then. According to the Commission on the Fair Administration of Justice, in 2008, maintaining the death penalty cost taxpayers more than $137 million a year beyond the cost of simply keeping the convicts locked up for life.[29] This figure does not count the millions more spent on court costs to prosecute capital cases.

The Effect of Plea Bargaining

Some have argued that the high cost of the death penalty is balanced by the savings incurred when capital defendants accept plea bargains with life sentences, thus saving the state the cost of a trial.[30] However, it appears that whatever savings occur through this ethically questionable practice are overwhelmed by the costs of *preparing* a death penalty case, even if it never goes to trial.

Some of the most thorough cost analyses have considered plea bargaining as an area that could lower the costs of the death penalty, including those in Indiana,[31] Kansas,[32] and California,[33] though some found it too speculative to measure. These studies nevertheless concluded that the death penalty added a significant net cost to the criminal justice system.

The flaw in assuming net savings by inducing plea bargains was underscored by a federal cost study. The Judicial Conference of the United States concluded that the average cost of representation in federal death penalty cases *that resulted in plea bargains* was $192,333. The average cost of representation in cases that were eligible for the death penalty but in which the death penalty was *not sought* was only $55,772.[34] Thus, it is the *seeking* of the death penalty that raises the cost, even when the case results in a plea bargain, because of the expensive preparations that must be begun as soon as a case is made capital. It would be far less expensive to prosecute murder cases if the death penalty were never on the table—even taking some noncapital cases to trial—than to threaten the use of the death penalty to induce an eventual plea bargain.

Moreover, the underlying assumption that more defendants will plead guilty if threatened with more severe penalties may not be correct. After the abolition of the death penalty in New Jersey in 2007, prosecutors said it has made no difference in their ability to secure guilty pleas.[35] A study by the National Institute of Justice found that in Alaska, where plea bargaining was abolished in 1975, "guilty pleas continued to flow in at nearly undiminished rates. Most defendants pled guilty even when the state offered them nothing in exchange for their cooperation."[36]

Other Hidden Costs

After paying for up to twenty years of investigations, trials, and appeals, the cost of the actual execution is usually hardly worth counting. However, recently even the drugs needed for lethal injections have become increasingly expensive as the major pharmaceutical companies have declined to provide them. The Arizona Department of Corrections, for example, ordered one thousand vials of pentobarbital to be shipped in unmarked jars and boxes at a cost of $1.5 million.[37]

The recent spate of executions in the federal system demonstrates the huge expenditures that can occur even in the last phase of the death penalty process. There had been no federal executions for seventeen years when President Donald Trump decided to jump-start the process as he approached the final year of his administration. Facilitated by Attorney General William Barr, the administration pushed through thirteen executions in the span of six months, a pace unseen in modern times. The last one occurred just four days before President Biden was sworn in with a promise to end federal executions.

In the race to carry out these executions, enormous resources were expended. According to Rick Winter of the Bureau of Prisons, the activation of an execution team included assembling more than forty employees from around the country who had to be removed from their normal duties. Another fifty members from the Special Operations Response and Disturbance Control Teams were posted to Terre Haute for security. Winter indicated that two hundred local staffers at Terre Haute were pulled away from their normal duties to provide support. Based on information obtained by the American Civil Liberties Union, the cost of just the five of the thirteen executions was about $4.7 million, or more than $900,000 per death, and it is not clear whether that included the personnel costs.[38]

The Cost of Mistakes

Still other expenses arise when governments have to pay for their mistakes in wrongful convictions. Although compensation for exonerees is uneven and very hard to achieve, states and municipalities have had to settle wrongful-conviction cases for millions of dollars.

Two brothers who were wrongfully convicted and sentenced to death in North Carolina in 1984 were recently awarded $75 million by a federal jury in a suit against the police investigators who presented false testimony.[39] Another set of capital co-defendants were given $18 million as compensation in 2020 in Ohio for the forty years they had been wrongly imprisoned, including years on death row.[40] While such substantial payouts are not the norm (and many exonerees receive nothing), the *risk* that such costs will be accrued represents another expense that state and local governments will have to prepare for if they continue using the death penalty. Theoretically, compensation could be paid in noncapital cases whenever someone is wrongly imprisoned, but death penalty cases draw the most attention, and the suffering inflicted by years on death row can result in larger payouts.

Additional Research

The death penalty was reinstated in the United States in 1976, but executions did not resume in significant numbers until about the mid-1980s. From then, the number of executions and the size of death row expanded steadily until about the year 2000.[41] As some states considered whether the new experiment with the death penalty was succeeding, research into the costs of the death penalty was undertaken as a factor in deciding whether to continue the practice. Since 2000, other issues such as the risk of executing the innocent and racial bias in death sentencing became particularly prominent in legislative circles. However, new research gathered by the Death Penalty Information Center has cast a spotlight on various parts of the cost question:

In 2017, a fiscal impact report prepared by the Legislative Finance Committee of the New Mexico legislature estimated that bringing back the death penalty for three types of homicides in the state would cost as much as $7.2 million over the first three years. Of course, any executions resulting from reinstatement would be a decade or more in the future.[42]

In 2016, a study by the Lewis and Clark Law School and Seattle University found that a death sentence in Oregon costs almost $1 million more than a life sentence in similar cases: sixty-one death sentences handed down in Oregon cost taxpayers an average of $2.3 million each, including

incarceration costs, while 313 non–death penalty murder cases cost an average of $1.4 million.[43]

Also in 2016, a Creighton University study of the costs of Nebraska's death
penalty found that the state spends $14.6 million per year to maintain its
capital punishment system. Over the past forty-five years, that system has
resulted in four executions.[44]

And in 2012, a study at the University of Nevada concluded that the eighty
pending capital murder cases in Clark County, Nevada, cost approximately
$15 million more than if they had been prosecuted without seeking the
death penalty, not including the costs of prosecution or appeals.[45]

In theory, a death penalty system might be devised that required short
trials with underpaid defense attorneys, followed by truncated appeals
and rapid executions. That system would be far less expensive than the
one that exists, but it would also violate our core principles of justice and
due process under the law.

Conclusion

A focus on the costs of the death penalty can evoke a response that
money is irrelevant when it comes to ensuring justice and a safer society.
However, the death penalty is not essential to those goals, as the twenty-
three U.S. states that have ended the practice, along with the growing
majority of abolitionist countries in the world, have demonstrated. Even
states with the death penalty rarely use it, belying its necessity. Justice
and safety can be pursued more consistently and equitably without the
death penalty, and at a far lesser cost. In many of the legislative debates
and official statements on death penalty repeal, the high costs of capital
punishment were underscored as a reason for ending it.

The death penalty should be carefully examined on a cost-benefit
basis, just as is done with other expensive programs that seem to no longer make sense in modern society. The hundreds of millions of dollars
spent yearly to achieve a handful of executions could be devoted more
productively to proven programs that really do make a difference in our
communities. There is no simple way to reduce the costs while ensuring
that innocent lives are protected and the accused are treated fairly. This
dilemma is one of the principal reasons that the use of the death penalty

has declined so dramatically in recent years. Tipping the scales further away from capital punishment are the immense intangible costs associated with racial bias, wrongful convictions, and the overall arbitrariness of the practice. Leaving aside whether the death penalty can any longer be defended constitutionally, its questionable value to society appears to be far outweighed by its costs.

Notes

1 Daniel Nagin and John Pepper, National Research Council, *Deterrence and the Death Penalty* (Washington, DC: National Academies Press, 2012).

2 Susan Bandes, "The Death Penalty and the Misleading Concept of 'Closure,'" *Crime Report*, January 8, 2021.

3 Tracy Snell, *Capital Punishment, 2018* (Washington, DC: Bureau of Justice Statistics, 2020).

4 The average number of murders per year for the five-year period 2013–17 was 15,775 (FBI Crime Data Explorer (CDE), FBI Uniform Crime Reporting Program, https://cde.ucr.cjis.gov). The average number of executions per year for the same period was twenty-nine (Execution Database, Death Penalty Information Center, https://deathpenaltyinfo.org.

5 Paul Hammel, "Pardons Granted to Five in Murder They Didn't Commit," *Omaha World-Herald*, January 27, 2009.

6 James S. Liebman, Jeffrey Fagan, and Valerie West, "A Broken System: Error Rates in Capital Cases" (Columbia Law School, Public Law Research Paper No. 15, Columbia University, New York, June 2000), i–iii.

7 Robert Dunham, *The Innocence Epidemic* (Washington, DC: Death Penalty Information Center, February 18, 2021).

8 Stephen B. Bright, "Counsel for the Poor: The Death Sentence not for the Worst Crime but for the Worst Lawyer," *Yale Law Journal* 103 (1994): 1843.

9 "Justice Backs Death Penalty Freeze," *CBS News*, April 10, 2001.

10 Liebman, Fagan, and West, "Broken System," ii.

11 Innocence Database, Death Penalty Information Center, https://deathpenaltyinfo .org.

12 Brandon Garrett, "The Decline of the Virginia (and American) Death Penalty," *Georgetown Law Journal* 105 (2017): 661–729.

13 Samuel Gross, "David Baldus and the Legacy of *McCleskey v. Kemp*," *Iowa Law Review* 97, no. 6 (2012): 1912.

14 Ngozi Ndulue, *Enduring Injustice: The Persistence of Racial Discrimination in the U.S.* (Washington, DC: Death Penalty Information Center, September 2020).

15 Equal Justice Initiative, *Lynching in America: Confronting the Legacy of Racial Terror*, 3rd ed. (Montgomery, AL: Equal Justice Initiative, 2017), 62.

16 Richard C. Dieter, *Struck by Lightning: The Continuing Arbitrariness of the Death Penalty* (Washington, DC: Death Penalty Information Center, 2011).

17 One thorough study at Duke University included the costs of the extra time spent on death penalty cases by prosecutors, judges, and other personnel and concluded that the death penalty costs North Carolina $2.16 million per execution *over* the costs of a non–death penalty system imposing a maximum sentence of imprisonment for life. The author updated this study in 2009, concluding that the state could save $11 million annually if it repealed the death penalty. Philip Cook, "Potential Savings from Abolition of the Death Penalty in North Carolina," *American Law and Economics Review* 11, no. 2 (2009): 1–32.

18 428 U.S. 153 (1976).

19 "Executions Overview," Death Penalty Information Center, https://deathpenaltyinfo.org.

20 Richard C. Dieter, *Smart on Crime: Reconsidering the Death Penalty in a Time of Economic Crisis* (Washington, DC: Death Penalty Information Center, 2009).

21 John Roman, Aaron Chalfin, Aaron Sundquist, Carly Knight, and Askar Darmenov, *The Cost of the Death Penalty in Maryland* (Washington, DC: Urban Institute Justice Policy Center, 2008), 2.

22 California Commission on the Fair Administration of Justice, *California Commission on the Fair Administration of Justice: Final Report* (Santa Clara, CA: Northern California Innocence Project, June 30, 2008), 116–17.

23 Since 2008, the per execution cost has risen even higher. The state has had no executions since 2006 but has continued to maintain a death penalty system involving over seven hundred people on death row, all of whom require enhanced security, attorneys for extensive appeals, and numerous court procedures.

24 Mary Forsberg, *Money for Nothing? The Financial Cost of New Jersey's Death Penalty* (Trenton, NJ: New Jersey Policy Perspective, 2005), 16.

25 Roman et al., *Cost of the Death Penalty*, 3.

26 David Von Drehle, "Bottom Line: Life in Prison One-Sixth as Expensive," *Miami Herald*, July 10, 1988.

27 S. V. Date, "The High Price of Killing Killers," *Palm Beach Post*, January 4, 2000, 1A.

28 Stephen Maganini, "Closing Death Row Would Save State $90 Million a Year," *Sacramento Bee*, March 28, 1988.

29 California Commission on the Fair Administration of Justice, *Final Report*, 117.

30 Kent Scheidegger of the Criminal Justice Legal Foundation stated, "Repeal of the death penalty would likely result in fewer pleas to life or long sentences, requiring that prosecutors either take more cases to trial at a substantial financial cost or accept bargains to lesser sentences at a substantial cost to public safety." Kent Scheidegger, *The Death Penalty and Plea Bargaining to Life Sentences* (Sacramento, CA: Criminal Justice Legal Foundation, February 2009), 13.

31 Indiana Criminal Law Study Commission, *The Application of Indiana's Capital Sentencing Law* (Indianapolis, IN: Indiana Criminal Justice Institute, January 10, 2002), 120.

32 Legislature of Kansas, Legislative Post Audit Committee, *Costs Incurred for Death Penalty Cases: A K-GOAL Audit of the Department of Corrections* (Topeka, KS: Legislative Division of Post Audit, December 13, 2003), 19.

33 California Commission on the Fair Administration of Justice, *Final Report*, 145–56.

34 Judicial Conference of the United States, Subcommittee on Federal Death Penalty Cases, *Federal Death Penalty Cases: Recommendations Concerning the Cost and Quality of Defense Representation* (Washington, DC: Administrative Office of the U.S. Courts, Defender Services Division, 1998), 7–8.

35 Rudy Larini, "A Year Later, State Assesses Justice without Death Penalty," *New Jersey Star Ledger*, December 15, 2008.

36 Ralph Fine, "Plea Bargaining: An *Unnecessary Evil*," *Marquette Law Review* 70, no. 4 (1987): 615, citing Michael Rubinstein, Stevens Clarke, and Teresa White, *Alaska Bans Plea Bargaining* (Washington, DC: National Institute of Justice, 1980), 80.

37 Ed Pilkington, "Revealed: Republican-Led States Secretly Spending Huge Sums on Execution Drugs," *The Guardian*, April 9, 2021.

38 Joe Davidson, "President Trump's Expensive Death Penalty Binge Could Continue Next Week," *Washington Post*, January 9, 2021.

39 Lateshia Beachum, "Two Brothers Were Wrongfully Convicted of Murder and Rape. Decades Later, a Jury Has Awarded Them $75 Million," *Washington Post*, May 16, 2021.

40 Chris Anderson, "3 Men Reach $18 Million Settlement with Cleveland for Wrongful Imprisonment in Connection to 1975 Murder," *Channel 19 News*, Cleveland, OH, May 8, 2020.

41 "Executions Overview."

42 New Mexico Legislative Finance Committee, *Fiscal Impact Report, HB72*, February 2, 2017, www.nmlegis.gov/.

43 Aliza Kaplan, Peter Collins, and Venetia Mayhew, "Oregon's Death Penalty: A Cost Analysis" (working paper, Lewis and Clark Law School and Seattle University, November 16, 2016), https://files.deathpenaltyinfo.org/.

44 Ernest Goss, Scott Strain, and Jackson Blalock, *The Economic Impact of the Death Penalty on the State of Nebraska: A Taxpayer Burden?* (Denver, CO: Goss and Associates Economic Solutions, August 15, 2016), https://files.deathpenaltyinfo.org/.

45 Terance Miethe, "Estimates of Time Spent in Capital and Non-capital Murder Cases: A Statistical Analysis of Survey Data from Clark County Defense Attorneys" (working paper, Department of Criminal Justice, University of Nevada, Las Vegas, February 21, 2012), https://files.deathpenaltyinfo.org/.

PART II

The Condemned and Their Stories

3

Juveniles and the Death Penalty

A Failure of Law and Morality

BHARAT MALKANI

There have been many grotesque features of the U.S. death penalty, but one of the most shameful has been the imposition of capital punishment on people who were under the age of eighteen at the time of the crime for which they were convicted. This practice, which was known as the "juvenile death penalty"[1] and was meted out from 1642 until 2005, was an abject failure of law, policy, and justice. It was inherently barbaric, and it also exacerbated problems with capital punishment generally, such as race discrimination, the risk of executing an innocent person, and the failure to abide by norms of international human rights law.

This chapter sets out the legal and moral controversies of the juvenile death penalty. Section 1 provides a brief overview of the law and practice from 1642 until 1972, when the U.S. Supreme Court temporarily outlawed all death penalties in *Furman v. Georgia*.[2] This overview provides the historical context for the primary focus of this chapter, an examination of the post-1972, or "modern," juvenile death penalty. Section 2 covers the period from 1972 until 1989, when the U.S. Supreme Court upheld the constitutionality of the death penalty for juveniles in *Stanford v. Kentucky*.[3] Section 3 covers the period from *Stanford* until 2005, when the Court reversed course and outlawed the juvenile death penalty in *Roper v. Simmons*.[4] In these sections, the legal and moral failings of the practice are considered, drawing on cases, scholarly research, the work of civil society organizations, and my own experiences of working on efforts to abolish the practice. Section 4 provides an outline of the Court's reasoning in *Roper*, which brought together the legal, moral, and criminological reasons for rejecting the punishment.

The story does not end with the abolition of the juvenile death penalty. Both the practice itself and the Court's reasoning in *Roper* have had long-lasting legacies, which are explored and evaluated in section 5. In particular, *Roper* inspired and enabled further reforms to juvenile justice, such as limitations to the sentence of life in prison without the possibility of parole. It also set out a framework for challenging other aspects of capital punishment. However, the potential of *Roper* has been stymied recently by the changing composition of the United States Supreme Court. Ultimately, despite some progress as a result of *Roper*, there is still much work to be done to overcome the failings of the juvenile death penalty.

The Juvenile Death Penalty, 1642–1972

On September 7, 1642, Thomas Graunger was hanged in Plymouth Colony, Massachusetts, for the crime of bestiality. He was sixteen years old at the time of the crime, trial, and execution and is the first juvenile known to have been executed in what is now the United States of America.[5] Over the next 330 years, a further 343 juveniles are known to have been executed across the United States. During this era, there was virtually no federal regulation of the death penalty, and people as young as ten years old at the time of their crimes were executed.[6]

This era also encompassed slavery and Jim Crow laws and practices. The juvenile death penalty exemplified the racism of these institutions. Of the eight people who were executed for crimes committed when aged twelve or younger, six were classed as Black or Native American. The races of the other two are unknown. All were executed for taking the life of a white person.[7] Perhaps the most infamous case of racism and the juvenile death penalty between 1642 and 1972 was that of George Stinney Jr., who was just fourteen years old when he was executed in South Carolina in 1944 for the murder of two white girls. His conviction and sentence were vacated in 2014, and it is now widely accepted that he was innocent and was targeted because of the color of his skin.[8]

In 1972, the death penalty in the United States was suspended when the U.S. Supreme Court ruled in *Furman v. Georgia* that the punishment as then applied was unconstitutional. At the time, decision-makers in states enjoyed unfettered discretion when deciding whether to impose the punishment in any given case, which led to inconsistencies in its application from state to state. The Court ruled that this rendered the practice unconstitutionally arbitrary. The majority of states responded to *Furman* by crafting death penalty statutes that either mandated capital punishment in certain circumstances, thus providing certainty, or purported to guide and constrain the discretion of decision-makers in capital cases, thus providing consistency in the administration of the penalty. The Court rejected the mandatory death penalty schemes, but approved the "guided discretion" death penalty schemes in *Gregg v. Georgia* in 1976.[9] This decision shaped the law and practice of the juvenile death penalty in the post-*Furman* era.

The Juvenile Death Penalty, 1972–1989

Although the *Furman* and *Gregg* Courts emphasized the need for decision-makers in capital cases to follow guidelines to ensure that only the most morally culpable people are sentenced to death, neither Court addressed the question of whether people must be a certain age before they are eligible for a death sentence. This was somewhat surprising, because legal authorities both in the United States and abroad have long recognized that young people are often not as morally culpable for criminal acts as older people, and lawmakers have therefore sought to demarcate the age at which people can be held criminally responsible and subject to certain punishments. These attempts have not been straightforward, though, because although we can observe biological changes in human bodies as they age, it is difficult to objectively observe developments in intellectual and emotional maturity. As a result, societies have, at different times and in different places, adopted different approaches to the legal age of criminal responsibility, just as they have to the questions of what age people must be to legally consume alcohol, or drive automobiles, or consent to sexual activity.[10] The lack of guidance from the U.S. Supreme Court, when coupled with these social and political disagreements, meant that in the aftermath of *Furman* and *Gregg*, states adopted different approaches to the question of age and the death penalty. We can classify the different approaches taken by death penalty states into five categories. The first category consisted of those states that did not specify a minimum age at all in statute, leaving open the possibility of sentencing even the youngest children to death. Delaware, Oklahoma, and South Dakota were the three states that fell into this category.[11] Second, there were states that also did not have a statutory minimum age, but where a minimum age could be inferred from other statutory provisions such as the minimum age for transfer from the juvenile court to stand trial in the adult criminal court. For example, in Indiana, a child had to be at least ten years old before being eligible for trial in the criminal court, and it could therefore be inferred that the minimum age of death eligibility in Indiana was ten. Louisiana and Virginia set the age at fifteen, and nine other states set ages between twelve and fourteen.[12]

A third category comprised seven states that did not set a minimum age but expressly included youthfulness as a statutory mitigating factor that had to be taken into account by the sentencer. Although a defendant's age was not an outright bar to the death penalty in these states, it was a factor that could prevent the imposition of a death sentence. A fourth category of states were those that did set a minimum age for death eligibility in statute, but set the age at sixteen or seventeen years old. This category comprised Nevada, Georgia, New Hampshire, and Texas.[13] The final category of death penalty states comprised ten states that set eighteen as the minimum age for death penalty eligibility, thus outlawing the death penalty for those classed as "juveniles."[14] The net result of this conglomeration of state laws meant that there was little uniformity across death penalty jurisdictions in the United States in the post-*Furman* years when it came to minimum ages and eligibility for capital punishment, despite the *Furman* Court's concern with inconsistencies in the use of capital punishment. Given the concerns expressed by the Court in *Furman* about arbitrariness, one might have expected the Court to address these inconsistencies at the earliest opportunity. However, the Court did not. In *Lockett v. Ohio*,[15] the Court tangentially addressed the issue when holding that sentencing authorities must be allowed to consider any mitigating factors, not just those enumerated in the relevant statute. This meant that a defendant's youthfulness could now be considered by sentencers in any death penalty jurisdiction, not just those that had specified age as a mitigating factor in statute.

Four years later, the Court expressly declined to rule on whether the Constitution set a minimum age for death penalty eligibility. In *Eddings v. Oklahoma*[16] the petitioner argued that since he was sixteen years old at the time of the crime, the death penalty should not even have been an option in his case. However, the Court sidestepped the question and instead decided *Eddings* on the basis of *Lockett*, sending the case back for resentencing on the grounds that the sentencer had not considered all mitigating factors, including Eddings's age. By avoiding the question, three of the five justices in the majority implied that there was no constitutional bar to the death penalty for those as young as sixteen;[17] they were merely concerned with the process by which Eddings's death sentence had been imposed. For example, Justice Lewis Powell stated, "We are not unaware of the extent to which minors engage increasingly in violent crime. Nor do we suggest an absence of legal responsibility where crime is committed by a minor. We are concerned here only with the manner of the imposition of the ultimate penalty: the death sentence imposed for the crime of murder upon an emotionally disturbed youth with a disturbed child's immaturity."[18] The four dissenting justices argued that on the facts of the particular case, there was no reason to interfere with the trial judge's decision to sentence Eddings to death. In other words, they expressly endorsed the death penalty for a person aged sixteen at the time of the crime. Taken together, the majority and dissenting opinions in *Eddings* signaled to states that it was permissible to impose the death penalty on juveniles, so long as proper procedures were followed.[19]

The judgment in *Eddings* was at odds with developments domestically and internationally. In the United States, there was an emerging belief that the age of death eligibility should be set at eighteen, which was, and continues to be, generally the minimum age to vote, to sit on a jury, and to get married without parental or judicial consent. In 1971, the National Commission on the Reform of Criminal Law had recommended setting the age of death eligibility at eighteen, and the American Law Institute adopted a similar position when drafting the Model Penal Code in 1980, two years before *Eddings* was decided.[20] In 1983, a year after *Eddings*, the American Bar Association adopted a resolution opposing the juvenile death penalty: "[T]he American Bar Association opposes, in principle, the imposition of capital punishment upon any person for the offense committed while under the age of eighteen (18)."[21] Between 1981 and 1988, five states took steps to ensure that juveniles were excluded from the scope of the death penalty.[22] Internationally, the picture was similar. In 1976, just two months before *Gregg v. Georgia* was decided, the

International Covenant on Civil and Political Rights (ICCPR) came into force. Article 6(5) of the ICCPR specifically prohibited the death penalty for those under the age of eighteen at the time of the crime. To be sure, the emerging domestic and international acceptance of eighteen as the appropriate age for death penalty eligibility was itself problematic. As noted earlier, societies have always struggled to determine appropriate ages for the enjoyment of legal rights or the burden of legal responsibilities, and the adoption of eighteen for the age of death penalty eligibility is better understood as a social construct based on prevailing views, rather than an objectively driven biological determination. As Corinne Field and Nicholas Syrett explain, "Not all people reach puberty or intellectual maturity or incapacity at exactly the same ages, and yet cultural expectations, not to mention legal disabilities and responsibilities, are fixed to precise ages. Human beings have approximated; they have chosen specific ages to stand in for the beginnings and endings of life stages and the societal expectations that accompany them."[23] However, even though the choice of eighteen as the age for death penalty eligibility was somewhat arbitrary, it is striking just how out of line U.S. law and policy was with contemporary international standards of human rights law.[24]

There were three groundbreaking developments on the topic of the juvenile death penalty in the last three years of the 1980s. In 1987, Victor Streib published *Death Penalty for Juveniles*, in which he collated details of all known juvenile executions from Graunger's in 1642 up until his book went to press. The cases and data led Streib to conclude that "the death penalty for juveniles makes no sense legally, criminologically, or morally."[25] At the time of publication, thirty-eight juveniles were on death rows, and just three had been executed in the post-*Furman* era. Opponents of the juvenile death penalty now had a wealth of data to draw on when making their arguments that the practice was "cruel and unusual," and thus contrary to the Eighth Amendment.

The next year, a constitutional challenge to the proposed execution of a fifteen-year-old was heard by the U.S. Supreme Court. However, in *Thompson v. Oklahoma*,[26] the Court again failed to rule definitively on the issue. At the time the case was decided, eighteen states with the death penalty had set a statutory minimum age for death eligibility at sixteen or older, and the remaining nineteen death penalty jurisdictions set no express minimum age at all. Writing for a plurality of four justices, Justice John Paul Stevens noted that all state legislatures that had expressly considered the question of death eligibility had set the age at sixteen or older, and just five of the 1,393 persons sentenced to death during the years 1982 and 1986 were under the age of sixteen at the time of the offense. In his view, the actions of state legislatures and sentencing juries provided evidence of a national consensus against sentencing those under sixteen to death, rendering the practice contrary to the Eighth Amendment prohibition on "cruel and unusual punishments."

Dissenting, Justices Antonin Scalia and Byron White and Chief Justice William H. Rehnquist interpreted the numbers differently. Since a majority of death penalty states had *not* set the age at sixteen or older, they argued that it could not be concluded that the Constitution categorially precludes the death penalty for those under sixteen. Writing separately, Justice Sandra Day O'Connor concurred with Justice Stevens's decision, but on narrower grounds. She was of the view that although the data seemed to suggest a national consensus against the practice, it was not strong enough to warrant a categorical prohibition on those grounds. Instead, she was of the view that Thompson's death sentence, and those of people in a similar position to him, were only unconstitutional because they had been imposed pursuant to a statute that did not specify a minimum age.[27] Although at the time it was generally understood that *Thompson* set a minimum age of sixteen for death eligibility, the ruling was fragile.

The next year, the Court was asked to rule on the constitutionality of imposing the death penalty on those under the age of eighteen at the time of the crime. Given that Justice O'Connor had expressed concern only with the lack of statutory clarity in *Thompson*, it was little surprise that she joined Justice Scalia's majority opinion in *Stanford v. Kentucky*,[28] holding that the Constitution does not forbid the juvenile death penalty, since a number of state legislatures had expressly decided on sixteen or seventeen as the minimum age for capital punishment. In the *Stanford* Court's view, there was "neither a historical nor a modern societal consensus forbidding the imposition of capital punishment on any person who murders at 16 or 17 years of age. Accordingly, we conclude that such punishment does not offend the Eighth Amendment's prohibition against cruel and unusual punishment."[29] From 1989, then, constitutional law was at last clear on the issue: the juvenile death penalty was not unconstitutional, and states were permitted to sentence people to death as long as they were aged sixteen years or older at the time of the crime.

The Juvenile Death Penalty, 1989–2005

The 1990s were something of a nadir in the United States' history of capital punishment generally, and the juvenile death penalty in particular. Armed with the Supreme Court's permission, states sentenced a further 123 juveniles to death and executed nineteen, until the practice was outlawed in *Roper v. Simmons*. While the United States embraced the juvenile death penalty, the rest of the world resolutely turned its back on the practice. During that same period, only seven other countries were known to have executed juveniles, but those countries did not defend the practice the way the United States did. Of those seven, Nigeria, Iran, and Saudi Arabia vehemently denied that they had executed any juveniles, most likely because they wanted to avoid any international opprobrium that an admission would entail. Yemen, Pakistan, and China acknowledged executions in their countries but amended their domestic laws to outlaw the practice. And in 2001, the Democratic Republic of the Congo commuted the death sentences of juveniles after pressure from the international community. The United States was alone in repeatedly defending the legality and morality of sentencing people to death for crimes committed when under the age of eighteen.[30]

U.S. law and practice were not just incongruent with the laws and practices of other countries—it was also contrary to international law. In 1991, just two years after *Stanford* was decided, the United Nations Convention on the Rights of the Child (CRC) came into force, which added to the wealth of international legal instruments that prohibited the juvenile death penalty. Most countries ratified the CRC and accepted the prohibition on the juvenile death penalty. Indeed, by the time *Roper* was decided in 2005, the United States and Somalia were the only two member states of the United Nations that had not ratified the CRC.[31] Even when the United States did ratify treaties that outlawed the juvenile death penalty, such as when it finally ratified the ICCPR in 1992, it entered a reservation exempting itself from the ban on the juvenile death penalty, demonstrating its willful rejection of international law on this point.[32]

The international community routinely denounced the United States' continued use of the juvenile death penalty, but international condemnation had little effect on domestic law and policy. Justice Scalia had stated in *Stanford* that non-American views on the juvenile death penalty are entirely irrelevant to constitutional interpretation and adjudication: "We emphasize that it is *American* conceptions of decency that are dispositive," Scalia wrote, "rejecting the contention of petitioners and their various amici that the sentencing practices of other countries are relevant."[33] Likewise, American policymakers were not ignorant of the international dimension, but they were driven instead by prevailing domestic views about the seriousness of youth crime. During the 1990s, there was a nationwide panic about so-called super-predators, a term that was coined by John J. Dilulio Jr. to describe "radically impulsive, brutally remorseless youngsters, including ever more pre-teenage boys, who murder, assault, rape, rob, burglarize, deal deadly drugs, join gun-toting gangs, and create serious communal disorders."[34] This sort of rhetoric encouraged policymakers to abandon the rehabilitative ideals of the juvenile justice system and implement more punitive measures and harsher punishments to assuage the public's fears about youth violence.[35] This political climate gave little oxygen to the argument that the juvenile death penalty should be abolished. In fact, in some cases the defendant's youth came to be viewed as a reason *for* sentencing them to death. When Christopher Simmons was on trial in 1994, the prosecutor urged the jury to hand down a death sentence in part *because* Simmons was just seventeen years old at the time of the crime: "Think about age. Seventeen years old. Isn't that scary? Doesn't that scare you? Mitigating? Quite the contrary I submit. Quite the contrary."[36] The myth of the "super-predator" had undeniable racial overtones too,[37] and it is little surprise to find that the juvenile death penalty in this era was riddled with the same sort of racism that had pervaded the premodern juvenile death penalty. Although ten of the twenty-two juveniles executed between 1972 and 2005 were white, not a single one was convicted for the killing of a Black, Latinx, or Native American person. In contrast, of the eleven Black juveniles executed in that same era, seven were convicted for killing a white person.

As with the death penalty generally, greater value was placed on the lives of those classed as white.

The modern juvenile death penalty was also plagued with error. Between 1972 and 2005, at least seven people who had been sentenced to death as juvenile offenders were exonerated.[38] Given that just twenty-two juvenile offenders were executed in that time, this means that for every three executions of juveniles, one juvenile on death row was innocent. Furthermore, six of those seven exonerees were Black, in line with research that shows that nonwhites are more susceptible to wrongful convictions.

There are several reasons why juveniles were more susceptible to wrongful convictions in capital cases than their adult counterparts. Juveniles are more likely to falsely confess to a crime because their brains are not fully developed, rendering them more vulnerable to pressure and impulsive decision-making. Researchers have found that younger people tend to focus on short-term rewards and will falsely confess if they think that is their way out of a police interrogation room."[39] Johnny Ross, for example, was convicted and sentenced to death in 1975 after falsely confessing to having committed rape, following physical assaults by the police as they were interrogating him.[40] Ross was a sixteen-year-old Black male; the victim in the case was a white woman. His conviction was overturned in 1981 when new evidence revealed that his blood type did not match the type in the semen found in the victim.

Leon Brown was fifteen when he and his nineteen-year-old half-brother Henry McCollum falsely confessed to the rape and murder of an eleven-year-old in North Carolina. Both had intellectual disabilities and confessed under duress. Brown was initially sentenced to death in 1984, but had his sentence commuted to life in prison. Thirty years later, on September 2, 2014, both brothers' convictions were finally overturned, and they were formally exonerated when DNA testing implicated another man who had been convicted of similar offences.[41]

False confessions were not the only cause of wrongful convictions. Shareef Cousin was sentenced to death for a crime committed when he was just sixteen, but it transpired that the prosecutor had withheld evidence that proved Cousin's alibi. Sabrina Butler was seventeen years old when she was sent to death row for causing the death of her nine-month-old son. Her conviction was overturned when the medical examiner on whose testimony the conviction rested changed his opinion.[42]

Even in cases where the defendant was factually guilty, there were legal, moral, and criminological reasons why the death penalty was particularly barbaric when imposed on juveniles. As explained in a report by Amnesty International in 2002, "The profile of the typical condemned teenager is not of a youngster from a stable, supportive background, but rather of a mentally impaired or emotionally disturbed adolescent emerging from a childhood of abuse, deprivation and poverty."[43] For example, Joseph Cannon had been severely sexually abused by his stepfather and grandfather from the age of seven and had developed a substance abuse problem from the age of ten. He had brain damage and suffered from schizophrenia and was expelled from school because of his mental impairments. He was executed for a crime committed when he was seventeen years old.

Even in cases where there was no history of abuse or mental impairment, it was difficult to argue that the death penalty was an appropriate punishment. Napoleon Beazley, for example, was sentenced to death in 1995 after the jury decided that he presented a future threat to society. Beazley had been a model student and star athlete, and his actions on the day of the crime were generally considered to be wholly out of character. For these reasons, his case attracted widespread concern, with several commentators questioning whether he really deserved death.[44] Beazley's final written statement before he was executed indicated that he was remorseful and, like virtually all seventeen-year-olds, capable of change: "The act I committed to put me here was not just heinous, it was senseless. But the person that committed that act is no longer here—I am."[45]

Toward the end of the 1990s, the picture was bleak for those who opposed the juvenile death penalty. To underscore just how entrenched the practice was, five juveniles were scheduled to be executed almost back-to-back in the first few weeks of 2000. However, as the proverb goes, the darkest hour is just before the dawn, and the new millennium was something of a new dawn. The proposed killing spree inspired a small but committed group of lawyers and activists to take action, and this action culminated in the abolition of the juvenile death penalty just five years later.

Patti Puritz, who was then director of the American Bar Association Juvenile Justice Center, circulated a memo about the impending executions to experts in juvenile justice and the death penalty, who took immediate steps to try and halt them. Among them were Stephen Harper and Steven Drizin, who drafted op-eds in an attempt to raise public awareness about the impending executions and to convince state authorities to grant clemency. Three of the scheduled five executions took place between January 10 and January 25, and it became clear that a more comprehensive and concerted effort was needed to bring the juvenile death penalty to an end. A meeting was convened in Chicago for November 2000, and from this meeting the Juvenile Death Penalty Initiative (JDPI) was created. The JDPI was a coalition of lawyers, civil society organizations, and others who opposed the practice. They took their cue from the opinions in *Thompson* and *Stanford*.

In both cases, the Supreme Court had emphasized the importance of using "objective indicia" such as the decisions of juries and the actions of state legislatures to determine whether the juvenile death penalty offended "evolving standards of decency." One of the JDPI's first tasks, then, was to stem the flow of juveniles being sentenced to death and executed, by locating and offering support to lawyers defending death-eligible juveniles around the country. Another task was to generate public opposition to the practice so that state legislators would feel compelled to support (or at least comfortable supporting) legislative efforts to outlaw the juvenile death penalty.

In both aspects, a key and innovative feature of the JDPI's work was to center the arguments for abolition around emerging scientific research on adolescent brain development. New methods of studying brain development suggested that the frontal lobes of brains, which control impulses and logical reasoning, are not fully developed at ages sixteen and seventeen. This cast doubt on the penological justifications for the death penalty, since it could not be said that juveniles were as morally culpable for their crimes as their adult counterparts. These physiological differences between adolescents and adults also pointed toward greater capacity for rehabilitation than had been previously understood.[46]

To add credibility to these arguments, the JDPI worked with experts in child psychological development, such as Professor Laurence Steinberg, and reached out to widely respected national organizations such as the American Psychiatric Association and the American Psychological Association to adopt policy positions such as the one the ABA had adopted in 1983. The JDPI also forged relationships with international partners, urging the European Union, for example, to exert greater diplomatic pressure.

The efforts of the JDPI paid dividends remarkably quickly. In the six-year period from 1994 to 1999, an average of thirteen juveniles were being sentenced to death each year, but in the five-year period from 2000 to 2004, that average dropped to just four. Juries were clearly turning their backs on the juvenile death penalty as lawyers became more adept at defending juveniles. In the eighteen-year period from 1981 to 1999, ten jurisdictions took steps to set the minimum age for the death penalty at eighteen, through either state legislative activity or state court decisions, at a rate of roughly one jurisdiction every two years. In just three years, from 2002 to 2004, a further four states took such steps. The rate at which states were turning their backs on the juvenile death penalty was accelerating.[47]

The year 2002 turned out to be something of a pivotal year in the United States' history of the juvenile death penalty. Over the course of a few months, a number of events occurred which propelled the United States toward nationwide abolition. On March 26, Indiana became the sixteenth state with the death penalty to prohibit the punishment for juveniles, with Missouri, South Dakota, and Wyoming joining that list over the next two years. On May 28, the arbitrariness of the juvenile death penalty was thrown into sharp relief when the fates of two juveniles on death row diverged dramatically on the same day.

Napoleon Beazley and Christopher Simmons had both been sentenced to death for crimes committed when seventeen years old, and both requested a stay of execution pending the outcome of a constitutional challenge to the execution of the intellectually disabled, which they argued had implications for the juvenile death penalty. On May 28, the Missouri State Supreme Court granted Simmons a stay pending the decision of the U.S. Supreme Court in *Atkins v. Virginia*.[48] Having already been denied a stay on the very same argument, Beazley, who was set to be executed that day, notified the Texas High Court of Missouri's decision, but was denied a stay again. On the same day that Simmons was reprieved, Beazley was killed by lethal injection shortly after 7:00 p.m.

The inconsistencies between the two cases did not go unnoticed.[49] Walter Long—Beazley's attorney and a central figure with the JDPI—publicly lamented how the events of that day "expose[d] the system's brutal arbitrariness."[50] The skin colors of Simmons and Beazley could not be ignored: Simmons was white and Beazley was Black. Beazley's execution was widely condemned and generated more vociferous opposition to the juvenile death penalty. Over thirty thousand individuals and organizations worldwide had appealed for clemency, including the judge who presided over Beazley's trial, as well as seven Nobel Peace Prize winners. Beazley's age was a crucial factor in these calls for clemency, with the former president of South Africa, F. W. de Klerk, stating, "I am not opposed in principle to the death penalty. . . . Nevertheless, I am opposed to the imposition of the death penalty where the perpetrator was under 18 years old at the time of the crime."[51]

On June 20, 2002, the United States Supreme Court outlawed the death penalty for those with intellectual disabilities in *Atkins v. Virginia*. As *Beazley* and *Simmons* had predicted, the Court's reasoning was just as applicable to juveniles as it was to those with intellectual disabilities, providing further support for abolitionist efforts. In September, Amnesty International released a seventy-two-page report titled *Indecent and Internationally Illegal: The Death Penalty against Child Offenders*, which outlined just how the reasoning in *Atkins* applied to juveniles, too. Although Texas had executed two more juveniles the previous month, it was clear that momentum toward abolition was building.

On October 21, 2002, the U.S. Supreme Court denied a writ of habeas corpus in *In re Stanford*, in which petitioner had asked the Court to revisit *Stanford v. Kentucky*. Although this seemed to set back the movement for abolition, four justices took the unusual step of issuing a dissent from the Court's refusal, and the even more unusual step of stating outright that they would find the practice unconstitutional: "The practice of executing such offenders is a relic of the past," Justice Stevens wrote, "and is inconsistent with evolving standards of decency in a civilized society. We should put an end to this shameful practice."

The very next day, the Inter-American Commission on Human Rights issued a report in the case of *Michael Domingues v. United States*. Domingues had been sentenced to death in Nevada for a crime committed at the age of sixteen, and the commission asserted that "a norm of international customary law has emerged prohibiting the execution of offenders under the age of 18 years at the time of their crime . . . and this rule has been recognized as being of a sufficiently indelible nature to now constitute a norm of jus cogens."[52] Norms of jus cogens are those rules of international law that are considered so important that they apply to all states, regardless of whether the state consents to the rule. Although this report had no legally binding effect, it had a powerful rhetorical effect: the juvenile death penalty was now in the same category as slavery and genocide. This made it much harder for the United States to defend the legality and morality of the practice.

Opponents of the juvenile death penalty were hopeful that these developments would quicken the demise of the juvenile death penalty, but on October 24, 2002, breaking news threatened the prospects for abolition. Throughout October, the news cycle in the United States had been dominated by reports of people being shot seemingly at random in the Beltway area around Washington, D.C. The first killings took place on October 2 and 3, when six people died from gunshot wounds. Over the next nineteen days, four more people were killed, and three others were injured at locations as mundane as gas stations, car parks, and bus stops. I had moved to D.C. from the United Kingdom in September to work with the JDPI, and I vividly remember the sense of fear that spread throughout the city and the concerns of my family and friends back home. I also remember the sense of relief that people felt on October 24 when it was announced that two people had been arrested in connection with the shootings. And I remember the concerns and anxieties among my colleagues in the JDPI when it transpired that one of the suspects— Lee Boyd Malvo—was just seventeen years old.

The nature of Malvo's crimes and the surrounding publicity made him something of a poster boy for those who wanted to retain the death penalty for juveniles, and we initially feared that his case would derail our efforts. Prosecutors announced that they would be seeking death sentences in Virginia, which still permitted the juvenile death penalty and where some of the killings occurred. It seemed almost certain that he would be sentenced to death. And as we assisted Malvo's lawyers, another juvenile neared his execution date. Despite our efforts to secure clemency, Scott Hain was executed in Oklahoma on April 3, 2003. The charge toward abolition appeared to be sputtering. However, Hain would be the last juvenile to be executed, as it transpired that counterintuitively, Malvo's case would help our cause.

In December 2003, the jury at Malvo's first trial, in Chesapeake, Virginia, spared him a death sentence, primarily because of his age. We could now argue that if the death penalty was deemed inappropriate for Malvo, then it must surely be inappropriate for all juveniles. One month later, on January 26, 2004, the U.S. Supreme Court granted certiorari in *Roper v. Simmons*. The juvenile death penalty was in its final throes.

Abolition at Last

On March 1, 2005, about 363 years after Thomas Graunger was executed in Plymouth Colony, and two years after Scott Hain's execution in Oklahoma, the Supreme Court ruled in *Roper v. Simmons* that the death penalty is "cruel and unusual" when imposed on juveniles, and therefore contrary to the Eighth Amendment to the Constitution.

Justice Anthony Kennedy wrote the majority opinion, which can broadly be split into two parts. The first focused on popular opinion and the juvenile death penalty, and the second focused on whether capital punishment is disproportionate when imposed on juveniles. With respect to the first part, Kennedy found that there was a national consensus against the practice of imposing death sentences on juveniles, thus rendering the practice contrary to "evolving standards of decency that mark the progress of a maturing society."[53] He noted that twelve states implicitly rejected the practice, since those states rejected the death penalty altogether, and a further nineteen states which retained the death penalty had explicitly excluded juveniles from the reach of capital punishment. Furthermore, just six states had actually executed people for crimes committed when under the age of eighteen since the Court last considered the issue in 1989.

In five of these six states, the practice was as rare as it could have been. Louisiana, Missouri, and Georgia had each executed just one juvenile; Oklahoma had executed two; and Virginia had executed three. Texas was responsible for the remaining eleven executions in the post-*Stanford* era, demonstrating just how unusual the practice was in the United States generally.[54] To compound these numbers, no state had reintroduced the death penalty for juveniles, yet five states had outlawed the practice since *Stanford*. In Kennedy's view, this was evidence of "consistency of direction of change." According to Kennedy, "the rejection of the juvenile death penalty in the majority of States; the infrequency of its use even where it remains on the books; and the consistency in the trend toward abolition of the practice—provide sufficient evidence that today our society views juveniles . . . as categorically less culpable than the average criminal."[55]

The finding of a national consensus against the juvenile death penalty was not the end of the inquiry, though. Kennedy went on to explain why the death penalty is a disproportionate punishment when imposed on juveniles, and thus contrary to the Eighth Amendment. In his words, there are "three general differences between juveniles under 18 and adults [that] demonstrate that juvenile offenders cannot with reliability be classified among the worst offenders."[56] First, scientific and sociological studies have consistently shown that those under eighteen have "a lack of maturity and an underdeveloped sense of responsibility," which result in "impetuous and ill-considered actions and decisions."[57] Second, young people are "more vulnerable or susceptible to negative influences and outside pressures."[58] Third, young people are more amenable to rehabilitation, and are not "irretrievably depraved."[59] As Kennedy wrote, "Once the diminished culpability of juveniles is recognized, it is evident that the penological justifications for the death penalty apply to them with lesser force than to adults."[60] This section of his judgment vindicated the JDPI's decision to place scientific arguments at the center of the case against the juvenile death penalty.

Justice Kennedy could have ended his analysis there, having established a national consensus against the practice, and having brought the Court's own "independent judgment to bear on the proportionality of the death penalty for a particular class of crimes or offenders."[61] However, he did not. In a remarkable passage, Kennedy surveyed international law and the laws of other countries in order to support the Court's ruling. This represented a sharp turn away from the *Stanford* Court's insistence that non-U.S. laws and practices were entirely irrelevant to constitutional interpretation. Kennedy reiterated what lawyers, scholars, and civil society organizations had long argued: "The United States is the only country in the world that continues to give official sanction to the juvenile death penalty."[62] He emphasized that "the opinion of the world community" did not control the decision of the Court, but provided "respected and significant confirmation for our own conclusions."[63]

Kennedy knew that this portion of this judgment would attract criticism, and he ended his judgment with a defense of the invocation of international and foreign law. In his view, "It is proper that we acknowledge the overwhelming weight of international opinion against the juvenile death penalty," and "[i]t does not lessen our fidelity to the Constitution or our pride in its origins to acknowledge that the express affirmation of certain fundamental rights by other nations and peoples simply underscores the centrality of those same rights within our own heritage of freedom."[64]

Justice Scalia issued a scathing dissent, which Chief Justice Rehnquist and Justice Clarence Thomas joined. In their view, the majority's entire approach to interpreting the Eighth Amendment was wrong. First, they argued that the Court's approach to finding a "national consensus" was erroneous. Non–death penalty states, in their view, should be taken out of the equation, with Scalia asserting that "consulting States that bar the death penalty concerning the necessity of making an exception to the penalty for offenders under 18 is rather like including old-order Amishmen in a consumer-preference poll on the electric car. Of course they don't like it, but that sheds no light whatever on the point at issue."[65] Second, they chastised the majority for bringing their own view to bear on the question of the proportionality of the punishment, asking, "By what conceivable warrant can nine lawyers presume to be the authoritative conscience of the Nation?"[66] Third, they criticized the majority for invoking international and foreign law, with Scalia sarcastically writing, "Though the views of our own citizens are essentially irrelevant to the Court's decision today, the views of other countries and the so-called international community take center stage."[67]

Justice O'Connor issued a separate, less hostile dissent, in which she agreed with the majority's general approach but disagreed with their conclusions. In her view, although international law was relevant to the question, there was no national consensus on the issue either way, and the death penalty was not always disproportionate when imposed on a sixteen- or seventeen-year-old. For O'Connor, retaining youthfulness as a mitigating factor was sufficient, but there could be no constitutional bar to the juvenile death penalty. By a 5–4 decision, then, the juvenile death penalty was declared unconstitutional. The immediate consequence of the judgment was that seventy-two juveniles on death rows in the United States had their death sentences overturned. However, the opinion was to have further-reaching consequences over the coming years.

The Legacy of the Juvenile Death Penalty and Its Abolition

I had left the United States before the Supreme Court handed down its judgment in *Roper*, so I could not celebrate the decision with my former colleagues. But I remember thinking that it would be inappropriate to "celebrate" the decision anyway. As always with the death penalty, there are the families of the deceased to consider. And any sense of relief that Simmons and the other juveniles on death row would be spared execution was tinged by the realization that many of them would now be sentenced to life in prison without the possibility of parole instead, which is tantamount to a death sentence in practice.[68] In this sense, the legacy of the juvenile death penalty and its abolition is complex.

The mere existence of the practice had the effect of levelling up punishments for young people, meaning that other harsh punishments for juveniles—such as life without parole and solitary confinement—went largely unnoticed and stayed in place after *Roper*. For example, even though people under the age of sixteen had been spared execution since 1988, many as young as thirteen or fourteen years old were still being sentenced to spend the rest of their lives in prison. Put another way, even when the juvenile death penalty was abolished, young people still tended to be punished much more punitively in the United States than in most other nations.[69] The manner of abolition, though, enabled challenges to these sorts of punishments. The successes and failures of these challenges are perhaps best understood by drawing a distinction between developments at the federal level and the state level in the years following *Roper*.

At the federal level, the legacy of *Roper* has been mixed. For just over a decade after *Roper*, the Supreme Court continued to exempt juveniles from the most severe punishments, but this progress seems to have come to an abrupt halt, and perhaps even gone into reverse, after the composition of the Court was radically changed during President Donald Trump's administration. To begin, it is worth clarifying that following *Roper*, the most serious punishment available for juveniles was life in prison without the possibility of parole (LWOP), which could be imposed for both homicide and nonhomicide offenses. In *Roper*, Justice Kennedy appeared to endorse LWOP for juveniles when he said that the death penalty was not necessary because "the punishment of life imprisonment without the possibility of parole is itself a severe sanction, in particular for a young person."[70] Despite this statement, advocates soon realized that they could use the reasoning in *Roper* to challenge the constitutionality of LWOP for juveniles.[71] Up until 2016, they were largely successful in their efforts.

In *Graham v. Florida*,[72] the Court invoked *Roper* to rule that the Eighth Amendment also prohibits the imposition of LWOP on juveniles convicted of nonhomicide offences, because "the limited culpability of juvenile nonhomicide offenders . . . and the severity of life without parole sentences all lead to the conclusion that the sentencing practice under consideration is cruel and unusual."[73] This was a remarkable decision because it was the first time that the Court deployed its death penalty jurisprudence in a noncapital case.[74] The *Graham* Court expressly drew on the reasoning in *Roper* that emphasized the special considerations that need to be taken into account when sentencing juveniles, such as their limited development and the potential for reform.

The domino effect of *Roper* continued in 2012, when the Court struck down mandatory sentences of life without parole for juveniles convicted of homicide. Evan Miller had been automatically sentenced to LWOP for a crime committed when he was just fourteen years old, but Justice Elena Kagan reasoned, "Mandatory life without parole for a juvenile precludes consideration of his chronological age and its hallmark features— among them, immaturity, impetuosity, and failure to appreciate risks and consequences. It prevents taking into account the family and home environment that surrounds him—and from which he cannot usually extricate himself—no matter how brutal or dysfunctional."[75] Four years later, in *Montgomery v. Louisiana*,[76] the Court confirmed that *Miller* applied retroactively and clarified that life without parole was prohibited "for all but the rarest of juvenile offenders, those whose crimes reflect permanent incorrigibility." Following *Montgomery*, it seemed clear that juveniles could now be sentenced to life without parole only if they were convicted of homicide and there was evidence that they were beyond all hope for rehabilitation. On this account, the legacy of *Roper* is a positive one. However, there are three reasons why we should be cautious of celebrating the legacy of *Roper* in the context of the Supreme Court.

First, the cases explicitly leave intact the constitutionality of life without parole for juveniles. This is contrary to international human rights law and the practice of the rest of the world.[77] A second reason for remaining pessimistic about the legacy of *Roper* is that the Court appears to be reversing course as a result of its changed composition since the *Graham–Miller–Montgomery* line of cases. Those cases had been decided by 5–4 and 6–3 majorities, but two of the justices on those majorities are no longer on the Court. Justice Kennedy retired in 2018, and Justice Ruth Bader Ginsburg passed away in 2020. They were replaced by conservative jurists who have indicated that they are willing to broaden the possibilities for imposing LWOP on juveniles. On April 22, 2021, the Court ruled by a 6–3 majority in *Jones v. Mississippi*[78] that a sentencer does not need to find that a juvenile is permanently incorrigible before imposing LWOP; they merely need to consider youth as a mitigating factor. As Justice Sonia Sotomayor wrote in her dissenting judgment, this ruling "guts" *Miller* and *Montgomery*. In those cases, the Court had explicitly stated that LWOP can only be imposed on the "rarest of juvenile offenders, those whose crimes reflect permanent incorrigibility."[79] Even Justice Thomas, who concurred with majority judgment in *Jones*, wrote separately to note that the ruling was inconsistent with *Montgomery*.

A third reason for reading the legacy of *Roper* cautiously lies in the fact that these cases only address the most severe sanction: life without parole. They say nothing about other lengthy terms of imprisonment for juveniles that amount to virtual life without parole sentences. Thus, while the impact of *Roper* should not be overlooked, the progress made through the Supreme Court decisions should not be overstated.

At the state level, the legacy of *Roper* and its progeny is similarly ambiguous. On the one hand, the reasoning in *Roper* has contributed to a decline in the use of LWOP for juveniles. When *Miller* was decided in 2012, just five states prohibited life without parole as a sentencing option for juveniles, but as of 2023 that number stands at twenty-eight, plus Washington, D.C.[80] And when *Montgomery* was decided in 2016, there were approximately 2,800 people serving sentences of LWOP for crimes committed as juveniles, but in 2020 the Sentencing Project found that that number had declined to 1,465.[81]

State authorities have also been inspired by *Roper* to engage with new scientific research that shows that the brain is not even fully developed at age eighteen. In Kentucky, for example, Judge Ernesto Scorsone declared that the age of death eligibility should actually be raised to twenty-one on the basis of new scientific understandings about culpability, and he was explicit about the influence of *Roper* on his ruling: "If the science in 2005 mandated the ruling in *Roper*, the science in 2017 mandates this ruling."[82] In Washington, D.C., in 2020, the Omnibus Public Safety and Justice Amendment Act was passed, which allows people sentenced to terms of life imprisonment for crimes committed when under the age of twenty-five to apply to have their sentence reduced after they have served fifteen years. Illinois, Washington State, and Maryland have taken similar steps, recognizing that the human brain keeps developing when a person is in their twenties.[83] These developments shed light on the arbitrariness of setting eighteen as a marker for adulthood.

On the other hand, several states have taken a more literal and narrow approach to the decisions in *Roper* and its progeny. Although twenty-eight states have now prohibited LWOP completely for juveniles, the other twenty-two have availed themselves of the opportunity to retain the punishment as a sentencing option.[84] Evan Miller, whose case led the U.S. Supreme Court to outlaw mandatory sentences of LWOP, was himself resentenced to life without parole in Alabama in 2021.[85]

Henry Montgomery—whose case was the subject of *Montgomery v. Louisiana* in 2016—fared better than Miller, but only after considerable struggle. Montgomery was initially resentenced to life with the possibility of parole following the U.S. Supreme Court decision in his case in 2016, but he was then denied parole on two occasions, in 2018 and 2019. In the latter hearing, one of the parole board members, Brennan Kelsey, said that Montgomery had not participated in enough classes during his incarceration. "I think that's a lack of maturity," Kelsey said, telling Montgomery that he should "continue to work hard on the inside [and] [t]ake as many programs as you can."[86] Montgomery was seventy-two years old at the time of this parole hearing. He was eventually granted parole in November 2021, five years after he won in the U.S. Supreme Court and fifty-seven years after his conviction at the age of seventeen in 1963, when President John F. Kennedy was still alive.[87]

In Florida, the state supreme court ruled in *Gridine v. State*[88] and *Henry v. State*[89] that seventy- and ninety-year terms of imprisonment, respectively, deny juveniles "a meaningful opportunity for early release" and are thus forbidden under the rationale of *Graham*. But the cases say nothing about terms of up to seventy years in prison. Moreover, in *Franklin v. State*,[90] the Court upheld a one thousand–year term of imprisonment on the basis that Franklin's sentence includes the opportunity for parole. The earliest date that Franklin will be eligible for parole, though, is 2352, nearly 370 years from the date of the offense.

Despite some important progress since *Roper*, then, there are still significant problems with legal responses to those who commit crimes when under the age of eighteen. Although many people have had their sentences of LWOP reduced as a result of the Supreme Court cases and subsequent state-level action, many have not. And although the *Roper* Court's use of science was relatively groundbreaking at the time, scientific understandings of moral blameworthiness have not dictated the issue. The Campaign for the Fair Sentencing of Youth goes so far as to argue that the "relief afforded to individuals serving JLWOP is based more on jurisdiction than on whether the individual has demonstrated positive growth and maturation."[91] And researchers have highlighted that racial disparities in the use of such sentences have actually increased since *Miller*, largely because JLWOP schemes are now discretionary, which means that white offenders tend to be spared by juries, while Black offenders are not. While Black youth made up 61 percent of the pre-*Miller* JLWOP population, they make up 70 percent of all sentences imposed since 2012. Similarly, courts and legislatures have been slow to address the problem of non-LWOP sentences that amount to life without parole in practical terms.

Conclusion

The juvenile death penalty was an abject failure of law, policy, and justice, but it received remarkably little attention until the new millennium. This is perhaps because it was so rarely used. Juveniles accounted for just 2 percent of all those executed in the 363 years between Graunger's execution and the decision in *Roper*, and at the time *Roper* was decided, juveniles similarly represented just 2 percent of the entire death row population: just seventy-two out of 3,471 people on death row at the time were classed as juveniles. However, as the outlines of some of the cases and issues demonstrate, the practice is better understood as emblematic of the broader problems of the U.S. death penalty: the prevalence of racial and social-class discrimination; the inherent risk of executing an innocent person; and exceptionalism from international human rights norms.

Although the phenomenon itself can be classed as a failure of law and morality, the manner of its abolition holds much promise. Some of this promise has been seen in the *Graham–Miller–Montgomery* line of cases, and in the actions of state authorities that have outlawed LWOP altogether for juveniles. The reasoning in *Roper* also initiated reforms to the protection afforded to children facing police interrogations; to the use of mandatory minimum sentencing schemes for youth; and to juvenile sex-offender registration requirements.[92] And *Roper* also provided hope to those who wished to see capital punishment curtailed further, with some arguing that the decision provides grounds for exempting the severely mentally ill from the death penalty.[93]

But the legacy of the juvenile death penalty and its abolition remains mixed. The Court has jettisoned the *Roper* approach to both juvenile justice and the death penalty, and people are still locked away in solitary confinement for offences committed when they were under eighteen. In 2015, ten years after the decision in *Roper*, Kalief Browder tragically took his own life after the trauma of being locked in Rikers Island at the age of sixteen without trial.[94] While some steps have been taken to atone for the United States' "ugly history of executing poor children,"[95] there is still considerable progress to be made.

Notes

1 Throughout this chapter, I use the term *juvenile* to refer to someone accused or convicted of a crime committed when under the age of eighteen. I use this term reluctantly, as it carries a certain stigma. However, it is the term that appears in the literature and in court judgments, and it is therefore used here for the sake of clarity.
2 *Furman v. Georgia*, 408 U.S. 238 (1972).
3 *Stanford v. Kentucky*, 492 U.S. 361 (1989).
4 *Roper v. Simmons*, 543 U.S. 551 (2005).
5 Lawrence M. Friedman, *Crime and Punishment in American History* (New York: Basic Books, 1993), 34–35.
6 Victor Streib, *Death Penalty for Juveniles* (Bloomington: Indiana University Press, 1987), 190–208.
7 Streib, 190–208.

8 Sheri Lynn Johnson, John H. Blume, and Hannah L. Freedman, "The Pre-*Furman* Juvenile Death Penalty in South Carolina: Young Black Life Was Cheap," *South Carolina Law Review* 68, no. 3 (2017): 331–72.

9 428 U.S. 153 (1976). The decision is often referred to as *Gregg* because that was the lead case. There were in fact five cases under consideration: *Gregg v. Georgia*, *Proffitt v. Florida*, *Jurek v. Texas*, *Woodson v. North Carolina*, and *Roberts v. Louisiana*. The Court upheld the constitutionality of the death penalty schemes of Georgia, Florida, and Texas since these provided frameworks that guided decision-makers' discretion in capital cases. Broadly speaking, these schemes limited the availability of the death penalty to specific circumstances (such as murder committed in the course of another felony) and either required or permitted sentencers to consider mitigating factors. The Court rejected schemes in North Carolina and Louisiana, which mandated the death penalty in certain circumstances.

10 Corrine T. Field and Nicholas L. Syrett, eds., *Age in America: The Colonial Era to the Present* (New York: New York University Press, 2015).

11 Streib, *Death Penalty*, 45.

12 Streib, 44.

13 Streib, 46.

14 Streib, 43.

15 438 U.S. 586 (1978).

16 *Eddings v. Oklahoma*, 455 U.S. 104 (1982).

17 Justice Brennan joined the majority but issued a concurring opinion to state that he would have held the death penalty to be unconstitutional in all circumstances. By implication, Brennan would have outlawed the juvenile death penalty. Although Justice Marshall did not write separately in this case, he had stated in *Furman* and *Gregg* that he considered the death penalty to be unconstitutional in all circumstances, and so it can be inferred that he too would have found the juvenile death penalty unconstitutional. In later cases, Marshall routinely joined Brennan in asserting the death penalty to be unconstitutional in all circumstances.

18 *Eddings*, 455 U.S. 104 at 116.

19 Streib, *Death Penalty*, 22, 50.

20 Streib, 30.

21 American Bar Association, Juvenile Death Penalty Resolution, adopted 1983.

22 Ohio (1981), Nebraska (1982), Colorado (1985), Oregon (1986), and New Jersey (1988).

23 Field and Syrett, *Age in America*, 1–2.

24 Joan F. Hartman, "Unusual Punishment: The Domestic Effects of International Norms Restricting the Application of the Death Penalty," *University of Cincinnati Law Review* 52, no. 3 (1983): 655–99.

25 Streib, *Death Penalty*, ix.

26 487 U.S. 815 (1988).

27 Justice Kennedy took no part in the decision, having only recently been appointed to the Supreme Court.

28 492 U.S. 361 (1989).

29 *Stanford*, 492 U.S. at 380.

30 Amnesty International, *Indecent and Internationally Illegal: The Death Penalty against Child Offenders*, AMR 51/143/2002 (London: Amnesty International, September 24, 2002), 46, www.amnesty.org.

31 Somalia was not able to ratify the treaty because it did not have a functioning government. At the time of writing in 2021, it has now ratified the Convention on the Rights of the Child, making the United States the only member of the United Nations that has not ratified the treaty.

32 Connie de la Vega and Jennifer Brown, "Can a United States Treaty Reservation Provide a Sanctuary for the Juvenile Death Penalty?," *University of San Francisco Law Review* 32 (1998): 735–72.

33 *Stanford*, 492 U.S. at 369 n.1.

34 W. J. Bennett, John J. Dilulio Jr., and J. P. Walters, *Body Count: Moral Poverty and How to Win America's War against Crime and Drugs* (New York: Simon and Schuster, 1996), 27.

35 Franklin E. Zimring, "The Power Politics of Juvenile Court Transfer in the 1990s," in *Choosing the Future for American Juvenile Justice*, ed. Franklin E. Zimring and David S. Tanenhaus (New York: New York University Press, 2014), 37–54.

36 Quoted in *Roper*, 543 U.S. at 558.

37 Rachel Leah, "The 'Superpredator' Myth Was Discredited, but It Continues to Ruin Young Black Lives," *Salon*, April 21, 2018, www.salon.com/.

38 Leon Brown was fifteen years old, Johnny Ross and Shareef Cousin were sixteen years old, and Sabrina Butler, Larry Osborne, Ryan Matthews, and Kwame Ajamu were all seventeen years old.

39 Megan Crane, Laura Nirider, and Steven A. Drizin, "The Truth About Juvenile False Confessions" *Insights on Law and Society* 16, no. 2 (Winter 2016): 10–15.

40 Ross was convicted before the U.S. Supreme Court outlawed the death penalty for rape in *Coker v. Georgia* (1977).

41 Center for Death Penalty Litigation, *Saved from the Executioner: The Unlikely Exoneration of Henry McCollum* (Durham, NC: Center for Death Penalty Litigation, 2017).

42 For details of Cousin's and Butler's cases, see the website of Witness to Innocence (www.witnesstoinnocence.org). This organization comprises exonerees from death row who now advocate for abolition in all circumstances.

43 Amnesty International, *Indecent and Internationally Illegal: The Death Penalty Against Child Offenders* (2002), 2.

44 Pamela Colloff, "Does Napoleon Beazley Deserve to Die?," *Texas Monthly*, April 2002.

45 Last Statement of Napoleon Beazley, Death Row Information, Texas Department of Criminal Justice, May 28, 2002, www.tdcj.texas.gov/.

46 Laurence Steinberg and Elizabeth S. Scott, "Less Guilty by Reason of Adolescence: Development Immaturity, Diminished Responsibility, and the Juvenile Death Penalty," *American Psychologist* 58, no. 12 (December 2003): 1009–18.

47 Victor L. Streib, "The Juvenile Death Penalty Today: Death Sentences and Executions for Juvenile Crimes, January 1, 1973–February 28, 2005" (Claude W. Pettit College of Law, Ohio Northern University, Ada, OH, 2005).

48 536 U.S. 304 (2002).

49 Sara Rimer, "In Similar Cases, One Inmate Is Executed, One Wins Stay," *New York Times*, May 29, 2002.

50 Walter Long, "Napoleon Beazley Should Have Been Granted Reprieve," *Austin American-Statesman*, June 6, 2002.

51 Amnesty International, *Indecent and Internationally Illegal*, 25.

52 *Michael Domingues v. United States*, Case 12.285, Report No. 62/02, Inter-American Commission on Human Rights, Doc. 5 rev. 1 at 913 (2002) (84–85).

53 *Roper*, 543 U.S. at 561.

54 Three executions took place in the modern era before *Stanford*. Two took place in Texas, and one occurred in South Carolina.

55 *Roper*, 543 U.S. at 567.

56 *Roper*, at 569.

57 *Roper*, at 569 (internal quotations omitted).

58 *Roper*, at 569.

59 *Roper*, at 570.

60 *Roper*, at 571.

61 *Roper*, at 574.

62 *Roper*, at 575.

63 *Roper*, at 578.

64 *Roper*, at 578.

65 *Roper*, at 610–11.

66 *Roper*, at 616.

67 *Roper*, at 622.

68 Most juveniles on death rows across the United States were resentenced to life without parole after *Roper*. Texas did not have life without parole as a sentencing option at the time of *Roper*, and so the thirty juveniles on Texas death row were sentenced to terms of imprisonment instead.

69 Brandon L. Garrett, "Life without Parole for Kids Is Cruelty with No Benefit," *The Atlantic*, October 19, 2020.

70 *Roper*, 543 U.S. at 572.

71 Jeffrey Toobin, "The Legacy of Lynching, on Death Row," *New Yorker*, August 15, 2016.

72 *Graham v. Florida*, 560 U.S. 48 (2010).

73 *Graham*, 560 U.S. at 74.

74 Mary Berkheiser, "Death Is Not So Different After All: *Graham v. Florida* and the Court's Kids Are Different Eighth Amendment Jurisprudence," *Vermont Law Review* 36 (2011): 1–62.

75 *Miller v. Alabama*, 567 U.S. 460, 477 (2012).

76 *Montgomery v. Louisiana*, 577 U.S. 190 (2016).

77 Connie de la Vega and Michelle Leighton, "Sentencing our Children to Die in Prison: Global Law and Practice," *University of San Francisco Law Review* 42, no. 4 (2008); Bharat Malkani, "Sentencing Children Who Kill: One Giant Leap for the US Supreme Court, One Small Step for International Human Rights Law," *Human Rights Law Review* 12, no. 4 (212): 801–13.

78 *Jones v. Mississippi*, 593 U.S. __ (2021).

79 *Montgomery*, 577 U.S. at 734.

80 Campaign for the Fair Sentencing of Youth, *National Trends in Sentencing Children to Life without Parole* (Washington, DC: Campaign for the Fair Sentencing of Youth, June 2022), www.cfsy.org.

81 Josh Rovner, *Juvenile Life without Parole: An Overview* (Washington, DC: Sentencing Project, 2023), www.sentencingproject.org/.

82 *Commonwealth of Kentucky v. Bredhold*, Fayette Circuit Court (Case No. 14-CR-161, 2017): 6.

83 Elizabeth Weill-Greenberg, "Maryland Bans Sentencing Children to Life without Parole," *The Appeal*, April 13, 2021.

84 Campaign for the Fair Sentencing of Youth, *National Trends*.

85 Kent Faulk, "Evan Miller, Youngest Person Ever Sentenced to Life without Parole in Alabama, Must Remain in Prison," *AL.com*, April 27, 2021.

86 Liliana Segura, "Henry Montgomery Paved the Way for Other Juvenile Lifers to Go Free," *The Intercept*, June 2, 2019.

87 Elyse Carmonisno, "Convicted of Murder at 17, His Case Changed Juvenile Sentences," *The Advocate*, November 17, 2021.

88 *Gridine v. State*, 175 So. 3d 672 (Fla. 2015).

89 *Henry v. State*, 175 So. 3d 675 (Fla. 2015).

90 *Franklin v. State*, 258 So. 3d 1239 (Fla. 2018).

91 Campaign for the Fair Sentencing of Youth, *National Trends in Sentencing Children to Life Without Parole* (June 2022), 2.

92 M. Levick and S. Drizin, "Celebrating the 10th Anniversary of *Roper v. Simmons*: One Small Step for Christopher Simmons, One Giant Step for Juvenile Justice Reform," *Huffington Post*, March 2, 2015.

93 Laura Ford, "Exempting the Severely Mentally Ill from the Death Penalty in the United States of America: The Concept of Human Dignity" (PhD diss., University of Birmingham, 2020); Robert Batey, "Categorical Bars to Execution: Civilizing the Death Penalty," *Houston Law Review* 45 (2009): 1493–528.

94 Jennifer Gonnerman, "Kalief Browder, 1993–2015," *New Yorker*, June 7, 2015.

95 Joan Jacobs Brumberg, *Kansas Charley: The Story of a 19th-Century Boy Murderer* (New York: Viking, 2003), 240.

4

Capital Sentencing and Mental Illness

Proportionality and Procedural Fairness

RICHARD J. BONNIE

This essay considers whether and to what extent prosecutors, judges, and defense attorneys have taken adequate account of serious mental illness of capital defendants (their fitness for adjudication or degree of culpability) or condemned prisoners (their decisional capacity for post-conviction review or fitness for execution) in the administration of the death penalty. The answer is and will continue to be no unless and until skillful legal representation is systematically provided to defendants in all capital prosecutions, particularly in connection with sentencing proceedings, and unless and until specialized counsel are provided to condemned prisoners in all post-conviction proceedings in both state and federal courts. Litigation outcomes convincingly document the fact that skillful representation saves lives. But not all states have made the necessary commitment to provide this representation. As a result, the administration of capital punishment in the United States has not taken adequate account of the morally and legally relevant effects of mental illness. Although this chapter focuses exclusively on mental illness, my observations for the most part also apply to the effects of intellectual and developmental disability, dementia, and traumatic brain injury.

Genuinely Narrowing the Class: A Constitutional Imperative

In its pathbreaking decisions in *Furman v. Georgia* (1972)[1] and *Gregg v. Georgia*[2] and the accompanying decisions in 1976, the Supreme Court was not in a position—juridically speaking—to declare the death penalty per se unconstitutional. It would have been an unprecedented exercise in judicial innovation and may well have triggered a constitutional amendment reinstating capital punishment. It was more sensible for the Court to invalidate the current generation of capital sentencing statutes, while laying out governing principles and giving states an opportunity to implement these principles faithfully. In my opinion, the Court did a reasonable job of formulating the necessary principles.

First, the 1976 decisions invited legislatures and courts to take meaningful steps to decrease the types of defendants eligible to be executed. This strategy was the only jurisprudential approach that had any plausible prospect of avoiding both the "freakishness" (arbitrariness) of capital sentencing and the insidious—and increasingly well documented— patterns of racial discrimination. Second, the Court properly ruled out mandatory death sentences, even for defendants convicted of committing the most aggravated offenses; in so doing, the Court properly insisted that—however aggravated the offense—the defendant is entitled to an opportunity to persuade the sentencing jury or judge to consider the "diverse frailties of humankind"[3] and to spare the defendant's life.

By narrowing the necessary predicates for a capital sentence to a small set of offenses most congruent with the community's demand for retributive justice, while leaving the door open to compelling individualized claims for leniency, the Court left sufficient room for the states most insistent on preserving the death penalty to do so while hoping that the desire for capital punishment would eventually wither away. This was the direction in which the Court seemed to be heading during the decade after *Furman*.

If the Court had stayed with the logic of "narrowing" the class to the most aggravated categories of murder that would predictably lead juries to impose death sentences untainted by racial bias, then Eighth Amendment[4] capital sentencing doctrine could have developed rationally. The class of lawful death sentences could have been gradually narrowed over time,[5] amounting to a strategy of de facto abolition, leading ultimately to legislative repeal or residual invalidation by state supreme courts (if not a coup de grâce by the Supreme Court itself). Notwithstanding sporadic political initiatives to salvage the death penalty in Congress and the states of the "Confederate" South, I believe this aggressive judicial strategy would have succeeded. It could have worked if the justices had stuck to it. Indeed, the Court might well have settled on an even more aggressive strategy (playing the race card, so to speak) if Justice Powell had voted differently in *McCleskey v. Kemp*.[6] If Georgia's capital sentencing statute had been declared *unconstitutional as applied*, the death penalty would have eventually been suspended while the door was kept open to definitive proof that it was being imposed in only a narrow class of cases ("the worst of the worst") untainted by race. Justice Powell later said he regretted his vote in *McCleskey*.[7]

It is conceivable that thoughtful justices, whatever their political orientations, will one day recognize that requiring aggressive supervision of capital sentencing by state supreme courts would be doing state legislatures a favor—not usurping their powers. In the meantime, though, opponents of the death penalty must continue to contest capital punishment one case at a time, in what has become a war of attrition. In that war, evidence of severe mental illness plays an indispensable role in preventing unjust outcomes in two ways: one is avoiding unjustified executions by enforcing the principle of proportionality; the other is assuring procedural fairness though aggressive, client-centered representation. This chapter addresses both challenges.

Proportionality: Mitigating Circumstances

The task of "narrowing" the class of capitally punishable offenses (aiming to reduce arbitrariness) can best be accomplished by identifying a small set of aggravating circumstances defined in terms of factors such as brutality, motivation, and prior serious offending, which are highly likely to arouse retributive emotions in an ordinary jury pool in the jurisdiction. The key point for present purposes is the role of specified *mitigating* circumstances. Most state capital sentencing statutes specify a list of mitigating factors without any indication of the weight they should carry in relation to aggravating circumstances.[8]

The question being posed now is whether it is possible to formulate a set of rules or criteria regarding mitigating circumstances that can be fairly and thoughtfully applied so as to exempt from the death penalty defendants whose culpability at the time of the offense was significantly diminished by understandable emotional arousal or distress or by mental disorder. Identifying the criteria is not as challenging as it might seem, because Anglo-American law has a rich legal tradition that has refined the factors of moral interest over many centuries. The most important question is whether the mitigating circumstance should preclude the death penalty altogether or, rather, should be "weighed" or "balanced" against the aggravating circumstances that provide the legal and moral predicate for a death sentence.

What mitigating circumstances should categorically preclude the death penalty regardless of degree of aggravation? Is it enough to tell the jury to weigh these mitigating factors? Does that satisfy the defendant's right to convince the jury that the death penalty is undeserved? The Supreme Court has concluded that sometimes the answer to the last question is no. In *Atkins v. Virginia* (2002),[9] the Court embraced a categorical exclusion of defendants with intellectual disability, and in *Roper v. Simmons* (2005),[10] the Court precluded execution of defendants who were younger than eighteen at the time of the offense.[11] Why did the Court take this rule-based position? Why was it insufficient for a state to tell the jury to take these mitigating characteristics into account in reaching the ultimate judgment? For example, why not tell the jury to pay "special attention" to the defendant's immaturity or intellectual disability? Or why not allow the state law to give evidence of diminished responsibility due to immaturity or intellectual disability "presumptive weight" in favor of a life sentence? Why should these mitigating circumstances *preclude* a death sentence?

The Court held that these circumstances *must be given preclusive weight* because there was too big a risk that the jury will not give the mitigating evidence the weight that it deserves, in part because they would often be so repulsed by the aggravating features of the killing that it would overwhelm the evidence of mitigation.[12] This per se rule (that youthfulness or intellectual disability precludes a death sentence) is designed to avoid disproportionate applications of the death penalty.

Aside from these examples, in many other cases, the weighing task is left to the sentencing jury. A death sentence recommended by the jury represents a collective judgment that the aggravating factors outweighed the mitigating ones. In many states, the jury is not required to make specific findings on the mitigating factors, even if they are required to specify their findings on the statutory aggravating circumstances. However, embedding the mitigating findings in the overall jury "recommendation" precludes meaningful appellate review. The only prospect for reviewing the jury's findings under such circumstances lies in a "thirteenth juror" review by the trial judge, a highly unusual structure. Giving preclusive weight to a finding of mitigation based on mental illness or intellectual disability exposes this finding to meaningful judicial review—by the sentencing judge or the appellate court or both.

Diminished Responsibility and Mental Illness

The *Atkins*[13] approach must be extended to defendants whose conduct was substantially affected by severe mental illness. This was the position taken in an important 2016 policy statement endorsed by the American Bar Association, the American Psychiatric Association, the American Psychological Association, and the National Alliance on Mental Illness:

> Defendants should not be executed or sentenced to death if, at the time of the offense, they had a severe mental disorder or disability that significantly impaired their capacity (a) to appreciate the nature, consequences or wrongfulness of their conduct, (b) to exercise rational judgment in relation to conduct, or (c) to conform their conduct to the requirements of the law. A disorder manifested primarily by repeated criminal conduct or attributable solely to the acute effects of voluntary use of alcohol or other drugs does not, standing alone, constitute a mental disorder or disability for purposes of this provision.[14]

The principle of diminished responsibility can be operationalized in many ways. However, the joint position statement of the ABA and the leading mental health organizations embraces a position with what appears to be unanimous and enthusiastic support. Accordingly, rather than parsing its elements, I will assume further that punishment should be mitigated (and, specifically, that execution is regarded as excessive) if serious mental illness "significantly impaired [the defendant's] capacity" either "to appreciate . . . the wrongfulness of [his or her] conduct . . . or . . . to conform [his or her] conduct to the requirements of the law." The latter phrase is the one most pertinent to our topic, and it can be more simply stated by saying that the symptoms of acute mental or emotional disturbance significantly affected the defendant's conduct. Obviously, this formulation is vague, difficult to apply, and ultimately rests on a complex clinical assessment and value judgment. However, a failure to take these contributing factors into account would allow or require imposition of death sentences in cases where such a punishment would be excessive in relation to the defendant's culpability. A just death penalty system must preclude the death penalty in cases where the defendant's capacity to appreciate the wrongfulness of his conduct or to conform his conduct to the requirements of the law was significantly impaired.

This formulation essentially transports the Model Penal Code formulation of the insanity defense to the sentencing phase of a capital case. A good example of a mitigating circumstance that would preclude a death sentence under this formulation is experiencing hallucinations or extreme disinhibition as a result of being high on alcohol or other disinhibiting substances. (It is important to emphasize that disordered conduct attributable to voluntary intoxication would not amount to a *defense* in any jurisdiction but would qualify as a ground for mitigation in a capital prosecution.)

Currently, under the capital sentencing law of every U.S. jurisdiction except Connecticut and Ohio, those claims could be considered by the jury, but they typically would not preclude the death penalty even if the jury found that the mitigating circumstance existed. The problem is that sentencing judges and juries in capital cases routinely find that the mitigating force of claims of mental illness is outweighed by the aggravating circumstances.

This is a profoundly serious problem. The tendency to devalue evidence of mental illness in capital cases is a significant impediment to morally defensible administration of capital punishment. This very problem led the Supreme Court to require a categorical exclusion based on intellectual disability in *Atkins*. A just system of capital sentencing must also provide a categorical basis for mitigation for defendants whose conduct was demonstrably affected by severe mental illness.

An Illustrative Case

Having observed numerous capital sentencing evaluations over the past forty years, I have had an ongoing opportunity to reflect on the legal and moral implications of the clinical narratives that emerge in these cases. One recurrent question is whether the aggravating circumstances will completely marginalize a defendant's compelling mitigation narratives derived from childhood abuse and deprivation, mental disability, situational pressures, or other "diverse frailties of humankind." Specifically—using Virginia's statute as an example (before Virginia abolished the death penalty)—will jurors, judges, and appellate courts ever allow compelling mitigating factors to override the momentum toward the death penalty created by a narrowed list of capital elements (e.g., multiple victims or an accompanying armed robbery) and a finding of "dangerousness" or "vileness"?

As in most states, defendants in Virginia had an opportunity to demonstrate specified statutory mitigating circumstances regarding mental illness. The defendant might cite extreme mental or emotional disturbance at the time of the offense or argue that the capacity of the defendant to appreciate the criminality of his conduct or to conform his conduct to the requirements of law was significantly impaired. Many defense attorneys worried, however, that introducing evidence of mental illness would amount to a "double-edged sword," and that mitigation would essentially be warped into aggravation. That is exactly what happened in Joe Giarratano's case.[15]

Giarratano was charged with the double murder of a mother and her daughter. After a bench trial in which the trial judge rejected an insanity plea, the court ordered Giarratano to undergo a psychiatric examination at the Forensic Psychiatry Clinic at the University of Virginia for possible use at the capital sentencing proceeding. I observed the clinical evaluation and consulted with the clinic staff as they developed their opinions and wrote the report. Because Giarratano had confessed to the killings, had already been convicted of committing them, and did not deny his guilt, the evaluators assumed he was guilty and focused entirely on possible mitigating factors, including whether Giarratano had experienced emotional disturbance and impaired volitional capacity at the time of the offenses.

In agreement with the findings in the clinic's report, the judge found that both of those statutory mitigating factors of diminished mental responsibility existed in Giarratano's case. Nevertheless, he sentenced Giarratano to death. He also interpreted one of the factors in a way that nullified its moral significance, reasoning that "by becoming an habituate of drugs and alcohol one does not cloak himself with immunity from penalty for his criminal acts." However, the judge ignored the fact that

Giarratano's severe addiction—and its resulting psychopathology and neuropathology—had its roots in his childhood, when he was exposed to his mother's habitual use of drugs and became addicted at a very early age. And Giarratano was not seeking "immunity from penalty for his criminal acts." Giarratano's compelling moral and legal claim was simply that the death penalty would be disproportionate to his culpability. Even if he did commit the crime—which was not contested at trial but was questioned in later post-conviction proceedings—he should not have received a death sentence.

Procedural Fairness

Assuming that the death penalty is retained, there can be no doubt, even among supporters of capital punishment, that the most important safeguard in preventing mistakes and assuring careful consideration of the suitability of the death penalty is skilled counsel, together with the resources required for adequate investigation, expert consultation, and advocacy. This nation's fifty-year experience with the post-*Furman* death penalty has shown convincingly that the frequency of death sentences has been reduced by providing skilled counsel at trial, and that the frequency of execution is reduced by providing specialized counsel in post-conviction proceedings. Those subjects are covered elsewhere in this book. What I want to add here are several observations on the highted importance of skillful representation of capital defendants and condemned prisoners with serious mental illnesses, together with the necessary clinical consultation and treatment. Given the proportion of capital defendants and condemned prisoners who need clinical attention, failure to respond effectively to these challenges undermines the integrity of the entire death penalty process. In this section, I will briefly highlight issues relating to the challenges of representing defendants and post-conviction clients with serious mental illnesses.

Overall, the nation's effort to design and implement a fair and just capital punishment system has improved, but progress is uneven, to say the least, and capital sentencing practice leaves much to be desired in many states. Even if the class of offenders subject to the death penalty is genuinely narrowed, and even if defendants with serious mental illnesses and intellectual disabilities are excluded, many imperfections remain.

Competence to Assist Counsel in a Capital Adjudication

Joe Giarratano's case presents a fairly common scenario in capital homicide cases.[16] He twice attempted to commit suicide in jail after his arrest, thereby triggering an evaluation of his competence to stand trial—as it virtually always does—even before counsel had been notified of the evaluation. He was also put on antipsychotics during the pretrial period. In many cases like this, the suicidal defendant is actively seeking a death sentence, and in others, the defendant may feel that a death sentence is inevitable. Either way, the defendant's lack of motivation to assist counsel is often accompanied by overt efforts to subvert counsel. What typically happens in these cases is that the defendant pleads guilty (sometimes over counsel's objection) and invites the judge to impose the death penalty. The tensions in the attorney-client relationship are often invisible to everyone except counsel. That is effectively what happened in Giarratano's case. We now know that he essentially undermined counsel every step of the way. He turned down a possible plea agreement and insisted on a bench trial. He wrote to the judge asking for a death sentence. He directed counsel not to appeal the conviction or the death sentence (though counsel filed a pro forma appeal because he concluded that he was required to do so).

Of what legal significance is this fairly common scenario? Is a capital defendant who seeks a death sentence and undermines counsel's efforts to defend him incompetent to stand trial? The law books are replete with cases where defendants such as this are ruled competent to stand trial. The psychiatrist who examined Giarratano at the psychiatric facility Central State after his suicide attempts found him competent to stand trial because Giarratano understood the charges and the proceedings against him, understood the role of counsel, and was able to communicate coherently with his attorney. Furthermore, the staff of the Forensic Psychiatry Clinic raised no doubts about his competence to stand trial. Indeed, the case file clearly shows that Giarratano understood his jeopardy and was not experiencing delusions, disorganized thinking, or other cognitive deficits that are usually the focus of assessments of competence to stand trial. It is clear that he did not lack the ability to assist counsel in the usual sense.

The issue is fundamentally about motivation. How should the courts respond to lack of motivation to defend oneself? Does it matter *why* the defendant isn't motivated? We have all seen obstreperous clients who provoke what I call "autonomy fights" with counsel—but capital cases raise the stakes qualitatively higher. Is a suicidal defendant competent to stand trial? A depressed defendant? A defendant who believes he deserves to die? A defendant who is traumatized by the homicidal encounter? There was plenty of evidence in Giarratano's case of acute emotional distress, but was he *unable* to assist counsel or did he *choose* not to assist counsel? This is a complicated clinical question that ultimately requires a value judgment. The forensic clinical experts at the University of Virginia concluded, based on expert consultation, that his depressed mental state and near-psychotic level of distress were attributable to psychopathological factors beyond his control. They found that his emotional distress and agitation became more intense as the proceedings neared a climax—initially, the trial itself and the pronouncement of a death sentence, and then the prospect of execution. It is likely that active treatment with antidepressants as well as psychotherapy could have been effective in restoring Giarratano's capacity to exercise reasoned judgment, but no such treatment was attempted.

We can easily see why courts might be reluctant to hold, categorically, that depressed or distressed defendants are not competent to proceed. Malingering could be a serious problem, for one thing, and even if the depression is genuine, bringing the criminal process to a halt while depressed defendants are treated on the basis of the diagnosis alone is probably not sensible. The key issue is functional impairment of decisional capacity. The question should be whether the defendant's emotional condition is symptomatic of a clinically diagnosable disorder *and* it is interfering materially with the defendant's ability to make a rational, self-interested decision about the defense or disposition of the case. The typical contexts in which this problem arises are cases in which the defendant insists on pleading guilty over counsel's objection, refuses to accept a plea agreement that would preclude a death sentence, refuses to put on a case in mitigation or otherwise contest a death sentence, or resolves the "autonomy fight" with counsel by waiving his right to counsel and invoking his right to represent himself under *Faretta v. California*.[17] Giarratano's case highlights the importance of distinguishing between, on the one hand, a defendant's abilities to understand the proceedings, appreciate his jeopardy, and communicate rationally with counsel, and on the other hand, his decisional capacity. What Giarratano lacked was the capacity to make rational, self-interested decisions. I hasten to add that I am not saying that every defendant who would prefer to be executed lacks decisional capacity. Indeed, I have taken the opposite position. Attorneys must, however, undertake a capacity assessment.

I have seen enough of these cases to convince me that a suicide attempt or other clinically significant symptoms of depression should raise a red flag and invite ongoing assessments of a defendant's competence for adjudication in capital cases. Moreover, even if the defendant is regarded as competent for adjudication, it does not follow that justice is well served by bringing the defendant to trial in this condition. The state should not be in a hurry to bring defendants with suicidal wishes and treatable depression to trial. Practice guidelines for capital representation should also advise counsel on how to recognize symptoms of depression, how to respond to those symptoms—especially suicidal ideation and behavior—and how to ameliorate possible adverse impacts on the attorney-client relationship and client decision-making.

None of this was done in Giarratano's case. As mentioned above, we argued in post-conviction proceedings that Giarratano had been incompetent to assist counsel during the pretrial period and that proceeding to adjudication under these circumstances violated his Sixth and Fourteenth Amendment rights to effective assistance of counsel and to a fair trial. Unfortunately, the claim never got any traction in the courts. The degree of Giarratano's emotional distress and its impact on the performance of trial counsel became apparent only in the habeas proceeding several years later.

I have not undertaken a comprehensive empirical investigation of the frequency with which post-conviction proceedings reveal genuine doubts about a capital defendant's trial competence that were not identified or properly assessed during the original proceedings. However, I have read hundreds of post-conviction opinions over four decades, and I feel reasonably comfortable offering the following impressions: during the first decade or two after capital punishment was reinstated in 1976, and before expert capital defenders were routinely appointed in capital cases, attorneys representing capital defendants often failed to recognize or respond effectively to deficits in decisional capacity that demonstrably undermined effective representation. Giarratano's case is a good example. As the quality of capital defense improved (largely through specialized representation) and access to clinical assistance became more routine, the likelihood of demonstrably tainted death sentences was reduced. Nevertheless, defense attorneys continue to face a subset of capital defendants whose psychopathology impedes effective representation, even though it does not amount to unfitness for trial or decisional incapacity. These cases would not be troubling if there were no death penalty, but as it is, they leave us wondering about whether execution is a morally defensible response to highly disturbed defendants who are nonetheless competent for adjudication.

Doubts about Decisional Incapacity in Post-conviction Proceedings

After Joe Giarratano was sentenced to death and the Virginia Supreme Court affirmed the conviction and sentence, he declined to seek any further judicial review. As the execution date neared, I went to see Giarratano at the request of anti–death penalty advocacy groups. Concluding that he was acutely distressed and possibly psychotic, I attempted to persuade him to authorize the initiation of post-conviction proceedings while efforts were also undertaken to obtain psychiatric treatment for him. He equivocated, but eventually authorized me and co-counsel to seek a stay and file a state habeas petition. However, for several years, Giarratano vacillated about whether he wanted to terminate the proceedings as they moved unsuccessfully through state courts and thereafter through the federal district court. Eventually, though, the entire narrative of the case changed as newly discovered evidence raised serious doubts about whether Giarratano had actually committed the murders.

Competence to Decide Whether to Seek or Terminate Post-conviction Relief

Much has been written on the ethical dilemmas faced by counsel in cases where clients seek to terminate post-conviction proceedings, and on the proper response of the legal system when a condemned prisoner "volunteers" for execution, seeking a "state-assisted suicide." I will not attempt to summarize that debate here. In brief, my view is that we should respect the dignity of condemned prisoners to make their own decisions about whether to abandon legally available opportunities to overturn their death sentences, as long as they are competent to make rational, self-interested decisions based on their own values. This view is reflected in the ABA's Mental Illness Resolution and in the companion position statements of the American Psychiatric Association and the American Psychological Association. The ABA statement reads:

> *Procedure in Cases Involving Prisoners Unable to Assist Counsel in Post-Conviction Proceedings.* If a court finds at any time that a prisoner under sentence of death has a mental disorder or disability that significantly impairs his or her capacity to understand or communicate pertinent information, or otherwise to assist counsel, in connection with post-conviction proceedings, and that the prisoner's participation is necessary for a fair resolution of specific claims bearing on the validity of the conviction or death sentence, the court should suspend the proceedings. If the court finds that there is no significant likelihood of restoring the prisoner's capacity to participate in post-conviction proceedings in the foreseeable future, it should reduce the prisoner's sentence to the sentence imposed in capital cases when execution is not an option.[18]

What should be done when a condemned prisoner decides to abandon post-conviction challenges to the death sentence? What is counsel's obligation in such circumstances? Does it depend on whether counsel has a good faith doubt about whether the prisoner has the capacity to make a rational decision on the matter? Does respecting the client's wishes amount to allowing "state-assisted suicide"? What does or should *competence* mean in this context? The joint statement by the ABA and the mental health organizations respects the prisoner's autonomy while endorsing a procedure for surrogate decision-making in the event of incapacity.

> *Procedure in Cases Involving Prisoners Seeking to Forgo or Terminate Post-Conviction Proceedings.* If a court finds that a prisoner under sentence of death who wishes to forgo or terminate post-conviction proceedings has a mental disorder or disability that significantly impairs his or her capacity to make a rational decision, the court should permit a next friend

acting on the prisoner's behalf to initiate or pursue available remedies to set aside the conviction or death sentence.[19]

Competence to Be Executed

The Eighth Amendment bars execution of a prisoner who does not appreciate the nature of the punishment and the reasons it is being imposed. Fortunately, this is an issue that did not arise in Giarratano's case. Unfortunately, it is tied to the other issues that I have addressed—not conceptually or doctrinally, but empirically. For most prisoners whose attorneys argue that they are not competent to be executed, the records indicate that usually they were incompetent at earlier stages of the case. Unlike Giarratano, these defendants typically have histories of severe mental illness, often including repeated episodes of psychiatric hospitalization. The records frequently indicate that their mental and emotional functioning was significantly impaired at the time of the offense and that their capacity to assist in their own defense was, at best, "borderline." Declaring the prisoner to be incompetent for execution is sometimes the last opportunity to rectify a moral error that was uncorrected at every previous stage of the criminal process. A case in point is Scott Panetti. After Panetti's conviction and sentence were upheld on collateral review, the trial court set an execution date, and Panetti filed a motion to stay the execution on the grounds that he was incompetent to be executed under *Ford v. Wainwright*.[20] After a highly convoluted sequence of state and federal proceedings relating to procedural and jurisdictional issues, The Supreme Court agreed to review Texas's denial of Panetti's execution competence claim. The substantive question was whether an admittedly delusional mentally ill prisoner who is aware that the state intends to execute him based on his conviction for a capital crime is, based on that finding alone, competent for execution under the Eighth Amendment.

In a 5–4 decision in *Panetti v. Quarterman*,[21] in 2007, the Supreme Court held that recognition that the execution is connected to the conviction is not sufficient. As Justice Kennedy explained, the court must also take into account whether the defendant's "psychological dysfunction . . . may have resulted in 'fundamental failure to *appreciate the connection between the petitioner's crime and his execution*.' . . . Gross delusions stemming from a severe mental disorder may put an awareness of a link between a crime and its punishment in a context so far removed from reality that the punishment can serve no proper purpose."[22] While rejecting the standard followed by the court of appeals, Justice Kennedy declined "to attempt to set down a rule governing all competency determinations" until Panetti's claims could be further developed on remand.[23] The ABA and its companion mental health organizations codified the Supreme Court's ruling as follows:

> *Procedure in Cases Involving Prisoners Unable to Understand the Punishment or its Purpose.* If, after challenges to the validity of the conviction and death sentence have been exhausted and execution has been scheduled, a court finds that a prisoner has a mental disorder or disability that significantly impairs his or her capacity to understand the nature and purpose of the punishment, or to appreciate the reason for its imposition in the prisoner's own case, the sentence of death should be reduced to the sentence imposed in capital cases when execution is not an option.[24]

The State of Texas vs. Scott Panetti: A Constitutional Embarrassment

As this essay is being written—more than fifteen years after the Supreme Court's ruling in *Panetti v. Quarterman*—Scott Panetti is still on death row awaiting execution and the case is still in litigation. Why does Texas insist on executing Scott Panetti?

Panetti's case[25] highlights two deeply troubling problems in death penalty adjudication reviewed in this essay. First, it exposes the utter failure of the Texas criminal justice system to take adequate account of the effects of severe mental illness in capital cases, specifically by failing to assure a fair defense for defendants with mental disabilities, by failing to give morally appropriate mitigating effect to claims of diminished responsibility at the time of the crime, and by failing to correct these deficiencies in post-conviction proceedings. Indifference to claims of incompetence on the eve of execution is only the last link in a long chain of indifference and neglect. Second, it highlights the futility of the Supreme Court's post-*Furman* capital sentencing jurisprudence.

It is painful to read the record in Panetti's case. His lengthy history of severe mental illness is well documented. He had been involuntarily committed to psychiatric hospitals in Texas and Wisconsin more than a dozen times during the decade preceding the crime. The recurrent diagnoses were chronic schizophrenia and schizoaffective disorder, characterized by tangential and circumstantial thinking, hallucinations, delusions, grandiosity, and paranoia, with acute psychotic exacerbations complicated by alcohol use. Over time, his paranoid delusions became more pronounced. Throughout this long period of chronic illness, there was no suggestion of malingering. Even after his arrest, the psychiatrist who evaluated his competence to stand trial (in November 1992) acknowledged Panetti's "chronic delusions, occasional hallucinations and an odd fragmentation of his personality," while concluding that he understood the charges against him and "appeared to be able to assist in his own defense and to process the information and questions given to him" in the course of two interviews.[26]

Some people with chronic schizophrenia and other major mental disorders have sufficient capacity to assist in their own defense in a criminal adjudication despite significant cognitive impairments, and it may be fair to proceed with the prosecution in such cases as long as defense counsel is aware of the defendant's impairments and is able to carry out his or her own tasks adequately. It appears clear, however, that Panetti's thought disorder was so severe that even with medication, he was unable to communicate rationally with his lawyers, one of whom later testified that he had never had a meaningful and rational conversation with Panetti about the legal issues in the case.

Panetti's lawyers had little choice except to challenge his competence to proceed. Under Texas law, competency proceedings are held before a jury. After hearing the opposing testimony of two psychiatrists, the jury deadlocked at 9–3 in favor of finding Panetti incompetent and the judge declared a mistrial. After a change in venue, Panetti was found to be competent at a second competency trial.

Seven months later, Panetti experienced what he called an "April Fool's Day revelation" that God had cured his schizophrenia, and he suddenly stopped taking his antipsychotic medication. His already severe condition worsened. Most significantly, his paranoid ideation swept his lawyers into the zone of suspicion and distrust, and he eventually sought to fire them and represent himself. His attorneys vehemently objected. Although the federal habeas record is sketchy, it appears that the trial judge did not hold a hearing on Panetti's competence to proceed to trial, with or without counsel, and allowed him to waive his right to counsel and represent himself.

Even if Panetti had been marginally able to assist counsel a year earlier, it seems highly doubtful that he was able to do so at this point—his abilities to communicate rationally and exercise judgment were substantially impaired by paranoid delusions and pervasive cognitive confusion. At the very least, the trial court should have suspended the proceedings to allow an inpatient evaluation of Panetti's competence to stand trial. However, even if Panetti remained competent to proceed to trial *with counsel*, he appears to have lacked the capacity to make a rational decision regarding self-representation and to make the decisions required of a defendant representing himself in a capital prosecution. Indeed, his fragile mental and emotional condition seems to have worsened as the trial went on. He lacked a "rational understanding" of the very task of self-representation and of the decisions that he was called on to make because he did not appreciate their significance or consequences. Yet, without even seeking further evaluation or holding a new hearing, the trial judge ruled that Panetti was competent to waive counsel and represent himself, and the trial went forward.

Scott Monroe, Panetti's standby counsel at his trial, characterized the trial as "truly a judicial farce, and a mockery of self-representation. It should have never been allowed to happen."[27] For example, Panetti never looked at the files prepared by counsel, and he sent them all to his family in Wisconsin to keep the jail guards from seeing them; he subpoenaed more than two hundred witnesses, including Jesus Christ, John F. Kennedy, and other dead people; he completely ignored the annotated materials on the law prepared by Monroe; he paid little attention to jury selection; and he never took advantage of the occasional "pow-wows" granted by the court to enable him to consult with Monroe, choosing instead to smoke a cigar. Panetti put on no case in mitigation whatsoever, notwithstanding his history of mental illness and the availability of many witnesses who could testify about the effects of his illness and the deterioration of his condition.

Courts trivialize mental illness and compromise the dignity of the law when they allow defendants as disturbed as Panetti to represent themselves in criminal trials. It is horrifying that judges would allow such a spectacle in a capital trial—even if the defendant fails to recognize that his behavior imperils his life, the courts should have no such illusions. Respect for autonomy does not require the courts to allow defendants as disturbed as Panetti to dig their own graves.

It is gruesomely ironic that less than two months after Panetti was sentenced to death, the trial court found him incompetent to waive the appointment of counsel to represent him in post-conviction proceedings. Thus, a severely disturbed capital defendant was allowed to forsake at trial every legal protection afforded by the law, including his right to counsel, while his desire to proceed pro se thereafter was overridden. Is it too cynical to attribute the trial court's otherwise puzzling decisions to a desire to secure a death sentence and then to insulate it from reversal in post-conviction review? Whatever the explanation, the death sentence was undisturbed on collateral review by both the state and federal courts in the face of claims that Panetti had been incompetent to stand trial or to waive his right to counsel and represent himself.

The second problem highlighted by the *Panetti* litigation is the futility of the Supreme Court's post-*Furman* capital sentencing jurisprudence. The *Panetti* litigation, seen in its entirety, documents the stubborn unwillingness of the Texas courts to take the necessary steps to assure the "heightened need for reliability" in capital adjudications. Ultimately, the success of the Supreme Court's post-*Furman* project depends on serious and sustained efforts by state appellate courts to implement the Eighth Amendment principles and values enunciated by the Supreme Court for a half century. The *Panetti* record reveals how unwilling the Texas courts have been to do so (and sadly, they are not alone), and how difficult it has become for federal courts to vindicate the values of the Eighth Amendment.

An even larger problem exposed by the *Panetti* litigation is the failure of the Supreme Court's capital sentencing jurisprudence. When a majority of the Supreme Court opted to reaffirm the constitutionality of capital punishment in 1976, they set out to develop and administer an aggressive "death is different" jurisprudence. As that effort continues to unfold, it is characterized by a rich body of principles and doctrines— together with an understandable unwillingness to enforce them aggressively by backstopping state courts—and by a byzantine body of habeas law that insulates state court judgments from collateral attack.

Successful implementation of capital sentencing jurisprudence depends on aggressive efforts by state appellate courts to enforce the values and principles articulated by the Supreme Court as "the supreme law of the land." While some state appellate courts have taken this responsibility seriously, others, such as the appellate courts of Texas, have not. The Texas courts failed miserably in Panetti's case, right from the beginning of the pretrial process and all the way through the multiple post-conviction proceedings (which continue as this book goes to press). Yet, Panetti's death sentence would have been carried out if Justice Kennedy had followed his usual inclination in 2007 to defer to state courts. And Texas continues its quest to execute a man who was clearly mentally ill both at the time of the crime and throughout three decades of litigation.

As this essay is being written, the future of capital punishment is clearly in the hands of the states. The Supreme Court has abandoned the death penalty project it initiated in 1972. State legislatures and supreme courts now bear the responsibility of harmonizing criminal punishment in the United States with our nation's proclaimed aspirations for fair and proportionate punishment and equality before the law.

Notes

1 *Furman v. Georgia*, 408 U.S. 238 (1972).
2 *Gregg v. Georgia*, 428 U.S. 153 (1976).
3 *Woodson v. North Carolina*, 428 U.S. 280, 304 (1976).
4 U.S. Const. amend. VIII.
5 I recognize that some narrowing did take place in *Atkins v. Virginia*, 536 U.S. 304 (2002), *Roper v. Simmons*, 543 U.S. 551 (2005), and *Kennedy v. Louisiana* 554 U.S. 407 (2008).
6 *McCleskey v. Kemp*, 481 U.S. 279 (1987).
7 David Von Drehle, "Retired Justice Changes Stand on Death Penalty," *Washington Post*, June 10, 1994.
8 "Aggravating Factors by State," Death Penalty Information Center, https://deathpenaltyinfo.org.
9 *Atkins v. Virginia*, 536 U.S. 304 (2002).
10 *Roper v. Simmons*, 543 U.S. 551 (2005).
11 *Roper*, 543 U.S. at 551.
12 *Roper*, 543 U.S. at 551.
13 *Atkins*, 536 U.S. at 304.

14 American Bar Association, Mental Illness Resolution, AM 122A, adopted August 7–8, 2006.

15 "Ex-Virginia Death-Row Prisoner with Strong Claim of Innocence Get[s] Parole after 38 Years," Death Penalty Information Center, November 21, 2017, https://deathpenaltyinfo.org.

16 The information on Giarratano's case comes from my previous writings as well as my review of relevant case materials. See, for example, Richard J. Bonnie, "Mental Illness, Severe Emotional Distress, and the Death Penalty: Reflections on the Tragic Case of Joe Giarratano," *Washington and Lee Law Review* 73, no. 3 (Summer 2016): 1445–68.

17 *Faretta v. California*, 422 U.S. 806, 806 (1975).

18 American Bar Association, Mental Illness Resolution.

19 American Bar Association, Mental Illness Resolution.

20 *Ford v. Wainwright*, 477 U.S. 399, 399 (1986).

21 *Panetti v. Quarterman*, 551 U.S. 930, 930 (2007).

22 *Panetti*, 960.

23 *Panetti*, 960–61.

24 American Bar Association, Mental Illness Resolution.

25 *Texas v. Panetti*, 2014 WL 6851502 (2014).

26 General background information on *Panetti* can be found in the following sources: Katie Arnold, "The Challenge of Rationally Understanding a Schizophrenic's Delusions: An Analysis of Scott Panetti's Subsequent Habeas Proceedings," *Tulsa Law Review* 50, no. 1 (Summer 2014): 243–70; Josh Sanburn, "Texas Plans to Execute a Schizophrenic Man Who Tried to Subpoena Jesus," *Time*, December 1, 2014; Michael Mello, "Executing the Mentally Ill—When Is Someone Sane Enough to Die?," *Criminal Justice* 22, no. 3 (Fall 2007): 30–41.

27 "Where Is the Compassion?: The Imminent Execution of Scott Panetti, Mentally Ill Offender," Amnesty International Report, January 2004, p. 10, https://www.amnesty.org.

5

Gender Matters

The Execution of "Unwomanly" Women

MARY WELEK ATWELL

Since 2007, when I first wrote about the women who had been executed in the United States in the modern period (since *Gregg v. Georgia* reinstated the death penalty in 1976),[1] the annual number of death sentences and executions has continued to decline.[2] Several states, most recently Virginia, have abolished the use of capital punishment.[3] According to a number of polls and based on the smaller number of sentences handed down by juries, public support has declined from its highest points in the late 1990s.[4] In addition, the United States stands even more starkly alone among modern democratic nations in its maintenance of capital sanctions and is thus even more subject to international criticism for human rights violations. In this environment, it is not surprising that no state has put a woman to death since Georgia executed Kelly Gissendaner in 2015.[5]

Although there have been no state executions of women since 2015, in the last days of the Trump administration the federal government put Lisa Montgomery to death on January 12, 2021. This is an important case that both Laura Schaefer (chapter 11) and I discuss in our respective essays. Montgomery was the first woman executed at the federal level since Bonnie Heady in 1953, a hiatus of almost seventy years.[6] Montgomery's case gained a great deal of public attention, in part because of the rarity of federal executions of women (only four in all U.S. history). But Montgomery also captured media notice based on her story. Her crime, her trial, and her death sentence were permeated with gendered issues. Aside from the jurisdictional difference, her case, like those of the other sixteen executed women and many of the fifty women remaining on death row, demonstrates how social conventions about women and womanly behavior can be factors that negatively determine the fate of those accused of capital offenses. Additionally, the interplay of gender and death sentences reflects contradictions in the capital system and give rise to questions of its ultimate utility and fairness.

Characteristics of Executed Women

Few Americans would recognize the names of the majority of women who have been executed in the last half century. Only two or three of the cases occupied much public attention. Perhaps people knew of Karla Faye Tucker, executed in Texas in 1998, because of her death row conversion and pleas from numerous famous evangelicals that Governor George W. Bush commute her sentence. (He refused.)[7] Many have heard of Aileen Wuornos, described as the first female serial killer and the subject of the movie *Monster*. But for the most part, the other fourteen women remain relatively anonymous. They were impoverished, often poorly educated, frequently suffering from mental disability, almost always experiencing a lifetime of abuse and mental illness. Most did not conform to majority definitions of attractiveness. With those characteristics, they do not differ greatly from the 1,550 men who have been put to death during the same period. However, because women represent such a small percentage of people executed in the United States, one is faced with two essential questions: "Why so few?" and "Why these few?" How does gender matter in explaining the small percentage of violent female offenders sentenced to death, and why did these particular women evoke the most extreme response the criminal justice system has to offer?

As they have historically, women continue to account for a small proportion of serious crimes. It is beyond the scope of this chapter to review the criminological literature that addresses this issue and to probe the theoretical reasons for the gender gap in offending. There is, however, an explanation for the disparity between men and women as it applies to death sentences. The reason is not chivalry, as some have suggested. There is little evidence that prosecutors, judges, or juries treat the women accused of capital murder with kid gloves.[8] In fact, as one looks at how the system regarded those women, the attitude was anything but gracious. A better explanation for the minority of women executed and

Table 5.1: Executed Women

Date of Execution	Name	State	Race
1984	Velma Barfield	North Carolina	W
1998	Karla Faye Tucker	Texas	W
1998	Judias Buenoano	Florida	W
2000	Betty Lou Beets	Texas	W
2000	Christina Riggs	Arkansas	W
2001	Wanda Jean Allen	Oklahoma	B
2001	Marilyn Kay Plantz	Oklahoma	W
2001	Lois Nadean Smith	Oklahoma	W
2002	Linda Lyon	Alabama	W
2002	Aileen Wuornos	Florida	W
2005	Frances Newton	Texas	B
2010	Teresa Lewis	Virginia	W
2013	Kimberly McCarthy	Texas	B
2013	Suzanne Basso	Texas	W
2014	Lisa Coleman	Texas	B
2015	Kelly Gissendaner	Georgia	W
2021	Lisa Montgomery	Federal	W

on death row is that women do not often commit the crimes that carry death sentences. Since *Gregg v. Georgia*, the Supreme Court has required that states opting to include the death penalty in their criminal code must specify aggravating factors that elevate a murder to the level of a capital crime. The majority of these offenses involve predatory crimes, especially murder in the commission of another felony such as rape or robbery. Women are seldom guilty of such crimes. On the other hand, on the relatively rare occasions when women do kill, their victims are likely to be part of their domestic circle. Table 5.1 lists the women who have been executed in the United States since 1984.

Perhaps the more relevant questions are why a few women do commit heinous murders and why a very small number of those women are singled out for execution. To account for serious offenses, feminist criminologists have advanced explanations beyond individual pathologies. They have examined how gendered social structures in a patriarchal environment channel behavior. The criminal justice system tends to focus on the crime—the snapshot or moment in time, separate from what went before and after. And yet, the single incident is incomprehensible without the context of the life that preceded it and the social (gendered) circumstances of that life. An integrated theoretical approach seems to offer the best explanation for why a woman, typically someone who had never before had a brush with the law, would commit murder.[9] Consider the sources of strain that are especially prevalent in women's lives: lower social status, lower-paying jobs, dependence on men, the social devaluation of femaleness, negative self-image related to appearance, low self-esteem, and a lack of self-confidence. Those who seek intimacy outside of traditional heterosexual, monogamous relationships are seen as violating social norms. Independence is hard, especially for those with disabilities. Such women work to preserve any valued relationship, even if it is abusive, and they often internalize the anger and hurt.

Girls and women have been socialized to suppress anger and often do not learn healthy strategies for expressing it. Most of the executed women had no history of violent behavior, yet at some point they burst out with rage and committed the most extreme form of violence, homicide. They often chose targets who were close by and vulnerable—family members and, in some cases, children. These women were exposed to especially gendered stressors. For long periods they responded in the socially conventional way, repressing their hurt and anger, until something triggered an extreme response.[10]

If one subscribes to such a feminist criminological theory to explain serious female offending, one may also look to the social context in which the miniscule number of women have actually been sentenced to death. Less than 2 percent of those executed in the United States are women. One can reject the theory that women on trial are the recipients of some "lingering paternalism"; the women accused of capital crimes seldom enjoy the social status that would evoke such chivalry. Poor, uneducated, mentally ill or mentally disabled women with a history of abuse and addiction seldom make good candidates for masculine protectiveness. Rather, their disadvantages are typically used against them to persuade juries that they have failed to live up to gendered social expectations. A prosecutor seeking a death sentence is likely to portray the defendant as so far outside the social mainstream as to have forfeited their claim to humanity, much less respect or deference based on their gender. Race, gender, sexuality, and sexual orientation can be used to marginalize. Those who are accused of being bad mothers, unfaithful wives, sexually promiscuous, or avaricious and self-indulgent have failed to conform to society's expectations. Although such moral deficiencies are not legally considered aggravating factors in a capital case, prosecutors typically paint a picture of the accused as someone who failed miserably as a woman as well as violated the law.[11]

A review of the women who have been executed in the modern period illustrates the significance of gendered norms, portraying them as evil women who did not deserve to live. Several of these women committed brutal crimes. In some cases, the victims were innocent children. The argument is not that these are not serious offenses deserving serious punishment, but rather that their cases, both in the courts and in the media, were shaped by ideas about gender—whether those ideas meant that a history of abuse was not taken seriously, that the failure to live up to gendered expectations was treated as an informal aggravating factor, or that unorthodox or promiscuous sexual behavior exacerbated a woman's blame for murder.

Who They Were: The Black Widows

Velma Barfield (executed in North Carolina, 1984) set the precedent that executing a woman did not violate contemporary standards of decency. Her case also revealed many of the ways in which gender and gendered expectations influenced the outcome. Barfield admitted to poisoning her fiancé because she was desperate for money to satisfy her addiction to prescription drugs. She also confessed to poisoning three other people. But this admission came after she had waived her Miranda rights during an interrogation when her thinking was befuddled by a mixture of prescription drugs. She claimed that her motive in each case was money to buy her "medicine," the drugs she depended on. She also claimed that her intention had been to make her victims sick, not to cause their deaths.

Velma had been the victim of incest, of physical and emotional abuse. From adolescence she had believed she must hide her feelings of worthlessness and depression. As a coping mechanism, she developed a serious dependence on prescription drugs—a dependence that got worse after the death of her first husband and ended only after she was incarcerated. She was poor and poorly educated. For a woman of her limited resources in a rural environment, the options for work were limited, while her mental health issues went untreated except for a cocktail of medications. Her crimes occurred when she was a live-in caretaker for a sick person—probably the worst possible job for someone with what was likely a bipolar disorder.

At trial, she was described as a "Black Widow" and as a woman who betrayed those who depended on her to look after them. The prosecutor portrayed a caretaker who failed in her nurturing role and chose instead to indulge her own cravings. Because her attorney was unexperienced and indifferent to his client, the jury heard little of Barfield's history of incest and physical and sexual abuse. He focused instead on her drug use and blamed her crimes on "the dope." Nor did the jury consider the irresponsibility of those who fostered her addiction to painkillers. And because the Democratic governor did not want to seem soft on crime in the face of a fiercely pro–death penalty political opponent, he gave short shrift to her petition for clemency, even though by the time of her death she had become a devout Christian and had supporters ranging from her own children to evangelical leaders.[12]

Elements of Velma Barfield's narrative would be echoed and repeated in the accounts of other executed women. Many of them had suffered abuse at the hands of family members, spouses, or intimate partners. Betty Lou Beets (executed in Texas, 2000) was accused of murdering her fifth husband and burying him in the backyard to collect his life insurance. Beets had been abused by a violent, alcoholic father and a series of brutal husbands. She suffered both physical and mental disabilities, making it difficult for her to hold a job and support herself and her children. Instead of viewing her crime as an act of self-defense by a battered woman, the state of Texas treated it as a brutal killing for financial gain, a motive that made it eligible for a death sentence. As was the case with several of the executed women, the mere fact that Beets was the beneficiary of her husband's life insurance policy created suspicion and gave the prosecutor a motive for murder—one that not only elevated the crime to a capital offense (murder for monetary gain) but also ignored abusive relationships and instead painted her as a greedy, grasping woman, a "Black Widow."[13] Judias Buenoano (Florida, 1998), Marilyn Kay Plantz (Oklahoma, 2001), and Teresa Lewis (Virginia, 2010) faced similar accusations. All of those women, according to the states' cases against them, wanted to experience an extravagant lifestyle and committed murder for the insurance money to finance it. Plantz's car and Lewis's clothes and manicures were the sort of luxuries prosecutors portrayed as evidence of their malevolence.[14]

Both Plantz and Lewis, along with Kelly Gissendaner (Georgia, 2015), were convicted of the murders of their husbands, although none of the three women actually killed anyone. All three cases fell under the "murder for hire" rubric, which in some states is the sole exception to the rule that only the actual "triggerman" can be convicted of capital murder. However, each of them was involved in an extramarital affair and in each case the boyfriend was the killer. Based on their agreements to share the insurance money with their paramours/accomplices, the women were sentenced to death while their partners in crime made deals with the prosecution for lesser sentences. In court, they were pictured as insatiable and avaricious money-grubbers as well as despicable mothers and cheating wives who betrayed their marriage vows. Plantz and Lewis, both of whom were borderline mentally disabled and had suffered abuse and mental illness, were described as the "masterminds" of their crimes. Allegedly they had used sex to lure unsuspecting young men to do their bidding, including the commission of brutal murders.

The Worst Mothers

Women convicted of killing their husbands or intimate partners violated one set of gendered norms, while those whose crimes involved the deaths of children departed even farther from the feminine ideal. Christina Riggs (Arkansas, 2000) was sentenced to death for the murder of her two preschool-aged children. A single mother, exhausted from working double shifts as a practical nurse and always short of money, Riggs felt hopeless enough to kill her son and daughter and to attempt to kill herself.[15] Although the prosecution would later claim otherwise, Riggs clearly intended to take her own life. She left several suicide notes, swallowed twenty-eight Elavil tablets, and gave herself a huge dose of a drug used in lethal injections.

Riggs was questioned by police while in the intensive care unit of the hospital. Although she waived her Miranda rights, she had not recuperated from the heavy doses of drugs, nor was her attorney present when she confessed, claiming that she intended to kill herself and did not want to leave her children motherless. The confession became the state's major argument against Riggs, although they chose to advance a different motive. The prosecution portrayed her as a thrill-seeking woman who found her children an inconvenience and wanted to get rid of them so she could go to clubs and enjoy a fun-filled life. They made no mention of her sexual abuse as a child, or her long history of depression and mental illness. Instead, when the defense raised those issues, the female prosecutor who made closing arguments called them "the excuse of the nineties." As was often the case, prosecutors dismissed years of abuse and misery as a mere "excuse." Not only was Riggs excoriated for her failures as a mother, but her weight was also presented as if it were an aggravating circumstance that suggested a lack of self-control. After less than an hour's deliberation, the jury found Riggs guilty. They sentenced her in fifteen minutes after she asked for the death penalty so she could be with her children.[16]

Michelle Oberman has written that the criminal justice system tends to portray female defendants as either mad or bad. This dichotomy is especially common if the victims are children, as infanticide is surely the crime most at odds with stereotypical womanly behavior. While "madness" may provide the accused with some mercy, "badness," often correlated with race and class, means she must receive the ultimate punishment.[17] The Riggs jury were focused on the image of irresponsibility and selfishness. They were not able or they chose not to see her mental illness—not as an excuse but rather an explanation that put her story in context.

If Riggs was one of the evil mothers who committed the most unnatural crime, Lisa Coleman (Texas, 2014) evoked an even stronger sense of badness. Coleman was found guilty and sentenced to death for killing nine-year-old Devontae Williams, the son of her partner, Marcella Williams.[18] The child died of pneumonia and malnutrition. He was severely underweight and showed signs of abuse, including dozens of scars. What made Davontae's death eligible for a capital sentence was that the Texas authorities included a charge of kidnapping as an aggravating factor. Coleman's appellate lawyers would challenge the charge, noting that Devontae was not taken away from home and arguing that witnesses said he came and went freely from the apartment to play out-side. However, the court upheld the allegation because he had marks of restraints on his body. One of her attorneys stated, "The state singled Lisa out and figured some way to get her the death penalty because she was black, a lesbian, and an easy target. . . . It was a slam dunk."[19]

It is puzzling that Coleman was executed for the murder while Devontae's natural mother was allowed to exchange a guilty plea for a life sentence. If indeed her race and sexual orientation helped to convict Coleman, the same could be said for Marcella Williams, also Black and a lesbian, who had been investigated by Child Protective Services on at least a dozen previous occasions. As for Coleman, the jury did not see her own history of physical and sexual abuse at the hands of family members, her teenage pregnancy as the result of rape, or her bipolar disorder as mitigating circumstances.[20] As with a number of the other executed women, no one was ever held responsible for the failure of the responsible agencies and adults to protect Lisa Coleman as a child. But when the horrors of her childhood and adolescence contributed to her own later damaging behavior, Coleman was forced to pay with her life.

Race as an Aggravating Factor

If race, poverty, and sexual orientation should be considered decisive factors in assuring a death sentence, Wanda Jean Allen (Oklahoma, 2001) makes a good argument for that hypothesis. Allen's execution also supports the thesis that the death penalty remains as arbitrary as a lightning strike.[21] Allen's crime was the murder of her partner, Gloria Leathers, on the steps of the Oklahoma City police station.[22] Normally, such an incident would be considered a domestic killing in the heat of passion, an unlikely candidate for a capital charge. It remains unclear why District Attorney Robert Macy, who sent a total of seventy-three people to death row during his tenure, chose to pursue the death penalty in Allen's case.[23] Perhaps the prospect of the media coverage surround-ing the trial of an African American lesbian woman was too tempting for the publicity-seeking district attorney to pass up.

In any event, Allen was represented by an underpaid, inexperienced attorney who, because the state denied him funds to hire an investiga-tor, failed to uncover evidence that she had been diagnosed as mentally disabled. Nor was the jury informed that she had suffered a traumatic brain injury at the age of twelve and was stabbed in the head at fourteen. Instead of acknowledging the cumulative cognitive effects of brain damage and the personality effects of years of deprivation, Macy focused attention on Allen's sexual orientation. In 1989, in the Bible Belt of Oklahoma, he portrayed her as the "man" of the couple who dominated her relationship with Leathers. In an appeal to both racism and homophobia, the district attorney repeatedly referred to a greeting card Allen had sent to Leathers that pictured a gorilla and which she had signed "Gene."[24] During the appellate process and even before the Oklahoma Pardon and Parole Board, the state denied Allen's mental disability. Instead, they evoked stereotypes based on race and sex to portray her as a "hunter" who would kill again if she were not executed.[25] The images employed to convict and sentence Allen were powerful enough to make her the first woman executed in Oklahoma since it had become a state, and the first Black woman executed in the United States in the modern period.

Frances Newton, a Black woman put to death in Texas in 2005, is the only one of the executed women whose actual guilt is in doubt.[26] Newton was an unlikely subject for a death sentence. She came from a loving family and had no history of addiction or abuse, no mental illness or disability. Her only brush with the law before her capital conviction was an $85 shoplifting charge. Yet the Houston district attorney, one of the nation's strongest proponents of capital punishment, succeeded in convincing a jury that Newton had killed her husband and her two young children for insurance money. He invoked the image of the grasping, greedy woman. He further persuaded them that she should die because of "future dangerousness."[27] The state of Texas described a crime in which a selfish woman (who once stole $85) sneaked up on her sleeping husband, killing him when he was defenseless, and then shot her two "babies." The crime was a perversion of natural womanly instincts; the perpetrator did not deserve to live. It was a terrible crime, and someone was worthy of the harshest punishment—except that Newton had an alibi that her incompetent attorney never investigated. As for the matter of future dangerousness, the state's psychiatrist, who had never laid eyes on Newton until the trial, persuaded the jury that she would be a continuing threat to society. As Maurice Chammah argues, the Texas law that makes future dangerousness one of the qualifications for a death sentence is especially troublesome in cases with African American defendants, given jurors' tendencies to associate dark skin with violence.[28]

The issue of future dangerousness helped to persuade a jury to sentence another Black woman to death in the Texas trial of Kimberly McCarthy in 2002.[29] To get money for her cocaine addiction, McCarthy robbed a neighbor, retired professor Dorothy Booth, stabbing her and cutting off her finger to get her diamond ring. She then took the victim's purse and credit cards and drove off in her Mercedes to an area where drugs were available. There was little doubt about McCarthy's guilt, but to ensure a death sentence, the prosecution claimed that "collateral offenses" for which McCarthy had been charged but not tried or convicted proved that she had a history of violence and that she would remain a threat to the community.[30] During her trial for Booth's robbery and murder, the state claimed that McCarthy had killed two other older women fourteen years earlier. She had not been tried at the time of those killings, but she was "linked" to the murders at the time of the capital charge against her. Although she was never found guilty of those earlier crimes, the Texas Court of Criminal Appeals stated that they could form a basis for the jury to conclude that she was dangerous "beyond a reasonable doubt."[31] Like Velma Barfield, McCarthy had worked as a home health aide, someone expected to provide care to elderly patients. The murder of Dorothy Booth was a dramatic contradiction to those expectations. It was a most "unwomanly" predatory crime—a murder in the course of a robbery to steal money to buy drugs.

Notorious

The two most famous executed women, Karla Faye Tucker and Aileen Wuornos, also committed more "masculine" crimes. Unlike the other women, who for the most part led conventional lives prior to committing murder, both Tucker and Wuornos worked as prostitutes. Tucker worked at the upper end of the field as a high-priced call girl; Wuornos solicited along the side of Florida highways. After three days and nights of "partying" with pills and booze, Tucker, along with her boyfriend and another meth-dealing friend, decided to "mess with" an acquaintance by stealing his motorcycle. During the robbery, Tucker repeatedly struck the victim, Jerry Lynn Dean, with a pickax. She used the same weapon to wound the woman sleeping in his bed (a total stranger to Tucker). In a taped statement used to incriminate Tucker and her cohorts, she admitted that she had reached sexual climax with every stroke of the pickax.[32] If the gruesome details of the crime were not enough, that statement sealed Tucker's fate and defined her as the most frightening and evil sort of woman. Although the defense tried to argue that Tucker was in a drug-induced psychotic state and could not form the intent to murder, the prosecution portrayed her as someone who got high and killed people voluntarily for sexual thrills and would surely continue to be dangerous in the future. One of the prosecutors remarked, "Her attitude and the way she looked and everything about her was the personification of evil."[33]

Tucker may personify evil a little less if one knows her backstory. She was raised by a mother who worked by day in an office and by night at a prostitute, a mother who introduced Karla to drugs and alcohol well before she reached her teens. School was optional, and drugs and men were plentiful. Tucker estimated that she was constantly high on something from the time she was fourteen years old until after her arrest at the age of twenty-three. A sober and incarcerated Tucker experienced a religious conversion, and for the first time in her life, she lived without drugs, men, or violence. She became a symbol of salvation for evangelical Christians and posed a dilemma for Texas governor George W. Bush when she asked for clemency. He ultimately determined that the political risk of executing a reformed and religious woman was less than the cost of seeming to be "soft on crime."[34]

The other "famous" executed woman, Aileen Wuornos, had none of the innocent charm of the converted Karla Faye Tucker. In fact, the movie of her story was called *Monster*.[35] Wuornos endured almost unmitigated abandonment, abuse, neglect, and horror in her life.[36] After their mother left Aileen and her brother to be raised by their grandparents, Aileen suffered physical and sexual abuse and became pregnant from a rape at age thirteen. Her grandparents failed to seek help for her hearing and cognitive difficulties. Her reactions to all this misery were, not surprisingly, anger and promiscuity accompanied by drinking and experimenting with drugs. When she was fifteen, her grandfather threw her out of the house for good. Aileen lived in abandoned cars, slept in the woods, and occasionally stayed with a friend. She "hit the road" permanently when she was sixteen and traveled from Michigan to Florida.

She supported herself with prostitution and minor property crimes, drifting on the edge of the law. After she met and fell in love with Tyria Moore, Wuornos committed a series of robberies and murders. Perhaps the thefts were a way to get the money to support Moore. The victims were "johns" who had picked her up for sex. All were killed in remote places, and several were left looking ridiculous, nude and wearing only a hat or a pair of socks. Wuornos claimed all the killings were in self-defense as the men were trying to rape and hurt her, but her claims of self-defense failed, and she was convicted and sentenced to death for one murder and later, at the urging of an incompetent attorney, pled guilty to five others.

Wuornos's crimes were both sordid and sensational. But as a relative of one of her victims commented, "She was off her rocker."[37] From the time of her arrest, psychiatrists repeatedly diagnosed Wuornos as psychotic and having a borderline personality disorder. Psychologists Stacey Shipley and Bruce Arrigo provided a retrospective analysis of her mental condition and found that she fit the profile for psychopathic antisocial personality disorder (ASPD). They further noted the connection with attachment theory, asserting that "the quality, frequency, and intensity of childhood bonds that do or do not form with parents or parental surrogates are extremely important to the formation of personality structure," including the development of psychopathology.[38] Wuornos's early experiences taught her that she was "wicked, worthless, and hated" by those who should have cared for her. She was convinced that they hurt her instead of loving her and that life was filled with "terror, rejection, and pain." Others could not be trusted. She was further dehumanized by the men who bought her services. She was to them an object of abuse, as she had been to her grandfather.[39] Yet, all the factors that were symptoms of her psychosis—poor behavior control, lack of appropriate emotional responses, absence of empathy, failure to accept responsibility, promiscuous sexual relationships—could also be seen as reasons to condemn her behavior and as factors that aggravated her guilt and blameworthiness.

Although Wuornos's life story was the embodiment of a marginalized woman, powerless in a patriarchal society, the prosecutors wanted to portray her as someone who upset established gender patterns, a celebrity-seeking and power-hungry "femme fatale" who used sex to create dominance over men, to murder them when they were most vulnerable.[40] Wuornos's defense was that "she did what you would do, she defended herself" from sexual assault. But according to the state of Florida and the media, she was not at all like you. She was outside the mainstream based on her life as a prostitute, and her lesbian relationship with Tyria Moore also figured prominently in the prosecution's strategy of defining her as "other."[41]

In an additional manifestation of how irrelevant gender characteristics might serve to aggravate a woman's guilt in the eyes of juries and the public, members of the prosecution team as well as journalists commented on Wuornos's appearance. One of the state's attorneys explained that her motive for the murders was financial—she was collecting her fees: "She's so ugly and overweight, even those who patronized her didn't want to pay."[42] Author Sue Russell described Wuornos's appearance in court, writing, "The defendant looked like some product of a less advanced nation, her uneven teeth veering off unchecked in conflicting directions, her skin rough and blotchy, her dishwater blond hair in lackluster condition." Russell labeled her a "creature" who "snarled and sneered."[43] Like most death penalty defendants, Wuornos was dehumanized, but words like *ugly* and *overweight* seem to have special resonance when applied to women.[44]

There is little doubt that Aileen Wuornos was severely mentally ill at the time of her execution, although the state of Florida pronounced her competent to proceed. Her last words offer evidence to the contrary: "I'd just like to say that I'm sailing with the rock, and I'll be back like Independence Day, with Jesus on June 6. Like the movie, big mother ship and all, I'll be back."[45]

Wuornos's death raised some unavoidable questions. Is death the appropriate, constitutional, or decent punishment for the mentally ill, regardless of the criminal acts they may have committed? How should courts account for a life history of abuse and exploitation and the effects of such horrors on the psyche of someone accused of serious crimes? How do factors like poverty, race, and gender exacerbate the effects of abuse and mental illness?

The last execution of a woman in the United States, the killing of Lisa Montgomery at the hands of the federal government, highlights the significance of those questions.

The Story of Lisa Montgomery

Amid the multiple dramas that marked the last days of the Trump presidency, including the January 6, 2021, insurrection in Washington, D.C., the outgoing administration engaged in a "historically aberrant federal execution spree."[46] Among the deviations from contemporary legal norms, Trump and his Justice Department, headed by Attorney General William Barr, presided over the largest number of federal civilian executions in any single year since 1896. They did this as the worst pandemic in a hundred years made visits between inmates and their attorneys difficult or impossible and at a time when states were carrying out the fewest executions in almost four decades. The Justice Department insisted and the Supreme Court agreed that executions would be performed while appeals were pending and unresolved. Two mentally ill inmates were put to death without any judicial review of their competency to be executed.[47] One of these was Lisa Montgomery, killed despite testimony from more than a thousand advocates—including forty-three current and former prosecutors and hundreds of representatives of mental health and anti–domestic violence and anti–sex trafficking organizations—that she suffered from severe mental illness.[48]

Montgomery admitted that she had committed a terrible crime. She killed a pregnant woman and took the baby from her womb. She then tried to claim that the baby was hers. The authorities charged her with murder and kidnapping across state lines, making her offense a federal crime and eligible for a sentence of death. There was no question of Montgomery's guilt. However, in the context of her life of appalling sexual and physical abuse and her mental deterioration on death row, there are many questions about her sentence and her execution.[49]

The abuse Lisa endured was horrific. Her life began with brain damage caused by her mother's alcoholism during pregnancy. Both her mother and her stepfather found creative ways to torture their children, and Lisa in particular was the target of their cruelty.[50] She was beaten with a variety of instruments and thrown into freezing cold showers. Her mouth was duct-taped to keep her from speaking out of turn or crying. Worst of all, Lisa was raped over and over by her stepfather. He had built a little room off the trailer where the family lived so he could assault her to his heart's content and no one would hear her scream. He threatened to rape her little sister or murder the rest of the family if Lisa told of the abuse.[51]

After social services removed her sister Diane from the home because their mother Judy had allowed friends to rape her, life became worse for Lisa. The mother knew that her husband was regularly molesting her daughter. She admitted as much when Lisa testified at their divorce trial. The judge reprimanded Judy for not reporting the abuse, but he also failed to tell the police.[52] This was only one of many instances where supposedly responsible adults neglected their duty to look after a severely mistreated child. Her mother took her to a doctor who never reported the abuse, nor did a school counselor who learned that the stepfather had beaten Lisa so severely that he broke a broom in the process.[53] When Lisa was in her early teens, her mother began prostituting her to men who paid to rape her orally, vaginally, and anally. Sometimes these tortures went on for hours and included several different men.[54] Lisa confided in her cousin, David Kidwell, who was a police officer. He later recalled that she told him, "It was over and over, one man right after the other, and went on for hours. They were also physically violent. They would beat her and slap her if she was 'doing it wrong.' When they were done, they urinated on her like she was trash."[55] Although Kidwell later claimed to regret his inaction, he did nothing at the time Lisa asked for his help.

Not surprisingly, Lisa began to develop a dissociative disorder, a mental condition that allows someone to escape reality. It usually occurs in children as a reaction to trauma, such as physical, sexual, or emotional abuse.[56] When Lisa was eighteen, her mother insisted that she marry her stepbrother, Carl Boman. Her husband continued to mistreat her sexually and physically. They lived in dire poverty and moved frequently. By the time Lisa was in her mid-thirties, she had moved sixty-one times. After giving birth to four children in five years, Lisa was involuntarily sterilized. With all these stressors—abuse, poverty, instability, cruelty, mistreatment—her mental health worsened. She finally divorced Boman and married Kevin Montgomery in 2000.

For unexplained reasons, in 2004 Lisa told Kevin she was pregnant. She may have become desperate when her former husband threatened to sue for custody of their children. That desperation seems to have triggered the crime that led to her death sentence. As Babcock wrote, her action "reflect[ed] the depth of her mental illness and despair."[57]

Like many of the other executed women, Montgomery was appointed ineffectual lawyers for her trial in federal court on capital charges of murder and kidnapping. This did not need to happen. At the outset, Judith Clarke, an exceptional defense attorney, was recommended as a member of her team. Lisa seemed to feel safe and comfortable working with Clarke. However, based on complaints from male lawyers on the defense team who resented her leadership, the judge removed Clarke from the case without consultation. After Clarke's removal, Lisa suffered emotional and mental anguish.[58] She wrote to the judge that she had lost all hope.[59] Nothing in her history would lead her to believe that a group of men were working to promote her best interests.

Defense lawyer Frederick Duchardt had the dubious distinction of having earned the most federal death sentences for his clients of any attorney in the United States.[60] He did not make much of an effort to understand anything about Lisa, as he visited her only three times before her trial.[61] Rather than building a narrative that detailed Lisa's life history of violent abuse and sexual exploitation and its likely result of traumatic brain injury (TBI), Duchardt tried to raise an insanity defense (with which it is notoriously difficult to prevail in a capital case) based on the notion that she suffered from pseudocyesis, a false belief in pregnancy. They introduced several expert witnesses whose testimony the prosecution was able to neutralize as unreliable and irrelevant. In less than five hours, the jury found Montgomery guilty.

The penalty phase of the trial was no better. Although American Bar Association standards state that capital cases should include a mitigation specialist, Duchardt did not hire one. He did call several witnesses, including Lisa's sister Diane Mattingly. But she stated that he failed to ask the questions that would reveal what the jury needed to hear about the mental and sexual abuse. After her testimony, Mattingly "started bawling because I felt like I'd let her down again." She thought Lisa's sentence would have been different with a different defense team. "If they would have heard the whole story, I think the jury would have come to a different conclusion. I think people nowadays would be more understanding of how the brain changes when you go through childhood abuse like Lisa had."[62] Perhaps even more damaging was that although Lisa's cousin David Kidwell, the former police officer and a credible witness, was prepared to testify to the gang rapes Lisa had endured, the defense did not bother to put him on the stand.[63]

Meanwhile, the prosecution offered witnesses who "questioned whether Montgomery had consented to the brutal violations of her own body," as a way of undermining the argument that her traumatic life had led to mental illness. One "expert" testified that she had willingly participated in the sexual abuse and trafficking.[64] The strategy was to belittle her history of sexual and physical torture as "the abuse excuse."[65] One journalist noted that the government used sexist tropes against her, citing her failures to live up to womanly expectations. She was accused of being a bad mother who did not cook or clean, who kept a filthy home, including a room filled with trash.[66] All of these things were true, but they should not have entered into the jury's consideration of aggravating factors. Lisa Montgomery was severely mentally ill. She could not be a good mother or a model housekeeper if she tried, but that did not add to her guilt for the murder of Bobbie Jo Stinnett.

After her 2007 trial in which the jury sentenced her to death, Lisa was incarcerated on death row at the Federal Medical Center, Carswell in Fort Worth, Texas. Ironically, her imprisonment meant some improvement in her overall mental state, as she was given psychotropic medication and treatment that helped to control her mental illness. Even so, she was still subject to anxiety and panic attacks if left alone in a room with a man.[67]

Lisa finally got the competent and committed representation she needed when experienced defense attorneys Kelly Henry and Amy Harwell took over her case during the appeal process. Even so, the Eighth Circuit denied her appeal, and the Supreme Court declined to consider her petition. Only days after her appeals were exhausted, on October 16, 2020, Attorney General William Barr scheduled Montgomery's execution for December 8. At that point, her mental state became even more precarious. Henry remembered that Lisa was so distressed she could barely speak on the phone. Although the COVID-19 pandemic was raging, her lawyers needed fly to Texas to meet in person as they prepared to try to avert the execution.[68] In the process, they contracted serious cases of the virus, and in Texas they found Montgomery in terrible shape. She had been placed under twenty-four-hour video surveillance and her clothes, including her underwear, had been taken away. In a frigid prison, she was given only a thin gown to wear. Even her visits to the toilet were monitored.[69] For a woman who had been repeatedly violated by men, the loss of every shred of dignity and privacy was the last straw. Her attorneys argued that she was no longer competent to understand what was happening to her, including her imminent death.[70] They included that claim in her clemency petition. As all of her appeals had been exhausted, the only hope to save Lisa's life was to appeal to President Donald Trump for clemency.

There was widespread support for Montgomery's petition for clemency—dozens of prosecutors wrote to point out that Lisa's history of abuse and sexual trafficking was not an "excuse," as the government had claimed, but "relevant to determining the appropriate punishment." Some prosecutors noted that other women who had committed almost identical crimes were not sentenced to death because their actions were the product of "serious mental illness."[71] Other supporters included eight hundred organizations devoted to ending violence against women, more than one hundred organizations opposed to child trafficking, and numerous child welfare advocates. Powerful opposition to her execution came in a statement from the National Alliance on Mental Illness, Mental Health America, and the Treatment Advocacy Center, who noted that "multiple experts have concluded that Mrs. Montgomery's crime was the product of her mental illness and brain injuries. Even today, her grip on reality is fragile, maintained only with a complex regimen of psychotropic medications that she never received before being incarcerated."[72]

Neither the arguments to delay the execution because Montgomery was incompetent nor the clemency petition made a difference. Although courts in three different circuits had granted stays based on various appeals, those were overturned as the Supreme Court refused to review any of the executions during the last days of the Trump administration. Justice Sonia Sotomayor found the rush to execute without adequate legal scrutiny to be unconstitutional. She wrote in her dissent in *United States v. Higgs*, "This is not justice." She found the Court had "sidestepped the usual deliberative process" and was putting people to death "before the courts had a meaningful opportunity to determine if the executions were legal." In the case of Lisa Montgomery, the Supreme Court never permitted a hearing, even after the district court had said that her "current mental state was so divorced from reality that she cannot rationally understand the government's rationale for her execution."[73]

In a final demonstration of cruelty, the authorities refused to allow a spiritual adviser to accompany Lisa to receive her lethal injection. She was described as bewildered and "detached from reality" as she went to her death.[74] One could only ask what purpose was served by executing a severely mentally ill woman with traumatic brain injury, post-traumatic stress disorder (PTSD), dissociative disorder, and bipolar disorder? Did it deter other persons detached from reality from committing crimes? Did it protect society from a woman who would otherwise spend the rest of her life in a maximum-security mental health facility? Was it meant to provide "closure" to the Stinnett family, fourteen years after their loss? Or was it a purely political gesture by a cold-hearted administration in its last days?

Gender Does Matter

What do the executed women have in common? Virtually every one of them had been the victim of abuse—sexual and physical abuse as young girls and intimate partner abuse as adults. Although many men who commit serious crimes have also suffered abuse, it is the victim's gender that characterizes both the abuse and the responses to it. As a number of criminologists have described, the experience of abuse at a young age often leads to desperate attempts to escape. Sometimes the escape involves running away from home; other times it involves an unfortunate marriage at a young age. Both of those solutions usually lead to more mistreatment.[75] Women who experience abuse have few socially sanctioned means to deal with their hurt and anger. To self-medicate, they often turn to drugs (either prescription or illegal) or alcohol or a combination of mind-altering substances. Addictions of one kind or another were common among the women put to death.

For casualties of abuse, mental illness is a common outcome. Traumatic brain injuries, PTSD, borderline personality disorder, and bipolar disorder were widespread among the women discussed here. Most went undiagnosed and untreated until after they were convicted of a capital offense, and the existence of addiction or mental illness did not have an effect on anyone's appeal. Executions went ahead, even for the most severely afflicted—Lisa Montgomery, Aileen Wuornos, Suzanne Basso, Judias Buenoano, and Lisa Coleman. The prosecutors, and in many cases even defense attorneys, tended to belittle or disparage claims of mental illness. Mental disabilities—perhaps sufficient to raise constitutional questions under *Atkins v. Virginia*[76]—afflicted Betty Lou Beets, Wanda Jean Allen, Marilyn Kay Plantz, Aileen Wuornos, Teresa Lewis, and Lisa Coleman.

A competent defense attorney should have raised issues of addiction and reduced responsibility, abuse, mental illness, or mental disability at trial. However, inadequate counsel was just about universal among the executed women. Perhaps Beets's and Wuornos's lawyers were the worst, as both tried to sell their clients' stories for books and movie deals while they were allegedly representing them. Their financial interests were tied to seeing their clients get death sentences, which made for a much more exciting story than life without parole. Frances Newton's lawyer—later disciplined by the Texas Bar Association for misconduct—met with her only twice and did not subpoena a single witness.[77] Almost without exception, the court-appointed lawyers treated their female clients with contempt and failed to take their life experiences seriously. Because they were poor or working class and could not afford a skilled private attorney, nearly every man and woman on death row could reasonably claim that their lawyers did not adequately represent them.

Those who were responsible for defending women, in particular, seemed unable or unwilling to understand the particularly gendered aspects of their life experiences. Thus, they were especially unqualified to respond when prosecutors hurled gendered tropes at their clients. The defendants were called bad mothers, unfaithful wives, greedy and selfish, and promiscuous sluts. They were pilloried for their failures as caregivers or as homemakers. They were reviled for their appearances, as if being unattractive or overweight could be considered a moral failure. On the other hand, some of the women's stories were oversexualized, with focus on the number or the gender of their intimate partners. None of those descriptions should have mattered to assessing their guilt or the appropriate punishment, yet all would make the accused women more unlike respectable people. Sentencing someone to death surely requires dehumanizing them—seeing them as "other." Once that has been accomplished, it is easier to see their life as expendable.

All of the executed women were judged within a framework that blamed each one for failing as a woman as well as for committing a crime. As David Baker writes, "The consequences of institutional sexism [in criminal justice processes and procedures] are not obscure and tangential, not the aberrations of rogue justice administrators." They are not fragmented and isolated. Rather, the way that capital punishment has been imposed shows that gender bias is "endemic, integral, and central."[78]

One of the most powerful insights the Supreme Court included in *Furman v. Georgia* was that the death penalty as administered was arbitrary and capricious in the same way that being struck by lightning was arbitrary and capricious. The gender bias embedded in the capital system has contributed to this arbitrariness. An examination of the stories of the women executed in the modern era has shown that they were not the most dangerous killers, not the worst of the worst. Instead, they were the unfortunate few whose lifestyles or failure to live as ideal women made them fair game to be demonized in the eyes of those who judged them.

We have no infallible way of knowing how much the accounts of their experiences have influenced efforts to abolish the death penalty. However, it is reasonable to assume that along with narratives that expose racism in the system, an examination of the role of gender bias also provokes opposition to capital punishment. The number of executed women is comparatively small, yet their cases illustrate the reasons why the application of the death penalty fails to meet the goal of justice.

Notes

1 *Gregg v. Georgia*, 428 U.S. 153 (1976).

2 Death Penalty Information Center, *Facts about the Death Penalty* (Washington, DC: Death Penalty Information Center, 2021), https://deathpenaltyinfo.org.

3 The states that have abolished the death penalty since 2007 are New York (2007); New Jersey (2007); New Mexico (2009); Illinois (2011); Connecticut (2012);

Maryland (2013); Delaware (2016); Washington (2018); New Hampshire (2019); Colorado (2020); and Virginia (2021).

4 See Death Penalty Information Center, *Facts about the Death Penalty*.

5 Kelly Gissendaner was executed on September 30, 2015. She was the first woman executed in Georgia in over seventy years.

6 Prior to the execution of Lisa Montgomery, only three women had been put to death by the federal government: Mary Surratt (1865); Ethel Rosenberg (1953); and Bonnie Heady (1953).

7 Alan Berlow, "The Texas Clemency Memos," *Atlantic Monthly* (July/August 2003).

8 See Janice L. Kopec, "Avoiding a Death Sentence in the American Legal System: Get a Woman to Do It," *Washington and Lee School of Law Capital Defense Journal* 15 (Spring 2003): 357.

9 Darrell Steffensmeier and Jennifer Schwartz, "Contemporary Explanations of Women's Crime," in *The Criminal Justice System and Women: Offenders, Prisoners, Victims, and Workers*, ed. Barbara Raffel Price and Natalie J. Sokoloff (New York: McGraw Hill, 2004), 114–15; Peggy C. Giardino and Sharon Mohler Rockwell, "Differential Association and Female Crime," in *Of Crime and Criminality: The Use of Theory in Everyday Life*, ed. Sally Simpson (Thousand Oaks, CA: Pine Forge Press, 2000), 4–5; Darrell Steffensmeier and Lisa Broidy, "Explaining Female Offending," in *Women, Crime, and Criminal Justice: Original Feminist Readings*, ed. Claire M. Rezetti and Lynne Goodstein (Los Angeles: Roxbury, 2001), 129.

10 Robbin S. Ogle, Daniel Maier-Katkin, and Thomas J. Bernard, "A Theory of Homicidal Behavior among Women," *Criminology* 33, no. 2 (1995).

11 Mary Welek Atwell, *Wretched Sisters: Examining Gender and Capital Punishment*, 2nd ed. (New York: Peter Lang, 2014); Elizabeth Rapaport, "The Death Penalty and Gender Discrimination," *Law and Society Review* 25, no. 2 (1991): 380–82; Joan W. Howarth, "Deciding to Kill: Revealing the Gender in the Task Handed to Capital Juries," *Wisconsin Law Review* (June/July 1994): 1348–51; Victor L. Streib, "Gendering the Death Penalty: Countering Sex Bias in a Masculine Sanctuary," *Ohio State Law Journal* 63 (2002): 18; Joan W. Howarth, "Executing White Masculinities: Learning from Karla Faye Tucker," *Oregon Law Review* 81 (Spring 2002): 194–95.

12 Velma Barfield's story is covered in the following sources: *State of North Carolina v. Margie Velma Barfield*, Bladen County (1978); *State of North Carolina v. Margie Velma Barfield* (259 S.E.2d 510), 1979; Velma Barfield, *Woman on Death Row* (Nashville, TN: Thomas Nelson, 1985); Jerry Bledsoe, *Death Sentence: The True Story of Velma Barfield's Life, Crimes, and Execution* (New York: Dutton, 1998); Joe Ingle, *Last Rights: Thirteen Fatal Encounters with the State's Justice* (Nashville, TN: Abingdon Press, 1990); Ann Jones, *Women Who Kill* (Boston: Beacon Press, 1996); Atwell, *Wretched Sisters*.

13 Details of Betty Lou Beets's case are available in *Ex Parte Betty Lou Beets*, Texas Court of Criminal Appeals, April 6, 1990; Joseph Margulis, "Memories of an Execution," *Law and Inequality* 20 (Winter 2002); Elizabeth Dermody Leonard,

"Stages of Gendered Disadvantage in the Lives of Convicted Battered Women," in *Gendered Justice: Addressing Female Offenders*, ed. Barbara Bloom (Durham, NC: Carolina Academic Press, 2003); Atwell, *Wretched Sisters*, chap. 5.

14 For details of Judias Buenoano's case, see *Judias Buenoano v. State of Florida*, 478 So. 2d 387 (1985); *Buenoano v. State of Florida*, 708 So. 2d 941 (1998); Chris Anderson and Sharon McGehee, *Bodies of Evidence: The Shocking True Story of America's Most Chilling Murderess . . . from Crime Scene to Courtroom to Electric Chair* (New York: St. Martin's Press, 1992); Atwell, *Wretched Sisters*, chap. 5.

    For Plantz, see *Plantz v. Massie*, 2000 10 Cir. 731, 216 F.3d 1088; Atwell, *Wretched Sisters*, chap. 6.

    For Lewis, see *Lewis v. Commonwealth* (Va. Cir. June 2–3, 2003); *Lewis v. Commonwealth* 593 S.E.2d 220 (Va. 2004); *Lewis v. Wheeler*, 609 F.3d (4th Cir. 2010); Atwell, *Wretched Sisters*, chap. 10.

15 Details of Christina Riggs's case may be found at *Riggs v. State of Arkansas*, 339 Ark. 111, 3 S.W.3d 305 (1999); Jennifer Furio, *Letters from Prison: Voices of Women Murderers* (New York: Algora, 2001); Atwell, *Wretched Sisters*, chap. 7.

16 Riggs was a "volunteer." She waived her post-conviction appeals and was executed on May 3, 2000.

17 Michelle Oberman, "Mothers Who Kill: Coming to Terms with Modern American Infanticide," *American Criminal Law Review* 34 (Fall 1996): 43–50.

18 Details of Lisa Coleman's case may be found at *Coleman v. Thayer*, 716 F.3d 895 (5th Cir. 2013).

19 Tom Dart, "Texas Set to Execute Lisa Coleman for Gruesome Murder of Child," *The Guardian*, September 17, 2014.

20 See "Lisa Ann Coleman," Office of the Clark County Prosecuting Attorney, www .clarkprosecutor.org.

21 In his concurrence in *Furman v. Georgia*, 408 U.S. 238 (1972), Justice Potter Stewart wrote that the death penalty was "cruel and unusual in the same way that being struck by lightening (*sic*) is cruel and unusual."

22 For information about Wanda Jean Allen and her case, see *Allen v. State*, 1995 OK CR 78, 909 P.2d 836; *Allen v. Massie*, 2000 10th Cir. 43, 236 F.3d 1243; Joey L. Mogul, "Equality: The Dykier, the Butcher, the Better: The State's Use of Homophobia and Sexism to Execute Women in the United States," *New York City Law Review* 8, no. 2 (Fall 2005); Atwell, *Wretched Sisters*, chap. 6.

23 Mark Fuhrman, *Death and Justice: An Expose of Oklahoma's Death Row Machine* (New York: Harper Collins, 2003), 235.

24 *Allen v. State*, 1995 OK CR 78, 909 P.2d.

25 Adam Buckley Cohen, "Who Was Wanda Jean? Black Woman Executed in the United States," *The Advocate*, March 13, 2001.

26 Frances Newton always maintained her innocence of the murders of her husband and children. There are a number of serious questions about the evidence used to convict her. Ballistics tests showed that she had not fired a gun. There were no bloodstains on her or her clothes. Witnesses made the timetable for Newton's

alibi and the murder inconsistent. Police made no effort to investigate whether the murders were drug related, despite her husband's history as a drug dealer. The forensics used as evidence by the prosecution were questionable if not nonsensical. Atwell, *Wretched Sisters*, chap. 9.

27 The basic facts of the crime are covered in the trial transcripts and in the appellate pleadings and opinions. See, for example, *State of Texas v. Frances Elaine Newton*, 263rd District (1988); *Newton v. Dretke*, 371 F.3d. 250 (5th Cir. May 20, 2004); Application for Postconviction Writ of Habeas Corpus and Motion for Stay of Execution, 2005.

28 Maurice Chammah, *Let the Lord Sort Them: The Rise and Fall of the Death Penalty* (New York: Crown, 2021), 253.

29 Information about Kimberly McCarthy's case may be found at *McCarthy v. State*, 65 S.W.3d 47 (Tex. Crim. App 2001); *McCarthy v. State*, 2004 WL 3099230 (Tex. Crim. App. 2004); *McCarthy v. Thaler* (2011) WL 1754199; *McCarthy v. Thaler* 483 Fed. App. 898 (5th Cir. 2012); Atwell, *Wretched Sisters*, chap. 11.

30 *McCarthy v. State*, 2004 WL 3099230 (Tex. Crim. App. 2004).

31 *McCarthy*, 2004 WL 3099230.

32 *State of Texas v. Karla Faye Tucker*, 263rd District (1984). See also Beverly Lowry, *Crossed Over: A Murder: A Memoir* (New York: Vintage, 2002) for the detailed story of Tucker's life, her crime, and her post-conviction conversion. Atwell, *Wretched Sisters*, chap. 4.

33 Lowry, *Crossed Over*, 13.

34 George Lardner, "Symposium: Forgiveness and the Law: Executive Clemency and the American System of Justice," *Capital University Law Review* 31 (2003): 181.

35 *Monster*, directed by Patty Jenkins (Denver and Delilah Films, 2003).

36 The basic facts of Wuornos's life can be found in Delores Kennedy, *On a Killing Day* (Chicago: Bonus Books, 1992); Sue Russell, *Lethal Intent* (New York: Pinnacle Books, 2002); Aileen Wuornos and Christopher Berry-Dee, *Monster: My True Story* (London: John Blake, 2004); and Stacey L. Shipley and Bruce A. Arrigo, *The Female Homicide Offender: Serial Murder and the Case of Aileen Wuornos* (Upper Saddle River, NJ: Pearson Prentice Hall, 2004); Atwell, *Wretched Sisters*, chap. 8.

37 Jim Ross, "Execution Evokes a Tide of Memories," *St. Petersburg Times*, October 10, 2002.

38 Shipley and Arrigo, *Female Homicide Offender*, 66–67.

39 Shipley and Arrigo, 109–15.

40 Kopec, "Avoiding a Death Sentence," 363.

41 Michael B. Shortnacy, "Guilty and Gay: A Recipe for Execution in American Courtrooms: Sexual Orientation as a Tool for Prosecutorial Misconduct in Death Penalty Cases," *American University Law Review* 51 (December 2001).

42 Kennedy, *On a Killing Day*, 222.

43 Russell, *Lethal Intent*, 485–86.

44 For example, one commentator described Suzanne Basso during her trial as a "murderous and manipulative freak of nature . . . who had shed an enormous

200 pounds in an attempt to look frail." Christopher Berry-Dee and Tony Brown, *Dead Men Walking: True Stories of the Most Evil Men and Women on Death Row* (London: John Blake, 2008), 9.

45 Ron Word, "Florida Executes Female Serial Killer," *St. Petersburg Times*, October 9, 2002.

46 "This Is Not Justice—Federal Execution Spree Ends with Planned Execution of African-American on Martin Luther King Jr.'s Birthday," Death Penalty Information Center, January 18, 2021, https://deathpenaltyinfo.org.

47 "This Is Not Justice."

48 "Coalition of More than 1000 Advocates Urge Federal Government to Halt December 8 Execution of Lisa Montgomery," Death Penalty Information Center, November 12, 2020, https://deathpenaltyinfo.org.

49 Lisa Montgomery's legal saga may be found at *U.S. v. Montgomery*, 635 F.3d 1074 (2011); *Montgomery v. Barr*, 2020 U.S. Dist. Lexis 217946 (November 19, 2020); *Montgomery v. Rosen*, 2020 U.S. Dist. Lexis 242403 (December 24, 2020); *Montgomery v. Rosen*, 2021 U.S. App. Lexis 1161 (January 11, 2021).

50 Meghan Roos, "Lisa Montgomery's Sister Blames Death Sentence in Part on Being Poor," *Newsweek*, December 24, 2020.

51 Sandra Babcock, "The Case of Lisa Montgomery: A Childhood of Torture, Rape, and Sex Trafficking Leading to Lifelong Mental Illness," Cornell Center on the Death Penalty Worldwide, October 23, 2020, https://deathpenaltyworldwide.org/.

52 Babcock, "Case of Lisa Montgomery."

53 Roos, "Lisa Montgomery's Sister."

54 Sandra Babcock, "Lisa Montgomery: A Victim of Child Incest, Child Prostitution, and Rape Faces Execution," Cornell Center on the Death Penalty Worldwide, November 23, 2020, https://deathpenaltyworldwide.org/.

55 Babcock, "Case of Lisa Montgomery."

56 "Dissociative Disorders," Mayo Clinic, www.mayoclinic.org.

57 Babcock, "Lisa Montgomery."

58 Babcock, " Case of Lisa Montgomery."

59 Natalie Schreyer, "A 'Prisoner of War' Story: The Life and Captivity of Lisa Montgomery—The First Women to be Executed by the Federal Government in 68 Years," *MS*, January 11, 2021.

60 Alison J. Lynch, Michael L. Perlin, and Heather Cucolo, "My Bewildering Brain Toils in Vain: Traumatic Brain Injury, the Criminal Trial Process, and the Case of Lisa Montgomery" (NYLS Legal Studies Research Paper No. 37775551, February 14, 2021), www.papers.ssrn.com.

61 Hannah Murphy, "Lisa Montgomery Suffered Years of Abuse and Trauma. The United States Killed Her Anyway," *Rolling Stone*, January 22, 2021.

62 Roos, "Lisa Montgomery's Sister."

63 Murphy, "Lisa Montgomery."

64 Schreyer, "Prisoner of War."

65 Babcock, "Lisa Montgomery."

66 Murphy, "Lisa Montgomery."

67 Babcock, "Case of Lisa Montgomery."

68 Amanda Robert, "Champion for the Condemned," *ABA Journal* 107, no. 2 (April/ May 2021): 62–64.

69 Robert, "Champion for the Condemned"; Schreyer, "Prisoner of War"; Ko Bragg, "Execution Delayed for Lone Woman on Federal Death Row," *The 19th*, November 19, 2020.

70 Robert, "Champion for the Condemned."

71 "Coalition of More than 1000."

72 "Coalition of More than 1000."

73 *United States v. Dustin John Higgs*, 529 U.S. _____ (2021), January 15, 2021.

74 Melissa Jeltson, "Lisa Montgomery's Final Hours before the Trump Administration Executed Her," *Huffington Post*, January 13, 2021.

75 See, for example, Meda Chesney-Lind and Lisa Pasko, eds., *Girls, Women, and Crime: Selected Readings* (Thousand Oaks, CA: Sage, 2004).

76 *Atkins v. Virginia*, 536 U.S. 304 (2002).

77 *Newton v. Dretke*, 371 F.3d 250 (5th Cir., May 20, 2004).

78 David V. Baker, *Women and Capital Punishment in the United States: An Analytical History* (Jefferson, NC: MacFarland, 2016), 12.

6

Discrimination and Capital Punishment

Will Persistent Racism Seal the Fate of the
U.S. Death Penalty?

NGOZI NDULUE

Racism has been central to the development of the U.S. death penalty. Despite changes in laws, procedures, and policies, capital punishment remains linked to race in a system that now promises equal justice for all. Though it is impossible to deny the mountain of accumulated evidence of racial bias in the death penalty, the United States Supreme Court has rejected challenges to the punishment based on this evidence. Attempts at addressing racial bias in the operation of the death penalty have gained renewed force in state legislatures and courts, but it remains to be seen whether the country is willing to recognize the full scope of the connections between long-standing systems of oppression and the foundations of the capital punishment system.

Created Unequal: The Early American Death Penalty

The death penalty was used in the American colonies from the earliest point of their existence, and when slavery was introduced to the colonies, capital punishment became a tool for maintaining a racial hierarchy. Southern states in the pre–Civil War period prescribed different crimes and penalties based on race and whether a person was enslaved.[1] Violence perpetrated by a white person against an enslaved person was seen less as an offense against a person than as a property crime against the person's owner. In northern states, Black people were executed in numbers disproportionate to their population.[2]

Race also affected how authorities carried out executions. In the colonies and early America, most people were executed by hanging, but

Black people were vulnerable to more severe and gruesome punishments.[3] Slave rebellions were seen as "petit treason" and punished in ways designed to send a strong deterrent message. In response to slave rebellions, murder, arson, or other crimes against white people, African Americans were burned at the stake, broken on wheels, gibbeted, decapitated, and dismembered.[4]

The use of the death penalty was also intrinsically connected to the conquest of Native American land and westward expansion. Throughout the eighteenth and nineteenth centuries, as the U.S. government seized large swaths of tribal land, Native Americans were executed for participation in resistance efforts. On December 26, 1862, following the U.S.-Dakota War of 1862, the federal government hanged thirty-eight members of the Dakota tribe in Minnesota.[5] It was the largest mass execution in United States history.[6] Executions of Native Americans also relied on stereotypes about their character and lack of "civilization."[7]

The Civil War ended slavery but not formal inequality under law. Instead, Southern states moved to legally entrench the racial caste system by creating Black Codes.[8] With the adoption of the Fourteenth Amendment in 1868, all Americans were formally guaranteed "equal protection of the laws."[9] Despite the promises of the new constitutional protection, the death penalty remained unevenly applied and intertwined with extralegal racial violence against people of color.

Between the end of the Civil War and the 1930s, lynchings and other forms of racial violence were an almost daily occurrence. During this period, the vast majority of lynchings took place in the South,[10] and after 1900, southern lynchings almost exclusively targeted African Americans. They also became more torturous and gruesome, serving both to terrorize the Black community and sometimes as an entertainment spectacle enjoyed by thousands of white celebrants.[11]

Although the vast majority of documented racial terror lynchings were perpetrated against Black people, the victims of lynching differed based on region, and other people of color and disfavored groups were at times the target of lynchings and mob violence. Several Native Americans and people of Asian descent were lynched in the western United States.[12] As the United States expanded westward in the nineteenth century, there were hundreds of instances of mob violence and lynchings of people of Mexican descent. The vast majority took place in Texas,

California, Arizona, and New Mexico, with a few occurring in other western and southern states.[13]

Racial terror lynchings and mass violence against African American communities often operated in tandem with formal executions. At times, the promise of a swift, officially sanctioned death penalty was used to deter would-be participants in lynch mobs. Executions following these show trials with little process and a preordained outcome were described by activists as "legal lynchings."[14] In debates about the abolition or reinstatement of capital punishment, public officials were concerned that the absence of capital punishment would result in more lynchings. For example, Tennessee abolished the death penalty for most murders in 1915. Within two years, the penalty was reinstated, in part because of lynchings that happened while the death penalty had been restricted.[15]

This same sentiment was echoed in the seminal decisions of the U.S. Supreme Court that ushered in the "modern" era of the death penalty. In *Furman v. Georgia*, the Supreme Court found the death penalty unconstitutional as it was administered throughout the United States. Justice Potter Stewart concurred in *Furman* because of the arbitrary and potentially racist way that the death penalty was being administered, but he disagreed with the argument that the death penalty violates the Eighth Amendment regardless of how it is implemented. He argued instead that retribution was an acceptable goal of capital punishment, writing that "[w]hen people begin to believe that organized society is unwilling or unable to impose upon criminal offenders the punishment they 'deserve,' then there are sown the seeds of anarchy—of self-help, vigilante justice, and lynch law."[16] Justice Stewart reiterated this sentiment four years later when he wrote the plurality opinion in *Gregg v. Georgia*, upholding the constitutionality of capital punishment statutes enacted in response to *Furman*.[17]

A "Reformed Death Penalty" with All the Same Racial Bias

Shortly after deciding *Gregg*, the Supreme Court had an opportunity to address one of the areas of the most extreme racial imbalance in capital punishment—the use of the death penalty for rape cases in which no murder was committed. Throughout U.S. history there is no evidence of any white man being executed for the rape of a Black woman, and the execution of a white man for the rape of a white woman was rare. For example, nationwide, between 1930 and 1967, 89 percent of those executed for rape were Black men.[18] Of the 125 people executed by Tennessee between 1916 and 1960, thirty-six were executed for rape—thirty-one Black men and just five white men.[19]

In the decade before *Furman*, the Supreme Court had declined to take up the issue of racial discrimination in capital rape cases brought by Black defendants.[20] The Court finally decided the issue of the constitutionality of imposing the death penalty for rape in 1977 when it was faced with the rare case of a white defendant sentenced to death for rape. The Court declared the death penalty an unconstitutionally disproportionate punishment for the rape of an adult woman when unaccompanied by a homicide. Although the briefing in the case described in detail the racially biased application of capital rape statutes, race was never mentioned in the Court's opinion.[21]

The Court would not deeply examine the role of race in capital sentencing until 1987, when the Court rejected a challenge to the death penalty based on statistical evidence of racial discrimination in its application. In *McCleskey v. Kemp*, Warren McCleskey presented evidence that in Georgia, the odds of a murder case resulting in a death sentence was 4.3 times greater when the victim was white.[22] The Court held that McCleskey needed to prove particularized discrimination in his own case and could not rely solely on systemic information. In 2020, researchers reviewed the final outcomes of the Georgia study that formed the basis for McCleskey's challenge and found that the disparities seen at sentencing increased as the cases wound through the court system. Cases with white victims were seventeen times more likely to result in executions.[23]

The disparities found in Georgia are not limited to that one state. The nation's death row has always had a higher percentage of Black persons than are represented in the overall population. Currently, 41 percent of death row is Black, even though Black people make up only 13.5 percent of the U.S. population.[24] Different rates of offending and victimization do not explain the racial differences in the capital punishment system. Seventy-five percent of the post-*Furman* executions involved homicides against white victims, but white victims make up less than half of those victimized by homicide.[25] Fifty years after *Furman*, the race of a murder victim remains a determining feature in which crimes are cleared with arrests, who is charged with a capital crime, who is sentenced to death, who succeeds in appeals and clemency, and who is ultimately executed.[26]

These disparities have been confirmed by empirical studies in death penalty jurisdictions throughout the country. For example, a 2022 study of Kentucky's post-1975 capital punishment system found "extraordinary racial disparities" in Kentucky's application of capital punishment based on the race and sex of both victims and defendants that "call into question the equity of the entire system."[27] The disparities reflected a strong white-victim preference—and in particular a white-female-victim preference—in whether a death sentence would be imposed. Death verdicts were more than five times as likely to be imposed in cases with white victims than in those with Black victims and were eleven times as likely in cases with white female victims than in those with Black male victims. "When the offender is black and the victim a white female," the study found, "odds are more than 20 times greater for a death sentence than in cases where both are black."[28]

A 2015 meta-analysis of capital charging and sentencing studies found that "each of the 30 studies [of prosecutors' decisions to charge a suspect with a capital crime] identified found that killers of Whites were more likely than killers of Blacks to face a capital prosecution. These studies cover a wide range of geographic areas and time periods and include different sets of statistical controls."[29] When evaluating studies about the decisions made at the capital sentencing stage, the researchers concluded that "the vast majority of studies found that killers of Whites are sentenced to death at higher rates than killers of Blacks." Of the seventy-eight studies examined, sixty-nine "found significant and substantial race-of-victim effects."[30]

Less information is available about Latinx defendants and victims, but available evidence demonstrates disparities.[31] Studies of San Diego County, Los Angeles County, and San Joaquin County, California have found that death-eligible offenses with Latinx victims are less likely to be pursued capitally than those with white victims.[32] In a 2005 study that evaluated all reported California homicides between 1990 and 1999 and the resulting death sentences, researchers found that those convicted of killing non-Latinx whites were three times more likely to be sentenced to death than those convicted of killing African Americans, and four times more likely to be sentenced to death than those whose victims were Latinx.[33] In Harris County, Texas, two county-level studies conducted over different time periods provided mixed results regarding disparities between the treatment of cases with Latinx victims when compared with white-victim cases.[34]

Women have always made up a small proportion of those sentenced to death, but Black women have been disproportionately subjected to the death penalty throughout U.S. history. Historians have documented 702 female executions; of this number, Black women and girls account for 436 executions, and white women and girls account for 229 executions. Black women and girls have been executed at two times the rate of white women and girls.[35] Four of the seventeen female executions in the modern era of the death penalty were of Black women.[36]

Glaring disparities persist in the use of the death penalty in interracial murders. Of the 1,586 executions between 1977 and April 2024, 305 Black prisoners were executed for murdering white victims and only twenty-one white prisoners were executed for murdering Black victims.[37] Several studies of state capital punishment systems have shown that cases with a Black defendant and white victim are most likely to result in the death penalty.[38] A study of Philadelphia capital sentencing found that when a murder victim was white, Black defendants who had more stereotypically Black physical features were more likely to be sentenced to death. No appearance effect was found when both the victim and defendant were Black.[39] Though the courts can no longer impose the death penalty for rape alone, when capital murders include allegations of sexual assault, Black defendants are more likely to be sentenced to death when the victims are white.[40]

The reasons for these persistent disparities are numerous, and the connection between historical racial terror lynchings and the contemporary death penalty cannot be overlooked. The states with the highest number of lynchings also have the highest numbers of post-*Furman* executions of Black defendants. States with higher numbers of lynchings and large Black populations have higher rates of death sentencing.[41] White residents of states with higher numbers of lynchings are more likely to support the death penalty than those in states where lynchings were not common.[42]

The continued salience of the history of lynching Black capital defendants accused of murdering white people has become explicit several times in recent years. In 2010, a number of commentors on local news sites suggested that lynching would be more appropriate than Andrew Ramseur's capital trial.[43] A Texas county judge responded to a November 2016 Facebook post about a Black capital defendant, "Time for a tree and a rope." Professional discipline for the judge's comment consisted of a public reprimand and required racial sensitivity training.[44]

Race, Youth, and the Death Penalty

The historical throughline of differential treatment based on race can be seen in the deployment of capital punishment against a category of defendants who have universally been considered less culpable and more capable of redemption.[45] The youngest children sentenced to death in U.S. history were African American and Native American boys. A ten-year-old Black boy whose name is unknown was reportedly hanged in Alexandria, Louisiana, in 1855.[46] James Arcene, a Cherokee, was sentenced to death for participating in a robbery-murder when he was ten years old. Because he avoided capture for over a decade, his execution took place on June 26, 1885, when he was in his early twenties.[47]

Young girls of color were also subject to the death penalty. In 1786, twelve-year-old Hannah Ocuish was executed in New London, Connecticut. Ocuish was executed for killing another child after a fight over strawberries. Ocuish had been abandoned by her mother and was likely intellectually disabled. She was described in local papers as "a fierce young savage," reflecting prevalent stereotypes of Native Americans.[48]

Mary was between twelve and sixteen years old when she allegedly killed her owner's child in Washington County, Missouri. She was interrogated by a neighbor while tied to a log. The neighbor described what took place: "I then commenced pulling up [Mary's] coat as if I was going to whip her. She then said if I would not whip her she would tell the truth. I told her then out with it. She then told me she had thrown [the child] in that hole of water."[49] Mary was tried and sentenced to death in 1837, and following a successful appeal and retrial she was resentenced to death. She was hanged in 1838.[50]

Most of the children executed in U.S. history were Black, and most executions were for crimes against white people.[51] At fourteen years old, George Stinney Jr. was among the youngest to be executed in the twentieth century. After a three-hour trial followed by ten minutes of deliberation by an all-white jury, Stinney was sentenced to death in 1944 for beating two white girls to death. His lawyer filed no appeals, and Stinney was electrocuted by South Carolina three months after the crime occurred.[52]

His case was widely reported, in part because of the gruesomeness of executing such a small child: "The guards had considerable difficulty strapping the small Black child (five feet one inch, ninety-five pounds) into the electric chair made for adults. As his electrocution began, Stinney's death mask slipped down to reveal the crying face of a frightened seventh-grader."[53] His descendants and community activists fought to clear his name posthumously, arguing that Stinney had been intimidated into confessing, that he did not have the physical strength or ability to beat the girls to death, that other suspects were not investigated, and that Stinney's lawyer put on no defense. Seventy years after his execution, Stinney's conviction was vacated because of the lack of due process in his rushed and perfunctory trial.[54]

Willie Francis was fifteen years old when he was sentenced to death for the murder of his employer. His death sentence came after a trial similar to Stinney's, in which his lawyers offered no defense. As with Stinney, there was no investigation of evidence pointing to other culprits, and a potentially coerced confession. Louisiana attempted to electrocute Francis in 1946, but because of a misconfigured electric chair, the execution attempt failed. A new lawyer unsuccessfully appealed to the U.S. Supreme Court to prevent a second execution attempt, and Francis was ultimately executed in 1947.[55]

In the post-*Furman* era of the death penalty, people of color were disproportionately sentenced to death and executed for crimes committed as children. From 1972 to the last juvenile execution in 2003, 55 percent of those executed for crimes committed as juveniles were people of color.[56] When the U.S. Supreme Court declared juvenile executions unconstitutional in 2005,[57] seventy-one people were on death row for crimes committed as juveniles. Of the juvenile death row population at that time, 66 percent were people of color.[58]

Now that the death penalty is available only for crimes committed after the age of eighteen, Black and Latinx youths are overrepresented in those sentenced to death and executed for crimes committed as young adults. Between 2000 and 2019, 164 people who were between eighteen and twenty-one years old at the time of the crime were executed. Of these, 60 percent were African American or Latinx.[59]

Responses to Racial Bias in the Death Penalty

In line with the United States Supreme Court's ruling in *McCleskey*, courts have been wary of granting relief based on statistical evidence of racial discrimination in capital punishment. However, a few state courts and legislatures have squarely addressed the issue.

Racial justice acts have been one tool that legislatures have used in response to evidence of racial bias in the administration of the death penalty. After the Kentucky legislature commissioned a study that showed significant racial disparities in the death penalty, it passed a racial justice act that allows a defendant to challenge a prosecutor's decision to capitally charge them. This challenge must be brought pretrial.[60] As a result of its limited scope, no Kentucky capital defendant has successfully pursued a challenge under this law.[61]

North Carolina enacted a racial justice act (RJA) in 2009 that allowed death row prisoners to overturn their sentences if they could prove that race was a "significant factor" in jury selection, prosecutors' decisions to seek a death sentence, or juries' decisions to impose the death penalty. Four prisoners successfully pursued RJA claims, but when the political composition of the state legislature changed in 2013, it passed a retroactive repeal of the RJA. In a series of 2020 rulings, the North Carolina Supreme Court struck down the state legislature's attempted retroactive repeal and restored the rights of approximately 140 death row prisoners to seek RJA relief.[62] It also restored the RJA relief granted to the four prisoners whose death sentences had been reinstated.[63]

In September 2020, California enacted a racial justice act that applies to all criminal cases. The act prohibits the state from seeking or obtaining a conviction or imposing a sentence "on the basis of race, ethnicity, or national origin." At the same time, the state enacted legislation to more effectively address discrimination in jury selection in all civil and criminal cases. The law bars the use of discretionary strikes to remove a prospective juror whenever "there is a substantial likelihood that an objectively reasonable person would view race, ethnicity, gender, gender identity, sexual orientation, national origin, or religious affiliation, or perceived membership in any of those groups, as a factor" in the challenge to the juror.[64] Given the newness of the laws, the extent of its impact on death sentencing is not yet apparent.

Some states have concluded that post-*Furman* racial disparities invalidate the death penalty altogether. In 2018, the Washington Supreme Court held that the death penalty violated the state constitution because it had been "imposed in an arbitrary and racially biased manner." In *State v. Gregory*, the court relied on a study of twenty-five years of Washington capital prosecutions that demonstrated that Washington juries were 4.5 times more likely to impose a death sentence on a Black defendant than on a white defendant in a similar case.[65] The *Gregory* court refused to dismiss these findings as the U.S. Supreme Court had in *McCleskey*; instead, it found that "[g]iven the evidence before this court and our judicial notice of implicit and overt racial bias against black defendants in this state, we are confident that the association between race and the death penalty is not attributed to random chance."[66]

In 2021, Virginia legislatively abolished the death penalty, in part based on racial justice concerns. The commonwealth—which from colonial times had carried out more executions than any other U.S. jurisdiction—became the first southern state to end capital punishment. The repeal effort emphasized the historical links between slavery, Jim Crow, lynchings, and the death penalty. Delegate Mike Mullin, the House sponsor of the bill, said, "We've carried out the death penalty in extraordinarily unfair fashion. Only four times out of nearly 1,400 [executions] was the defendant white and the victim Black."[67] In signing the bill, Governor Ralph Northam characterized the death penalty as "fundamentally flawed," based in large part on its racial inequity.[68] That history underlined the symbolic importance of the death penalty being abolished in the former capital of the Confederacy.

Conclusion

The United States' death penalty has always been a reflection of the strength of systems of racial oppression. Equality was formally enshrined more than 150 years ago in post–Civil War constitutional amendments, but the United States Supreme Court remains unwilling to ensure that equal justice is extended to the administration of capital punishment. Given existing Supreme Court precedent and the current Court's composition, the road to abolition of the death penalty in the United States runs through state courts and legislatures. Since the current strongholds of the death penalty are mostly in southern states with courts and legislatures dominated by white conservatives, it is tempting to downplay or ignore racial justice issues in order to secure abolition. However, pursuing abolition without centering the current practice in an established legacy of racism results in a flattening of the racial justice issues central to the death penalty's continued existence. Racial injustice was central to the establishment of the U.S. death penalty, it is central to its continued existence, and ending racial injustice must be central to its abolition.

Notes

1 Barbara O'Brien, Catherine M. Grosso, George Woodworth, and Abijah Taylor, "Untangling the Role of Race in Capital Charging and Sentencing in North Carolina, 1990–2009," *North Carolina Law Review* 94 (2015): 1997; Stuart Banner, "Traces of Slavery: Race and the Death Penalty in Historical Perspective," in *From Lynch Mobs to the Killing State*, ed. Charles J. Ogletree Jr. and Austin Sarat (New York: New York University Press, 2006), 81. For more on the racial history of the death penalty, see Ngozi Ndulue, *Enduring Injustice: The Persistence of Racial Discrimination in the U.S. Death Penalty*, ed. Robert Dunham (Washington, DC: Death Penalty Information Center, September 2020), https://deathpenaltyinfo .org.

2 Jeffrey Kirchmeier, *Imprisoned by the Past: Warren McCleskey, Race, and the American Death Penalty* (New York: Oxford University Press, 2015).

3 Banner, "Traces of Slavery," 103.

4 Carol S. Steiker and Jordan M. Steiker, "The American Death Penalty and the (In)Visibility of Race," *University of Chicago Law Review* 82, no. 1 (2015): 243–94; Daniel J. Flanigan, "The Criminal Law of Slavery and Freedom, 1800–1868" (PhD diss., Rice University, May 1987), 2. Maryland criminal laws in the eighteenth century allowed that "for murder, or arson of a dwelling trial courts could sentence slaves to have their right hands cut off before they were hanged. Later, they would be beheaded, quartered, and their bodies left exposed to serve as a warning to their fellows" (Flanigan, 2).

5 Gary C. Anderson, *Massacre in Minnesota: The Dakota War of 1862* (Norman: University of Oklahoma Press, 2019), 2.

6 Carol Chomsky, "The United States–Dakota War Trials: A Study in Military Injustice," *Stanford Law Review* 43 (1990): 13.

7   For example, in 1786, twelve-year-old Hannah Ocuish, who was executed in
    Connecticut, was described in local papers as "a fierce young savage." David V.
    Baker, *Women and Capital Punishment in the United States: An Analytical History*
    (Jefferson, NC: McFarland, 2016), 131; Victor L. Streib and Lynn Sametz, "Executing
    Female Juveniles," *Connecticut Law Review* 22 (1989): 3.

8   John K. Cochran, Christopher J. Marier, Wesley G. Jennings, M. Dwayne Smith,
    Beth Bjerregaard, and Sondra J. Fogel, "Rape, Race, and Capital Punishment: An
    Enduring Cultural Legacy of Lethal Vengeance?," *Race and Justice* 9, no. 4 (Octo-
    ber 2019): 383–406.

9   U.S. Const. amend. XIV.

10 Equal Justice Initiative, *Reconstruction in America: Racial Violence after the Civil
    War* (Montgomery, AL: Equal Justice Initiative, 2020), https://eji.org/; Amy Kate
    Bailey and Stewart E. Tolnay, *Lynched: The Victims of Southern Mob Violence*
    (Chapel Hill: University of North Carolina Press, 2015), 2.

11 Equal Justice Initiative, *Lynching in America: Confronting the Legacy of Racial
    Terror*, 3rd ed. (Montgomery, AL: Equal Justice Initiative, 2017), http://eji.org/;
    David Garland, "Penal Excess and Surplus Meaning: Public Torture Lynchings
    in Twentieth-Century America," *Law and Society Review* 39 (2005): 793; Amy L.
    Wood, *Lynching and Spectacle: Witnessing Racial Violence in America, 1890–1940*
    (Chapel Hill: University of North Carolina Press, 2009).

12 Bailey and Tolnay, *Lynched*. See Bureau of the Census, *Historical Statistics of the
    United States: Colonial Times to 1970* (Washington, DC: U.S. Department of Com-
    merce, Bureau of the Census, 1972) (noting estimates that 45 Native Americans,
    12 people of Chinese descent, 1 person of Japanese descent, and 20 people of
    Mexican descent were lynched between 1882 and 1903).

13 William D. Carrigan and Clive Webb, *Forgotten Dead: Mob Violence against Mexi-
    cans in the United States, 1848–1928* (New York: Oxford University Press, 2013)
    (declining to use the term *lynching*, but documenting 547 victims of anti-Mexican
    mob violence and asserting that there are thousands more unnamed victims);
    William D. Carrigan and Clive Webb, "The Lynching of Persons of Mexican Origin
    or Descent in the United States, 1848 to 1928," *Journal of Social History* 37, no. 2
    (2003): 411–38; see also Richard Delgado, "The Law of the Noose: A History of
    Latino Lynching," *Harvard Civil Rights–Civil Liberties Law Review* 44 (2009): 297.

14 Steiker and Steiker, "American Death Penalty"; Charles J. Ogletree Jr., "Black
    Man's Burden: Race and the Death Penalty in America," *Oregon Law Review* 81
    (2002): 15.

15 Jeffrey Kirchmeier, *Imprisoned by the Past: Warren McCleskey, Race, and the
    American Death Penalty* (New York: Oxford University Press, 2015).

16 *Furman v. Georgia*, 408 U.S. 238, 310 (1972) (Stewart, J., concurring) ("[I]f any
    basis can be discerned for the selection of these few to be sentenced to die, it is
    the constitutionally impermissible basis of race.").

17 *Gregg v. Georgia*, 428 U.S. 153, 183 (1976) (plurality opinion) (stating that society
    must have an outlet to express its moral outrage, asserting that "it is essential in

an ordered society that asks its citizens to rely on legal processes rather than self-help to vindicate their wrongs.").

18 Brief for the American Civil Liberties Union, the ACLU of Louisiana, and the NAACP Legal Defense and Educational Fund, Inc., in Support of Petitioner, at 10, *Kennedy v. Louisiana*, 554 U.S. 407 (2008) (citing Wolfgang, Marvin E., and Marc Riedel, "Race, Judicial Discretion, and the Death Penalty," *Annals of the American Academy of Political and Social Science* 407, no. 1 (1973): 119–33); see generally Jack Greenberg, "Capital Punishment as a System," *Yale Law Journal* 91, no. 5 (1982): 908.

19 "Tennessee Executions," Tennessee Department of Corrections, www.tn.gov/.

20 See *Maxwell v. Bishop*, 393 U.S. 997 (1968); *Rudolph v. Alabama*, 375 U.S. 889 (1963).

21 *Coker v. Georgia*, 433 U.S. 584 (1977). The death penalty for rape of a child was found unconstitutional in 2008, but no one had been executed for such a crime in the post-*Furman* era. *Kennedy v. Louisiana*, 554 U.S. 407 (2008). In *Kennedy*, the Court followed the same pattern in considering the constitutionality of the death penalty for child rape. Once again, it did not acknowledge overwhelming evidence of extreme racial disparities but still found the death penalty unconstitutionally disproportionate when imposed for child rape.

22 *McCleskey v. Kemp*, 481 U.S. 279, 339 (1987).

23 Scott Phillips and Justin Marceau, "Whom the State Kills," *Harvard Civil Rights–Civil Liberties Law Review* 55, no. 2 (2020): 585–656.

24 Death Penalty Information Center, *Facts about the Death Penalty* (Washington, DC: Death Penalty Information Center, updated August 30, 2024), https://deathpenaltyinfo.org; "Population Estimates, July 1, 2023," U.S. Census Bureau, QuickFacts: United States, www.census.gov/.

25 "Easy Access to the FBI's Supplementary Homicide Reports: 1980–2020," Office of Juvenile Justice and Delinquency Prevention, https://www.ojjdp.gov/; see Samuel Gross et al., *Race and Wrongful Convictions in the United States 2022* (Ann Arbor, MI: National Registry of Exonerations, September 2022), 4 n.10, https://www.law .umich.edu/ (noting the overestimate of white murder victims in the FBI's Supplementary Homicide Reports).

26 Ndule, *Enduring Injustice*, 33–50.

27 Frank R. Baumgartner, "A Statistical Overview of the Kentucky Death Penalty" (University of North Carolina at Chapel Hill, January 11, 2022), http://fbaum.unc .edu/.

28 Baumgartner, "Statistical Overview."

29 Frank R. Baumgartner, Amanda J. Grigg, and Alisa Mastro, "#BlackLivesDon'tMatter: Race-of-Victim Effects in US Executions, 1976–2013," *Politics, Groups, and Identities* 3, no. 2 (2015): 1–13.

30 Baumgartner, Grigg, and Mastro, "#BlackLivesDon'tMatter," 4.

31 Sheri Lynn Johnson, "The Influence of Latino Ethnicity on the Imposition of the Death Penalty," *Annual Review of Law and Social Science* 16, no. 1 (2020): 421–31.

32 Steven F. Shatz, Glenn L. Pierce, and Michael L Radelet, "Race, Ethnicity, and The Death Penalty in San Diego County: The Predictable Consequences of Excessive

Discretion," *Columbia Human Rights Law Review* 51, no. 3 (2020): 1070–98; Nick Peterson, "Cumulative Racial and Ethnic Inequalities in Potentially Capital Cases," *Criminal Justice Review* 45, no. 2 (2017): 225–49; Catherine Lee, "Hispanics and the Death Penalty: Discriminatory Charging Practices in San Joaquin County, California," *Journal of Criminal Justice* 35, no. 1 (2007): 17–27.

33 Glenn L. Pierce and Michael L. Radelet, "The Impact of Legally Inappropriate Factors on Death Sentencing for California Homicides, 1990–1999," *Santa Clara Law Review* 46 (2005): 1.

34 Scott Phillips, "Continued Racial Disparities in the Capital of Capital Punishment: The Rosenthal Era," *Houston Law Review* 50 (2012): 131 (studying death sentencing between 1992 and 1999 and finding no disparities in the treatment of cases with Latinx victims when compared to the treatment of cases with white victims); Scott Phillips, "Racial Disparities in the Capital of Capital Punishment," *Houston Law Review* 45 (2008): 807 (using a different methodology to examine death-eligible sentences between 2001 and 2007 and finding that cases with Latinx victims were less likely to lead to a death sentence than cases with white victims).

35 Baker, *Women and Capital Punishment.*

36 "Executions of Women," Death Penalty Information Center, https://deathpenaltyinfo.org/.

37 Death Penalty Information Center, *Facts about the Death Penalty.*

38 See, e.g., Glenn L. Pierce, Michael L. Radelet, and Susan Sharp, "Race and Death Sentencing for Oklahoma Homicides Committed between 1990 and 2012," *Journal of Criminal Law and Criminology* (1973–) 107, no. 4 (2017): 733–56; Tim Lyman, Frank R. Baumgartner, and Glenn L. Pierce, "Race and Gender Disparities in Capitally-Charged Louisiana Homicide Cases, 1976–2014," *Southern University Law Review* 49 (2021): 153.

39 Jennifer L. Eberhardt, Paul G. Davies, Valerie J. Purdie-Vaughns, and Sheri Lynn Johnson, "Looking Deathworthy: Perceived Stereotypicality of Black Defendants Predicts Capital-Sentencing Outcomes," *Psychological Science* 17, no. 5 (2006): 383–86.

40 John K. Cochran, Christopher J. Marier, Wesley G. Jennings, M. Dwayne Smith, Beth Bjerregaard, and Sondra J. Fogel, "Rape, Race, and Capital Punishment: An Enduring Cultural Legacy of Lethal Vengeance?" *Race and Justice* 9, no. 4 (October 2019): 383–406; Phyllis L. Crocker, "Crossing the Line: Rape-Murder and the Death Penalty," *Ohio Northern University Law Review* 26, no. 3 (2000): 689–724.

41 David Jacobs, Jason T. Carmichael, and Stephanie L. Kent, "Vigilantism, Current Racial Threat, and Death Sentences," *American Sociological Review* 70, no. 4 (2005): 656–77.

42 Steven F. Messner, Eric P. Baumer, and Richard Rosenfeld, "Distrust of Government, the Vigilante Tradition, and Support for Capital Punishment," *Law and Society Review* 40, no. 3 (2006): 559–90.

43 Brief of Defendant-Appellant at 9–10, *State v. Ramseur*, 843 S.E.2d 106 (No. 388A10), 2020 WL 3025852 (N.C. June 5, 2020) (internal citations omitted).

44 Public Reprimand and Order of Additional Education, Texas State Commission on Judicial Conduct, April 5, 2018, http://www.scjc.texas.gov/.

45 See generally *Miller v. Alabama*, 567 U.S. 460 (2012); *Roper v. Simmons*, 543 U.S. 551 (2005).

46 *Thompson v. Oklahoma*, 487 U.S. 815, 828 (1988) (plurality opinion) (citing Victor L. Streib, "Death Penalty for Children: The American Experience with Capital Punishment for Crimes Committed While under Age Eighteen," *Oklahoma Law Review* 36 (1983): 613.

47 Victor L. Streib, *Testimony on the Death Penalty for Juveniles Offered to the Subcommittee on Criminal Justice Regarding House Bill 343 and Related Bills*, 99th Cong. 5 (June 5, 1986), https://www.ncjrs.gov/.

48 Streib and Sametz, "Executing Female Juveniles," 3.

49 Amy Kostine and Ashley Brown, *Snelson-Brinker House Historic Structure Report* 7 (Murfreesboro, TN: MTSU Center for Historic Preservation, 2016), 7.

50 Kostine and Brown, *Snelson-Brinker House*.

51 Victor L. Streib, "The Juvenile Death Penalty Today: Death Sentences and Executions for Juvenile Crimes, January 1973—February 28, 2005" (Ohio Northern University, October 6, 2005), https://deathpenaltyinfo.org/; Streib, *Testimony on the Death Penalty*; Streib, "Death Penalty for Children." See also Sheri Lynn Johnson, John H. Blume, and Hannah L. Freedman, "The Pre-*Furman* Juvenile Death Penalty in South Carolina: Young Black Life Was Cheap," *South Carolina Law Review* 68, no. 3 (2016): 331 ("[O]ver 80% of all juvenile offenders executed in the United States between 1865 and 1972 were children of color. . . . Specifically, of the 133 juveniles executed in the United States between 1865 and 1972, 100 were black and 25 were white.").

52 Johnson, Blume, and Freedman, "Pre-*Furman*," 31.

53 Streib, *Testimony on the Death Penalty*.

54 Order, *State v. George Stinney, Jr.*, Clarendon Cty., S.C. 3d Jud. Dist. Ct. Dec. 17, 2014); Johnson, Blume, and Freedman, "Pre-*Furman*," 331.

55 *Louisiana ex rel. Francis v. Resweber*, 329 U.S. 459 (1947).

56 Streib, "Juvenile Death Penalty Today."

57 *Roper v. Simmons*, 543 U.S. 551 (2005).

58 Streib, "Juvenile Death Penalty Today."

59 Research on file with the Death Penalty Information Center.

60 Ky. Rev. Stat. Ann. § 532.300(1).

61 Rees Alexander, "A Model State Racial Justice Act: Fighting Racial Bias without Killing the Death Penalty," *George Mason University Civil Rights Law Journal* 24 (2013): 113.

62 *State v. Ramseur*, 843 S.E.2d 106 (N.C. 2020); *State v. Burke*, 843 S.E.2d 246 (N.C. 2020).

63 "In New Round of Racial Justice Act Litigation, North Carolina Judge Orders Prosecutors to Disclose Data on Decades of Jury Strikes," Death Penalty Information Center, May 28, 2021, https://deathpenaltyinfo.org.

64 "California Legislature Passes Racial Justice Package Affecting Death-Penalty Practices," Death Penalty Information Center, September 4, 2020, https://deathpenaltyinfo.org.

65 *State v. Gregory*, 427 P.3d 621, 630 (Wash. 2018) (citing Katherine Beckett and Heather Evans, "The Role of Race in Washington State Capital Sentencing, 1981–2014" (University of Washington, October 13, 2014)).

66 *State v. Gregory*, 427 P.3d at 635.

67 Death Penalty Information Center, *The Death Penalty in 2021: Year End Report* (Washington, DC: Death Penalty Information Center, December 16, 2021), https://deathpenaltyinfo.org.

68 "Governor Northam Signs Law Repealing Death Penalty in Virginia," news release, March 24, 2021, www.governor.virginia.gov/.

PART III

Actors and Decision-Makers

7

Conflicted Justices and a Divided Court

The U.S. Supreme Court's Death Penalty Jurisprudence

JOHN D. BESSLER

When the law punishes by death, it risks its own sudden descent into brutality, transgressing the constitutional commitment to decency and restraint.
—Justice Anthony Kennedy

The justices of the United States Supreme Court have long been divided—and personally conflicted—about the U.S. death penalty and its administration. In 1949, for example, the Supreme Court considered the case of Samuel Williams—a man convicted of first-degree murder after a killing during a burglary. The jury had recommended life imprisonment, but the trial judge imposed a death sentence.[1] In the Court's majority opinion in *Williams v. People of State of New York*, Justice Hugo Black reflected, "This whole country has traveled far from the period in which the death sentence was an automatic and commonplace result of convictions—even for offenses today deemed trivial."[2] As Justice Black emphasized, "Retribution is no longer the dominant objective of the criminal law. Reformation and rehabilitation of offenders have become important goals of criminal jurisprudence."[3] The trial judge had considered information outside the record in imposing the death sentence, but the *Williams* Court nonetheless affirmed that sentence, concluding, "We cannot say that the due-process clause renders a sentence void merely because a judge gets additional out-of-court information to assist him in the exercise of this awesome power of imposing the death sentence."[4]

In a dissent, Justice Frank Murphy emphasized that "in spite of the shocking character of the crime of which they found him guilty," the jurors had "unanimously recommended life imprisonment as a suitable punishment for the defendant."[5] In objecting to the trial judge's reliance on inadmissible hearsay, Justice Murphy wrote, "[I]n a capital case, against the unanimous recommendation of a jury, where the report would concededly not have been admissible at the trial, and was not subject to examination by the defendant, I am forced to conclude that the high commands of due process were not obeyed."[6]

The following year, in *Solesbee v. Balkcom*, the Supreme Court considered a habeas corpus petition filed by George Solesbee, seeking to prevent his execution in Georgia on the grounds that he'd become insane after his conviction.[7] In another opinion written by Justice Black, the Court—citing *Williams*—concluded in 1950, "We cannot say that it offends due process to leave the question of a convicted person's sanity to the solemn responsibility of a state's highest executive with authority to invoke the aid of the most skillful class of experts on the crucial questions involved."[8]

Justice Felix Frankfurter—a Franklin D. Roosevelt appointee—dissented, taking issue with the Court's ruling. "In the history of murder," his dissent began, "the onset of insanity while awaiting execution of a death sentence is not a rare phenomenon."[9] Seeing a denial of due process in the failure to consider Solesbee's claim, Justice Frankfurter observed, "That it offends our historic heritage to kill a man who has become insane while awaiting sentence cannot be gainsaid. This limitation on the power of the State to take life has been part of our law for centuries, recognized during periods of English history when feelings were more barbarous and men recoiled less from brutal action than we like to think is true of our time."[10] Since the early 1950s, Supreme Court justices have—time and time again—remained divided about capital punishment and the law's contours. In *Rosenberg v. United States*, in an opinion delivered in the midst of the Cold War on the very day (June 19, 1953) that Julius and Ethel Rosenberg were executed for espionage in Sing Sing Prison's electric chair, the Supreme Court vacated their stay of execution, allowing the electrocutions to proceed. The majority opinion itself evidenced the controversial nature of the executions: "Vacating this stay is not to be construed as indorsing the wisdom or appropriateness to this case of a death sentence. That sentence, however, is permitted by law and . . . is therefore not within this Court's power of revision."[11]

"Though the penalty is great and our responsibility heavy," the Court ruled, "our duty is clear."[12]

Justices Black, William O. Douglas, and Frankfurter all filed dissents. "Judicial haste is peculiarly out of place where the death penalty has been imposed for conduct part of which took place at a time when the Congress appears to have barred the imposition of the death penalty by district judges acting without a jury's recommendation," Justice Black wrote.[13] "No man or woman should go to death under an unlawful sentence merely because his lawyer failed to raise the point," Justice Douglas stressed.[14] And Justice Frankfurter, adding a dissent three days after the executions, emphasized, "To be writing an opinion in a case affecting two lives after the curtain has been rung down upon them has the appearance of pathetic futility. But history also has its claims."[15]

The history of Supreme Court cases pertaining to the death penalty is, in fact, replete with critiques of capital punishment and scores of 5–4, 6–3, and 7–2 decisions. In 1972, *Furman v. Georgia*—perhaps the most famous 5–4 decision of all—held that death penalty laws, as then applied, violated the U.S. Constitution's Eighth and Fourteenth Amendments.[16] But after upholding the constitutionality of newly enacted death penalty laws in 1976 in *Gregg v. Georgia*,[17] *Proffitt v. Florida*,[18] and *Jurek v. Texas*[19]—7–2 decisions that drew dissents from Justices William Brennan and Thurgood Marshall[20]—the Supreme Court has, ever since, allowed executions to proceed. Justices Brennan and Marshall believed any execution to be a cruel and unusual punishment, and other American jurists also came to see it that way.

Many judges have weighed in by authoring judicial opinions. "[F]or over a half-century," law professor Kevin Barry wrote in 2017, "at least thirty-five federal and state judges have concluded that the death penalty is unconstitutional per se."[21] He adds, "[T]hey have done so for remarkably similar reasons—namely, objective criteria detailing the death penalty's unacceptability to contemporary society, the subjective determination that the death penalty no longer serves any legitimate penological purposes, and a recognition that the death penalty violates human dignity."[22] In their landmark 2015 dissent in *Glossip v. Gross*, Justices Stephen Breyer and Ruth Bader Ginsburg concluded that "it highly likely that the death penalty violates the Eighth Amendment," and specifically called for a "full briefing on the basic question" of "whether the death penalty violates the Constitution."[23] The history of the United States' death penalty is one of successive restrictions on its use, though death sentences and executions continue to linger even as their annual numbers have declined precipitously in the last few decades.[24] Capital punishment is akin to a state-run lottery, the gravity of its blatant arbitrariness eclipsed only by its highly discriminatory application and torturous nature.[25]

Judging Capital Punishment in Post–World War II America:
The Supreme Court Justices Wrestle with Capital Punishment

Justice Frankfurter had questioned the death penalty's use even before joining the nation's highest court. A founder of the American Civil Liberties Union (ACLU), Frankfurter—as a Harvard Law School professor—had publicly sought a new trial for Nicola Sacco and Bartolomeo Vanzetti, the Italian immigrants infamously condemned to die on questionable evidence for first-degree murder. Prior to their highly publicized executions at Massachusetts's Charlestown Prison on August 23, 1927, Frankfurter had published an article in *The Atlantic* that laid out the case for a new trial in the matter.[26]

After joining the Supreme Court, Frankfurter continued speaking out in other cases. In 1948, in a concurring opinion in the Supreme Court's 5–4 decision in *Haley v. Ohio*,[27] Justice Frankfurter candidly wrote, "A lifetime's preoccupation with criminal justice, as a prosecutor, defender of civil liberties, and scientific student, naturally leaves one with views. Thus, I disbelieve in capital punishment."[28] At that time, only a few U.S. states barred executions. "But, as a judge," Justice Frankfurter opined in *Haley*, taking a position that other justices would echo in decades to come, "I could not impose the views of the very few States who, through bitter experience, have abolished capital punishment upon all the other States by finding that 'due process' proscribes it."[29]

The *Haley* case illustrates how the United States' system of capital punishment was once applied to juvenile offenders—and how African American suspects were frequently subjected to the "third degree," the euphemistic phrase for torturous or coercive interrogations. In *Haley*, a fifteen-year-old African American youth, John Haley, was accused of a capital crime, and he signed a confession at 5:00 a.m. after being interrogated for five hours without the benefit of counsel or speaking to his mother.[30] It was alleged in that case that Haley acted as "a lookout" while two other teenagers, Willie Lowder, sixteen, and Al Parks, seventeen, robbed a confectionary store around midnight on October 14, 1945, and that, in the course of the robbery, William Karam—the store's owner—was shot and killed. Five days after the crime, Haley had been arrested and taken to police headquarters for questioning.[31]

In 1946, Haley stood trial for the capital offense, but the jury recommended mercy, and he was sentenced to life imprisonment, thus saving him from the electric chair.[32] Ultimately, the Supreme Court—which, in prior cases, had denounced coercive interrogation techniques[33] even as it had generally failed to intervene to stop the death penalty's then widespread use[34]—held that the way in which Haley's confession had been obtained violated the Fourteenth Amendment's Due Process Clause.[35] "We do not think the methods used in obtaining this confession can be squared with that due process of law which the Fourteenth Amendment commands," the Court ruled.[36]

With the Supreme Court in *Haley* adjudicating whether John Haley's confession was improperly coerced or voluntarily obtained, the Court's opinion—written by Justice Douglas—observed that Haley's mother testified that Haley was "bruised and skinned" and that his clothes were "torn and blood-stained" when she was first allowed to see him days after his arrest.[37] Although the details of Haley's interrogation were disputed, there was—as the Supreme Court put it—"undisputed testimony" laying out this sequence of events: "Beginning shortly after midnight, this 15-year-old lad was questioned by the police for about five hours. Five or six of the police questioned him in relays of one or two each. During this time, no friend or counsel of the boy was present. Around 5 a.m.—after being shown alleged confessions of Lowder and Parks—the boy confessed."[38] What was at stake in the Court's review of the facts of the case was made abundantly clear. "If the undisputed evidence suggests that force or coercion was used to exact the confession," the Court emphasized of its approach to the law, "we will not permit the judgment of conviction to stand even though, without the confession, there might have been sufficient evidence for submission to the jury."[39]

After taking note of Haley's young age[40] and describing the teenager's middle-of-the-night interrogation and how Haley had been "held incommunicado" for more than three days,[41] the Supreme Court expressed its judgment, writing initially of Haley's youth, "Age 15 is a tender and difficult age for a boy of any race. He cannot be judged by the more exacting standards of maturity. That which would leave a man cold and unimpressed can overawe and overwhelm a lad in his early teens." Pointing out that as many as a half-dozen police officers questioned Haley over the course of the night, the Court added, "A 15-year-old lad, questioned through the dead of night by relays of police, is a ready victim of the inquisition."[42] Finding Haley's treatment showed a "disregard of the standards of decency,"[43] the Supreme Court reversed Haley's murder conviction and life sentence.[44] "The Fourteenth Amendment," the Court held, "prohibits the police from using the private, secret custody of either man or child as a device for wringing confessions from them."[45] Coerced confessions—whether obtained "by the torture of fear" or otherwise— are "inherently untrustworthy,"[46] the Court has emphasized. Justice Frankfurter provided the decisive fifth vote to overturn John Haley's conviction and sentence.

In *State of Louisiana ex rel. Francis v. Resweber* (1947), the Supreme Court justices were likewise sharply divided as to whether Louisiana should be allowed to execute Willie Francis, another African American teenager. On May 3, 1946, pursuant to a death warrant, Francis had been placed in Louisiana's electric chair in the presence of the official witnesses. The executioner had thrown the switch, but there were mechanical difficulties and, consequently, death did not occur. Francis was then removed from the electric chair and returned to prison, with Louisiana's governor later fixing a new execution date. Francis then claimed that his rights under the Fifth Amendment's Double Jeopardy Clause, the Eighth Amendment's Cruel and Unusual Punishments Clause, and the Fourteenth Amendment's Due Process Clause would be violated if another attempt was made to execute him "because he had once gone through the difficult preparation for execution and had once received through his body a current of electricity intended to cause death." Father Charles Hannegan, the prison chaplain, had assured Willie that his electrocution would be painless, but Willie reported that it felt like "being cut and pricked by . . . thousands . . . of razor-sharp needles and pins."[47]

After the Supreme Court of Louisiana denied relief to Francis, the nation's highest court agreed to consider the case. In an opinion announcing the Court's judgment, Justice Stanley Reed—writing for himself and three other justices—found no constitutional violation and thus affirmed the death sentence. "We find nothing in what took place here which amounts to cruel and unusual punishment in the constitutional sense," Justice Reed observed, adding of Francis's claim,

> Petitioner's suggestion is that because he once underwent the psychological strain of preparation for electrocution, now to require him to undergo this preparation again subjects him to a lingering or cruel and unusual punishment. Even the fact that petitioner has already been subjected to a current of electricity does not make his subsequent execution any more cruel in the constitutional sense than any other execution. . . . The situation of the unfortunate victim of this accident is just as though he had suffered the identical amount of mental anguish and physical pain in any other occurrence, such as, for example, a fire in the cell block. We cannot agree that the hardship imposed upon the petitioner rises to that level of hardship denounced as denial of due process because of cruelty.[48]

Four justices dissented in *Resweber*, with that dissent—written by Justice Harold Burton—expressing the view that "the unusual facts before us require that the judgment of the Supreme Court of Louisiana be vacated." When the Fourteenth Amendment was ratified in 1868, Justice Burton wrote, "there long had been imbedded deeply in the standards of this nation a revulsion against subjecting guilty persons to torture culminating in death." In arguing in favor of a remand for further proceedings, Burton's dissent—written long before the Supreme Court, in 1962, held the Eighth Amendment applicable to the states[49]—emphasized, "Preconstitutional American history reeked with cruel punishment to such an extent that, in 1791, the Eighth Amendment to the Constitution of the United States expressly imposed upon federal agencies a mandate that 'Excessive bail shall not be required, nor excessive fines imposed, nor cruel and unusual punishments inflicted.' Louisiana and many other states have adopted like constitutional provisions." Justice Burton's dissent further editorialized, "The capital case before us presents an instance of the violation of constitutional due process that is more clear than would be presented by many lesser punishments prohibited by the Eighth Amendment or its state counterparts."[50]

A civil rights leader, Justice Frankfurter personally opposed capital punishment,[51] but his concurring opinion in *Resweber*—couched in abstract terms about the role of judges "as the organs of the Law" in constitutional interpretation[52]—provided the pivotal fifth vote to let the execution of Willie Francis go forward. "The notion that the Privileges or Immunities Clause of the Fourteenth Amendment absorbed, as it is called, the provisions of the Bill of Rights that limit the Federal Government has never been given countenance by this Court," Frankfurter wrote, citing Supreme Court precedents, including the *Slaughter-House Cases*. "[T]his Court," Frankfurter opined, deferring to the Supreme Court of Louisiana's decision, "must abstain from interference with State action no matter how strong one's personal feeling of revulsion against a State's insistence on its pound of flesh." As Justice Frankfurter articulated his version of judicial restraint, "One must be on guard against finding in personal disapproval a reflection of more or less prevailing condemnation. Strongly drawn as I am to some of the sentiments expressed by my brother Burton, I cannot rid myself of the conviction that were I to hold that Louisiana would transgress the Due Process Clause if the State were allowed, in the precise circumstances before us, to carry out the death sentence, I would be enforcing my private view rather than that consensus of society's opinion which, for purposes of due process, is the standard enjoined by the Constitution."[53] Yet, so troubled was Justice Frankfurter by the consequences of his vote that he appealed directly to Louisiana's governor, Jimmie Davis, in an unsuccessful effort to seek a commutation of Francis's death sentence. "I have little doubt that if Louisiana allows Francis to go to his death," Frankfurter wrote, "it will needlessly cast a cloud upon Louisiana for many years to come, and, what is more important, probably leave many of its citizens with disquietude."[54] In 1950, Justice Frankfurter also took the extraordinary step of testifying before the British Royal Commission on Capital Punishment.[55] When asked, "Would you be in favour of reducing the scope of capital punishment?" Frankfurter bluntly replied, "I myself would abolish it."[56] Frankfurter recognized the horror of state-sanctioned executions, but voted against his own conscience in *Resweber* because of his judicial philosophy.[57]

Conflicting Judicial Philosophies and Evolving Standards: Debating Capital Punishment

The concept of the "evolving standards of decency," the test created to interpret the Constitution's Eighth Amendment, first debuted in the Supreme Court's jurisprudence in 1958. In its decision that year in *Trop v. Dulles*,[58] the Supreme Court observed that "[t]he exact scope of the constitutional phrase 'cruel and unusual' has not been detailed by this Court," but that "the basic policy reflected in these words is firmly established in the Anglo-American tradition of criminal justice."[59] After observing that the Constitution's Cruel and Unusual Punishments Clause was derived from the English Declaration of Rights of 1688, the Supreme Court declared, "The basic concept underlying the Eighth Amendment is nothing less than the dignity of man. While the State has the power to punish, the Amendment stands to assure that this power be exercised within the limits of civilized standards."[60] "Fines, imprisonment and even execution may be imposed depending upon the enormity of the crime," the Court ruled in *Trop*, "but any technique outside the bounds of these traditional penalties is constitutionally suspect."[61]

In another case, *Rhodes v. Chapman*,[62] the Court had this to say: "The Eighth Amendment, in only three words, imposes the constitutional limitation upon punishments: they cannot be 'cruel and unusual.' The Court has interpreted these words 'in a flexible and dynamic manner,' and has extended the Amendment's reach beyond the barbarous physical punishments at issue in the Court's earliest cases."[63] After citing *Weems v. United States*,[64] in which "a punishment of 12 years in irons at hard and painful labor for the crime of falsifying public records" was declared in 1910 to be "cruel in its excessiveness and unusual in its character," a plurality of the Court in *Trop* held in 1958 that the Eighth Amendment prohibits stripping a deserter of his U.S. citizenship. The Court further declared that *Weems* recognized that the words of the Eighth Amendment "are not precise, and that their scope is not static." "The Amendment," the Court in *Trop* announced in its landmark judgment, "must draw its meaning from the evolving standards of decency that mark the progress of a maturing society."[65]

Calling it the "total destruction of the individual's status in organized society," the Court in *Trop* underscored that "denationalization . . . is a form of punishment more primitive than torture, for it destroys for the individual the political existence that was centuries in the development. The punishment strips the citizen of his status in the national and international political community."[66] "In short," the *Trop* plurality opinion stated, "the expatriate has lost the right to have rights."[67]

In dicta, the Court in *Trop* also took a swipe at capital punishment, even though its intent at that time was not to strike down as unconstitutional the punishment of death. As the Court wrote, "At the outset, let us put to one side the death penalty as an index of the constitutional limit on punishment. Whatever the arguments may be against capital punishment, both on moral grounds and in terms of accomplishing the purposes of punishment—and they are forceful—the death penalty has been employed throughout our history, and, in a day when it is still widely accepted, it cannot be said to violate the constitutional concept of cruelty." "But it is equally plain," the Court stressed, "that the existence of the death penalty is not a license to the Government to devise any punishment short of death within the limit of its imagination."[68]

After 1958, the Supreme Court utilized the evolving standards of decency test in a number of capital cases.[69] "Evolving standards of societal decency," the Supreme Court observed in one case decided thirty years after *Trop*, "have imposed a correspondingly high requirement of reliability on the determination that death is the appropriate penalty in a particular case."[70] In that appeal, *Mills v. Maryland* (1988), the Supreme Court—in an opinion written by Justice Harry Blackmun—vacated a death sentence and made this observation: "The decision to exercise the power of the State to execute a defendant is unlike any other decision citizens and public officials are called upon to make." Expressing its concerns about "arbitrariness" in the death penalty's infliction, the Court in *Mills*—citing prior decisions, including *Lockett v. Ohio*[71]—observed, "It is beyond dispute that, in a capital case 'the sentencer [may] not be precluded from considering, *as a mitigating factor*, any aspect of a defendant's character or record and any of the circumstances of the offense that the defendant proffers as a basis for a sentence less than death.'"[72] "To enforce the Constitution's protection of human dignity," Justice Kennedy pointed out in *Hall v. Florida* (2014), "this Court looks to the 'evolving standards of decency that mark the progress of a maturing society.'"[73] "The Eighth Amendment's protection of dignity," he stressed in a ruling protecting the intellectually disabled from execution, "reflects the Nation we have been, the Nation we are, and the Nation we aspire to be."[74]

An Historical Analysis of U.S. Jurisprudence: The Supreme Court's Approach Changes over Time

It actually took considerable time before the Supreme Court, aside from reviewing the propriety of individual death sentences, meaningfully involved itself in the capital punishment debate.[75] A few U.S. state legislatures—Michigan (1846), Rhode Island (1852), and Wisconsin (1853)—abolished the death penalty for homicide before the Civil War.[76] However, the Supreme Court—which rejected legal challenges to the firing squad[77] and electrocution[78] in the late nineteenth century—did not engage in a full-throated debate about the death penalty's constitutionality until the 1960s. Most notably, in 1963, Justice Arthur Goldberg penned an internal memorandum to his colleagues about six pending capital cases, with Goldberg raising this legal issue: "Whether, and under what circumstances, the imposition of the death penalty is proscribed by the Eighth and Fourteenth Amendments to the United States Constitution."[79] That same year, he wrote a dissent—one joined by Justices Brennan and Douglas—from the Court's denial of certiorari in *Rudolph v. Alabama*.[80] In that dissent, Justice Goldberg wrote that he would have granted certiorari to consider whether the Eighth and Fourteenth Amendments "permit the imposition of the death penalty on a convicted rapist who has neither taken nor endangered human life."[81]

In the 1960s and 1970s, the Supreme Court justices were divided in their views, just as they are today. Among other things, Justice Goldberg's dissent in *Rudolph* cited a United Nations report finding that many countries and U.S. states no longer permitted the death penalty's imposition for rape and—in light of that reality—urged the Supreme Court to consider this question: "In light of the trend both in this country and throughout the world against punishing rape by death, does the imposition of the death penalty by those States which retain it for rape violate 'evolving standards of decency that mark the progress of [our] maturing society' or 'standards of decency more or less universally accepted?'"[82] Justice Goldberg's dissent from the denial of certiorari laid the intellectual foundation for the Supreme Court's subsequent 7–2 decision in *Coker v. Georgia*,[83] in which the Court ruled in 1977 that "a sentence of death is grossly disproportionate and excessive punishment for the crime of rape, and is therefore forbidden by the Eighth Amendment as cruel and unusual punishment."[84] "The murderer kills; the rapist, if no more than that, does not," the Court in *Coker* held, adding, "We have the abiding conviction that the death penalty, which 'is unique in its severity and irrevocability,' is an excessive penalty for the rapist who, as such, does not take human life."[85]

It was during the early 1970s that the Supreme Court, for the first time, substantively addressed the constitutionality of capital punishment head-on through a number of high-profile rulings. The 1971 decision of the Court in *McGautha v. California*[86] rejected a due process challenge to the death penalty, but the Court's landmark 1972 ruling in *Furman v. Georgia*[87] held, in a short per curiam opinion, that "the imposition and carrying out of the death penalty" constitutes "cruel and unusual punishment in violation of the Eighth and Fourteenth Amendments."[88] The Court's 5–4 decision, with all nine justices writing separately in more than 230 pages of concurring or dissenting opinions to express their own views,[89] cleared U.S. death rows, resulted in scores of commutations to life sentences, and produced a de facto moratorium on executions.[90] *Furman*'s five concurring opinions focused on the death penalty's arbitrary and discriminatory application; the punishment's severity, inhumanity, and violation of human dignity; the discretion in capital sentencing; that innocent people had been executed; and the excessive, unnecessary, and morally unacceptable nature of executions.[91]

After a legislative backlash to the *Furman* decision, with thirty-five states reenacting death penalty laws,[92] the Supreme Court ultimately reversed course. In 1976, the year of the United States' bicentennial, the Court thus upheld the death penalty's constitutionality in *Gregg v. Georgia*[93] and in companion cases,[94] although it struck down statutes imposing mandatory death sentences following offenders' convictions.[95] Writing for the Court in *Gregg*, Justice Potter Stewart had this to say: "We now hold that the punishment of death does not invariably violate the Constitution."[96] The Eighth Amendment's requirements "must be applied with an awareness of the limited role to be played by the courts," the Court held, rejecting the idea that the death penalty violates the

Eighth and Fourteenth Amendments. "[I]t is now evident," Stewart concluded of that punishment, "that a large proportion of American society
continues to regard it as an appropriate and necessary criminal sanction."[97] Only Justices Brennan and Marshall were willing to declare—as
they did so consistently thereafter—that the death penalty constitutes a
per se violation of the Eighth and Fourteenth Amendments.[98]

Justice Blackmun's intense and personal struggle with capital cases
illustrates the human toll that capital cases and state-sanctioned executions have taken on jurists and many others through the years. In his
dissent in *Furman*, Justice Blackmun freely admitted that he had "first
struggled silently with the issue of capital punishment" as an Eighth Circuit judge, describing how, in deciding death penalty cases, he had laid
bare his "distress and concern."[99] In addition, he wrote in *Furman* of
the capital cases under review before the nation's highest court in 1972,
"Cases such as these provide for me an excruciating agony of the spirit.
I yield to no one in the depth of my distaste, antipathy, and, indeed,
abhorrence, for the death penalty, with all its aspects of physical distress
and fear and of moral judgment exercised by finite minds." "That distaste," Blackmun emphasized, "is buttressed by a belief that capital punishment serves no useful purpose that can be demonstrated. For me, it
violates childhood's training and life's experiences, and is not compatible
with the philosophical convictions I have been able to develop." "Were I
a legislator," Blackmun observed, "I would vote against the death penalty
for the policy reasons argued by counsel for the respective petitioners
and expressed and adopted in the several opinions filed by the Justices
who vote to reverse these judgments."[100]

Shortly before retiring, Justice Blackmun reevaluated his judicial role
and, despite his earlier dissent in *Furman*, concluded in *Callins v. Collins*
(1994) that the death penalty should be struck down as unconstitutional.
"[D]espite the effort of the States and courts to devise legal formulas and
procedural rules" to ensure that death sentences were imposed fairly
and with reasonable consistency, Blackmun dissented from the denial
of certiorari in that case, specifically finding "the death penalty remains fraught with arbitrariness, discrimination, caprice, and mistake."
"From this day forward, I no longer shall tinker with the machinery of
death," Blackmun concluded, adding this coda: "For more than 20 years
I have endeavored—indeed, I have struggled—along with a majority

of this Court, to develop procedural and substantive rules that would lend more than the mere appearance of fairness to the death penalty endeavor. Rather than continue to coddle the Court's delusion that the desired level of fairness has been achieved and the need for regulation eviscerated, I feel morally and intellectually obligated simply to concede that the death penalty experiment has failed." For Blackmun, there were no rules that the Court could fashion that would "save the death penalty from its inherent constitutional deficiencies."[101] "The problem," Blackmun wrote, "is that the inevitability of factual, legal, and moral error gives us a system that we know must wrongly kill some defendants, a system that fails to deliver the fair, consistent, and reliable sentences of death required by the Constitution."[102]

A Grave Injustice and the Justices: Capital Punishment before the Nation's Highest Court

The fierce debate over the death penalty's constitutionality continues to the present day, with originalists—following the lead of the late Justice Antonin Scalia—taking a much different view of the punishment than living constitutionalists. In fact, the justices have been sharply divided in many death penalty cases, including in challenges to lethal injection protocols, to the death penalty's propriety for particular categories of offenders, and to the use of victim impact statements.[103] For example, in *Glossip v. Gross* (2015), a 5–4 decision upholding the constitutionality of Oklahoma's three-drug lethal injection protocol, Justice Samuel Alito—writing for the Court—found that the petitioning death row inmates had "failed to identity a known and available alternative method of execution that entails a lesser risk of pain." "[T]he prisoners failed to establish that Oklahoma's use of a massive dose of midazolam in its execution protocol entails a substantial risk of severe pain," he wrote. In effect, the Court's *Glossip* decision—turning the adversarial system upside-down—now requires that a *death row inmate* making an Eighth Amendment method-of-execution claim actually propose a different method of execution by which the execution can be carried out.[104] Referring to the prospect of physical pain at the moment of a death row inmate's death, Justice Alito's opinion asserted that "some risk of pain is inherent in any method of execution" and that the Constitution "does not require the avoidance of all risk of pain." "Holding that the Eighth Amendment demands the elimination of essentially all risk of pain," he wrote, "would effectively outlaw the death penalty altogether."[105]

By contrast, Justice Sonia Sotomayor's dissent in *Glossip*—joined by Justices Breyer, Ginsburg, and Kagan—worried that the lethal injection protocol's maladministration "leaves petitioners exposed to what may well be the chemical equivalent to being burned at the stake." In a separate dissent joined by Justice Ruth Bader Ginsburg, Justice Stephen Breyer concluded that it is "highly likely that the death penalty violates the Eighth Amendment." Their rationale: "Today's administration of the death penalty involves three fundamental constitutional defects: (1) serious unreliability, (2) arbitrariness in application, and (3) unconscionably long delays that undermine the death penalty's penological purposes. Perhaps as a result, (4) most places within the United States have abandoned its use."[106] The dissent laid out the death penalty's many defects, including the pervasiveness of wrongful convictions, the punishment's arbitrary and discriminatory application, the cruelty of death row inmates languishing on death row in solitary confinement for years or decades, and the infrequency with which executions are carried out, thus demonstrating their unusualness.[107] In prior dissents, Justice Breyer—now retired and replaced by Justice Ketanji Brown Jackson—had repeatedly called on the Court to review whether prolonged stays on death row, part of the so-called death row phenomenon, make the carrying out of executions unconstitutional.[108] In one case, Justice Breyer pointed out that the death row inmate was first sentenced to death more than forty-four years earlier—and had thus long endured a threat of execution.[109]

The Supreme Court's handling of a spate of federal executions from mid-2020 to early 2021 during the Trump administration highlights the sharp divide over capital punishment that persists to the present day. For example, in *Barr v. Purkey*, decided a few months before Justice Ginsburg's death, Justices Breyer, Ginsburg, Sotomayor, and Kagan all dissented. They objected to the federal government's plans "to put to death Wesley Purkey, a 68-year-old federal inmate who has Alzheimer's disease and, according to a recent in-person evaluation by a forensic psychiatrist, 'lack[s] a rational understanding of the basis for his execution.'"[110]

In a separate dissent, Justices Breyer and Ginsburg also lamented the "serious legal defects" they'd observed that "have long plagued the administration of the death penalty in the United States"; emphasized that Purkey "has undergone many years of what this Court has called the 'immense mental anxiety' of confinement on death row awaiting an uncertain date of execution"; and stressed that they remained "convinced of the importance of reconsidering the constitutionality of the death penalty itself."[111] In comparison, a majority of the Court, including Justice Amy Coney Barrett (who now occupies Justice Ginsburg's seat and, in 1998, called capital punishment "evil"),[112] has voted to allow executions to go forward on multiple occasions.[113]

The Supreme Court's unwillingness to declare capital punishment unconstitutional—something that the Constitutional Court of Hungary, the Constitutional Court of South Africa, and other national courts did years ago[114]—has meant that U.S. death sentences and executions continue to be imposed and carried out. While the continent of Europe has barred the death penalty's use[115] in both wartime and peacetime,[116] some U.S. jurisdictions still allow death sentences and executions even though many retentionist states have not executed anyone in decades or years.[117] Meanwhile, the Supreme Court has engaged in denialism about all the human rights abuses associated with capital punishment.[118] Indeed, scores of innocent people have been convicted and horrifyingly condemned to die, only to be later exonerated;[119] pervasive arbitrariness and racial and geographic discrimination in the death penalty's administration has stubbornly persisted;[120] and death row inmates—often subjected to multiple execution warrants and, in the case of Curtis Flowers, six separate murder trials[121]—have been continuously subjected to credible death threats while awaiting decisions as to their fate.

In 2021, Oklahoma governor Kevin Stitt commuted Julius Jones's death sentence just *hours* before Jones was scheduled to be executed—and after Jones received his "last meal"—for a 1999 murder he says he didn't commit. "The racism that tainted Mr. Jones' case is a shameful and intractable feature of the death penalty's administration in the United States," Cassandra Stubbs, the director of the ACLU Capital Punishment Project said of the case, with another civil rights organization—the National Association for the Advancement of Colored People (NAACP)—also calling for a new trial.[122] The Rev. Cece Jones-Davis, a lead organizer of the Justice for Julius Campaign, specifically emphasized the torment experienced by Julius Jones and his friends and family members. "We should not have received this news four hours before an execution," she said, adding, "This was torture for Julius and for his family and for the people who love him."[123]

A Failing (or, at Best, an "Incomplete") Grade: Assessing the Supreme Court's Eighth and Fourteenth Amendment Jurisprudence

The Supreme Court's Eighth and Fourteenth Amendment jurisprudence is unprincipled, and it has a Dr. Jekyll and Mr. Hyde quality to it.[124] On one hand, the Eighth and Fourteenth Amendments are regularly used to *safeguard* the rights of prisoners. For example, those two constitutional amendments have been used to *protect* inmates from gratuitous assaults by guards or other inmates,[125] credible threats of death,[126] prison over-crowding,[127] the failure to provide necessary medical care,[128] and exposure to secondhand smoke.[129] In 1968, in an opinion written by then circuit judge Harry Blackmun, the Eighth Circuit explicitly held that the Cruel and Unusual Punishments Clause barred the lashing of Arkansas prisoners.[130] After writing that the Eighth Amendment's guarantee against the infliction of cruel and unusual punishments had "come to be regarded as directly applicable to the states" through the Fourteenth Amendment's Due Process Clause,[131] the Eighth Circuit in *Jackson v. Bishop* concluded, "[W]e have no difficulty in reaching the conclusion that the use of the strap in the penitentiaries of Arkansas is punishment which, in this last third of the 20th century, runs afoul of the Eighth Amendment; that the strap's use, irrespective of any precautionary conditions which may be imposed, offends contemporary concepts of decency and human dignity and precepts of civilization which we profess to possess. . . ."[132]

In *Hope v. Pelzer*,[133] the Supreme Court itself described allegations that an Alabama inmate was subjected to cruel and unusual disciplinary punishment as an "obvious" Eighth Amendment violation. In that case, prison guards handcuffed the inmate to a hitching post and left him out in the hot sun, shirtless for seven hours, and in that seven-hour period, he was given water only once or twice and had no bathroom breaks. As the Court observed of the "obvious cruelty" and "punitive treatment" associated with those specific allegations, the inmate was "knowingly subjected" to "a substantial risk of physical harm, to unnecessary pain caused by the handcuffs and the restricted position of confinement for a 7-hour period, to unnecessary exposure to the heat of the sun, to prolonged thirst and taunting, and to a deprivation of bathroom breaks that created a risk of particular discomfort and humiliation."[134] Existing case law is clear that prison officials may be held liable for "deliberate indifference" to a prisoner's Eighth Amendment right to protection against violence while in custody if such officials know that the inmate faces a substantial risk of serious harm and disregards that risk by failing to abate it.[135]

On the other hand, while the Constitution generally protects prisoners from harm, and while corporal punishments once put to use (e.g., branding, ear cropping, the pillory, and the whipping post) have been abolished or abandoned in the United States' penal system,[136] the Eighth and Fourteenth Amendments have not stopped the carrying out of state-sanctioned executions—which, by their very nature, involve torturous threats of death associated with the bringing of capital charges, the imposition of death sentences, and the setting of specific execution dates.[137] No longer are American offenders branded on the forehead or burned in the palm of a hand, as they once were, with the Supreme Court of North Carolina ruling in 1837 that someone convicted of manslaughter "may be sentenced to be burned in the hand."[138] "A common form of mutilation or maiming was the detachment of an ear," a Third Circuit judge once explained, noting that "[t]he effect of branding, mutilation, or maiming was often to cast the offender out of society once and for all."[139] The retention of executions is thus an enigmatic anomaly in U.S. constitutional law[140] because the Cruel and Unusual Punishments Clause is now effectively understood to bar *nonlethal* punishments while still tolerating *lethal* ones.[141]

In the past few decades, the Supreme Court has barred the use of the death penalty for some offenders while permitting executions for others. In a series of cases utilizing the dynamic duo of the Eighth and Fourteenth Amendments and the "evolving standards of decency" test, the Supreme Court has declared unconstitutional imposing the death penalty on the insane,[142] those under the age of eighteen,[143] the intellectually disabled,[144] those without a rational understanding of the reasons for a death sentence,[145] nonhomicidal kidnappers and rapists,[146] and other offenders who did not take a life, attempt to take a life, or intend to take a life.[147] But the execution of other offenders (e.g., those convicted of first-degree murder, even those suffering from dementia or severe mental illnesses) continues.[148] Consequently, while the Eighth and Fourteenth Amendments are already interpreted to bar nonlethal corporal punishments and the execution of certain classes of offenders, state-sanctioned executions are still occurring for some offenders and offenses, albeit in a smaller number of locales and with less frequency, under the auspices of U.S. law and the Supreme Court's judicial power.[149]

To make matters worse, the Supreme Court's Eighth and Fourteenth Amendment jurisprudence has utterly failed to eliminate racial discrimination in the death penalty's administration. Most notably, in *McCleskey v. Kemp*,[150] the Supreme Court considered the implications of a statistical study known as the Baldus study that showed the presence of substantial racial prejudice in the death penalty's administration in Georgia.[151] That study—as the Court acknowledged—showed that "defendants charged with killing white victims were 4.3 times as likely to receive a death sentence as defendants charged with killing blacks."[152] In *McCleskey*, an African American man, Warren McCleskey, was convicted of armed robbery and murder and sentenced to death, but he asserted that Georgia's capital punishment regime violated the Eighth Amendment and the Fourteenth Amendment's Equal Protection Clause.[153] The Supreme Court notoriously rejected his legal challenge, finding that McCleskey "must prove that the decisionmakers in *his* case acted with discriminatory purpose" and had failed to do so.[154] "[T]he Baldus study," the Court determined, "is clearly insufficient to support an inference that any of the decisionmakers in McCleskey's case acted with discriminatory purpose."[155] "McCleskey's claim, taken to its logical conclusion," the Court stated, "throws into serious question the principles that underlie our entire criminal justice system," with Justice Lewis Powell writing, "[I]f we accepted McCleskey's claim that racial bias has impermissibly tainted the capital sentencing decision, we could soon be faced with similar claims as to other types of penalty."[156]

In response to McCleskey's legal challenge to Georgia's capital sentencing system, the Supreme Court—in its 5–4 decision written by Justice Powell—decided that "[s]tatistics, at most, may show only a likelihood that a particular factor entered into some decisions."[157] The majority opinion in *McCleskey*, essentially resigning itself to blatant and ongoing discrimination in the death penalty's administration, emphasized, "At most, the Baldus study indicates a discrepancy that appears to correlate with race. Apparent disparities in sentencing are an inevitable part of our criminal justice system."[158] After observing that Georgia's statute "generally follows the standards" of the American Law Institute's Model Penal Code, the Court in *McCleskey* affirmed Warren McCleskey's death sentence[159] and he was later executed.[160]

Not only have the Model Penal Code's death penalty provisions since been deleted,[161] but Justice Powell—having written the case's majority opinion—told his biographer after he retired from the Court that he regretted his votes in death penalty cases, including his decision in *McCleskey*.[162] Fast-forward to the twenty-first century, and the racial discrimination identified in the Baldus study clearly continues. In 2020, California governor Gavin Newsom and six district attorneys—in a damning condemnation—signed onto a friend-of-the-court brief describing how capital punishment is plagued by racial prejudice and disparities. "Since its inception, the American death penalty has been disproportionately applied, first, to enslaved Africans and African Americans, and, later to free Black people," Governor Newsom said.[163]

In recent years, Supreme Court justices have continued to spar over the death penalty's constitutionality, with Justice Breyer, in *Barr v. Purkey*, highlighting "the inherent arbitrariness of the death penalty." As Justice Breyer wrote in that dissent, "A modern system of criminal justice must be reasonably accurate, fair, humane, and timely. Our recent experience with the Federal Government's resumption of executions adds to the mounting body of evidence that the death penalty cannot be reconciled with those values."[164] Justice Breyer's successor, Justice Jackson, never wrote a decision in a capital case before her Senate confirmation, but the NAACP's preconfirmation report on her record concluded that "her tenure as an appellate defender and her public remarks . . . inspire confidence that she would recognize that 'death is different,' and carefully assess whether the adjudicatory process was fair, rational, and reliable."[165]

As a factual matter, while Justice Jackson, since joining the Supreme Court, has frequently dissented in capital cases, a majority of the justices continue to affirm death sentences. For example, in *Bucklew v.*

Precythe,[166] Justice Neil Gorsuch—in delivering the Court's opinion—held that "[t]he Constitution allows capital punishment."[167] As Justice Gorsuch, the self-avowed "originalist," wrote in that 2019 decision, "[D]eath was 'the standard penalty for all serious crimes' at the time of the founding. Nor did the later addition of the Eighth Amendment outlaw the practice. On the contrary—the Fifth Amendment, added to the Constitution at the same time as the Eighth, expressly contemplates that a defendant may be tried for a 'capital' crime and 'deprived of life' as a penalty, so long as proper procedures are followed." "[T]he first Congress, which proposed both Amendments," Gorsuch added, alluding to the Crimes Act of 1790,[168] "made a number of crimes punishable by death." "The same Constitution that permits States to authorize capital punishment also allows them to outlaw it," Gorsuch asserted, his opinion in *Bucklew* notably conducting no legal evaluation of the torturous nature of state-sponsored death threats and, oddly, making no reference to the Court's long-standing "evolving standards of decency" test.[169]

Eighteenth-century practices should not dictate the outcome of twenty-first-century court rulings—a principle in line with the Eighth Amendment's long-standing "evolving standards of decency" jurisprudence.[170] It should be recalled that the United States' founders made use of slavery, mandatory death sentences,[171] and grotesque corporal punishments, with executions then carried out in a matter of days or months following convictions.[172] With Justice Gorsuch focusing on how *eighteenth-century lawmakers* had authorized capital punishment, he conducted no analysis whatsoever of the contemporary definition of torture and, unfortunately, saw no place for judicial intervention to stop a clearly torturous practice *in the twenty-first century*. "[T]he judiciary," Justice Gorsuch wrote, ignoring the modern reality of the death penalty's highly arbitrary, discretionary, discriminatory, and torturous administration, "bears no license to end a debate reserved for the people and their representatives."[173] But it is the objective *characteristics* of a practice, not how it is *characterized* by judges or lawmakers, that must determine whether a practice is torturous or cruel. Needless to say, burying one's head in the sand, deferring to long-dead founders, or turning a blind eye to injustice does nothing to stop injustice; it only multiplies it, "adding deeper darkness to a night already devoid of stars," as the Rev. Dr. Martin Luther King Jr. once said of returning hate for hate.[174]

In assessing the Supreme Court's existing Eighth and Fourteenth Amendment jurisprudence, it should get a failing (or, at best, an "incomplete") grade—especially in this, the twenty-first century. The Supreme Court's Eighth and Fourteenth Amendment jurisprudence has protected the individual rights of some offenders,[175] but criminal defendants continue to be wrongfully convicted and sentenced to death.[176] Indeed, a recent report by the Death Penalty Information Center (DPIC) found that, in 2019 alone, "[t]he use or threat of the death penalty was a factor in more than 13% of exonerations across the United States."[177] The report's analysis of data from the National Registry of Exonerations indicate that a number of false confessions resulted from law enforcement threats to seek the death penalty. "The numbers show that the death penalty has dangerous effects on the criminal justice system that go far beyond the already significant risk of executing innocent people," observed then DPIC executive director Robert Dunham, who stressed, "Innocent people confess to crimes they didn't commit to avoid the possibility of being executed. Suspects, both innocent and guilty, who are threatened with the death penalty if they do not cooperate with law enforcement provide false testimony that sends innocent people to jail, often for decades. The data suggest that the misuse of the death penalty as a coercive interrogation and plea bargaining tool poses a far greater threat to the fair administration of the criminal laws than we had previously imagined."[178]

A September 1, 2020, report of the National Registry of Exonerations clearly documents "the role of official misconduct in the conviction of innocent people." That report focused on misconduct contributing to wrongful convictions of later exonerated defendants—"misconduct that distorts the evidence used to determine guilt or innocence." The report pointed out that "misconduct in interrogation and fabrication are two parts of a single course of action," citing specific cases in which threats of the death penalty led to false confessions. Regarding Charles Johnson—a man wrongfully convicted of murder—the report noted of his twelve-hour interrogation that "Chicago detectives told him that if he did not 'tell the truth' he would 'never see his family again,' would get the death penalty, and would be raped in prison. At the end of that ordeal, he signed—without reading—a few documents that were said to be 'release papers.' One was a confession written by the police." In 2022, the city of

Idaho Falls, Idaho, paid out a $11.7 million settlement to Christopher Tapp, an exoneree cleared by DNA evidence who spent twenty years in prison for a murder and rape he didn't commit after police coerced a false confession from him by threatening him with the death penalty.[179]

In truth, the death penalty is a clear affront to human dignity, the rule of law, and the notion of universal human rights, including the right to be free from cruelty and torturous punishments and threats of violence.[180] The right to be free from torture—as reflected in the Universal Declaration of Human Rights[181] and the International Covenant on Civil and Political Rights[182]—is a universal, nonderogable right,[183] and the law is clear that prisoners are entitled to be protected against cruelty and torture. As the Supreme Court observed in *Roper v. Simmons*, "By protecting even those convicted of heinous crimes, the Eighth Amendment reaffirms the duty of the government to respect the dignity of all persons."[184] There continues to be rampant arbitrariness and racial discrimination in the death penalty's administration,[185] and death sentences have become rare as juries—conviction-prone "death-qualified" juries, no less—have in recent years frequently rejected death sentences in preference to sentences that do not involve putting offenders to death.[186] Of the diminishing number of inmates put to death at the hands of the state, they now spend—on average—more than twenty years on death row before their executions, often facing serial death warrants and execution dates before their lives are extinguished in execution chambers.[187] Because of the prolonged periods of time inmates typically spend on death row, they actually often die of natural causes before their cases can be resolved by appellate judges.

In reality, an inherent and immutable characteristic of any death penalty regime is that it involves the regular use of credible threats of death.[188] *Torture*, as the United Nations Convention against Torture and Other Cruel, Inhuman or Degrading Treatment or Punishment and other modern definitions make clear, can be either physical or psychological in nature, with credible death threats and mock (or simulated) executions already classified as mental torture.[189] Case law interpreting the Constitution has already held that the Eighth Amendment forbids not only physically torturous punishments,[190] but also non–physically barbarous punishments,[191] including psychological torture.[192] To date, the Supreme Court—in affirming the death penalty's constitutionality—has not yet categorized the death penalty as a torturous act, in spite of its inherent characteristics. But back in 1972—in *People v. Anderson*—the California Supreme Court offered this candid assessment: "The cruelty of capital punishment lies not only in the execution itself and the pain incident thereto, but also in the dehumanizing effects of the lengthy imprisonment prior to execution during which the judicial and administrative procedures essential to due process of law are carried out." "Penologists and medical experts agree," the California Supreme Court wrote, "that the process of carrying out a verdict of death is often so degrading and brutalizing to the human spirit as to constitute psychological torture."[193]

Executions irretrievably end lives, thus depriving individuals of what political theorist Hannah Arendt, in another context, spoke of as "the right to have rights."[194] But while the Supreme Court in recent decades has repeatedly declined to declare the death penalty unconstitutional, state court decisions in criminal cases reveal how torture is commonly understood in the twenty-first century. In those cases decided under state law, *psychological torture* has been clearly defined in aggravated or torture-murder prosecutions as an awareness of, but a helplessness to prevent, one's impending death.[195] "Psychological torture," the Court of Criminal Appeals of Alabama has held, "can be inflicted where the victim *is in intense fear and is aware of, but helpless to prevent, impending death.*"[196] As their execution dates approach and become imminent, of course, death row inmates are put in extreme and intense fear yet are utterly helpless to prevent their own deaths as they are moved to prison death houses and strapped down on lethal injection gurneys.[197] In short, applying a standard definition of psychological torture, the death penalty subjects offenders to torturous treatment and punishment.

Conclusion

The United States Supreme Court's death penalty jurisprudence is highly disturbing, depriving Eighth and Fourteenth Amendment case law of its humanity—and thus, of our collective humanity. For decades, the Supreme Court explicitly held that the Eighth Amendment's Cruel and Unusual Punishments Clause must take into consideration modern standards of decency, laudably allowing American jurists to strike down dehumanizing punishments such as the lashing of prisoners and other practices violative of human dignity. In *Ford v. Wainwright*,[198] the Supreme Court specifically observed, "[T]he Eighth Amendment's proscriptions are not limited to those practices condemned by the common law in 1789. Not bound by the sparing humanitarian concessions of our forebears, the Amendment also recognizes the 'evolving standards of decency that mark the progress of a maturing society.' In addition to considering the barbarous methods generally outlawed in the 18th century, therefore, this Court takes into account objective evidence of contemporary values before determining whether a particular punishment comports with the fundamental human dignity that the Amendment protects."[199] Yet, the present-day Supreme Court perversely continues to allow state-sanctioned executions simply because the United States' founders permitted capital punishment.[200] With the majority of current Supreme Court justices upholding the death penalty's constitutionality, the Court's own actions and indifference to human suffering must not escape scrutiny. For starters, the "originalist," eighteenth century–centric bent of today's justices who permit executions utterly ignores the overt racism and brutality of the United States' founding era. The judicial philosophy of originalism also fails to take into account the importance of the Fourteenth Amendment's guarantee of "equal protection of the laws."[201]

It is impossible to predict how the Court will rule in future cases, but it's fair to say that history will not be kind to the authors of the Court's current approach to the law. By embracing an increasingly rigid and originalist approach to the Constitution and the Cruel and Unusual Punishments Clause, the Court—as now composed—has hollowed out constitutional guarantees. Instead of recognizing the modern-day understanding of torture, the inherently torturous nature of credible death threats in the capital punishment context, and the arbitrary and discriminatory nature of death sentences, the Supreme Court has neglected its duty to safeguard individual rights and to ensure "EQUAL JUSTICE UNDER LAW." Indeed, so long as U.S. law allows death sentences and executions, the Court's Eighth and Fourteenth Amendment jurisprudence will be unprincipled, totally incoherent, and deserving of a failing grade.

When future historians write their histories of capital punishment's ultimate demise, they will—in their own postmortems—no doubt describe the punishment's long, sordid pattern of discrimination and arbitrariness. But they will also write of the death penalty's incompatibility with *universal* human rights, including the right to be free from torture. Since 1878, the Supreme Court has read the Constitution's Cruel and Unusual Punishments Clause to prohibit "punishments of torture."[202] Yet, the Court has failed to keep up with the times by failing to fully recognize—and take seriously—universal human rights and the *modern conception* of torture.[203] International law prohibits all forms of torture,[204] with many countries now refusing to extradite anyone who might face a capital charge without assurances that the death penalty will not be sought.[205] *Mock executions* are already barred throughout the world—including in U.S. law—as impermissible acts of psychological torture.[206] If *simulated* executions are prohibited by law as torture (and they are), how can the Supreme Court possibly continue to allow *real* executions? If the concept of *universal* human rights is ever to be actualized, then *everyone*—even those who've committed heinous crimes in the past—must be protected from torture.[207]

Credible death threats backed by state power plainly inflict severe pain and suffering amounting to mental torture (not only on those accused and condemned to die, but also on their family members).[208] Until the Supreme Court recognizes that—and outlaws executions—it will be functioning as a modern-day equivalent of the Star Chamber.[209] In 2015, the Connecticut Supreme Court in *State v. Santiago* acted decisively, declaring capital punishment to be unconstitutional as a cruel and unusual punishment.[210] The United States Supreme Court's own failure to immediately stop *all* executions will forever mar its history, although the Court plainly has the power to make a similar ruling. An immutable characteristic of capital punishment is that it makes routine use of official death threats—threats that, in other contexts, are already treated by the law as acts of torture. The death penalty is, consequently, an inherently torturous punishment, and the Supreme Court needs to say so. Until it does, it will be complicit in the severe pain and suffering—the torture and inhuman barbarism—inflicted on offenders and their family members by capital punishment regimes.

Notes

Epigraph: *Kennedy v. Louisiana*, 554 U.S. 407, 420 (2008).
1   *Williams v. People of State of New York*, 337 U.S. 241 (1949).

2   *Id.* at 247–48.

3   *Id.* at 248.

4   *Id.* at 252.

5   *Id.* at 252–53 (Murphy, J., dissenting).

6   *Id.* at 253.

7   *Solesbee v. Balkcom*, 339 U.S. 9, 10 (1950).

8   *Id.* at 13.

9   *Id.* at 14 (Frankfurter, J., dissenting).

10 *Id.* at 16–17.

11 *Rosenberg v. United States*, 346 U.S. 273, 292–93 (1953).

12 *Id.* at 296.

13 *Id.* at 299 (Black, J., dissenting).

14 *Id.* at 312 (Douglas, J., dissenting).

15 *Id.* at 310 (Frankfurter, J., dissenting).

16 *Furman v. Georgia*, 408 U.S. 238 (1972).

17 428 U.S. 153 (1976).

18 428 U.S. 242 (1976).

19 428 U.S. 262 (1976).

20 *Gregg v. Georgia*, 428 U.S. 153, 227 (1976) (Brennan, J., dissenting); *id.* at 231
    (Marshall, J., dissenting).

21 Kevin M. Barry, "The Law of Abolition," *Journal of Criminal Law and Criminology*
    107 (2017): 521, 523.

22 *Id.*

23 *Glossip v. Gross*, 576 U.S. 863, 908, 946 (2015) (Breyer, J., dissenting).

24 *E.g.*, John D. Bessler, "Foreword: The Death Penalty in Decline: From Colonial
    America to the Present," *Criminal Law Bulletin* 50 (2014): 245.

25 *See generally* John D. Bessler, *Cruel and Unusual: The American Death Penalty and
    the Founders' Eighth Amendment* (Boston: Northeastern University Press, 2012);
    John D. Bessler, *The Death Penalty's Denial of Fundamental Human Rights: Inter-
    national Law, State Practice, and the Emerging Abolitionist Norm* (New York: Cam-
    bridge University Press, 2022); John D. Bessler, "The Inequality of America's Death
    Penalty: A Crossroads for Capital Punishment at the Intersection of the Eighth and
    Fourteenth Amendments," *Washington and Lee Law Review Online* 73 (2016): 487.

26 Felix Frankfurter, "The Case of Sacco and Vanzetti," *The Atlantic*, March 1927.

27 332 U.S. 596 (1948).

28 *Id.* at 602 (Frankfurter, J., concurring).

29 *Haley*, 332 U.S. at 602 (Frankfurter, J., concurring). Although some jurisdictions
    had abolished the death penalty by the 1950s, a number of countries and U.S.
    states did not abolish the death penalty until much later.

30 *Haley*, 332 U.S. at 598 (Douglas, J., announcing the Court's judgment); *id.* at 607
    (Burton, J., dissenting).

31 *Id.* at 597 (Douglas, J., announcing the Court's judgment); "Canton Boy Gets Life
    Sentence in Robbery-Murder," *Sandusky Register Star-News* (Sandusky, OH),

April 13, 1946; "Youth May Get Life," *Circleville Herald* (Circleville, OH), April 4, 1946; "New Trials Denied Two Life Termers," *Greenville Daily* (Greenville, OH), February 7, 1947.

32 "Boy, 15, Gets Life," *Kentucky Advocate* (Danville, KY), April 7, 1946.

33 *Chambers v. Florida*, 309 U.S. 227 (1940); *Ashcraft v. Tennessee*, 322 U.S. 143 (1944); *Malinski v. New York*, 324 U.S. 401 (1945).

34 Carol S. Steiker and Jordan M. Steiker, *Courting Death: The Supreme Court and Capital Punishment* (Cambridge, MA: Belknap Press, 2016), 26.

35 *Haley*, 332 U.S. at 597 (Douglas, J., announcing the Court's judgment).

36 *Id.* at 599.

37 *Id.* at 597.

38 *Id.* at 598.

39 *Id.* at 599.

40 *Id.*

41 *Id.* at 598, 600.

42 *Id.* at 598–99.

43 *Id.* at 600.

44 *Id.* at 597.

45 *Id.* at 601.

46 *Dickerson v. United States*, 530 U.S. 428, 433 (2000) (citations omitted).

47 Willie Francis (as told to Samuel Montgomery), "My Trip to the Chair," in *Demands of the Dead: Executions, Storytelling, and Activism in the United States*, ed. Katy Ryan (Iowa City: University of Iowa Press, 2012), 33; Gerald Caplan, review of *Death by Installments: The Ordeal of Willie Francis*, by Arthur S. Miller and Jeffrey H. Bowman, *George Washington Law Review* 57 (1989): 1643–44.

48 *State of Louisiana ex rel. Francis v. Resweber*, 329 U.S. 459, 461–66 (1947).

49 *Robinson v. California*, 370 U.S. 660 (1962).

50 *Resweber*, 329 U.S. at 472–74 (Burton, J., dissenting).

51 Helen Shirley Thomas, *Felix Frankfurter: Scholar on the Bench* (Baltimore: Johns Hopkins University Press, 2019), 158–160.

52 *Resweber*, 329 U.S. at 470 (Frankfurter, J., concurring)

53 *Id.* at 466–67, 471 (Frankfurter, J., concurring).

54 Gilbert King, "The Two Executions of Willie Francis," *Washington Post*, July 19, 2006.

55 Thomas, *Felix Frankfurter*, 158–160 (discussing *Louisiana ex rel. Francis v. Resweber*, 329 U.S. 459 (1947), which held that a second attempt at electrocution did not violate the Eighth Amendment, and observing, "During 1950 on a visit to Great Britain, he testified before the Royal Commission on Capital Punishment and made mention of the *Resweber* case as one that 'told on my conscience a good deal. . . . I was very bothered by the problem, it offended my personal sense of decency to do this. Something inside of me was very unhappy, but I did not see that it violated due process of law.' Frankfurter's vote in *Resweber* probably did cause him a good deal of personal anguish in view of his deep humanitarian instincts. . . .").

56 Melvin F. Wingersky, "Report of the Royal Commission on Capital Punishment (1949–1953): A Review," *Journal of Criminal Law, Criminology and Police Science* 44 (1954): 695, 701. "I am strongly against capital punishment for reasons that are not related to concern for the murderer or the risk of convicting the innocent," Justice Frankfurter told the Royal Commission. "When life is at hazard in a trial, it sensationalizes the whole thing almost unwittingly; the effect on juries, the Bar, the public, the judiciary, I regard as very bad." Justice Frankfurter's testimony continued: "I think scientifically the claim of deterrence is not worth much. Whatever proof there may be in my judgment does not outweigh the social loss due to the inherent sensationalism of a trial for life." Paul A. Freund, Mr. Justice Frankfurter, *University of Chicago Law Review* 26 (1959): 205, 211.

57 William Cohen, "Justice Douglas and the Rosenberg Case: Setting the Record Straight," *Cornell Law Review* 70 (1985): 215 n.22 ("Justice Frankfurter agonized over cases involving the death penalty, often torn between his opposition to capital punishment and his general theories of judicial restraint in constitutional adjudication.").

58 356 U.S. 86 (1958) (plurality opinion).

59 *Id.* at 99–100.

60 *Id.* at 100.

61 *Id.*

62 452 U.S. 337 (1981).

63 *Id.* at 345–46 (citations omitted); *id.* at 346 ("No static 'test' can exist by which courts determine whether conditions of confinement are cruel and unusual, for the Eighth Amendment 'must draw its meaning from the evolving standards of decency that mark the progress of a maturing society.'" (quoting *Trop*, 356 U.S. at 101)). "Today," the Court wrote in *Rhodes v. Chapman*, "the Eighth Amendment prohibits punishments which, although not physically barbarous, 'involve the unnecessary and wanton infliction of pain,' or are grossly disproportionate to the severity of the crime." *Id.* at 346.

64 217 U.S. 349 (1910).

65 *Trop*, 356 U.S. at 100–101.

66 *Id.* at 101.

67 *Id.* at 102.

68 *Id.* at 99.

69 William W. Berry III, "Individualized Sentencing," *Washington and Lee Law Review* 13 (2019): 59–60 (noting that in capital cases, the U.S. Supreme Court has "applied a much higher level of procedural scrutiny under the Eighth Amendment to assess the imposition of death sentences," and that "the Court applied its evolving standards of decency doctrine to make substantive determinations about the scope of the Eighth Amendment," including "relating to the imposition of the death penalty for certain crimes and certain types of offenders").

70 *Mills v. Maryland*, 486 U.S. 367, 383–84 (1988); *see also Gardner v. Florida*, 430 U.S. 349, 357 (1977) ("[T]his Court has acknowledged its obligation to re-examine

capital-sentencing procedures against evolving standards of procedural fairness in a civilized society.").

71 438 U.S. 586, 604 (1978) (plurality opinion).

72 *Mills*, 486 U.S. at 369, 374, 383–84 (italics in original; citations omitted).

73 *Hall v. Florida*, 572 U.S. 701 (2014).

74 *Id.*

75 For example, in *In re Medley*, 134 U.S. 160 (1890), the U.S. Supreme Court—responding to a petition by death row prisoner James Medley, sentenced to death for first-degree murder—held that a Colorado statute enacted after the crime's commission that added to the punishment the further punishment of imprisonment by solitary confinement until execution constituted an impermissible ex post facto law. *Id.* at 161–67. In that case, the Supreme Court emphasized of the period of solitary confinement that an inmate was subjected to under the new Colorado law: "Nor can we withhold our conviction of the proposition that when a prisoner sentenced by a court to death is confined in the penitentiary awaiting the execution of the sentence, one of the most horrible feelings to which he can be subjected during that time is the uncertainty during the whole of it, which may exist for the period of four weeks, as to the precise time when his execution shall take place." *Id.* at 172. The Court in *In re Medley* specifically noted of the use of solitary confinement by U.S. states: "[E]xperience demonstrated that there were serious objections to it. A considerable number of the prisoners fell, after even a short confinement, into a semi-fatuous condition, from which it was next to impossible to arouse them, and others became violently insane; others still committed suicide, while those who stood the ordeal better were not generally reformed, and in most cases did not recover sufficient mental activity to be of any subsequent service to the community." *Id.* at 168.

76 Kara E. Stooksbury, John M. Scheb II, and Otis H. Stephens Jr., eds., *Encyclopedia of American Civil Rights and Liberties*, vol. 1 (Santa Barbara, CA: ABC-CLIO, 2017), 218.

77 *Wilkerson v. Utah*, 99 U.S. 130 (1879).

78 *In re Kemmler*, 136 U.S. 436 (1889).

79 Arthur J. Goldberg, "Memorandum to the Conference RE: Capital Punishment—October Term, 1963," *South Texas Law Review* 27 (1985–86): 493. Arthur Goldberg later co-authored a law review article with Harvard Law School professor Alan Dershowitz—one of Justice Goldberg's former law clerks—arguing that the death penalty should be declared unconstitutional. Arthur J. Goldberg and Alan M. Dershowitz, "Declaring the Death Penalty Unconstitutional," *Harvard Law Review* 83 (1970): 1773.

80 375 U.S. 889 (1963) (dissenting from denial of certiorari).

81 *Id.* at 889.

82 *Id.* at 889–90 & n.1.

83 433 U.S. 584 (1977).

84 *Id.* at 592.

85 *Id.* at 598.
86 402 U.S. 183 (1971).
87 408 U.S. 238 (1972).
88 *Id.* at 239–40.
89 Martha Dragich Pearson, "Revelations from the Blackmun Papers on the Development of Death Penalty Law," *Missouri Law Review* 70 (2005): 1184–85.
90 Frank R. Baumgartner, Marty Davidson, Kaneesha R. Johnson, Arvind Krishnamurphy, and Colin P. Wilson, *Deadly Justice: A Statistical Portrait of the Death Penalty* (New York: Oxford University Press, 2018) (noting how the California Supreme Court's 1972 decision in *People v. Anderson* and the U.S. Supreme Court's 1972 decision in *Furman v. Georgia* invalidated more than six hundred death sentences).
91 *Furman v. Georgia*, 408 U.S. 238, 256–57 (Douglas, J., concurring); *id.* at 271–91 (Brennan, J., concurring); *id.* at 306–10 (Stewart, J., concurring); *id.* at 310–14 (White, J., concurring); *id.* at 358–64 (Marshall, J., concurring).
92 Austin Sarat, Charlotte Blackman, Elinor Scout Boynton, Katherine Chen, and Theodore Perez, "After Abolition: Acquiescence, Backlash, and the Consequences of Ending the Death Penalty," *Hastings Journal of Crime and Punishment* 1 (2020): 33, 35 n.14 ("At the time of the *Furman* decision, 40 states had the death penalty on the books. That 35 of these 40 states restored capital punishment is indicative of the severity of the post-*Furman* backlash").
93 428 U.S. 153 (1976).
94 *Proffitt v. Florida*, 428 U.S. 242 (1976); *Jurek v. Texas*, 428 U.S. 262 (1976).
95 *Woodson v. North Carolina*, 428 U.S. 280 (1976) (the mandatory imposition of a death sentence violated the Eighth Amendment's Cruel and Unusual Punishments Clause and the Fourteenth Amendment's Due Process Clause); *Fowler v. North Carolina*, 428 U.S. 904 (1976) (vacating mandatory death sentence in light of *Woodson*); *Roberts v. Louisiana*, 428 U.S. 325 (1976) (a death penalty law is unconstitutional under the Eighth and Fourteenth Amendments when it makes capital punishment mandatory on conviction for first-degree murder).
96 *Gregg*, 428 U.S. at 169.
97 *Id.* at 174, 176, 179.
98 Michael Mello, *Against the Death Penalty: The Relentless Dissents of Justices Brennan and Marshall* (Boston: Northeastern University Press, 1996).
99 *Furman*, 408 U.S. at 361 (Blackmun, J., dissenting).
100 *Id.* at 359 (Blackmun, J., dissenting).
101 *Callins v. Collins*, 510 U.S. 1141, 1145 (1994) (Blackmun, J., dissenting from denial of cert.).
102 *Id.* at 1145–46.
103 *Baze v. Rees*, 553 U.S. 35 (2008) (upholding the constitutionality of Kentucky's lethal injection protocol); *Glossip v. Gross*, 135 S. Ct. 2727 (2015) (upholding the constitutionality of Oklahoma's lethal injection protocol); *Bucklew v. Precythe*, 139 S. Ct. 1112 (2019) (upholding the constitutionality of Missouri's lethal injection protocol); *Ford v. Wainwright*, 477 U.S. 399 (1986) (a 5–4 decision holding unconstitutional the

execution of the insane); *Tison v. Arizona*, 481 U.S. 137 (1987) (a 5–4 decision hold-ing that the death penalty may be imposed on a felony murder defendant who was a major participant in the underlying felony); *Kansas v. Marsh*, 548 U.S. 163 (2006) (a 5–4 decision finding the imposition of the death penalty is constitutional when mitigating and aggravating factors are in equipoise); *Kennedy v. Louisiana*, 554 U.S. 407 (2008) (a 5–4 decision holding that the death penalty is unconstitutional for non-homicidal child rape); David W. Neubauer and Henry F. Fradella, *America's Courts and the Criminal Justice System*, 13th ed. (Boston: Cengage Learning, 2019), 275 (noting that the U.S. Supreme Court's decision in *Payne v. Tennessee*, 501 U.S. 808 (1991) overruled *Booth v. Maryland*, 482 U.S. 496 (1987) and *South Carolina v. Gathers*, 490 U.S. 805 (1989), two cases that had held the use of victim impact state-ments unconstitutional in capital cases).

104 *See also Nance v. Ward*, 2022 WL 2251307 (U.S. June 23, 2022), at *4 (setting forth the Court's new legal standard).

105 John Bessler, introduction to *Against the Death Penalty*, by Stephen Breyer, ed. John D. Bessler (Washington, DC: Brookings Institution Press, 2016), 14.

106 *Id.* at 9–11, 26–29.

107 Breyer, *Against the Death Penalty*, 72–96.

108 *E.g.*, Andrew Novak, "The Rule of Law, Constitutional Reform, and the Death Penalty in the Gambia," *Richmond Journal of Global Law and Business* 12 (2013): 217, 228 n.75 ("Justice Stephen Breyer of the United States Supreme Court has recognized the death row phenomenon may be a violation of the Eighth Amend-ment of the United States Constitution.") (citing *Knight v. Florida*, 528 U.S. 990 (1990) (Breyer, J., dissenting from denial of cert.)); *see also Reynolds v. Florida*, 139 S. Ct. 27 (2018) (Breyer, J., statement respecting denial of cert.) (asserting that "the unconscionably long delays that capital defendants must endure as they await execution" is "a serious flaw in the death penalty system," with Justice Breyer adding, "I have previously written that lengthy delays—made inevitable by the Constitution's procedural protections for defendants facing execution—deepen the cruelty of the death penalty and undermine its penological rationale.").

109 *Smith v. Shinn*, 142 S. Ct. 1714 (2022) (Breyer, J., statement respecting denial of cert.); *see also Buntion v. Lumpkin*, 142 S. Ct. 1464 (2022) (Breyer, J., statement respecting denial of application for stay) ("Carl Wayne Buntion has been on death row under threat of execution for 30 years").

110 *Barr v. Purkey*, 140 S. Ct. 2594, 2597 (2020) (Sotomayor, J., dissenting).

111 *Id.* at 2595–96 (Breyer, J., dissenting).

112 John H. Garvey and Amy V. Coney, "Catholic Judges in Capital Cases," *Marquette Law Review* 81 (1998): 303, 325 ("The evil of capital punishment is certainly grave—the taking of human life.").

113 Amy Howe, "In 6–3 Ruling, Court Reinstates Death Penalty for Boston Marathon Bomber," *SCOTUSblog*, March 4, 2022, www.scotusblog.com; Nathan Goetting, "The *Furman* Filtration Problem: Why the Death Penalty Will Always Be a Cruel and Unusual Punishment," *Toledo Law Review* 53 (2022): 407, 409–10 ("Recent

eloquent dissents of Justices Breyer and Sotomayor notwithstanding, the Supreme Court's agonizing over the constitutionality of the death penalty ended long ago. No fewer than six sitting supreme court justices, including the freshly seated Amy Coney Barrett, have given it their imprimatur.").

114 *State v. Makwanyane* 1995 (6) BCLR 665 (CC) (S. Afr.); Alkotmánybíróság (AB) [Constitutional Court] Oct. 31, 1990, Decision No. 23/1990 (Hung.).

115 John Quigley and S. Adele Shank, "Why Europe Abolished Capital Punishment," *Ohio State Journal of Criminal Law* 17 (2019): 95.

116 Protocol Nos. 6 & 13 to the European Convention on Human Rights.

117 *E.g.*, Eric Berger, "Courts, Culture, and the Lethal Injection Stalemate," *William and Mary Law Review* 62 (2020): 1, 69 ("Twenty-eight states currently have capital punishment, but since 2015, only twelve have carried out executions. Some of these dormant death penalty states are ambivalent about capital punishment and not really making serious efforts to resume executions. In other states, though, problems with lethal injection explain the inability to carry out executions.").

118 Jenny-Brooke Condon, "Denialism and the Death Penalty," *Washington University Law Review* 97 (2020): 1397.

119 The Death Penalty Information Center has documented more than 190 exonerations in the modern era. https://deathpenaltyinfo.org.

120 *Glossip v. Gross*, 576 U.S. 863, 916–23 (2015) (Breyer, J., dissenting) (discussing studies).

121 *Flowers v. Mississippi*, 139 S. Ct. 2228, 2234 (2019).

122 Amir Vera and Dakin Andone, "Oklahoma Governor Grants Clemency to Julius Jones, Halting His Execution," *CNN*, November 19, 2021.

123 Deon Osborne, "Governor's Clemency Delay 'Terrorized' Julius Jones' Family, Traumatized Nation," *Black Wall Street Times*, November 22, 2021.

124 John D. Bessler, "What I Think About When I Think About the Death Penalty," *St. Louis University Law Review* 62 (2018): 781, 790.

125 *Hudson v. McMillian*, 503 U.S. 1 (1992); *id.* at 8–9 (noting that the Eighth Amendment's prohibition of cruel and unusual punishments "'draw[s] its meaning from the evolving standards of decency that mark the progress of a maturing society'"; "When prison officials maliciously and sadistically use force to cause harm, contemporary standards of decency always are violated."); *Farmer v. Brennan*, 511 U.S. 825 (1994) (to show an Eighth Amendment violation, a prisoner must show that a defendant act with "deliberate indifference"); *id.* at 833–34 ("Prison conditions may be 'restrictive and even harsh,' but gratuitously allowing the beating or rape of one prisoner by another serves no 'legitimate penological objectiv[e],' any more than it squares with "'evolving standards of decency.'" Being violently assaulted in prison is simply not 'part of the penalty that criminal offenders pay for their offenses against society.'") (citations omitted).

126 John D. Bessler, "Taking Psychological Torture Seriously: The Torturous Nature of Credible Death Threats and the Collateral Consequences for Capital Punishment," *Northeastern University Law Review* 11 (2019): 1, 14–21.

127 *Brown v. Plata*, 563 U.S. 493 (2011); *see also id.* at 510 ("Prisoners retain the essence of human dignity inherent in all persons. Respect for that dignity animates the Eighth Amendment prohibition against cruel and unusual punishment."); *id.* at 510–11 ("Just as a prisoner may starve if not fed, he or she may suffer or die if not provided with adequate medical care. A prison that deprives prisoners of basic sustenance, including adequate medical care, is incompatible with the concept of human dignity and has no place in civilized society.").

128 *See Hudson v. McMillian*, 503 U.S. 1, 5 (1972) ("deliberate indifference to medical needs amounts to an Eighth Amendment violation only if those needs are 'serious'").

129 *Helling v. McKinney*, 509 U.S. 25 (1993).

130 *Jackson v. Bishop*, 404 F.2d 571, 579 (8th Cir. 1968); *see also Estelle v. Gamble*, 429 U.S. 97, 102 (1976) ("The [Eighth] Amendment embodies 'broad and idealist concepts of dignity, civilized standards, humanity, and decency . . . ,' against which we must evaluate penal measures.") (quoting *Jackson*, 404 F.2d at 579).

131 *Jackson*, 404 F.2d at 576.

132 *Id.* at 579.

133 536 U.S. 730 (2002).

134 *Id.* at 733–35, 738, 741.

135 *Ortiz v. Jordan*, 562 U.S. 180, 190 (2011) (citing *Farmer v. Brennan*, 511 U.S. 825, 834 (1994)).

136 John D. Bessler, "The Anomaly of Executions: The Cruel and Unusual Punishments Clause in the 21st Century," *British Journal of American Legal Studies* 2 (2013): 297, 430–33.

137 *See generally* John D. Bessler, *The Death Penalty as Torture: From the Dark Ages to Abolition* (Durham, NC: Carolina Academic Press, 2017); Bessler, *Death Penalty's Denial of Rights*.

138 *State v. Henderson*, 2 Dev. & Bat. 543, 1837 WL 498 (N.C. 1837); Lyle S. Evans, ed., *A Standard History of Ross County, Ohio: An Authentic Narrative of the Past, with Particular Attention to the Modern Era in the Commercial, Industrial, Civic and Social Development,* vol. 1 (Chicago: The Lewis Publishing Co., 1917), 152.

139 *E. B. v. Verniero*, 119 F.3d 1077, 1116 (3d Cir. 1997) (Becker, J., concurring in part and dissenting in part).

140 Bessler, "Anomaly of Executions."

141 *E.g.*, John D. Bessler, "Tinkering around the Edges: The Supreme Court's Death Penalty Jurisprudence," *American Criminal Law Review* 49 (2012): 1913.

142 *Ford v. Wainwright*, 477 U.S. 399 (1986); *id.* at 406 ("[T]he [Eighth] Amendment also recognizes the 'evolving standards of decency that mark the progress of a maturing society.'"); *compare Kahler v. Kansas*, 140 S. Ct. 1021 (2020) (the Eighth and Fourteenth Amendment did not require states to adopt an insanity defense in criminal cases).

143 *Roper v. Simmons*, 543 U.S. 551 (2005); *see also id.* at 560–61 ("The prohibition against 'cruel and unusual punishments,' like other expansive language in the

Constitution, must be interpreted according to its text, by considering history, tradition, and precedent, and with due regard for its purpose and function in the constitutional design. To implement this framework we have established the propriety and affirmed the necessity of referring to 'the evolving standards of decency that mark the progress of a maturing society' to determine which punishments are so disproportionate as to be cruel and unusual.") (quoting *Trop*, 3456 U.S. at 100–101).

144 *Atkins v. Virginia*, 536 U.S. 304 (2002); *see also id.* at 311–12 ("A claim that punishment is excessive is judged not by the standards that prevailed in 1685 when Lord Jeffreys presided over the 'Bloody Assizes' or when the Bill of Rights was adopted, but rather by those that currently prevail. As Chief Justice Warren explained in his opinion in *Trop v. Dulles* . . . : 'The basic concept underlying the Eighth Amendment is nothing less than the dignity of man. . . . The Amendment must draw its meaning from the evolving standards of decency that mark the progress of a maturing society.'").

145 *Panetti v. Quarterman*, 551 U.S. 930 (2007); *Madison v. Alabama*, 139 S. Ct. 718 (2019).

146 *Coker v. Georgia*, 433 U.S. 584 (1977) (finding the imposition of the death penalty for the nonhomicidal rape of an "adult woman" to be unconstitutional); *Kennedy v. Louisiana*, 554 U.S. 407 (2008) (finding the imposition of the death penalty for nonhomicidal child rape to be unconstitutional); *see also id.* at 420 ("Evolving standards of decency must embrace and express respect for the dignity of the person, and the punishment of criminals must conform to that rule."); *Eberheart v. Georgia*, 433 U.S. 917 (1977) (vacating the death penalty for a defendant convicted of kidnapping and rape in a case in which the victim was severely beaten, and ruling that "[t]he death penalty constitutes cruel and unusual punishment in violation of the Eighth and Fourteenth Amendment").

147 *Enmund v. Florida*, 458 U.S. 782, 797 (1982) ("Although the judgments of legislatures, juries, and prosecutors weigh heavily in the balance, it is for us ultimately to judge whether the Eighth Amendment permits imposition of the death penalty on one such as Enmund who aids and abets a felony in the course of which a murder is committed by others but who does not himself kill, attempt to kill, or intend that a killing take place or that lethal force will be employed. We have concluded, along with most legislatures and juries, that it does not."); *compare Tison v. Arizona*, 481 U.S. 137, 154 (1987) ("[W]e note the apparent consensus that substantial participation in a violent felony under circumstances likely to result in the loss of innocent human life may justify the death penalty even absent an 'intent to kill.'").

148 "Mental Illness," Death Penalty Information Center, https://deathpenaltyinfo.org/ (noting that the U.S. Supreme Court has not barred the death penalty for those suffering from serious mental illnesses); *see also* "US Carries Out Second Execution in a Week, Killing Man Lawyers Say Had Dementia," *The Guardian*, July 16, 2020.

149 Ngozi Ndulue, *Enduring Injustice: The Persistence of Racial Discrimination in the U.S. Death Penalty*, ed. Robert Dunham (Washington, DC: Death Penalty Information Center, September 2020), 61 ("When researchers examine the places of greatest concentration of executions and death sentences, it is clear that a small minority of jurisdictions are responsible for the majority of capital punishment activity. A 2013 Death Penalty Information Center report compiled data on death sentences and executions across the country to find that 2% of the counties in the U.S. have been responsible for the majority of modern executions, and the same percentage of counties are responsible for the majority of the death row population. By 2020 just 1.2% of U.S. counties accounted for half of the nation's death row. And just three high-execution states—Texas, Missouri, and Virginia—accounted for more than half of the federal death row.").

150 481 U.S. 279 (1987).

151 *Id.* at 282–83, 286.

152 *Id.* at 287.

153 *Id.* at 283, 291.

154 *Id.* at 292 (italics in original).

155 *Id.* at 297.

156 *Id.* at 315.

157 *Id.* at 308.

158 *Id.* at 312.

159 *Id.* at 282, 301–302 nn.23–24.

160 *Sawyer v. Whitley*, 505 U.S. 333, 355 (1992) (Blackmun, J., concurring) ("The Court refused to address Warren McCleskey's claim of constitutional error, and he was executed on September 24, 1991.").

161 Carol S. Steiker and Jordan M. Steiker, "No More Tinkering: The American Law Institute and the Death Penalty Provisions of the Model Penal Code," *Texas Law Review* 89 (2010): 353, 354.

162 John Charles Boger, "*McCleskey v. Kemp*: Field Notes from 1977–1991," *Northwestern University Law Review* 112 (2018): 1673, 1682–83 ("Justice Powell's change of mind and heart is well known. In 1990, less than a year after he retired from the Court and lobbied Congress to curtail prisoners' access to habeas corpus procedures, Justice Powell told his biographer that the one vote he regretted in his sixteen-year career of Supreme Court service was the one he cast in *McCleskey v. Kemp*. Asked if he meant that he had come to accept the statistical case, he responded: 'No, I would vote the other way in any capital case.'").

163 "California Governor, 6 District Attorneys File Briefs Saying State's Death Penalty Is Arbitrary and 'Infected by Racism,'" Death Penalty Information Center, October 28, 2020, https://deathpenaltyinfo.org.

164 *Barr v. Purkey*, No. 20A9 (U.S. Sup. Ct.), July 16, 2020 (Breyer, J., dissenting).

165 NAACP Legal Defense and Educational Fund, *The Civil Rights Record of Judge Ketanji Brown Jackson* (New York: NAACP Legal Defense and Educational Fund, March 2022), 27. Since joining the Court, Justice Ketanji Brown Jackson has

dissented multiple times in capital cases. *E.g.*, King v. Emmons, 144 S. Ct. 2501, 2501 (2024) (Jackson, J., dissenting from denial of cert.); Thornell v. Jones, 144 S. Ct. 1302, 1315 (2024) (Jackson, J., dissenting); Compton v. Texas, 144 S. Ct. 916, 916 (2024) (Sotomayor, J., dissenting from denial of cert.; joined by Justice Jackson).

166 139 S. Ct. 1112 (2019).

167 *Id.* at 1122.

168 Crimes Act of 1790, Statute II, ch. IX, 1 Stat. 112.

169 Jenny-Brooke Condon, "A Cruel and Unusual Term: The Distortion of Decency and Restraint in the Supreme Court's 2018–2019 Death Penalty Decisions," *Federal Sentencing Reporter* 32 (2019): 15, 17 ("[G]iven that adherence to precedent is a powerful curb on judicial overreach, *Bucklew*'s failure to cite to the Court's 'evolving standards of decency' doctrine, which has guided the Court's Eighth Amendment precedents since 1958, provides an additional reason to question the majority's professed commitment to judicial restraint. . . . [S]ignificantly, the Court utilized an originalist approach to evaluate whether Bucklew's execution would be cruel and unusual, assessing the degree of pain countenanced by the Eighth Amendment at the time of its adoption. Within this analysis, the Court never discussed whether historical execution practices can or should be squared with the Court's well-settled 'evolving standards of decency' doctrine. While the Court did not overtly call into question the doctrine, its failure to discuss 'evolving standards of decency' and its originalist analysis of the Eighth Amendment could set the stage for significant disruption to Eighth Amendment doctrine away from the norms of decency and anti-brutality."). Justice Clarence Thomas has written that the Supreme Court's prior Eighth Amendment ruling in *Robinson v. California* (1962) was "wrongly decided," and—in rejecting the Supreme Court's "evolving standards of decency" test—asserted: "I continue to believe that we should adhere to the Cruel and Unusual Punishment Clause's fixed meaning in resolving any challenge brought under it." *City of Grants Pass, Oregon v. Johnson*, 144 S. Ct. 2202, 2226–27 (2024) (Thomas, J., concurring).

170 *E.g.*, *Graham v. Florida*, 560 U.S. 48, 58 (2010) ("To determine whether a punishment is cruel and unusual, courts must look beyond historical conceptions to the 'evolving standards of decency that mark the progress of a maturing society.'").

171 *Harmelin v. Michigan*, 501 U.S. 957, 995 (1991) ("[M]andatory death sentences abounded in our first Penal Code. They were also common in the several States—both at the time of the founding and throughout the 19th century.").

172 Jacob Leon, "*Bucklew v. Precythe*'s Return to the Original Meaning of 'Unusual': Prohibiting Extensive Delays on Death Row," *Cleveland State Law Review* 68 (2020): 485, 497–99 (analyzing the average sentence-to-execution delay of a sample of executions from 1770 to 1791 in Connecticut, Maine, Massachusetts, New Hampshire, New Jersey, New York, Rhode Island, and Vermont, and finding that "the average sentence-to-execution delay was 1.14 months" and that "only 3.77% of prisoners awaited execution for more than three months from 1770 to 1791").

173 *Bucklew*, 139 S. Ct. at 1122–23.

174 Jerry Windley-Daoust, *Living Justice and Peace: Catholic Social Teaching in Practice*, 2nd ed. (Winona, MN: St. Mary's Press, 2008), 302.

175 Shawn E. Fields, "Constitutional Comparativism and the Eighth Amendment: How a Flawed Proportionality Requirement Can Benefit from Foreign Law," *Boston University Law Review* (2006): 963, 981 ("[T]he Bill of Rights (including the Eighth Amendment), since the addition of the Fourteenth Amendment, has been construed to protect individual liberties from offensive state action.").

176 Since 1973, 200 death row inmates have been exonerated. "Innocence," Death Penalty Information Center, https://deathpenaltyinfo.org.

177 "DPIC Analysis: Use or Threat of Death Penalty Implicated in 19 Exoneration Cases in 2019," Death Penalty Information Center, October 23, 2020, https://deathpenaltyinfo.org.

178 "DPIC Analysis."

179 "Idaho Falls Will Pay $11.7 Million to Exoneree Coerced into False Confession by Threat of the Death Penalty," Death Penalty Information Center, June 24, 2022, https://deathpenaltyinfo.org/.

180 *See generally* Bessler, *Death Penalty as Torture*.

181 G.A. Res. 217 (III) A, Universal Declaration of Human Rights, art. 5 (Dec. 10, 1948).

182 G.A. Res. 2200 (XXI), International Covenant on Civil and Political Rights, art. 7 (Dec. 16, 1966).

183 David Weissbrodt and Cheryl Heilman, "Defining Torture and Cruel, Inhuman, and Degrading Treatment," *Law and Inequality* 29 (2011): 343, 351–55; Karen Parker, "Jus Cogens: Compelling the Law of Human Rights," *Hastings International and Comparative Law Review* 12 (1989): 411, 437–38.

184 *Roper v. Simmons*, 543 U.S. 551, 560 (2005).

185 John D. Bessler, "The Concept of 'Unusual Punishments' in Anglo-American Law: The Death Penalty as Arbitrary, Discriminatory, and Cruel and Unusual," *Northwestern Journal of Law and Social Policy* 13 (2018): 307 (discussing the arbitrary and discriminatory nature of death sentences and executions); Ndulue, *Enduring Injustice*, 3.

186 Ndulue, *Enduring Justice*, 28 ("Each year since 2015, states have conducted fewer than 30 executions and imposed fewer than 50 new death sentences. This starkly contrasts with the peak of executions and death sentences in the late 1990s, with more than 300 sentences imposed in 1996 and almost 100 executions in 1999. Since then, death sentences have fallen by more than 85%, and executions are down by more than three-quarters."). The decline in death sentences has occurred even though capital juries are "death-qualified."

187 Carol S. Steiker and Jordan M. Steiker, "Capital Clemency in the Age of Constitutional Regulation: Reversing the Unwarranted Decline," *Texas Law Review* 102, no. 7 (2024), 1467 ("This past year saw the longest average time of death row incarceration prior to execution in American history—about 23 years."); *see also* Michael Johnson, "Fifteen Years and Death: Double Jeopardy, Multiple Punishments, and

Extended Stays on Death Row," *Boston University Public Interest Law Journal* 23, no. 1 (2014): 85; John H. Blume, Hannah L. Freedman, Lindsey S. Vann, and Amelia Courtney Hritz, "Death by Numbers: Why Evolving Standards Compel Extending *Roper*'s Categorial Ban against Executing Juveniles from Eighteen to Twenty-One," *Texas Law Review* 98, no. 5 (2020): 921, 938 n.104 ("When examining the executions, it is important to note the length of time between a death sentence and an execution. Across the country, there are significant lags from when a sentence of death is announced to when the sentence is carried out. For example, in 2013, the most recent year for which accurate data is available, the average time between sentencing and execution in the United States was 186 months (or 15.5 years).").

188 Bessler, "Taking Psychological Torture Seriously," 59.

189 *Id.* at 12.

190 *See Wilkerson v. Utah*, 99 U.S. 130, 136 (1879) ("[I]t is safe to affirm that punishments of torture . . . and all others in the same line of unnecessary cruelty, are forbidden by that amendment."); *In re Kemmler*, 136 U.S. 436, 447 (1890) ("Punishments are cruel when they involve torture or a lingering death. . . ."); *see also Gregg v. Georgia*, 428 U.S. 153, 169–70 (1976) ("The American draftsmen, who adopted the English phrasing in drafting the Eighth Amendment, were primarily concerned . . . with proscribing 'tortures' and other 'barbarous' methods of punishment."); *Bucklew v. Precythe*, 139 S. Ct. 1112, 1141 (2019) (Breyer, J., dissenting) ("The majority acknowledges that the Eighth Amendment prohibits States from executing prisoners by 'horrid modes of torture' such as burning at the stake.").

191 *Estelle v. Gamble*, 429 U.S. 97 (1976) ("Our more recent cases . . . have held that the [Eighth] Amendment proscribes more than physically barbarous punishments. The Amendment embodies 'broad and idealistic concepts of dignity, civilized standards, humanity, and decency . . . , against which we must evaluate penal measures.'") (citations omitted).

192 Bessler, "Taking Psychological Torture Seriously"; *see also* Alyssa M. Knappins, "Setting the Record Straight: Why Threats of Physical Violence Made towards Inmates Violate the Eighth Amendment," *Roger Williams University Law Review* 27 (2022): 113, 126–27 (discussing threats of violence in the prison context).

193 *People v. Anderson*, 493 P.2d 880, 894 (Cal. 1972).

194 *See generally* Stephanie DeGooyer, Alastair Hunt, Lida Maxwell, and Samuel Moyn, *The Right to Have Rights* (London: Verso, 2018) (discussing Hannah Arendt's views).

195 Bessler, "Taking Psychological Torture Seriously."

196 *Shanklin v. State*, 187 So. 3d 734, 808 (Ala. Crim. App. 2014) (italics in original).

197 *See generally* John D. Bessler, "Torture and Trauma: Why the Death Penalty Is Wrong and Should Be Strictly Prohibited by American and International Law," *Washburn Law Journal* 58 (2019): 1, 6, 47–55.

198 477 U.S. 399 (1986).

199 *Id.* at 406 (citations omitted).

200 *Bucklew v. Precythe*, 139 S. Ct. 1112, 1122–23 (2019).

201 The Fourteenth Amendment was ratified in part in 1868 to ensure the constitutionality of the Civil Rights Act of 1866. Bessler, "Inequality of America's Death
Penalty." That act required "like punishment, pains, and penalties" for offenders
without regard to race. Civil Rights Act of 1866, 14 Stat. 27, § 1; *General Building
Contractors Ass'n, Inc. v. Pennsylvania*, 458 U.S. 375, 384 n.10 (1982).

202 *Wilkerson v. Utah*, 99 U.S. 130, 136 (1878).

203 The leading international convention prohibiting its use defines *torture* as "any
act by which severe pain or suffering, whether physical or mental, is intentionally
inflicted on a person" for a prohibited purpose such as obtaining information or
a confession, punishment, or discrimination. U.N. Convention Against Torture
and Other Cruel, Inhuman or Degrading Treatment or Punishment (adopted
by General Assembly resolution 39/46 of Dec. 10, 1984; entry into force June 26,
1987), Art. 1(1).

204 *E.g., Filártiga v. Peña-Irala*, 630 F.2d 876, 884–85 (2d Cir. 1980) ("[O]fficial
torture is now prohibited by the law of nations. The prohibition is clear and
unambiguous. . . . [I]nternational law confers fundamental rights upon all people
vis-a-vis their own governments. While the ultimate scope of those rights will
be a subject for continuing refinement and elaboration, we hold that the right to
be free from torture is now among them.").

205 Nkem Adeleye, "The Death Row Phenomenon: A Prohibition against Torture,
Cruel, Inhuman and Degrading Treatment or Punishment," *San Diego Law
Review* 58 (2021): 875, 890–900.

206 David R. Dow, Jim Marcus, Morris Moon, Jared Tyler, and Greg Wiercioch, "The
Extraordinary Execution of Billy Vickers, the Banality of Death, and the Demise
of Post-conviction Review," *William and Mary Bill of Rights Journal* 13 (2004): 521,
550 n.150 ("Mock executions and other threats of imminent death are widely recognized to be a form of unconscionable torture. Legislation passed by the United
States Congress on April 30, 1994, implementing the United Nations Convention
Against Torture and Other Cruel, Inhuman or Degrading Treatment or Punishment, identifies 'the threat of imminent death' as a form of torture. This provision
was designed to bring 'mock executions' within the ambit of the legislation.")
(citing 18 U.S.C. § 2340(2)(C) (2004)).

207 *See generally* John D. Bessler, "The Rule of Law: A Necessary Pillar of Free and
Democratic Societies for Protecting Human Rights," *Santa Clara Law Review* 61
(2021): 467.

208 *E.g., Sotloff v. Syrian Arab Republic*, 525 F. Supp.3d 121, 136–37 (D.D.C. 2021) (noting that "threats of execution" are "severe enough to qualify as torture" under
the Torture Victim Protection Act (TVPA), 28 U.S.C. § 1605A(h)(7)); *Kilburn v.
Islamic Republic of Iran*, 699 F. Supp.2d 136, 152 (D.D.C. 2010) (including "mock
executions" among the acts constituting torture under the TVPA).

209 *Culombe v. Connecticut*, 367 U.S. 568, 581–82 (1961) (discussing the Star Chamber's
use of torture).

210 *State v. Santiago*, 122 A.3d 1, 10 (2015).

8

Leveling the Playing Field

*Quality Representation in the Capital
Defense Community*

MAYA PAGNI BARAK AND JON B. GOULD

The public, along with many attorneys, tend to hold capital defense work
in low regard. From the stigma of defending "the worst of the worst" to
the stigma of criminal defense work more generally, capital defenders
are often painted as morally corrupt, legally inept, or both.[1] Yet, such
assumptions are not only misleading but also inaccurate.

Capital defense attorneys are tasked with a very difficult job. They are
frequently confronted with horrible case facts, mentally ill clients, jury
bias, prosecutorial misconduct, uncooperative witnesses, and unreasonable judges—and the list goes on. They are also generally underfunded.
Most capital defendants are indigent, and the state has notoriously been
reluctant to adequately fund defense teams' requests.[2] This is particularly
problematic, as good capital defense is costly and time consuming, and
it requires specialized training and skills. In light of these challenges,
however, capital defense attorneys provide some of the best representation in all of criminal defense.

Still, there is no shortage of subpar representation in the world of
capital defense—both past and present. Inexperienced attorneys often
approach capital cases with a "cowboy mentality," likening them to "any
old" felony case and assuming they can go to trial with little preparation. Out of ignorance or ego, they may eschew the idea of a negotiated
plea deal. Others may be in it for the payday, attracted to capital work
by higher hourly rates.[3] These attorneys don't file motions or advocate
zealously, rarely ask the court for sufficient funds to investigate or hire
experts, and generally avoid "making waves" so that judges continue
appointing them and they continue getting paid. Such run-of-the-mill

capital failings have been documented in criminological and legal scholarship, as well as evidenced by numerous capital conviction reversals.[4] There are, of course, more serious examples of shoddy capital defense.

Among the most notable instances of ineffective assistance of counsel in a capital case is that of Joe Frank Cannon, who fell asleep while representing Calvin Burdine at trial. On habeas appeal, a panel of the Fifth Circuit Court of Appeals concluded that Burdine's rights had not been violated despite Cannon being, quite literally, "asleep at the wheel." Only later, on review by the court en banc, did the Fifth Circuit conclude that a defendant facing the death penalty has a constitutional right to an attorney who is *awake* at trial.

Although an outlier, this case serves as an example of particularly egregious ineffective assistance of counsel. More importantly, however, it shines a light on systemic barriers to quality capital representation. That a circuit court of appeals would entertain the idea that a sleeping attorney can effectively represent a capital defendant at trial, let alone find this to be true, is outrageous. Yet, this behavior and its tacit approval from the judicial community is not unfathomable in the context of a criminal justice system that has long been stacked against capital defendants.[5]

The institution of capital punishment was not constructed with quality in mind, and certainly not with quality defense representation in mind. Indeed, decades of substandard capital representation and its consequences—including the many wrongful convictions and executions of which we are aware, as well as those we will never discover—have contributed to ongoing calls to abolish the death penalty. Admittedly, capital punishment has evolved significantly in the fifty years since *Furman v. Georgia*.[6] Still, despite advanced guidelines for attorneys, judges, and juries, enhanced due process protections for defendants, and restrictions barring the pursuit of capital charges in all but the most serious of cases, U.S. capital punishment presents numerous structural obstacles to quality representation.

Confronted with the complex rules and realities of U.S. capital punishment, a specialized community of capital practice has emerged. Driven by the many challenges they face, adept, creative, and persistent attorneys, along with talented investigators and mitigation specialists, have been forced to develop dynamic strategies to save their capital clients' lives. In so doing, they've also formed a legal community with shared norms, resources, and social networks. Those who find themselves "on the outside" of this community, whether by choice or due to its elite and seemingly exclusive nature, may contribute to the perception of poor-quality lawyers among the capital defense bar. Those who find themselves "on the inside" of this community have contributed to a cutting-edge canon of criminal defense practice, with implications that extend far beyond the world of capital punishment.

A Community of Practice

Death is different, or so goes the common refrain among the capital defense community.[7] The American Bar Association (ABA), too, recognizes this distinction. The ABA's *Guidelines for the Appointment and Performance of Defense Counsel in Death Penalty Cases* states that "the [capital] defense team should consist of no fewer than two attorneys . . . an investigator, and a mitigation specialist."[8] Moreover, since the Supreme Court's decision in *Wiggins v. Smith* in 2003, it has become de rigueur for the defense to conduct a social history of the defendant. As such, capital defense teams often rely on a myriad of skilled actors including investigators, mitigation specialists, psychologists or psychiatrists, social workers, and various other experts who can offer insight into the defendant's past, including his IQ, psychological or physical abuse, and addictions. The result is a defense team that may include two named lawyers, law clerks or associates, an investigator or mitigation specialist, a psychologist, and two or three other experts. Contrast this with typical representation in capital criminal trials, or even in similarly situated non–capital murder trials, which often consists of representation by a single attorney who may or may not have funding to support experts and investigators—or even the training needed to realize the value of them.

The evolution of such guidelines, along with key legal decisions and the abolition movement, has contributed to the emergence of capital defense as a geographically diverse community of practice. The term *community of practice* was first put forward by Mather, McEwen, and Maiman to describe the norms created and reinforced in legal networks among divorce lawyers.[9] Such communities consist of "elites" and "commonplace" lawyers, "insiders" and "outsiders" who make the field both a specialized community and a distinct culture within law.

What distinguishes the "insiders" and "outsiders" in the case of capital defense? In large part, this is incumbent on the amount of one's practice that is dedicated to capital defense. Few attorneys set out to do capital work. Instead, most "fall into" capital defense by chance.[10] For many, this is part of a natural progression of taking on more serious criminal cases as one becomes more experienced, either by choice or by promotion within a public defender office. Indeed, capital cases are often considered the pinnacle of criminal defense work among the criminal defense community. However, capital defense is not for everyone. Few attorneys transition from the "one-off" capital case to a regular capital practice.

There are clear differences between the defense attorney who takes on the occasional capital case and those who consider themselves to be capital defenders. While capital defenders work in a variety of settings, including solo practice and small private firms, public defender offices, and nonprofits, the typical insider's practice consists almost entirely, if not solely, of capital cases. Insiders regularly attend capital training conferences. They recognize the value of mitigation and teamwork, as well as the importance of building strong relationships with their capital clients and engaging in outreach to victims' family members. They also stay abreast of the most recent academic literature in fields such as neuropsychology and toxicology. They have listservs and reach out to one another for advice.

Capital defense insiders also tend to have similar educational and professional backgrounds. They often hold elite legal pedigrees, having attended top law schools and obtained prestigious clerkships, fellowships, and internships. Many have worked with, learned from, or idolized the capital community's "inner circle," often said to consist of Judy Clarke, David Bruck, Mark Olive, John Blume, Bryan Stevenson, Stephen Bright, and Denny Leboeuf, among several others. It is these lawyers who set the tone, expectations, and standards for capital representation. Like this inner circle, many capital defenders have practiced in the South. Indeed, southern states are considered by those in the capital community to be among the toughest areas to practice capital defense and, thus, an excellent place to "learn the ropes"—a capital defense boot camp of sorts.

The outsiders, those who occasionally represent capital clients, do not generally share in the beliefs and experiences of insiders. They rarely attend capital conferences or trainings. They may not know the key national players, nor are they on the capital defender listservs, and they shy away from seeking advice from the capital community. They are not as likely to stay up to date with cutting-edge research or practice in the field. They fail to see the value of experts, mitigation, relationship building, and teamwork. Perhaps most significantly, they approach capital cases as they would any other criminal case—at least according to insiders. Ultimately, there is an assumption within the field that although attorneys who take on the occasional capital case may provide their clients adequate representation, the best capital defense work is done by those who specialize in it.

The Contours of Quality Capital Defense

Just what constitutes quality capital defense in the eyes of the capital community? Certainly, strong analytical and writing skills are important. This is particularly helpful given the robust motions practice of most successful capital defense attorneys. Motions slow down the system. They buy the defense team time to work toward the ultimate goal: the plea bargain and "taking death off the table."

Indeed, the goal is rarely acquittal in a capital trial. Seasoned capital defenders insist that the goal in a capital case is to avoid trial altogether. In most capital cases, the facts are quite horrific and evidence of guilt is overwhelming. Juries often tilt in favor of the prosecution, particularly in conservative southern states with higher usage of capital punishment. Under these circumstances, not only is it difficult to argue that one's client is innocent, it is often reckless. Capital trials are bifurcated, consisting of the "guilt" phase, during which guilt or innocence is decided, and the "penalty" or "sentencing" phase, during which a sentence of death or life without the possibility of parole is handed down after a guilty verdict. A defense strategy resting on innocence during the first stage of a capital trial leaves little room to change course and introduce mitigating factors during the sentencing phase should the defendant be found guilty.

Yet, avoiding trial is not always an option. Obtaining a plea bargain requires that capital defense attorneys persuade both prosecutors and their clients to accept a life sentence. Similarly, escaping a guilty verdict at trial is unlikely, and convincing death-qualified jurors not to sentence a guilty defendant to execution requires his humanization. None of this is possible without mitigation. Mitigation entails uncovering the defendant's background in an attempt to make sense of—but not excuse—his crimes. Put differently, mitigation centers the case around the capital defendant while at the same time situating him, and his alleged actions, within the context of his own life history. Examining the facts of the case through this lens, capital defenders hope that prosecutors and jurors come to see beyond the "worst thing" the client ever did and spare his life.

Relationship building and teamwork lay the foundation for quality mitigation. As the ABA's *Guidelines for the Appointment and Performance of Defense Counsel in Death Penalty Cases* stress, "Establishing a relationship of trust with the client is essential both to overcome the client's natural resistance to disclosing the often personal and painful facts necessary to present an effective penalty phase defense, and to ensure that the client will listen to counsel's advice on important matters such as whether to testify and the advisability of a plea."[11]

Uncovering a capital defendant's deepest secrets and darkest traumas is no easy task. Most capital defendants suffer from severe mental illness, addiction, or childhood trauma and abuse; many have struggled with all of these. Clients and their family members do not open up easily. They are often ashamed, embarrassed, and reluctant to disclose such information, especially to a stranger, and especially if it casts them or others with whom they are close in a disparaging light.

Mental illness and trauma, in and of themselves, present barriers to the trust that disclosure requires. Many capital defendants have had negative experiences with attorneys or the legal system. Many have also been abused, disregarded, or ignored by people who were close to them, including their parents, other family members, and teachers. It is not uncommon for capital defendants to act out or refuse to cooperate with their own defense attorneys at the outset of their relationship. Met with such challenges, inexperienced defense attorneys might write their clients off as too difficult or problematic. Yet, the success of a capital case is dependent on building a strong relationship between the defendant and the defense team, as well as one between the defense team and other central figures in the defendant's life.

These relationships, in turn, require substantial interpersonal and time investments that begin long before a capital case goes to trial. Veteran capital defense attorneys, along with investigators and mitigation specialists, spend dozens if not hundreds of hours with the client and those in his social network, establishing the kind of rapport that generates trust and cooperation. They listen. They pay attention. They follow through. They help meet their client's immediate needs, such as putting money in their commissary account or following up on questions they have about their case. They get to know the client as a person, initially visiting numerous times to talk about anything and everything *except* the facts of the case, like food, sports, and weather. Ultimately, relationship building requires capital defenders to walk a fine line, balancing care, compassion, and empathy with professional objectivity and reasonable expectations about the client and the case. Such relationship building can be understood through the lens of "emotional labor," or the management of one's own or others' emotions as required in a given job, which is work traditionally associated with women.[12] It includes both the performance of emotion,[13] such as feigning concern, and authentic exhibition of emotion,[14] such as expressing remorse. Emotional labor is generally overlooked, minimized, or even looked down on in many occupations. Yet, within the capital defense community it is often venerated—to a point. While those well versed in capital defense pinpoint caring skills and activities as integral to the success of a capital case— emotional labor is essential to building a relationship with the client and demonstrating their humanity to the jury—this work is still highly gendered in the capital context. Women are often shunted into performing this work whether they want to or not (their abilities are framed as "innate" or "natural"), and their professionalism is questioned if they are ever deemed to be "too close" to capital defendants.[15]

Still, the immense amount of effort and skill that goes into relationship building, as well as mitigation overall, cannot be accomplished without teamwork. There is no room for ego or pride in capital defense. Again, defense teams often consist of two named lawyers, law clerks or associates, an investigator or mitigation specialist, a psychologist, and sometimes two or three other experts, as the case facts require. While everyone must work toward accomplishing what is in the best interests of the case and client, the core of the team—attorneys, investigators, and mitigation specialists—must be able to work together without regard to hierarchy. This is often particularly difficult for many criminal defense attorneys, especially for those among the private bar who are used to working alone.

In addition to being able to work collectively, capital defense attorneys must have the wherewithal and expertise to build a defense team that can function successfully as a whole. Team members must have not only complementary strengths but also, ideally, complementary identities spanning class, gender, race, and even language divides. Having a diversity of team membership is key, as it maximizes the likelihood that at least someone on the team—often but not always a woman—will be able to connect with the client in a meaningful way and help the rest of the team to do so, too.

Quality capital representation is also demanding. Capital defense is not a sprint, it is a marathon. It requires immense amounts of highly skilled coordinated efforts around intensely emotional and traumatic subjects over long periods of time, as cases stretch on for years. Seasoned capital defenders are up for the challenge. They are meticulous, and often perfectionists. They compulsively leave no stone unturned, no lead or possibility unexplored. Still, this work places defense attorneys under extreme pressure—one mistake, and the client dies, or at least that is how it seems to many. Inevitably, quality capital representation takes its toll on these zealous advocates, whether they realize it or not.

Emerging literature on the effects of trauma in "helping professions"—such as law enforcement, medicine, rescue work, therapy, social work, and law[16]—suggests that capital defenders may face increased risks of anxiety, depression, stress, substance abuse, and vicarious traumatization from their work. Indeed, for many, capital defense work is accompanied by troubling side effects: addiction, compulsion, depression, divorce, fatigue, nightmares, physical problems such as chronic back pain and heart attacks, and stress. It can also result in vicarious or secondary trauma, defined as indirect traumatization from exposure to others' trauma.[17] This includes exposure to the trauma of both victims and perpetrators, such as exposure to horrifying case facts and devastating life histories.

Capital defenders employ a variety of coping mechanisms—self-destructive or helpful—that allow them to continue with their work.

These include detaching from work or using work to avoid others; compulsive habits and substance use and abuse; hobbies such as art, reading, or watching television; playing sports, working out, or enjoying the outdoors; and relying on family, friends, peers, or therapist for support. Still, avoiding burnout and coping with the effects of capital defense work is a never-ending battle. For many, the work is ultimately debilitating.

Post-abolition: Lessons for Criminal Defense

What is to be gained from explorations of quality representation among the capital defense community? Moreover, what can capital defense offer us in a post-abolition world? We need look no further than the realm of juvenile life sentences to find traces of lessons learned from capital practitioners. Indeed, since the Supreme Court's decision in *Roper v. Simmons*[18] striking down the juvenile death penalty, some of the "best of the best" capital defenders have moved on to addressing juvenile LWOP (life in prison without the possibility of parole), and their efforts are promising.[19] Hence, were the death penalty abolished, it is likely that those same talented former capital defenders might address cases involving adult LWOP, crimmigration,[20] mass incarceration, or unjust prison conditions.

Working in any such specialty areas would allow capital defenders to continue doing what drives many of them to defense work in the first place: affording representation to the most vulnerable among us.[21] Alternatively, they might defend persons accused of terrorism, treason, or war crimes, providing representation to some of the most despised among us. After all, many capital defenders have a "soft spot" for outcasts and underdogs, believing that they are just as deserving of zealous advocacy as anyone else. Or, perhaps some would go on to represent the Julian Assanges of the world, the whistleblowers who don't just take the fight to the government's doorstep, they *start* the fight on the government's doorstep; this would satiate some capital defenders' desires for excitement and the chance to challenge the state's authority.

In addition to making tangible contributions to challenging, high-profile, or prestigious areas of law, quality capital representation offers a pathway toward humanizing the law in a *postmortem* world, just as it does in the present. The irony that such insights could be gleaned from one of the most inhumane realms of the U.S. legal system is not lost on us. Through mitigation, relationship building, and teamwork, capital defense attorneys reveal the law at its best and its worst, from the ways capital defendants are treated in the system to the collateral consequences experienced by attorneys in the course of zealous advocacy. Ultimately, the work of capital defenders shows us that humanizing defendants, legal practice, and legal systems is not only possible, but imperative.

Notes

1 Jon B. Gould and Maya Pagni Barak, *Capital Defense: Inside the Lives of America's Death Penalty Lawyers* (New York: New York University Press, 2019); Jack Ladinsky, "Careers of Lawyers, Law Practice, and Legal Institutions," *American Sociological Review* 28 (1963): 47; Barbara Babock, "Defending the Guilty," *Cleveland State Law Review* 32 (1983).

2 Testimonies of Richard Burr, Anthony Ricco, and U.S. District Judge Marcia Crone at a hearing of the Ad Hoc Committee to Review the Criminal Justice Act Program (2016), http://cjastudy.fd.org/.

3 The state supplies most capital defendants with their attorneys, as most are indigent. Because not all jurisdictions have public defense systems—and those that do often lack the capacity to take capital cases—state-selected members of the private bar defend most capital clients. These "panel attorneys" are paid at an hourly rate that is considerably higher for capital cases than for others. For instance, federal panel attorneys are authorized to receive upward of $202 per hour to defend a capital case, as compared with $158 for lower-level felonies (United States Courts, *Defender services*, 2022, https://www.uscourts.gov). Still, those familiar with capital defense know that this funding falls short of the needs of quality capital defense.

4 For example, the late Welsh White, a law professor at the University of Pittsburgh and an expert on capital defense, detailed many of these failings in his book, *Litigating in the Shadow of Death* (Ann Arbor: University of Michigan Press, 2005). Similarly, analyzing death sentences imposed between 1973 and 1995, James Liebman and his team concluded that "68% of all death verdicts imposed . . . were reversed by courts due to serious errors." See James Liebman, Jeffrey Fagan, Valerie West, and Jonathan Lloyd, "Capital Attrition: Error Rates in Capital Cases, 1973–1995," *Texas Law Review* 78 (1999–2000): 1850.

5 For discussions situating capital punishment as an extension of racially motivated southern lynchings, see Equal Justice Initiative, *Lynching in America: Confronting the Legacy of Racial Terror* (Montgomery, AL: Equal Justice Initiative, 2015); Charles J. Ogletree Jr. and Austin Sarat, eds., *From Lynch Mobs to the Killing State: Race and the Death Penalty in America* (New York: New York University Press, 2006).

6 *Furman v. Georgia*, 408 U.S. 238 (1972).

7   In this chapter we draw primarily on insights from our interview study of capital defense attorneys conducted between 2013 and 2015 and detailed in our book, *Capital Defense*.

8   American Bar Association, *Guidelines for the Appointment and Performance of Defense Counsel in Death Penalty Cases* (Chicago: American Bar Association, 2003).

9   Lynn Mather, Craig A. McEwen, and Richard J. Maiman, *Divorce Lawyers at Work: Varieties of Professionalism in Practice* (New York: Oxford University Press, 2001).

10 Gould and Barak, *Capital Defense*.

11 American Bar Association, *Guidelines*.

12 Arlie Russell Hochschild, "Emotional Labor, Feeling Rules, and Social Structure," *American Journal of Sociology* 85 (1979): 551–75; Arlie Russell Hochschild, *The Managed Heart: Commercialization of Human Feeling* (Berkeley: University of California Press, 1983); Ronnie J. Sternberg and Deborah M. Figart, "Emotional Demands at Work: A Job Content Analysis," *Annals of the American Academy of Political and Social Science* 561 (1999): 177–91; Ronnie J. Sternberg and Deborah M. Figart, "Emotional Labor since *The Managed Heart*," *Annals of the American Academy of Political and Social Science* 561 (1999): 8–26.

13 Hochschild, *Managed Heart*; Hochschild, "Emotional Labor"; Sternberg and Figart, "Emotional Demands at Work"; Sternberg and Figart, "Emotional Labor."

14 Blake E. Ashforth and Ronald H. Humphrey, "Emotional Labor in Service Roles: The Influence of Identity," *Academy of Management Review* 18 (1993): 88–115; Martin O'Brien, "The Managed Heart Revisited: Health and Social Control," *Sociological Review* 42 (1994): 393–413.

15 Gould and Barak, *Capital Defense*.

16 Mary Ann Dutton, Adriana Serrano, Sharias Dahlgren, Maria Franco-Rahman, Monica Martinez, and Mihriye Mete, "A Holistic Healing Arts Model for Counselors, Advocates, and Lawyers Serving Trauma Survivors: Joyful Heart Foundation Retreat," *Traumatology* 23 (2017); Charles R. Figley, ed., *Compassion Fatigue: Coping with Secondary Traumatic Stress Disorders in Those Who Treat the Traumatized* (New York: Routledge, 1999); Grace Maguire and Mitchell K. Byrne, "The Law Is Not as Blind as It Seems: Relative Rates of Vicarious Trauma among Lawyers and Mental Health Professionals," *Psychiatry, Psychology, and Law* 24 (2017); Susannah Sheffer, *Fighting for Their Lives: Inside the Experience of Capital Defense Attorneys* (Nashville, TN: Vanderbilt University Press, 2013).

17 Figley, *Compassion Fatigue*; Maguire and Byrne, "Law Is Not as Blind"; Martha D. Burkett, "Practicing Wellness: Stress Management for Lawyers: An Ounce of Prevention," *Michigan Bar Journal* 89 (2010).

18 *Roper v. Simmons*, 543 U.S. 551 (2005).

19 Joshua Rovner, "Juvenile Life without Parole: An Overview," Sentencing Project, April 7, 2023, https://www.sentencingproject.org.

20 Crimmigration is broadly defined as issues at the intersection of the criminal justice and immigration systems, including the criminalization of immigrants as

well as the increasing adoption of criminal justice practices and strategies in the realm of immigration enforcement Alissa R. Ackerman and Rich Furman, eds., *The Criminalization of Immigration: Contexts and Consequences* (Durham, NC: Carolina Academic Press, 2014); Juliet Stumpf, "The Crimmigration Crisis: Immigrants, Crime, and Sovereign Power," *American University Law Review* 56 (2006).

21 In our research, lawyers remarked on at least six central motives for their decisions to take on capital work, including (1) moral conviction, including attorneys' religious devotion; (2) natural, although sometimes unintentional, professional progression from traditional criminal defense to the greater complexity of capital matters; (3) the desire for excitement or an "adrenaline rush"; (4) prestige and ambition; (5) oppositional personalities and past psychological trauma; and (6) financial gain. Gould and Barak, *Capital Defense.*

9

Mitigation and the Death Penalty

Successes, Obstacles, and Forced Constraints

RUSSELL STETLER

Mitigation is the engine of self-destruction for the modern U.S. death penalty. This is not an example of intelligent (or unintelligent) design. Engineers now design land mines and rocket boosters to self-destruct to prevent malfunctions that endanger large numbers of innocent lives. However, no one person or institution designed the modern death penalty. Multiple legislatures crafted statutes and the Supreme Court of the United States shaped the final creation by applying constitutional principles. Over a half century, the modern death penalty has been well defined, and mitigation is a core element in the constitutional requirement of individualized sentencing mandated by the Eighth Amendment.[1] However, this requirement—meant to ensure fairness and to avoid arbitrary outcomes—has largely backfired and produced results as arbitrary as those it was striving to avoid.

As Carol Steiker and Jordan Steiker have astutely observed,

> The irony, of course, was that the Court seemed to be protecting as a matter of constitutional law the very discretion *Furman* [*v. Georgia*[2]] had identified as constitutionally problematic. But according to the Court, the discretion to *withhold* the death penalty based on mitigating factors is categorically different from the discretion to *impose* the death penalty based on amorphous perceptions of the aggravating aspects of the offense. So was born the central tension in American death penalty law: its simultaneous command that states cabin discretion of who shall die while facilitating discretion of who shall live.[3]

The effort to define mitigation in the broadest possible terms based on the Eighth Amendment has been a remarkable success. Nonetheless, in assessing the impact of mitigation on the fairness of the U.S. death penalty, we must recognize three key points: (1) it works in the majority of cases; (2) it fails in individual cases because of racism, inadequate funding of the defense function, and legal barriers insulating decision-makers from the power of mitigation; and (3) the structural forced choice of death or life without parole has so dehumanized people facing the death penalty that it has obscured the capacity for rehabilitation that mitigation might otherwise have demonstrated.

Mitigation's Breadth and Success

First, and most importantly, mitigation has worked. Throughout the modern era, death sentences have been rare.[4] The Death Penalty Information Center's census captured 8,842 cases in which a total of 9,820 death sentences had been imposed between the *Furman* decision in 1972 and January 1, 2022.[5] Regrettably, neither the Death Penalty Information Center nor any other data repository has tracked the number of cases in which prosecutors sought the death penalty. Although the total number of death sentences seems large at first glance (an overall average of nearly two hundred per year), that number must be compared to the immense universe of death-eligible cases. Jeffrey Fagan and colleagues attempted to estimate the number of cases that might have been prosecuted capitally in the period 1976 to 2003, using case characteristics data in the FBI Supplementary Homicide Reports.[6] This macrosurvey found 123,485 cases with death-eligible characteristics,[7] but it did not exclude homicides from states that did not authorize capital punishment, and it used broad parameters for death eligibility rather than actual statutory criteria. Even without a more precise comparison, it is clear that death sentences have been imposed in a tiny subset of eligible cases, which are, in turn, a fraction of the annual homicides in the United States (usually exceeding fifteen thousand).[8]

There are of course many reasons why death sentences are avoided in potentially eligible cases, including prosecutorial discretion (i.e., electing not to seek the death penalty or accepting negotiated dispositions). However, there is abundant evidence that mitigation has persuaded jurors to reject death sentences over and over, even in the most highly aggravated cases. These include not just high-profile cases, such as those of the so-called twentieth hijacker from September 11, Zacarias Moussaoui;[9] the Atlanta courthouse shooter, Brian Nichols;[10] the perpetrator of the Aurora, Colorado, movie theater massacre, James Holmes;[11] and Nikolas Cruz, who pled guilty to the Parkland, Florida, shootings in which fourteen high school students and three teachers were killed.[12]

Life outcomes rejecting the death penalty have been common in more mundane cases as well. To illustrate this point, my colleagues and I published a list of over six hundred cases in which jurors rejected the death penalty in three highly aggravated categories: child killing, cop killing, and multiple murder.[13] These categories are clear-cut, with no room for subjective interpretation of aggravating circumstances. They have also been identified by social scientists from the Capital Jury Project as the types of cases in which jurors thought that the death penalty was the only appropriate penalty when presented with case-type categories (compared to, for example, killing during another crime or killing by a gang member).[14]

The cases we identified span the entire history of the modern death penalty. Some thirty-five state legislatures responded to the Supreme Court's *Furman* decision in 1972 by passing new death penalty laws. Some sought to avoid unfettered jury discretion and arbitrary outcomes by making the death penalty automatic for a narrow category of murders, but the *Woodson* Court rejected this approach and established individualized sentencing as a constitutional requirement when the punishment is death. However, the Court approved new statutory frameworks that required a sentencing proceeding in which jurors could consider aggravating factors favoring execution and mitigating factors favoring life sentences. A footnote in the *Gregg* decision[15] specifically identified the mitigating factors proposed by the American Law Institute in its Model Penal Code as guidance intended to avoid capricious or arbitrary results:

(a) The defendant has no significant history of prior criminal activity.
(b) The murder was committed while the defendant was under the influence of extreme mental or emotional disturbance.
(c) The victim was a participant in the defendant's homicidal conduct or consented to the homicidal act.

(d) The murder was committed under circumstances which the defendant believed to provide a moral justification or extenuation for his conduct.

(e) The defendant was an accomplice in a murder committed by another person and his participation in the homicidal act was relatively minor.

(f) The defendant acted under duress or under the domination of another person.

(g) At the time of the murder, the capacity of the defendant to appreciate the criminality [wrongfulness] of his conduct or to conform his conduct to the requirements of law was impaired as a result of mental disease or defect or intoxication.

(h) The youth of the defendant at the time of the crime.[16]

It is hardly surprising that defense counsel were initially confused. Did these statutory factors prevent traditional arguments for mercy that rely on the defendant's background and character? A veteran public defender in California wrote in the syllabus of a 1978 Strategy Session on Death Penalty Trials that "most of the doubt and uncertainty lies within the penalty phase. Although strong arguments can be made for allowing the defendant to produce evidence going to such matters as common mercy, defendant's total value within the community, his character, history, and background, the more strict and severe interpretation is one that admits the production of evidence of only specifically enumerated factors."[17] The eight factors from the Model Penal Code include two, (a) and (h), that are either/or choices. In other words, factor (a) identifies whether a defendant has or does not have a significant history of criminal activity. The language was subject to interpretation, since it designated "criminal activity," not convictions, and adversaries could debate what made a history significant. However, the defense generally had to rely on police and prosecutors to concede this mitigating factor. Factor (h), youth, was undefined. It would be nearly three decades before the Supreme Court barred the execution of individuals whose capital offenses occurred prior to age eighteen.[18]

According to the Death Penalty Information Center execution database, twenty-two juveniles had been executed prior to this decision, and executions continue for individuals who were eighteen or nineteen at the time of the offenses, including, for example, Brandon Bernard and Christopher Vialva, executed in 2020 for federal crimes committed when they were eighteen and nineteen, respectively.[19] As a statutory mitigating factor, youth has not always been effective. Factor (c), victim participation, is simply rare. Few prosecutors seek the death penalty if the only deceased victim was a crime partner.

The remaining factors relate entirely to the time of the crime; the rest of the defendant's life is irrelevant. They are mainly imperfect versions of traditional affirmative defenses: extreme emotional disturbance or impairment that does not rise to the level of an insanity defense or diminished capacity but can be counted as mitigation; duress or relatively minor participation; and the accused's mistaken belief that he was morally justified in taking a life (i.e., self-defense). No wonder the California public defender was concerned about whether the new death penalty laws would be strictly and severely interpreted to allow only enumerated mitigating factors that made no mention of the adversities and vulnerabilities in someone's life or his positive qualities. In 2009, the American Law Institute deleted the death penalty provisions from the Model Penal Code because they simply did not work.[20]

Fortunately, the Supreme Court provided some guidance to confused defense counsel in the early years of the modern death penalty. James Woodson, an African American, had only been a lookout when two others robbed a convenience store, so when the Court required individualized sentencing in his case, some members may have been mindful of his relatively minor role. He had been drinking and was asleep in a trailer when two other men woke him, struck him, and threatened him to compel his participation in the robbery.[21] What little is known of Woodson from the Supreme Court opinion might have fit neatly under the model mitigating factors for duress and relatively minor participation.

Sandra Lockett was another minor participant sentenced to death in the early years. She was prosecuted in 1975 under an Ohio statute that left sentencing to the court.[22] The case went to trial only three months after the crime. The prosecution theory was that Sandra was the getaway driver in a pawnshop robbery, although her lawyer disputed whether she was even in the car at the time of the homicide. The robbery involved Sandra's brother, a girlfriend, and two visitors from New Jersey. No one had a gun, but one of the out-of-state visitors had some bullets. He borrowed a gun from the pawnbroker, inserted the bullets, demanded money, and then killed the pawnbroker with a single shot when they struggled.

The Ohio statute required a death sentence unless one of three mitigating factors was established: victim participation, duress or coercion, or the offense was primarily the product of psychosis or mental deficiency. The judge reviewed a presentence report, as well as psychiatric and psychological assessments. However, the judge concluded that Sandra Lockett did not qualify for mercy under the statute.

There was mitigating evidence in the various reports that the judge received, but he said he could not consider it. Sandra was twenty-one at the time of the crime, and her prior record was minor. Her intelligence was average or low average. Although she had used heroin, her drug treatment had been effective, and she was "on the road to success." Her "prognosis for rehabilitation if returned to society was favorable."

The Ohio Supreme Court affirmed the death sentence, but the Supreme Court of the United States overturned it, holding that statutes could not preclude consideration of, *as a mitigating factor*, any aspect of a defendant's character or record, as well as the circumstances of the offense that defense counsel offered as a basis for a sentence less than death.

The Supreme Court applied the *Lockett* rule to overturn the Oklahoma death sentence of a sixteen-year-old boy who did not contest that he had killed a highway patrol officer.[23] The Court recognized that there was more mitigation than the mere fact of Monte Eddings's age, and its eloquent language inspired a focus on childhood as a central segment of mitigation investigation:

> But youth is more than a chronological fact. It is a time and condition of life when a person may be most susceptible to influence and to psychological damage. Our history is replete with laws and judicial recognition that minors, especially in their earlier years, generally are less mature and responsible than adults. Particularly "during the formative years of childhood and adolescence, minors often lack the experience, perspective, and judgment" expected of adults. Even the normal 16-year-old customarily lacks the maturity of an adult. In this case, Eddings was not a normal 16-year-old; he had been deprived of the care, concern, and paternal

attention that children deserve. On the contrary, it is not disputed that he was a juvenile with serious emotional problems, and had been raised in a neglectful, sometimes even violent, family background. In addition, there was testimony that Eddings' mental and emotional development were at a level several years below his chronological age. All of this does not suggest an absence of responsibility for the crime of murder, deliberately committed in this case. Rather, it is to say that just as the chronological age of a minor is itself a relevant mitigating factor of great weight, so must the background and mental and emotional development of a youthful defendant be duly considered in sentencing.[24]

The *Eddings* opinion also held that the sentencer had to do more than simply "consider" mitigation. The constitutional requirement was to give effect to the mitigation—not just consider it. The *Eddings* opinion also noted that there were virtually no limits on relevant mitigating evidence.

Just as *Lockett* and *Eddings* had established the importance of a capital defendant's developmental years (not just her mental condition and role at the time of the offense), the *Skipper* decision in 1986 stretched the mitigation boundaries to include post-offense capacity to change.[25] Ronald Skipper had been a model inmate, but the trial court in South Carolina excluded testimony on his adjustment because it did not reduce his culpability at the time of the offense. The Supreme Court of the United States agreed that it did not reduce his culpability but held that such evidence was nonetheless mitigating in that it could provide a basis for a sentence less than death. In addition, in cases where future dangerousness was alleged, it was crucial rebuttal.

The Court also reiterated the importance of narrowing the factors that made any case eligible for a potential death sentence. The Supreme Court overturned another Georgia death sentence because the state's highest court had relied on the subjective and ambiguous language that described the offense as "outrageously or wantonly vile, horrible, or inhuman."[26] The Court noted that almost every murder could be so characterized: "There is nothing in these few words, standing alone, that implies any inherent restraint on the arbitrary and capricious infliction of the death sentence."

For many years, the courts in Texas (and some elsewhere as well) interpreted mitigation as requiring a nexus, or connection, to the crime.

In 2008, the Supreme Court disabused the Texas courts of that notion, reiterated (quoting *Eddings*) that mitigation is virtually unlimited,[27] and stated simply that some things are "inherently" mitigating. Intellectual impairment, for example, is mitigating in its own right and does not require a showing of how it affected intent.

For mitigation evidence to be relevant, the threshold is low: it need only *tend* to prove or disprove some fact or circumstance that a fact finder *could* reasonably deem to have mitigating value, regardless of whether the fact finder accepts or rejects it.[28] Justice Anthony Kennedy even referred to "potentially infinite" mitigators.[29] Jurors need not be unanimous about mitigation,[30] which must be proved only by a preponderance of the evidence (not beyond a reasonable doubt).

One case summed up everything about the narrowing process of eligibility for capital punishment and the broad selection process to be sure that the penalty would be reserved for a minuscule, most deserving few. The Supreme Court had decided long ago that the death penalty was unconstitutional for the rape of an adult.[31] Three decades later, the Court held that execution was precluded even for the rape of a child. In *Kennedy v. Louisiana*, the Court said that the culpability of the "average murderer" is not sufficient for the death penalty. Capital punishment must "be limited to those offenders who 'commit a narrow category of the most serious crimes' and whose extreme culpability makes them 'the most deserving of execution.'"[32]

This case also provided a context for the Court's decisions barring the execution of people with intellectual disabilities (*Atkins v. Virginia*)[33] and those whose crimes occurred prior to age eighteen (*Roper v. Simmons*).[34] These categorical exemptions from execution were simply subsets of the vast universe of "average murderers" for whom the death penalty was unconstitutional and unfair.

The Duty to Investigate Mitigation

Just as the Supreme Court had expanded the parameters of mitigation under the Eighth Amendment in the 1980s and 1990s, a line of cases beginning in 2000 established a duty to conduct thorough mitigation investigation under the Sixth Amendment. In all these cases, post-conviction, counsel conducted the investigations that should have been done by trial counsel. In the case of Terry Williams, trial counsel had waited until a week before trial to look into mitigation.[35] The result was too little, too late. In this Virginia case, the Supreme Court held that "trial counsel did not fulfill their obligation to conduct a thorough investigation of the defendant's background."[36]

Three years later, the Court elaborated on this duty in the Maryland case of Kevin Wiggins, finding that, despite "well-defined norms," his public defenders had abandoned their mitigation investigation after acquiring "only rudimentary knowledge of his history from a narrow set of sources."[37] The Court outlined a broad range of investigative areas consistent with the breadth of mitigation, including "medical history, educational history, employment and training history, *family and social history*, prior adult and juvenile correctional experience, and religious and cultural institutions."[38] The *Wiggins* Court also stressed that if the jury had been able to place Wiggins's "excruciating life history on the mitigating side of the scale, there is a reasonable probability that at least one juror would have struck a different balance."[39]

In the case of Ronald Rompilla from Pennsylvania, the Supreme Court stressed the importance of record gathering "even when a capital defendant's family and the defendant himself have suggested that no mitigating evidence is available."[40] In other words, the obligation to investigate is there, even if the client is "uninterested," "bored," and "actively obstructive" in sending trial counsel off in pursuit of false leads.[41]

In a case from Florida, the Supreme Court criticized the state courts for discounting evidence of William Porter's childhood maltreatment because he was fifty-four years old at the time of the capital offense. The Court also credited the power of mitigation based on Porter's service to his country and combat trauma during the Korean War. The Court explained negative behavior in his history (including alcohol abuse and going AWOL) as understandable in light of Porter's struggle to return to normality after returning from the war.[42]

In a Georgia case, trial counsel presented seven mitigation witnesses to say that Demarcus Sears came from a loving, middle-class family who would be devastated by his execution. The Court said that a mitigation theory that was "reasonable in the abstract" did not excuse a failure to conduct a thorough mitigation investigation that would have discovered major mental health evidence.[43] According to the Court, "This evidence might not have made Sears any more likable to the jury, but it might well have helped the jury understand Sears" and his crime.[44]

Recent Trends

In the post-*Furman* era, the Supreme Court of the United States has not been friendly to death-sentenced prisoners generally. Nonetheless, I have already shown that, in opinions largely written by justices appointed by Republican presidents prior to Donald J. Trump, the Court not only interpreted the Eighth Amendment to view mitigation in the broadest possible terms, but also established the obligation to conduct thorough mitigation investigation as a core element of capital defense counsel's obligations under the Sixth Amendment. Through the years, mitigation has prevailed.

Even when capital sentencing and executions were at their zenith in the modern era in the 1990s, annual death sentences never exceeded 315 (in 1996) and executions peaked at ninety-eight (in 1999), while the number of annual homicides has ranged from fifteen thousand to twenty thousand.[45] However, it would be wrong to infer that the carefully regulated capital punishment system has been working and only the "worst of the worst" have received death sentences and been executed. Mitigation has worked to forestall the application of the death penalty in an overwhelming majority of cases, but those that ended with death sentences and executions were just as random and capricious as what inspired Justice Stewart's comparison a half century ago to being "struck by lightning."[46]

In the twenty-first century, annual death sentences and executions have been in steep decline. There has been a twenty-year decline in the number of states conducting executions and imposing death sentences, from nearly thirty states imposing death sentences and over fifteen conducting executions in the early 2000s to seven states imposing death sentences and five conducting executions in 2023. The death row population has decreased from a peak of 3,682 in 2000 to 2,331 as of January 1, 2023. The number of executions, which peaked at ninety-eight in 1999, dropped to twenty-four in 2023.[47] Annual death sentences, which peaked in the 1990s at over three hundred, had decreased more than 90 percent to twenty-one in 2023. For the ninth consecutive year in 2023, fewer than thirty people were executed and fewer than fifty were sentenced to death.

Of course, these trends have been influenced by many factors, including declining murder rates, the availability of life without parole as a sentencing alternative, wrongful convictions and exonerations, increasingly long delays between sentences and executions, cost, public opinion (and related juror attitudes), geography, and changing prosecutorial regimes.[48] Access to lethal injection drugs and ongoing challenges to execution methods based on "botched" executions have independently contributed to declining numbers of executions, but the other factors affecting death sentencing have been mutually reinforcing. The declining murder rate[49] may reduce public fear of violent crime. Wrongful convictions, not just on death row but in the DNA exonerations that have made headlines, have shaken public confidence in irreversible sentences. Cost, appellate reversals, and long delays between sentencing and executions have given prosecutors second thoughts about seeking the death penalty, and the election of new prosecutors with reservations about the death penalty have contributed to the geographic disparities where only a small number of counties account for the majority of new death sentences and executions. Although polls continue to show a majority in favor of the death penalty (53% to 44% in a 2023 Gallup poll), a record-high 50 percent of Americans think the death penalty is applied unfairly (compared to 47% who think it is fairly applied). In the end, these many concerns may also have made jurors more receptive to mitigation.

Eleven states have abolished the death penalty in this century, and governors have imposed a moratorium on executions in three others.[50] What the Supreme Court once called "the consistency of the direction of change" is clear.[51] In the states that have funded—even underfunded—dedicated capital defense offices with guaranteed mitigation investigation and robust presentations at sentencing, there are almost no death sentences. Public opinion polls show a corresponding decline in popular support for the death penalty. It has become a damaged brand.

Mitigation's Failures

Nonetheless, for several reasons, mitigation has failed to prevent numerous wrongful death sentences and executions. There are many different reasons in individual cases, but the main causes are inadequate funding, racial effects (from systemic racism to implicit bias), and legal obstacles to post-conviction review. These problems affect every aspect of capital defense, not just the ability to investigate and present mitigation. They have resulted in wrongful convictions, as well as wrongful sentences and executions.

Inadequate Funding

The failure to adequately fund the work of developing mitigation in some jurisdictions continues to thwart effective representation.[52] Brandon Garrett scrutinized the impact of funding in the pretrial context. Before Virginia repealed its capital statute, Garrett contrasted how death sentences were reduced to near zero once a statewide capital defense system (instituted in 2002) guaranteed thorough investigation and presentation of mitigation. He noted succinctly, "It doesn't take a 'dream team' to turn the tide. It just takes a team, working out of a state-supported office, which saves money by using nonlawyers like social workers and mitigation investigators."[53]

As a practical matter, mitigation matters most in the trial courts, where adequate funding for defense counsel, mitigation investigation, and experts is often unavailable: no money, no mitigation. In the jurisdictions where state-funded capital defense agencies have been created—with dedicated staffing to investigate mitigation—such as New York, Georgia, and Virginia, death sentences became vanishingly rate.[54] However, indigent defense remains chaotic in most jurisdictions around the country. Some have state public defenders, some have public defenders at the county level, and some rely on private lawyers appointed by local judges. Funding at the trial level remains the difference between life and death in many jurisdictions.

Systemic Racism

In some cases, powerful mitigation simply cannot overcome what some social scientists have called "the empathic divide" between white jurors (and judges) and Black defendants. Racism so pervades the modern U.S. death penalty that sometimes no amount of mitigation will matter.[55] Two researchers who have studied capital jurors, Mona Lynch and Craig

Haney, described the "empathic divide" between white jurors and Black capital defendants[56] such that mitigation that might have inspired mercy in the case of white defendants falls short when the accused is a person of color. Another study even found a correlation between "stereotypical Black features" (e.g., broad nose, thick lips, dark skin) and "death worthiness" in cases involving white victims.[57]

These researchers built on the studies by the late Iowa law professor David C. Baldus, who, over his long career, examined race effects in numerous jurisdictions and employed painstaking statistical analyses to demonstrate how race of victim and race of defendant affected outcomes in real cases. His most famous study went before the Supreme Court of the United States in the case of Warren McCleskey.[58] Between 1973 and 1979, seventeen defendants were prosecuted in Fulton County (Georgia's most populous county) for murdering police officers. Only one, a Black man, was sentenced to death, and he was convicted of killing a white officer. Only one other case went to a sentencing proceeding. In that one, a white defendant who had killed a Black officer received a life sentence. This anecdotal information was suggestive, but the attorneys working on McCleskey's case insisted on having incontrovertible evidence before claiming that racial bias was at work. They wanted the sort of evidence that had been used effectively in other contexts, such as real estate and employment law, to support discrimination claims in violation of the Equal Protection Clause of the Fourteenth Amendment.

Baldus and his team sifted through massive amounts of data and crunched the numbers on all the murder cases in the state of Georgia in the 1970s, examining over two thousand cases and controlling for some 230 variables. After controlling for all the other variables in multiple regression analyses, they found powerful race-of-victim effects: defendants charged with killing white victims were 4.3 times more likely to receive a death sentence. Moreover, Black defendants who killed white victims had the greatest likelihood of receiving the death penalty.

More recent scholarship has not only confirmed the Baldus findings but also demonstrated that the race-of-victim effects on *executions* are even more striking than the effects on which defendants receive a death sentence. Analyzing the same Georgia prosecutions after the cases had reached their conclusions, two professors from the University of

Denver[59] found that the execution rate was roughly seventeen times greater in white victim cases.

Legal Obstacles

The law itself has sanctioned numerous undeserved executions by denying post-conviction opportunities to consider powerful mitigation that trial lawyers had failed to discover and present. Robert J. Smith and colleagues, for example, examined one hundred recent executions and found that 87 percent were carried out in spite of significant mitigation evidence, which often was barred from consideration by labyrinthine procedural obstacles.[60]

Warren McCleskey was doubly unlucky in the Supreme Court. When his racial-bias litigation failed, his lawyers raised another claim about how the prosecution had used a jailhouse informant (in fact, a jailed police officer) to elicit statements from him, in clear violation of the Court's precedents. The Supreme Court used this case to decree that all habeas corpus claims must be submitted in a single petition; in colloquial terms, petitioners should have only one bite of the habeas corpus apple. A few years later, this principle was codified in the Antiterrorism and Effective Death Penalty Act of 1996 (AEDPA), which created further obstacles to post-conviction review and most frequently closed the courthouse doors to new mitigation evidence that prior lawyers had failed to discover.

AEDPA and subsequent Supreme Court decisions have made it harder for federal judges to overturn state court appellate and post-conviction rulings. Counsel have an obligation to exhaust their state-court remedies (often before the same judges who had presided at trial).

Redemption: The Forgotten Potential for Rehabilitation

The humanizing mission of mitigation has been distorted by the statutory frameworks that offer a forced binary choice between death and life without parole. Once the prosecution has decided that a case is eligible for capital punishment, these are the only options in most contemporary death penalty jurisdictions. That decision channels the mitigation function into a limited practice that fails to challenge mass incarceration and implicitly accepts the premise that some crimes evince such depravity, or some persons are so damaged, that the accused should die in prison, whether naturally or at the hands of the state. Instead of taking on the fear of future dangerousness,[61] capital defenders have too often been content simply to say that prisons are effective in keeping the public safe. The relatively recent application of the methodology of mitigation from death penalty litigation to the cases of children sentenced to life without parole has reawakened our understanding of redemption[62] and the capacity to change, even for many individuals convicted of murder.

Life without parole (LWOP) is a sentencing option in every U.S. state except Alaska.[63] LWOP is an alternative to the death penalty in all the states that retain capital punishment, as well as under the federal and military capital schemes. This forced choice between execution and "death by prison" developed in spite of the fact that the majority of former death-sentenced prisoners who were released after the *Furman* decision did not go on to commit another crime.[64] One irony in the era of mass incarceration is that capital defense counsel have been forced to urge jurors to impose life-without-parole sentences rather than sentence their clients to execution. Everyone operates in a universe where it has been unthinkable to release anyone convicted of a death-eligible murder. Defense counsel often insist that the court instruct the jury that life without parole means exactly what it says.

We forget that it was not always like this. The most celebrated death penalty case of the early twentieth century was the kidnapping and murder trial of Nathan Leopold and Richard Loeb, two white Chicago teenagers whose wealthy families were able to retain the legendary attorney Clarence Darrow. Darrow's closing argument in 1924 went on for hours, and he persuaded the judge to spare the lives of both clients. Loeb was murdered in prison, but Leopold was later released on parole in 1958.[65]

While incarcerated in Stateville Penitentiary, Leopold and Loeb helped to establish a library and a rudimentary education program where they tutored other prisoners. Leopold also worked as an X-ray technician and volunteered as a test subject for a malaria experiment during the Second World War. He first faced the parole board in 1953 and was denied release. Five years later, he had the support of the Brethren Service Commission to work as a volunteer laboratory technician at Castañer Hospital in a tiny village in the mountains of central Puerto

Rico. The church had internally debated whether to sponsor Leopold, fearing that prison might have taught him "anti-social habits." Leopold flourished as a volunteer at the hospital, completed his term of service, and went on to earn a social work degree at the University of Puerto Rico. He remained in Puerto Rico, worked as a social worker, married, and in 1964 became the director of a $125,000 medical research project. He died in 1971.[66]

Sandra Lockett, an African American, was originally tried in 1975. She went to trial only three months after the crime in which she was alleged to have been only a getaway driver. The Supreme Court overturned her death sentence in 1978. When she returned to the trial court, she received a parole-eligible life sentence. She was released in 1993, married, raised a son, worked, and in her later years often spoke at law school discussions of the death penalty. In 2018, she participated in a symposium at the University of Akron Law School on the fortieth anniversary of her case.[67] Lockett subsequently had a stroke and died in 2020, having lived productively for more than a quarter century outside the prison walls.

Bobby Moore, also African American, was sentenced to death in Harris County, Texas, in 1980. This was long before Texas adopted life without parole as an alternative to the death penalty, and those sentenced to life were eligible for parole after serving twenty years. His lawyers litigated an intellectual disability claim for many years, but the Texas courts created their own rules for deciding who qualified for the exemption, relying on popular stereotypes rather than science. The U.S. Supreme Court twice ordered Texas to respect the clinical criteria of the medical community before the court of criminal appeals did so.[68] When Bobby Moore's death sentence was finally overturned, he became eligible for parole immediately. The parole board granted Moore's release in 2020 at age sixty. Moore has since been campaigning on behalf of those he left behind on death row.

Wilbert Rideau, an African American from Louisiana, was sentenced to death twice. His original prosecution in 1961 so deprived him of his rights that the U.S. Supreme Court labeled the trial "kangaroo court proceedings."[69] Rideau continued to litigate his case until 2005, when a jury found him guilty of a lesser degree of homicide, for which he had already served twice the maximum term of years. In his forty-four years of imprisonment, Rideau became the self-educated editor of the prison newspaper at Angola and earned numerous journalistic prizes. His career as a writer has continued. Rideau is the author of a powerful memoir, and he has been a frequent speaker at training seminars for lawyers and other programs on criminal justice reform.

Two hundred other prisoners have been released from death row because they were wrongfully convicted.[70] Failure to conduct thorough mitigation investigation has set aside many more death sentences, but the default punishment is almost always life without parole. Nonetheless, mitigation has had immense impact in the cases of prisoners who were originally sentenced to life without parole for crimes committed prior to age eighteen.[71] When the Supreme Court in *Miller* and *Montgomery*[72] gave these individuals a second chance at sentencing, lawyers and mitigation specialists began utilizing the methodology of mitigation not only to develop the evidence that might have been presented at their clients' original trials, but also to show how they have matured in prison and now bear little resemblance to the teenagers who were considered so depraved and permanently incorrigible that they were sentenced to die in prison. Their litigation aims at giving them a second chance and potentially an opportunity for release.

Over two thousand people received life without parole sentences for crimes they committed prior to age eighteen. Many of those who are seeking a second chance are now middle-aged prisoners who have spent decades behind bars. Those who have been released have benefited from rich presentations of mitigation evidence that demonstrates not only what should have been considered at the time of their trials but also their capacity for rehabilitation. Like Lockett, Moore, and Rideau, they help us to imagine what capital clients might look like decades into the future.

There is a risk that the binary choice of a sentence of death or life without parole has led to overpathologizing capital defendants and uncritical presentation of mental health evidence that suggests to jurors that these individuals are damaged—and dangerous—forever. Some experts respond to this implication of future dangerousness by simply saying that the structured setting of a maximum-security prison will incapacitate the individual effectively and minimize the risk that he will harm anyone. The individuals who were sentenced to LWOP as juveniles but are now free clearly have benefited from the brain development that we now understand continues years beyond adolescence. No one has yet had an opportunity to study other symptoms of trauma and mental illness that may have manifested for these individuals as youths and how they managed to survive prison, mature, and overcome previously diagnosed conditions. Given the evidence that the carceral environment exacerbates mental disorders, it could be important to examine the lives of these former prisoners to understand their transformations and to include these capacities when we think about mitigation in the years ahead.

Conclusion

I recognize that death sentences and executions have been imposed in spite of mitigation, and that the death-versus-LWOP framework has had unintended consequences that have affected mitigation practice. However, this recognition should not obscure or diminish my main points. Mitigation matters. Mitigation works. For the overwhelming majority of people who have faced capital prosecution, it has saved them from execution. It has given jurors the evidence they need to render reliable and empathic moral sentencing decisions. And it has been the driving force of the modern death penalty's self-destruction.

Bryan Stevenson has observed that with regard to racial justice, we won the legal battle with school integration and legislative enactments promoting civil rights, voting rights, and fair housing, but we lost the narrative battle because the ideology of white supremacy continues to prevail.[73] I want to suggest that with regard to the death penalty, we have lost the legal battle (with the impact of Donald J. Trump's appointments on the whole federal judiciary, especially on the Supreme Court), but we are winning the narrative battle. We are succeeding in telling mitigating, humanizing stories about capital clients, not just in court but in the realm of public opinion.

The barriers to effective mitigation that I have identified—systemic racism, inadequate indigent defense funding, and legal obstacles to postconviction review of constitutional claims—have broader consequences than their impact on mitigation, and they must be addressed in more general efforts at criminal law reform. However, until such reforms are enacted, we must expect the barriers to continue to thwart the mitigation function.

The individuals sentenced to die in prison for crimes they committed as children have given us an opportunity to examine hundreds of cases of people who have demonstrated their redemptive capacity. What we learn from these cases must inform future mitigation practice and also strengthen the efforts to end mass incarceration and challenge life without parole as a sentencing option not just in capital cases but even for nonviolent offenses under "three strikes" and habitual offender laws.

The need for mitigation investigation and presentation will not cease with the abolition of the death penalty. The Supreme Court long ago described individualized sentencing as an enlightened policy in general and a constitutional requirement when the potential punishment is death.[74] A return to that enlightened policy is long overdue.

Notes

1 *Woodson v. North Carolina*, 428 U.S. 280, 304 (1976) ("While the prevailing practice of individualizing sentencing determinations generally reflects simply enlightened policy rather than a constitutional imperative, we believe that in capital cases the fundamental respect for humanity underlying the Eighth Amendment . . . requires consideration of the character and record of the individual offender and the circumstances of the particular offense as a constitutionally indispensable part of the process of inflicting the penalty of death." Citation omitted.).

2 *Furman v. Georgia*, 408 U.S. 238 (1972) (per curiam).

3 Carol S. Steiker and Jordan M. Steiker, *Courting Death: The Supreme Court and Capital Punishment* (Cambridge, MA: Harvard University Press, 2016), 165.

4 Russell Stetler and W. Bradley Wendel, "The ABA Guidelines and the Norms of Capital Defense Representation," *Hofstra Law Review* 41, no. 3 (Spring 2013): 635–96; Russell Stetler, "The Past, Present, and Future of the Mitigation Profession: Fulfilling the Constitutional Requirement of Individualized Sentencing in Capital Cases," *Hofstra Law Review* 46, no. 4 (Summer 2018): 1161–256.

5 The Death Penalty Census, Death Penalty Information Center. All DPIC databases and reports cited in this chapter can be found at https://deathpenaltyinfo.org/.

6 Jeffrey Fagan, Franklin Zimring, and Amanda Geller, "Capital Punishment and Capital Murder: Market Share and the Deterrent Effects of the Death Penalty," *Texas Law Review* 84 (2006): 1810–14.

7 *Id.* at 1818–19, table 1.

8 FBI Crime Data Explorer (CDE), FBI Uniform Crime Reporting Program, https://cde.ucr.cjis.gov (reporting 15,407 U.S. homicides in 2022).

9 Jerry Markus and Timothy Dwyer, "Jurors Reject Death Penalty for Moussaoui," *Washington Post*, May 4, 2006, A1.

10 Steve Visser and J. Scott Trubey, "Nichols Gets Life without Parole," *Atlanta Journal Constitution*, December 13, 2008.

11 Jack Healy, "Life Sentence for James Holmes, Aurora Theater Gunman," *New York Times*, August 8, 2015.

12 Patricia Mazzei and Nicholas Burgo-Burroughs, "Gunman Who Killed 17 in Parkland Is Spared the Death Penalty," *New York Times*, October 13, 2022.

13 Russell Stetler, Maria McLaughlin, and Dana Cook, "Mitigation Works: Empirical Evidence of Highly Aggravated Cases Where the Death Penalty Was Rejected at Sentencing," *Hofstra Law Review* 51, no. 1 (Fall 2022): 89–229. *See also* Stetler, "Past, Present, and Future" (predecessor study identifying nearly two hundred cases in the same categories where sentencer rejected death penalty).

14 Marla Sandys, Sara M. Walsh, Heather Pruss, and Dylan Cunningham, "Stacking the Deck for Guilt and Death: The Failure of Death Qualification to Ensure Impartiality," in *America's Experiment with Capital Punishment: Reflections on the Past, Present, and Future of the Ultimate Penal Sanction*, ed. James R. Acker, Robert M. Bohm, and Charles S. Lanier, 3rd ed. (Durham, NC: Carolina Academic Press, 2014), 411, table 1.

15 *Gregg v. Georgia*, 428 U.S.153, 193–95, n.44 (1976).

16 American Law Institute, Model Penal Code § 210.6 (Proposed Official Draft 1962).

17 Russell Stetler and Aurélie Tabuteau, "The ABA Guidelines: A Historical Perspective," *Hofstra Law Review* 45, no. 3 (Spring 2015): 735.

18 *Roper v. Simmons*, 543 U.S. 551 (2005). *See also Commonwealth v. Mattis*, Supreme Judicial Court of Massachusetts, No. SJC-11693, slip op. Jan. 11, 2024 (barring life without parole sentences for crimes committed prior to age twenty-one).

19 Execution Database, Death Penalty Information Center.

20 Stetler and Tabuteau, "ABA Guidelines," 734, n.23. *See also* Carol S. Steiker and Jordan M. Steiker, "No More Tinkering: The American Law Institute and the Death Penalty Provisions of the Model Penal Code," *Texas Law Review* 89, no. 2 (2010): 353, 354 (2010). The article includes their report to the American Law Institute that led to the withdrawal of the death penalty provisions in the Model Code (367–421).

21 *Woodson*, 428 U.S. at 283.

22 *Lockett v. Ohio*, 438 U.S. 586, 593 (1978).

23 *Eddings v. Oklahoma*, 455 U.S, 104, 108, 110 (1982).

24 *Id.* at 115–16.

25 *Skipper v. South Carolina*, 476 U.S. 1, 4–5 (1986).

26 *Godfrey v. Georgia*, 446 U.S. 420, 428 (1980).

27 *Tennard v. Dretke*, 542 U.S. 274, 285 (2008).

28 *McKoy v. North Caroina*, 494 U.S. 433, 440 (1990).

29 *Ayers v. Belmontes*, 549 U.S. 7, 21 (2006).

30 *Mills v. Maryland*, 486 U.S. 367, 384 (1988).

31 *Coker v. Georgia*, 433 U.S. 584, 598 (1977).

32 *Kennedy v. Louisiana*, 554 U.S. 407 (2008).

33 *Atkins v. Virginia*, 536 U.S. 304 (2002).

34 *Roper v. Simmons*, 543 U.S. 551 (2005).

35 *Williams v. Taylor*, 529 U.S. 362, 395 (2000).

36 *Id.* at 396.

37 *Wiggins v. Smith*, 539 U.S. 510, 524 (2003).

38 *Id.* (emphasis in original).

39 *Id.* at 537.

40 *Rompilla v. Beard*, 545 U.S. 374, 377 (2005).

41 *Id.* at 381.

42 *Porter v. McCollum*, 558 U.S. 30 (2010) (per curiam).

43 *Sears v. Upton*, 561 U.S. 945, 958 (2009) (per curiam).

44 *Id.* at 951.

45 Centers for Disease Control and Prevention 2020; FBI Uniform Crime Report, Crime in the U.S. 2019, Expanded Homicide Data Table 8 (reporting 2015–2019), https://ucr.fbi.gov/.

46 *Furman*, 408 U.S. at 309.

47 Death Penalty Information Center, *The Death Penalty in 2023: Year End Report* (Washington, DC: Death Penalty Information Center, December 1, 2023); Execution Database, Death Penalty Information Center.

48 *See* Stetler, "Past, Present, and Future," 1195–98.

49 *See* German Lopez, "Crime on the Decline: Murders Likely Fell at Record Speed Last Year," *New York Times*, January 11, 2024 (reporting decline in murder rate of 68 per 10,000 people in 2021 to an estimated 53 per 10,000 in 2023; prior high rate reached over 100 per 10,000 decades earlier).

50 "State by State: States with and without the Death Penalty," Death Penalty Information Center.

51 *Atkins*, 536 U.S. at 315.

52 *See* Meredith Martin Rountree and Robert C. Owen, "Overlooked Guidelines: Using the Guidelines to Address the Defense Need for Time and Money," *Hofstra Law Review* 41, no. 3 (Spring 2013): 623–34.

53 Brandon L. Garrett, *End of Its Rope: How Killing the Death Penalty Can Revive Criminal Justice* (Cambridge, MA: Harvard University Press, 2017), 113.

54 Stetler, "Past, Present, and Future," 1189–94.

55 *See also* Ngozi Ndulue, "Discrimination and Capital Punishment," chapter 6 of this book.

56 Mona Lynch and Craig Haney, "Mapping the Racial Bias of the White Male Capital Juror," *Law and Society Review* 45 (2011): 69–102.

57 Jenifer L. Eberhardt, Paul G. Davies, Valerie J. Purdie-Vaughns, and Sheri Lynn Johnson, "Looking Deathworthy: Perceived Stereotypicality of Black Defendants Predicts Capital Sentencing Outcomes," *Psychological Science* 17, no. 5 (May 2006): 383–86.

58 *McCleskey v. Kemp*, 481 U.S. 279 (1987).

59 Scott Phillips and Justin F. Marceau, "Whom the State Kills," *Harvard Civil Rights–Civil Liberties Law Review* 55 (2020): 585–656.

60 Robert J. Smith, Sophia Cull, and Zoë Robinson, "The Failure of Mitigation," *Hastings Law Journal* 65, no. 5 (2014): 1225–56.

61 John H. Blume, Stephen P. Garvey, and Sheri Lynn Johnson, "Future Dangerousness in Capital Cases: Always 'At Issue,'" *Cornell Law Review* 86, no. 2 (January 2001): 397–410.

62 Dana Cook, Lauren Fine, and Joanna Visser Adjoian, "*Miller, Montgomery*, and Mitigation: Incorporating Life History Investigations and Reentry Planning into Effective Representation of 'Juvenile Lifers,'" *The Champion*, April 2016, 44–46, 48–50, 52, 54–55, 58.

63 "Sentencing Alternatives: Life without Parole," Death Penalty Information Center.

64 James W. Marquart and Jonathan R. Sorenson, "A National Study of the *Furman-*Commuted Inmates: Assessing the Threat to Society from Capital Offenders," *Loyola Los Angeles Law Review* 23 (1989): 5–28 (finding that 80% of those released after the *Furman* decision converted their sentences to life with parole did not go on to commit another crime). *See also* Joan M. Cheever, *Back from the Dead: One Woman's Search for the Men Who Walked Off America's Death Row* (Chichester, UK: John Wiley and Sons, 2008), 5–6. Cheever reported that some were subsequently exonerated by courts or pardoned. She also noted that the majority of those who returned to prison did so for technical violations, such as failing to report a change of address or pay an administrative fee, or for nonviolent offenses (5–6).

65 Russell Stetler, "Keynote Address: Why Mitigation Matters, Now and for the Future," *Santa Clara Law Review* 61, no. 3 (Fall 2021): 699–743.

66 Haley Steinhilber, "A Second Chance at Life: From Convicted Murderer to Brethren Service Volunteer," Church of the Brethren, Brethren Historical Library and Archives, August 16, 2018, www.brethren.org/bhla/.

67 Margery B. Koosed, "Introduction to the '*Lockett v. Ohio* at 40 Symposium': Rethinking the Death Penalty 40 Years after the U.S. Supreme Court Decision," *ConLawNOW* 10, no. 1 (2018): 1–12.

68 *Moore v. Texas*, 581 U.S. 1 (2017); *Moore v. Texas*, 586 U.S. ___, 139 S. Ct. 666 (2019) (per curiam).

69 Wilbert Rideau, *In the Place of Justice: A Story of Punishment and Deliverance* (New York: Alfred A. Knopf, 2010), 726.

70 Innocence Database, Death Penalty Information Center.

71 Cook, Fine, and Adjoian, "*Miller, Montgomery*, and Mitigation."

72 *Miller v. Alabama*, 567 U.S. 460 (2012) (barring mandatory life without parole for juvenile homicide offenders); *Montgomery v. Louisiana*, 577 U.S. 190 (2016) (holding that Miller applies retroactively).

73 Bryan Stevenson, "'Just Mercy' Attorney Asks United States to Reckon with Its Racist Past and Present," NPR Fresh Air, January 20, 2020, http://www.npr.org.

74 *Woodson*, 428 U.S. at 304.

10

The Capital Jury as the Community's Conscience

From Illusion to Reality (and Back Again?)

SCOTT E. SUNDBY

The story of the capital jury's role in the United States' death penalty saga is a vivid reminder that unless legal rights and institutions have life breathed into them, they will remain unanimated. As this chapter will chronicle, in the beginning of the modern death penalty, the capital jury's ability to fulfill its role as the community's conscience was largely dormant because of unrepresentative jury selection, poor lawyering, and legal rules that failed to provide the defendant with the ability to meaningfully make his argument for his life to the jurors. It was only as those deficiencies were gradually addressed that life was slowly breathed into capital juries and they began to become powerful actors in bringing about a dramatic decline in the death penalty. The moral of the capital jury's creation story, therefore, is one that extends far beyond the death penalty: if society is going to rely on legal rights to imbue our justice system with legitimacy, we must recognize that a right does not stand alone; it can only become fully animated if interconnected legal doctrines and institutions breathe life into it.

The Capital Jury as the Community's Conscience

The jury has long been heralded as a centerpiece of the U.S. criminal justice system because of its potential to serve as a critical link between everyday citizens and the criminal justice system. As Alexis de Tocqueville famously wrote, "The institution of the jury . . . places the real direction of society in the hands of the governed . . . and not in that of the government. . . . [I]t invests the people, or that class of citizens, with the direction of society."[1] This link is especially important because by "anchoring convictions and punishment in the defendant's community," the jury serves to "legitimize the criminal justice system."[2]

Unsurprisingly then, the Supreme Court has relied heavily on the jury in its Sisyphean effort through the years to imbue the death penalty with legitimacy. In a 1968 case, *Witherspoon v. Illinois*, the Court expressly noted that "one of the most important functions any jury can perform in making [the death penalty decision] is to maintain a link between contemporary community values and the penal system—a link without which the determination of punishment could hardly reflect 'the evolving standards of decency that mark the progress of a maturing society.'"[3] And after the Court temporarily struck down the death penalty in the 1972 landmark case of *Furman v. Georgia*[4] because capital punishment was being applied in an "arbitrary and capricious" manner, the Court relied heavily on the role of the jury to justify its 1976 decision in *Gregg v. Georgia*[5] that allowed capital punishment to regain constitutional footing. Capital juries, the *Gregg* Court argued, would serve as a reassuring check on capital punishment's legitimacy going forward, because the juries would act as a "significant and reliable objective index of contemporary values."[6]

The Court in effect deemed the capital jury the Eighth Amendment's Geiger counter to measure and ensure that the death penalty was being used as a fair and just punishment. And if one accepted the capital jury as a "significant and reliable objective index of contemporary values," early measurements suggested that the Court, in allowing the death penalty to return, was acting in accord with community concerns over deterrence and retribution. In the two decades following the Court's renewed constitutional blessing, the number of annual death sentences trended steadily upward until its crescendo at 315 death sentences in 1996. And as the number of death sentences escalated, the judicial and political process relied heavily on the fact that a jury—twelve members drawn from the community—had heard all of the evidence and determined that the defendant deserved to die. The criminal justice system, in other words, actively used the capital jury to provide an imprimatur of rationality and fairness in conjunction with other procedural protections that the Court touted.[7]

This reliance on the capital jury to justify capital punishment, however, was a dangerously misleading illusion. If the capital jury was supposed to serve as the Court's Geiger counter, it was giving off an alarming number of false readings due to a combination of confounding factors that the Court was very slow to recognize. It was only when these factors began to be acknowledged and addressed that the capital jury was able to serve its vaunted role. To fully comprehend how these factors affected the jury's role in the rise and fall in the number of death sentences, it is first necessary to understand the jury's role in the death penalty decision.

The Capital Trial as Narrative

In a run-of-the-mill homicide trial, the jury is asked to decide a series of questions focused on historical facts. Did the defendant kill the victim? If she did the killing, did she intend to kill, or was it an accident? Did she act in self-defense because she believed she was in mortal danger? While the answers to these questions may be vigorously contested by the prosecution and defense and heatedly debated in the jury room, they do exist as a factual matter: either the defendant killed the victim or she didn't; she either intended to kill or she didn't; she either acted in self-defense or she didn't. And depending on the jury's answers to those questions of fact, the law will dictate whether a crime was committed or not. If she killed intentionally, it will be murder; if she did it in self-defense or with some other excuse the law recognizes, she will be acquitted. We know from DNA exonerations that juries do not always answer these questions correctly, but they are posed as questions of fact to which a factual answer exists.

The jury's death penalty decision, by contrast, is not an answer to a factual question. While the law attempts to dress up the death penalty decision in legal garb, at bottom it is not a question of fact but a naked moral question posed to each individual juror: Based on what you know of the crime, the defendant, and your own beliefs about punishment, does this defendant deserve to die?

The penalty phase of a capital trial, in other words, is all about storytelling because it is a modern-day morality tale. In trying to tell a story that calls for a death sentence, the prosecution will present a narrative about the heinousness of the murder, the tragic loss of the victims, and the defendant's remorselessness. The defense, by contrast, will highlight how the defendant's own life story was so full of tragedy (for example, severe child or sexual abuse) and hardship (such as mental illness) that it calls for an ending to the story that does not excuse the murder but acknowledges the defendant as human, even if deeply flawed. And, of course, it is the jurors as the audience for these two versions of the morality tale who decide after their deliberations which conclusion they choose to embrace on behalf of society.

The reliability of the jury's choice as a reflection of the community's conscience, therefore, is based on a number of presuppositions: that the storytellers will be capable at their craft; that the storytellers will be aware of everything about the defendant's character that they need to know to effectively weave their narrative; and that the jury as the audience reflects the community they are representing. In the immediate aftermath of *Gregg*, however, a jury's verdict of death far too often reflected a failure in the storytelling process rather than an informed expression of the community's conscience. Once improvements in the process occurred, juries started choosing life sentences with greater frequency.

The Storyteller

On paper, the Supreme Court in using the jury as its Geiger counter could point to a host of procedural protections that appeared to help ensure that a jury would have a full picture of the defendant and his life. Most notably, the Court had ruled as early as 1978 in *Lockett v. Ohio* that a defendant was entitled to present "any evidence about the defendant or the crime that argues for a sentence less than death."[8] This broad definition of what is called 'mitigating evidence' was essential in the Court's view because the Eighth Amendment required that before a defendant could be sentenced to death he must be judged not as part of a "faceless, undifferentiated mass" of murderers, but as a "unique[] individual."[9]

And, in the hands of a skilled defense attorney, *Lockett* mitigating evidence has indeed proven to be a powerful tool in persuading juries to return life sentences, even in extremely aggravated cases.[10] Presenting a defendant's 'case for life,' however, is a labor-intensive undertaking requiring considerable skill. Even in cases that ultimately result in a life sentence, many jurors are likely to favor a death sentence after the guilt-innocence phase, which is understandable given that they just convicted the defendant of first-degree murder. The defense attorney's challenge is to present a 'case for life' that humanizes her client and allows the jury to understand the defendant as someone with a unique life story.[11] The more a juror reports that they felt sympathy for the defendant, found the defendant likeable as a person, and imagined being in the defendant's situation, the more likely the juror is to cast her first vote for a sentence of life imprisonment.[12]

In making a persuasive case for life, though, the defense attorney must become as much storyteller as legal expert in presenting the case for life. This means that the lawyer in constructing the narrative for life must have an understanding of a diverse range of topics unique to capital litigation: matters such as how trial strategy affects jury's perceptions, how jurors view remorse, how jurors respond to different types of witnesses, how jurors respond to certain types of mitigation, and how to ensure that one's audience of jurors will be receptive to mitigating evidence.

In far too many cases in the decades immediately following *Gregg*, however, juries never fully heard the defendant's life story, never had the opportunity to give life to *Lockett*'s promise, were never given a meaningful chance to function as the community's conscience. These were cases where the lawyer failed to do even rudimentary mitigation investigation, such as interviewing family members, getting school records, or requesting mental health exams. One wishes that these failures could be chalked up to capital defenders still mastering the learning curve of how to tell the story for life and how to obtain the resources to find the material for the narrative, but the truth is far more distressing.

Attorneys were being appointed who had no business being in the courtroom let alone handling the most difficult and challenging cases in the criminal law. The case law is replete with sleeping attorneys, drunk attorneys, stoned attorneys, attorneys who despised their client and told the jury they despised them, attorneys who had been previously disbarred, attorneys who were about to be disbarred, and attorneys who had never handled a murder case let alone a death penalty case.[13] In short, forget about mastering a learning curve, these were attorneys who could not even find the classroom. And perhaps most scandalous of all, the judiciary largely turned a blind eye for a quarter of a century to these "walking violations of the Sixth Amendment [right to counsel]."[14]

Because poor lawyering had deprived the jurors of the defendant's story for life, the capital jury often was not functioning as the community's conscience. Lacking the defendant's life story was like asking an audience to judge Hamlet's moral culpability knowing only that he has caused the deaths of five victims, two stabbed by his own hand. And imagine that audience's later reaction when they learned of Hamlet's torments. Their reaction is what is often heartbreakingly on display when jurors learn *after* imposing a death sentence what a competent defense team would have presented as mitigation.[15]

Through a variety of means and fueled by public alarm at the number of DNA exonerations of death row inmates, capital lawyering eventually improved, especially in weeding out the worst of the worst lawyers. Studies by organizations such as the American Bar Association highlighted the abysmal state of capital representation and states began responding by passing minimum standards that a lawyer must meet before handling a capital case.[16] Indeed, the concern over competent capital representation reached such a level of national concern that President Bush pledged in his 2005 State of the Union "to fund special training for defense counsel in capital cases, because people on trial for their lives must have competent lawyers by their side."[17] Even the Supreme Court eventually began to reverse course and acknowledge the grim reality that incompetent attorneys were undermining its claim that the death penalty could be fairly administered.[18]

Unsurprisingly, once competent representation became far more prevalent, capital juries began returning life sentences in cases that undoubtedly would have been death sentences if they had not heard a compelling 'story for life.' The lesson is clear: if capital juries were to function as the community's conscience, a competent defense attorney was essential to giving them a full accounting of the defendant's life.

Developing the Characters and the Plot

Even the best storyteller, however, must have compelling material with which to work, and in a capital case this means an exhaustive investigation of the defendant's background and mental health. It is from this investigation that the witnesses will emerge who have the life stories and insights that will humanize the defendant for the jury.[19] Unsurprisingly, then, the rise of the mitigation specialist—the person charged with gathering the mitigation material that will become the narrative for life—is crucial to understanding why juries eventually began returning far more life sentences. From a few individuals who pioneered mitigation investigation after the death penalty was reinstituted following *Gregg*, mitigation specialists gradually developed into a discipline with extensive training and became recognized by the American Bar Association as a crucial and indispensable part of a capital defense team.[20]

A properly investigated and litigated capital case, however, is undeniably labor-intensive and expensive, especially compared to a murder case where the death penalty is not sought. We already have seen that far too many defense counsel did not understand the necessity of a thorough mitigation investigation in the years following *Gregg*, but, even for those who did, the funds and resources needed to undertake the mitigation investigation were frequently lacking. Eventually, however, courts came to understand that mitigation specialists were as fundamental to a capital defense as a lawyer trained in capital litigation and began providing the funding needed so that juries could hear the full production of the defendant's life story.

Other developments were necessary as well before the jury could begin to fulfill its role as the community's conscience. For instance, even jurors who are strongly moved by a defendant's story for life understandably will still choose a death sentence if they believe that the defendant might someday be released and have the chance to kill again. Predictably, therefore, as an increasing number of states made life-without-parole (LWOP) the alternative sentence to death, rather than a life sentence that would allow the defendant to someday be eligible for release, an increasing number of juries chose life sentences since their concerns about community safety could be assuaged without having to choose execution.[21] Even then, some states played off of jurors' concerns that a defendant might someday be released by keeping juries in the dark and refusing to tell them that if they chose a life sentence there would be no possibility of parole. Eventually, however, the Supreme Court recognized that capital juries could not fulfill their role if they were being misled as to the meaning of a life sentence, and required states to be honest with jurors and inform them that a life sentence was in fact without parole.[22]

Several other Supreme Court actions similarly aided capital jurors in hearing the full story before deciding between life and death. The Court, for example, in *Ake v Oklahoma*[23] required that indigent capital defendants have access to expert witnesses, such as psychiatrists, who are essential to the preparation of their defense. Prior to the Court's decision, the state could present *their* expert psychiatric witnesses without an indigent defendant having a reciprocal right to their own expert; the result was, of course, that the jury would hear only the prosecution's side regarding the defendant's sanity or mental health mitigation. This right to make sure that the jury hears from experts on both sides has been extended by courts to other essential experts such as DNA and forensic experts.[24]

The Court has over time also exercised increasing scrutiny of prosecutorial failures to turn over what is known as "*Brady* material," evidence that tends to show that the defendant was innocent or is not deserving of the death penalty.[25] While under current law a prosecutor has a constitutional duty to turn over such exculpatory evidence, it is the prosecutor herself who makes the decision whether the evidence qualifies as exculpatory. This creates an obvious problem of cognitive dissonance: The prosecutor who presumably believes in her case must identify for the defense evidence that she possesses and undermines her case. As would be expected, this psychologically difficult (if not impossible) requirement has led to a number of cases where the prosecutor's failure to turn over *Brady* evidence has resulted in the conviction of innocent individuals who were sentenced to Death Row.[26]

Eventually the Court, much as it did with ineffective assistance of counsel claims, gradually awakened to the fact that a key constitutional right was being underenforced. In a string of capital cases, the Court began to stress with renewed vigor the prosecutor's constitutional obligation to turn over exculpatory evidence that raised doubts about the jury's verdict and death sentence.[27] These cases focused not only on proof going to the defendant's innocence, such as evidence casting doubt on the veracity of key prosecution witnesses, but also evidence that juries could have seen as arguing against a death sentence, such as the defendant's severe intoxication at the time of the crime.[28] Although the Court's efforts still fall far short of the need to ensure that prosecutors turn over all exculpatory evidence, more rigorous enforcement of *Brady* is another example of how better execution of other rights is necessary for ensuring capital juries knew the full story before entering the jury room to deliberate.

The Jury as Audience

We have seen so far how dramatic improvements in the quality of capital defense, the development of the field of mitigation specialists, and strides toward providing juries with better information all contributed to helping the capital jury to hear the full "story for life" and were crucial to the eventual dramatic decline in the number of juries returning death sentences. However, even having a lawyer with Shakespearean skills weave a compelling narrative for life is pointless if the narrative is told to an audience that is unreceptive to the possibility of a life sentence for a murder. The final aspect of understanding the capital jury's role in the decline of the death penalty thus requires us to look at how capital juries themselves changed over time.

As we all know from personal experience—and social science studies have confirmed[29]—an individual's world view largely dictates how he or she perceives a situation. Even the most stunning Picasso will not impress someone who does not believe that abstract art is "real art." Unsurprisingly, it turns out that whether a capital juror finds a defendant's mitigating evidence compelling also largely turns on one's worldview. Having a diverse jury that is representative of the entire community and receptive to the idea of mitigation, therefore, is an absolute prerequisite if the jury is to function as the community's conscience.

This, however, was not the case in the decades immediately following *Gregg*. The composition of capital juries was distinctly tilted toward "placing a thumb [on] death's side of the scales"[30] for two primary reasons: the lack of diversity on capital juries and the weighting of juries toward jurors favoring death.

Making Juries More Diverse and Representative

The death penalty's underpinnings in racial discrimination are well documented. Dating back to the nation's founding and on through the Civil War, in many states the law expressly authorized the death penalty only for Blacks, both enslaved and free, for certain crimes.[31] Although express forms of death penalty racism eventually were banished, a number of studies have shown that less overt but every bit as pernicious forms of discrimination persist, such as the fact that someone who kills a white victim is far more likely to receive the death penalty than someone who murders a Black victim.[32] The sources of discrimination are varied, but the lack of jury diversity is undeniably one that contributed to the high number of death sentences at capital punishment's peak.

One study in particular discovered the profound effect that the presence or absence of minority jurors can have on the likelihood of a death sentence. Where a Black defendant was on trial, the inclusion of a single Black male juror reduced the rate of death verdicts by almost thirty percent from 71.9 percent to 42.9 percent. As a statistically independent factor, if five or more white male jurors were on a jury the death sentence rate *increased* by forty percentage points.[33] The study found that Black jurors on the whole brought a different perspective to the evidence in a capital trial that was more favorable to a life sentence. Black jurors were particularly more likely than white jurors to hold views favorable to the defendant on three issues that are often decisive for jurors in deciding between life and death: harboring lingering doubts about the defendant's guilt or role in the crime; having a belief that the defendant was remorseful; and in not seeing the defendant as posing a future danger.[34]

Unsurprisingly, prosecutors in seeking to shape the jury to favor a death sentence often tried to exclude Black jurors. One of the most prevalent ways was through the use of *peremptory challenges*.[35] In picking the jury, each side is given a certain number of peremptory challenges that allow them to remove a potential juror for any reason they want (as compared to a *challenge for cause* through which a potential juror is removed because they cannot be fair or follow the law—for example, because they knew the victim of the crime or had read news accounts and already made up their mind on the defendant's guilt). Because prosecutors were often using peremptory challenges to strike all of the potential Black jurors, capital defendants, many of whom were Black, frequently were being convicted and sentenced to death by all-white juries.

In 1986, the Supreme Court finally stepped in, ruling in *Batson v. Kentucky*[36] that attorneys using a peremptory strike to remove a potential juror solely because of their race violated the Equal Protection Clause (the Court later extended the ruling to also prohibit strikes based on gender). While *Batson* has justifiably been criticized as not having fully ended racial discrimination in the use of peremptories, the decision undoubtedly has led to the seating of more Black jurors on capital juries. Prosecutors contemplating using a peremptory challenge on a minority juror must now anticipate a *Batson* challenge and the possibility of a death sentence later being reversed if they proceed with the peremptory. This deterrent effect against using peremptories to strike minority jurors has likely been strengthened by a series of Supreme Court rulings in capital cases harshly condemning the lower courts' failures to find *Batson* violations.[37] And, keep in mind, although *Batson* is anything but a foolproof safeguard against the removal of minority jurors, if a prosecutor's concerns over facing a *Batson* challenge results in even one more Black juror being seated on a capital jury in a case, the odds increase dramatically that the audience will be far more receptive to the defense's story for life.

The Colorado Method: Leveling the Playing Field and Enabling Jurors to Vote Their Conscience

The second primary change in jury composition that led to the decline in death sentences was a change in who the Supreme Court deemed "qualified" to sit on a capital jury based on their views about capital punishment. Even prior to *Gregg*, it had long been held that before an individual could sit on a capital jury, they must first be "death qualified;" that is, since a juror must follow the law, and the law allows for the death penalty as a possible sentence, if a potential juror's personal beliefs would "substantially impair" them from voting for a death sentence or conviction, they must be dismissed "for cause." Potential jurors who are excluded from the jury on this basis are referred to as "*Witherspoon* excludables."[38] As one would expect, social science studies have shown that a "death-qualified" jury (i.e., a jury consisting only of jurors willing to impose a death sentence) tends to be not only more likely to favor a death sentence but also more prone to convict in the first place. Death-qualified jurors also are more likely to be white and male.[39]

In 1992, the Supreme Court finally took an important step in leveling the playing field in a case called *Morgan v Illinois*.[40] Recall that even when the law recognizes a death sentence as a permissible sentence, the law *also* requires that a juror first consider mitigating circumstances and a life sentence before imposing it. In other words, just as the Supreme Court has said that a juror cannot serve who could never vote for a death sentence, a juror who would always impose a death sentence for murder and never consider a life sentence (usually on an "eye for an eye" rationale) likewise should be excluded from the capital jury because they too cannot follow the law; consequently, the Court held, a juror must be "life-qualified" as well as "death-qualified" to ensure that they can follow the law. Potential jurors who are dismissed on this basis are referred to as "*Morgan*-excludables" or "reverse-*Witherspoon* excludables."

Morgan had several important effects in making capital juries more likely to return life sentences. Most obviously, it meant that juries could no longer start off with locked-in votes for death no matter how strong the case for life. Given the social dynamics of how juries reach a death sentence—the social science shows that the pressure on an individual juror to vote death increases with each additional juror who votes for death[41]—even one juror on the jury automatically voting death (and, of course, there may be more) immediately increases the chances a jury will return a death sentence. Moreover, and unsurprisingly, jurors who are convinced that the death penalty is the *only* appropriate sentence for the defendant tend to be the most zealous voices in the jury room in arguing for death and the most likely to strongly pressure jurors voting for life to change their votes.[42] By holding that *Morgan*-excludables could no longer serve on capital juries, therefore, the Court altered both the composition and the internal dynamics of capital juries.

Morgan also had one more critical effect. The holding provided further impetus to what capital defense attorneys already were beginning to understand: a potential juror's attitudes about the death penalty are a critical tool for divining which jurors will be most receptive to mitigating evidence and whose presence on the jury would thus increase the chances of a life sentence. Even when we exclude jurors at both ends of the spectrum (i.e., jurors who would always vote death and those who would always vote life), a wide range of attitudes about the death penalty will exist among the remaining pool of jurors. Some of those jurors, for example, may initially be open to a life sentence for someone they convict of murder, but after further questioning it turns out they will only consider certain types of mitigation and not others, or will not vote for life for certain types of murder (for example, if the victim was a child). These views can only be ascertained, however, if voir dire (the process when potential jurors are questioned) allows inquiry into a potential juror's attitudes on the death penalty.

Questions based on *Morgan* provided the means during voir dire to more accurately ascertain potential jurors' views on the death penalty decision. This allowed defense attorneys to better identify jurors who are not excludable (because theoretically they are open to a life sentence) but have such strong leanings toward a death sentence that they are unlikely to vote for life. Since both the prosecution and defense are given a limited number of peremptory challenges to strike potential jurors whom they believe are not likely to favor their side, more information can be extremely helpful in using peremptory challenges most effectively. With a more accurate sense of whether a potential juror is likely to give much weight to their mitigation, defense attorneys can exercise their peremptory challenges to remove jurors who are unlikely to be persuaded by the defense's case for life (some jurors, for instance, are highly skeptical of mental illness or addiction as mitigation evidence, but this evidence plays an extremely important role in many defendants' cases for life).

This use of voir dire that focuses intently on jurors' attitudes about the death penalty as the crucial touchstone for capital jury selection is sometimes referred to as the "Colorado method," based on its development by several leading Colorado public defenders.[43] The method is effective not only because it identifies jurors who are receptive to mitigation, but also because it entails constantly reinforcing for the jurors, beginning with voir dire, that the law itself sees the decision of whether to sentence the defendant to death as a personal moral decision for each individual juror. In what might be thought of as the "Capital Jurors' Bill of Rights," the method ensures that jurors understand (1) that each juror must make their own personal assessment of mitigation in deciding between a life and death sentence, (2) that the law never requires a juror to vote for death, and (3) that jurors must respect each other's judgment.[44]

By repeatedly stressing to jurors that the death penalty determination is a moral decision qualitatively distinct from the "usual" factual decisions that jurors are asked to make (e.g., whether the defendant pulled the trigger), the method has helped empower jurors who favor a life sentence to resist the pressures of jurors who are insisting on a death sentence. Once the entire jury understands that the death penalty decision is meant to be an individual juror's moral decision, it becomes far less likely that other jurors will "browbeat" a juror who is in favor of a life sentence, since no one person can claim to know what the correct moral decision for another person is based on their values and beliefs. Likewise, if a juror understands that they are entitled to their own moral opinion, an individual juror in favor of a life sentence is far more likely to be able to resist their own self-doubts and other jurors' pressure to change their vote if they find themselves alone in their judgment.

The elimination of "automatic death jurors" and the empowering of individual jurors favoring life sentences yielded predictable outcomes. In states where a single juror's vote for life results in a life verdict, the number of life sentences rose. And even in states that require that a life sentence be unanimous, jurors favoring life became increasingly able to resist majority pressures, leading to a "hung jury" rather than a death sentence.[45]

The Cascade Effect and the Death Penalty's Decline

The capital jury's role in bringing about the decline of capital punishment went beyond refusing to return death sentences in cases where the prosecution had sought death. As juries across the nation returned life verdicts in cases that would likely have resulted in a death sentence in the immediate post-*Gregg* era, a cascade effect was created as other actors in the legal system took notice.

Prosecutors now knew that filing a capital case and seeking the death penalty meant that the defense would be far better funded and more capable than in a noncapital case. The prosecution would be facing at least two experienced attorneys who would be trained in capital litigation and have access to expert witnesses. In addition, the demand on state and local resources to fund a capital prosecution had to be taken into account, given the large sums spent seeking the death penalty. As juries returned life sentences even in cases where the aggravating evidence was extremely strong (e.g., in cases with multiple victims, child victims, or law enforcement victims), the cost/benefit calculus for prosecutors began to skew against pursuing death sentences. From a prosecutor's viewpoint, it often made more sense to make a guilty plea agreement for a life sentence than to spend enormous sums on a capital trial that was likely to end in a life sentence anyway.[46]

Legislatures and the public also started to question the wisdom of maintaining an expensive system of capital punishment in the face of the dwindling number of death sentences, especially after a jury would return a life sentence in a notorious case like that of James Holmes, whose attack in an Aurora, Colorado theater left twelve dead and seventy wounded.[47] As a former proponent of Colorado's death penalty who came to support abolition remarked, after life sentences were returned for Holmes and the defendant in another Colorado case who had stabbed five people to death, "The juries sent a message to our public officials that it was time to abolish the death penalty."[48] In states that legislatively abolished the death penalty, like Virginia and Colorado, the fact that no jury had imposed a death sentence in the decade preceding abolition made it far less politically risky for legislators to vote for abolition.

Once capital juries, therefore, were given the chance to actually function as the community's conscience, they played a pivotal role in the decline of the death penalty. It turned out that when the humanity of a defendant was brought vividly and fully to life—when jurors learned of a defendant's mental illness or the horrendous abuse he suffered as a child and also saw that he was loved by his family—even jurors who were death-qualified would often choose life over death. And as these individual juries began consistently spurning death in favor of life even in cases that had highly sympathetic victims or particularly gruesome facts, the community as a whole started to notice and to turn away from capital punishment. In a very real sense, then, the capital jury was living up to Tocqueville's grand vision of the jury Still, before any champagne corks are popped in celebration of the capital jury fulfilling its noble role, we must not forget the far more sobering part of the saga: no right, including that of the jury, can live up to its noble intentions unless the surrounding law and legal actors first bring it to life.

Postscript

As this chapter was being finalized, events in Florida demonstrated once again the important role the capital jury will play in the future of the death penalty. Like other states, Florida had experienced a distinct downturn in the number of juries imposing death sentences. The most high-profile rejection of the death penalty was in the case of Nikolas Cruz, who killed seventeen classmates and staff (and injured seventeen others) in a mass shooting at Parkland High School in February 2018. Even after viewing the highly graphic evidence and hearing heart-wrenching victim impact testimony, three of the twelve jurors found that the compelling mitigating evidence presented by the defense called for sparing Cruz's life.

In other states, juries' rejections of death sentences in similar cases had prompted the state legislatures to retire the death penalty. But Florida governor Ron DeSantis, eyeing a run for the White House, called for changing the rules to make it far easier to obtain a death sentence; if prosecutors could no longer obtain death sentences under the traditional standard of a unanimous jury of twelve, Florida would simply move the goalposts to make it easier for prosecutors. Since the Cruz case had three jurors voting for life, the state enacted legislation allowing a death sentence to be imposed if only eight jurors voted for death.

It remains to be seen if the legislation survives constitutional scrutiny, but Florida's actions highlight the primary theme of this chapter: capital juries are representative of community sentiment only if they are given the means to live up to their constitutional tasks. As the Cruz life sentence demonstrated, even in the most aggravated murder case, competent counsel and a skilled mitigation specialist are almost always able to present a compelling case for life that will convince some jurors.

The only way to obtain the number of death sentences necessary to justify the elaborate and expensive apparatus of capital punishment is to deliberately skew the jury's operation toward returning a sentence of death. But manipulating the rules to obtain more death sentences, as Florida has done, comes at a price. When the rules render powerless jurors who vote for a life sentence—as much as one third of the jury—then the legal system has forfeited its ability to claim that the death penalty is justified as a reflection of a community's values and sentiments.

Notes

1 Alexis de Tocqueville, *Democracy in America*, ed. Philip Bradley (New York: Vintage Books, 1945), 293–94.

2 J. Harvie Wilkinson III, "In Defense of American Criminal Justice," *Vanderbilt Law Review* 67 (2014): 1099, 1159. A less romantic view of the jury is reflected in Mark Twain's famous quip that jury selection places a premium on "ignorance, stupidity, and perjury."

3 391 U.S. at 519 & n.15 (1968) (quoting *Trop v. Dulles*, 356 U.S. 86, 101(1958)).

4 408 U.S. 238 (1972).

5 428 U.S. 153 (1976).

6 *Id.* at 181.

7 *See, e.g., Penry v. Lynaugh*, 492 U.S. 302, 340 (1989) (refusing to adopt a ban on imposing the death penalty on intellectually disabled defendants because "[a jury] can consider and give effect to [intellectual disability] in imposing sentence"); *McCleskey v. Kemp*, 481 U.S. 279, 311–13 (1987) (heralding the role of the jury in assuring fairness of death sentences despite statistical studies suggesting racial bias). In rare instances, the Court did use the fact that juries were rarely returning death sentences for certain types of crimes as a justification for not allowing the death penalty. *See, e.g., Enmund v. Florida*, 458 U.S. 782 (1982) (death penalty not allowed for felony murder if the defendant was not the triggerman or did not foresee likelihood of death).

8 438 U.S. 586 (1978).

9 *Woodson v. North Carolina*, 428 U.S. 280, 304 (1976).

10 One study found that juries had returned life sentences in over two hundred cases between 1979 and 2018 involving child victims, law enforcement victims, or multiple victims—the types of victims that studies have found jurors are most likely to view as warranting a death sentence. *See* Russell Stetler, "The Past, Present, and Future of the Mitigation Profession: Fulfilling the Constitutional Requirement of Individualized Sentencing in Capital Cases," *Hofstra Law Review* 46 (2018): 1161.

11 John H. Blume, Sherri Lynn Johnson, and Scott Sundby, "Competent Capital Representation: The Necessity of Knowing and Heeding What Jurors Tell Us about Mitigation," *Hofstra Law Review* 36 (2008): 1035, 1037–38. *See generally* Scott Sundby, *A Life and Death Decision: A Jury Weighs the Death Penalty* (New York: St. Martin's Press, 2005), 133–61 (describing how defense counsel changed the jurors' views by humanizing the defendant).

12 Stephen Garvey, "The Emotional Economy of Capital Sentencing," *New York University Law Review* 75 (2000): 25, 63.

13 *See generally* Stephen B. Bright, "Counsel for the Poor: The Death Sentence Not for the Worst Crime but for the Worst Lawyer," *Yale Law Journal* 103 (1994): 1835 (summarizing capital cases with abysmal lawyering). For a poignant in-depth look at one case, *see* "The Lawyer Who Drank His Client to Death" in Marc Bookman, *A Descending Spiral: Exposing the Death Penalty in 12 Essays* (New York: New Press, 2021), 77–96.

14 David L. Bazelon, "The Defective Assistance of Counsel," *University of Cincinnati Law Review* 42 (1973): 1, 4.

15 On learning that they had not heard compelling mitigating evidence, jurors often express regret and join the defense's efforts to overturn the death sentence. *See, e.g.*, Robert Patrick, "Juror Who Voted to Execute Glendale Killer Now Hopes for Mercy," *St. Louis Post-Dispatch*, December 22, 2015.

16 Scott E. Sundby, "The Death Penalty's Future: Charting the Crosscurrents of Declining Death Sentences and the McVeigh Factor," *Texas Law Review* 84 (2006): 1929, 1945–47.

17 President George W. Bush, State of the Union Address, *Washington Post*, February 3, 2005.

18 Sundby, "Death Penalty's Future," 1947. Some states that had a particular poor history of capital lawyering, such as Virginia, Georgia, and North Carolina, established statewide capital defense units that dramatically improved the overall quality of capital defense work. *Id.*

19 Blume, Johnson, and Sundby, "Competent Capital Representation," 1037–42.

20 Stetler, "Past, Present, and Future."

21 Sundby, "Death Penalty's Future," 1941–45.

22 *Simmons v. South Carolina*, 512 U.S. 154 (1994); *Shafer v. South Carolina*, 532 U.S. 36 (2001).

23 470 U.S. 68 (1985).

24 *See Rey v. State*, 897 S.W.2d 333 (Tex. Crim. App. 1995) (en banc) (cataloguing cases extending *Ake* to nonpsychiatric experts and holding that *Ake* gave defendant right to appointment of pathologist).

25 373 U.S. 83 (1963).

26 As of 2020, 185 individuals on death row had been exonerated. Innocence Database, Death Penalty Information Center, https://deathpenaltyinfo.org/. Perjury and official misconduct are the leading causes of wrongful convictions of death row exonerees. Robert Dunham, "The Most Common Causes of Wrongful Death Penalty Convictions: Official Misconduct and Perjury or False Accusation," Death Penalty Information Center, May 31, 2017, https://deathpenaltyinfo.org/.

27 *Kyles v. Whitley*, 514 U.S. 419 (1995) (*Brady* applies where "cumulative" effect of withheld evidence would be exculpatory); *Strickler v. Greene*, 527 U.S. 263 (1999) (failure to turn over exculpatory evidence in police files violated *Brady* even though prosecutor unaware of the evidence); *Banks v. Dretke*, 540 U.S. 668 (2004) (prosecutors' failure to turn over key exculpatory evidence like a state witness's prior inconsistent statements rendered trial unfair); *Cone v. Bell*, 556 U.S. 449 (2009) (suppressed evidence of defendant's drug use at time of crime was possible *Brady* material as to sentencing even if not material as to guilt); *Smith v. Cain*, 565 U.S. 73 (2012) (defendant's conviction reversed where the prosecution failed to turn over a sole eyewitness's initial statements that he could not have not seen the intruders' faces and could not describe them). *Wearry v. Cain*, 135 S. Ct. 1002 (2016) (reversing capital conviction for failure to turn over exculpatory evidence).

28 *Cone v. Bell*, 556 U.S. 449 (2009) (suppressed evidence of defendant's drug use at time of crime was possible *Brady* material as to sentencing, even if not material as to guilt).

29 The Cultural Cognition Project illustrates this phenomenon through an interdisciplinary look at various scenarios. *See* http://www.culturalcognition.net/.

30 The phrase comes from *Sochor v. Florida*, 504 U.S. 527, 532 (1992).

31 Stuart Banner, *The Death Penalty: An American History* (Cambridge, MA: Harvard University Press, 2002), 140–43 (detailing how for certain crimes, the antebellum South allowed the death penalty only for Blacks and not whites).

32 "The Death Penalty in Black and White: Who Lives, Who Dies, Who Decides," Death Penalty Information Center, June 4, 1998, https://deathpenaltyinfo.org/.

33 William J. Bowers, Benjamin D. Steiner, and Maria Sandys, "Death Sentencing in Black and White: An Empirical Analysis of the Role of Jurors' Race and Jury Racial Composition," *University of Pennsylvania Journal of Constitutional Law* 3 (2001): 171, 193.

34 *Id.* at 203–26.

35 *See generally* David C. Baldus, George Woodworth, David Zuckerman, and Neil Alan Weiner, "The Use of Peremptory Challenges in Capital Murder Trials: A Legal and Empirical Analysis," *University of Pennsylvania Journal of Constitutional Law* 3 (2001): 3. Underrepresentation of Blacks on capital juries also takes place at the initial stage through underrepresentation in the jury pool from which the jury is selected. *See* Ashish S. Joshi and Christina T. Kline, "Lack of Jury Diversity: A National Problem with Individual Consequences," American Bar Association, September 1, 2015, www.americanbar.org/.

36 476 U.S. 79 (1986).

37 *Miller-El v. Dretke*, 545 U.S. 231 (2005); *Snyder v. Louisiana*, 552 U.S. 472 (2008); *Foster v. Chatman*, 136 S. Ct. 1737 (2016); *Flowers v. Mississippi*, 139 S. Ct. 2228 (2019).

38 The term comes from a Supreme Court case dealing with the death qualification of jurors, *Witherspoon v. Illinois*, 391 U.S. 510 (1968).

39 Mona Lynch and Craig Haney, "Death Qualification in Black and White: Racialized Decision Making and Death-Qualified Juries," *Law and Policy* 40 (2018): 148.

40 504 U.S. 719 (1992).

41 Scott E. Sundby, "War and Peace in the Jury Room: How Capital Juries Reach Unanimity," *Hastings Law Journal* 62 (2010): 103.

42 Sundby, *Life and Death Decision*, 128–30 (describing how jurors who strongly favor the imposition of the death penalty influence deliberations).

43 *See* Matthew Rubenstein, "Overview of the Colorado Method of Capital Voir Dire," *The Champion*, November 2010, 8. The term *Colorado Method* has also made into popular usage; *see, e.g.*, Macradee Aegerter, "Defense Attorneys Use 'Colorado Method' to Save Theater Shooter from Death Penalty," Fox 31 News, August 10, 2015, https://kdvr.com/.

44 Sophie Honeyman, "Escaping Death: The Colorado Method of Capital Jury Selection," *John Marshall Law Review* 54 (2021): 247, 281–82.

45 In states requiring unanimity for either a death or life sentence, a "hung jury" on the sentence means that the first-degree murder conviction still stands, but the prosecutor must decide whether to seek another trial solely on the penalty. If the prosecutor decides not to have a retrial of the penalty phase, the defendant will receive a life sentence without parole.

46 *See generally* Sundby, "Death Penalty's Future," 1148–52. Defense counsel in the Eric Rudolph bombing case, for example, despite the defendant's notorious crimes that led him to be on the FBI's Ten Most Wanted Fugitives List for the five years until he was caught, were able to negotiate a life plea given the prosecution's concerns about "risking an acquittal or spending the millions of dollars it would take to bring the cases to trial." Jonathan Ringel, "Rudolph Defenders Read Feds' Signals to Make a Plea Deal," *Fulton County Daily Reporter*, April 19, 2005.

47 *See* "James Holmes Sentenced to Life in the Aurora Theater Shooting," *Denver Post*, August 7, 2015.

48 Doug Friednash, "I Helped Expand the Colorado Death Penalty; Now I Support Its Repeal," *Denver Post*, February 1, 2019 (also noting that Holmes's trial lasted six months and "cost Colorado taxpayers an estimated $5 million").

11

The Death and Life of Clemency

Mercy versus Finality

LAURA SCHAEFER

On January 6, 2021, the same day that rioters surged past barricades to
swarm the Capitol in Washington, D.C., a clemency hearing was underway for federal death row prisoner Lisa Montgomery. As Mary Atwell
notes in chapter 5 of this volume, Lisa was to be the eleventh person executed during the Trump administration's unprecedented federal execution spree, which claimed thirteen lives before President Trump's term
in office expired. As a result of the ongoing COVID-19 pandemic and
limitations on travel and in-person gatherings, however, the hearing was
taking place virtually via Zoom. In "attendance" were Lisa's attorneys, as
well as Acting Pardon Attorney Rosalind Sargent-Burns and her staff.
Lawyers from the Department of Justice's capital case unit were also present virtually. The hearing lasted about two hours, during which time
Lisa's case for mercy was laid out in painstaking detail.[1]

In the months leading up to Lisa's execution, the media had seized
on the sensational story of the first woman scheduled to be executed
by the federal government in nearly seventy years. Thanks to Lisa's attorneys, however, the stories the media ran did not simply detail the
shocking crime she had committed, as so many such stories do; rather,
they sought to contextualize Lisa and her crime against the backdrop of
the staggering trauma, abuse, and mental illness that had defined her
life. By the time Lisa's clemency petition came before the White House
on December 24, 2020, nearly 313,000 supporters[2] had signed on in support, and she had garnered the public support of the Office of the UN
High Commissioner for Human Rights[3] and other groups.

In making the public case for clemency, Lisa's attorneys were able to
make some sense of the horrendous crime Lisa had committed without

ignoring her individual responsibility or remorse. And in clemency cases where guilt is not at issue but significant grounds for mercy exist, this is precisely what attorneys should aim to do—offer the clemency decision-maker an opportunity to see that the person set for execution is not the "worst of the worst," but more typically, "the most broken of the broken."[4]

Although the Trump administration had overseen ten executions in the space of five months prior to Lisa's scheduled execution date of January 11, 2021—refusing to intervene or grant clemency in a single one—there was still a feeling that Lisa's case might end up differently. Mary Atwell has powerfully described the sexual abuse that Lisa had suffered as a child and young adult. The abuse was so extreme, and her mental illness and detachment from reality as her execution date approached so profound, that it did seem that if Trump were to show mercy in any of the cases scheduled for execution in the last year of his presidency, this would be the one.

There is a tradition of U.S. clemency decision-makers picking just one case of which to make a merciful example. In Alabama, where there has only ever been *one* death penalty case resolved via clemency, it was a woman who was spared. Rumor was, the governor at the time thought it would be unseemly for the state to kill a woman, no matter how horrendous the crime, although he publicly cited the judge's decision to override the jury's verdict of life as the rationale for the unusual grant.[5] It was not unthinkable that a similar "savior" logic might work on Trump, who as president held the ultimate clemency power over individuals on federal death row.

Lisa's attorneys knew that clemency depends in large part on the ability to appeal to your individual decision-maker and his or her interests and idiosyncrasies. If you can make a clemency decision-maker feel heroic and powerful in the act of commutation, you are more likely to entice them to look away from the potential political pitfalls of a grant. Lisa's attorneys wrote in their clemency petition that if President Trump were to spare Lisa, he could "send a message of hope" to the "countless women [who] have suffered silently under the weight of the shame and humiliation of the trauma inflicted by sexual and physical violence."[6] He could "make a difference in women's lives" and "maybe even save lives."[7] He could stand up against the stigmatization of mental illness and showcase his capacity for mercy. Unspoken in all this was an offer to Trump to get himself some good press and to take back the narrative about his one-term presidency that was rapidly escaping him. Lisa's clemency petition smartly focused on Trump's sole power to make a difference in the resolution of this case: "You alone have the power to temper Justice with Mercy. You alone have the power to protect her children and grandchildren from more heartache and pain. You alone have the power to join the growing chorus to end the stigmatization of mental illness. You alone have the power to send a message to the thousands of women who have been the victim of childhood rape and trafficking that their pain matters—that they matter—that their lives have value. You alone write the ending to this story."[8] Despite this strategic appeal to Trump's ego, Lisa was executed as scheduled on January 11, 2021. And perhaps Lisa's pleas for mercy were always going to fall on deaf ears. Perhaps the intervening circumstances of the January 6th riot on the same day as her clemency hearing made no difference in the White House's consideration of her request. It is impossible to know, because the law says the president is not even required to make a decision on a clemency application one way or another—let alone publicize why clemency has been denied.[9] A denial can simply come in the form of doing nothing and allowing the execution to proceed—which, in the cases of the thirteen prisoners executed during Trump's term, is exactly what happened.[10] Thousands of hours of attorney work, organizing, and advocacy, all in the midst of a global pandemic, were met with deafening silence as the federal machinery of death was switched on and cranked forward.

This is the paradox of clemency in the modern era of the death penalty—without it, the last remaining sliver of hope for death penalty defendants boxed out of the court system would be gone; but even with a system for clemency firmly in place, a defendant is guaranteed little more than the opportunity to ask for it. They say that good facts make bad law. Similarly, an extreme case for clemency set against the extraordinary circumstances of the Trump presidency, the COVID-19 pandemic, and the January 6th riot seems like it should be an impossible example from which to extrapolate. How can one comment on whether a given system is working amid so much external dysfunction?

I would posit, however, that it is precisely because the facts surrounding Lisa's bid for clemency were so extraordinary that we are able to draw some conclusions about the way death penalty clemency functions (and does not) in the United States today. It is only because the clemency power is still considered so separate from the ordinary administration of justice, and so outside the purview of traditional judicial review, that such extreme circumstances do not themselves give rise to an obvious claim before the courts. And while clemency has long been understood to occupy an uncomfortable space between law and executive fiat, it is also a fact that it is an indispensable component of a legal system that continues to put people to death despite significant, documented problems with the way capital punishment operates and is applied in this country. As unusual as the circumstances of January 2021 were, they highlight yet another enduring problem in the functioning of the death penalty in the United States today: the inability to vindicate rights in clemency despite the critical status of the "mercy function" in the U.S. death penalty scheme.

Lisa Montgomery's Case for Clemency

As discussed in chapter 5, Lisa Montgomery was convicted and sentenced to death for the 2004 murder of eight-months-pregnant Bobbi Jo Stinnet and the forcible extraction and kidnapping of her infant daughter.[11] As experienced capital defenders know, the more horrific the facts of a crime, the more likely it is that the defendant suffers from one or more serious mental illnesses or disabilities. That this was true in Lisa's case was immediately evident to all involved in her legal representation, although the jury that ultimately sentenced Lisa to death was never painted a clear picture of how significant and repeated emotional and sexual abuse led her to Bobbi Jo Stinnett's house that day. Instead, this picture only emerged years after Lisa's initial conviction and sentence, when new attorneys were assigned to her case to represent her through the remainder of her available judicial appeals and, eventually, in her plea for federal clemency.

Despite her obvious mental illness, Lisa was found competent to stand trial. After significant infighting among the legal teams initially appointed to represent her,[12] Lisa was ultimately appointed a solo practitioner defense attorney who seized on pursuing a "not guilty by reason of insanity" verdict, premised on the theory that Lisa suffered from pseudocyesis, a condition in which one falsely believes oneself to be pregnant.[13] While it was clear that Lisa had desperately *wanted* to be pregnant in the lead-up to her crime, it was also clear from the facts known at the time that she knew that she was not; it was *because* she was not that she had killed Bobbi Stinnett. This theory of the case was doomed to fail, not least because it didn't make sense. It should have been clear to her counsel that the task at hand was to understand how Lisa got to a place where she sincerely thought that she could murder a woman, steal her unborn baby, and effectively convince her family, who had themselves forced her to undergo sterilization, that she had somehow still become pregnant and birthed an infant. Lisa's trial attorney was not wrong to assume that mental illness had played an acute role in this crime; but without conducting the sort of background investigation that her attorneys undertook years later, finally weaving together how a person can get to the place where Lisa was mentally and emotionally when she murdered Ms. Stinnett, her jury was given little help to make sense of this brutal crime.

Needless to say, left without a coherent mitigating narrative to weigh against the gruesome facts of the crime, Lisa's jury sentenced her to death. And while a deeper trial presentation of Lisa's history of trauma, victimization, abuse, and mental illness—including evidence of her profound and lifelong disassociation—may not have made an impact on the jury's assessment of guilt, such context would have been critical to convincing the jury to spare her life. (Indeed, research conducted by Lisa's post-conviction attorneys revealed that Lisa was the only woman in the United States serving a death sentence for the crime of forcibly extracting another woman's baby. This research shows that a death sentence is not a forgone conclusion for this sort of offense, in spite of its brutality, as it is so frequently indicative of significant and enduring mental illness.)[14]

About a decade after being convicted and sentenced, Lisa was finally appointed counsel who would thoroughly investigate her case and uncover and develop the wealth of mitigating evidence that is touched on only briefly here. But because it is a feature of the U.S. criminal legal system that finality is prized above almost all else, it is exceptionally difficult to overturn a conviction or sentence once it has been handed down. Thus, although death penalty cases famously undergo multiple layers of appellate review before the sentence is finally carried out, the presumption of review at these stages of a case is always set against overturning the conviction and sentence. Even in a case like Lisa's, where her trial attorney failed to present even a fraction of the significant mitigating evidence that existed to contextualize her crime, reviewing courts deemed the representation she received at trial "good enough" for her death sentence to stand.[15] As a result, by January 6, 2021, all Lisa and her attorneys had left to hope for was a chance at clemency.

But at the same time Lisa's attorneys were making a final plea for her life, the Capitol riot was underway. The five days between Lisa's clemency hearing and her January 11, 2021, execution date were consumed by mention of little else aside from the attempted insurrection. This was devastating to Lisa's clemency efforts, particularly because a successful clemency petition often has to have the ability to capture media focus and public attention. If decision-makers feel they have "cover" for granting mercy—meaning, public support sufficient to outweigh any backlash—they are much more likely to do so. A favorable media environment can go a long way toward securing that outcome. And although one may like to assume that clemency decisions are made on the merits of the case alone, there is no question that clemency decision-makers consider the public and political consequences of any action they take. (This does not have to be an inherently problematic part of the clemency power; in a way, it allows for a sort of "democratic correction" of the judicial process.)

In any other sort of executive branch adjudication where a decision is so likely to be impacted by outside circumstances, however, one expects to be entitled to go to court to ask—Did the fact of the January 6th riot on the same day as Lisa's clemency hearing prejudice consideration of her request for mercy? If so, could her clemency hearing date be reset for a less chaotic time, when the only decision-maker standing between her and execution was not potentially facing impeachment proceedings and accusations of treason? Was President Trump still even legally president after his actions and/or inactions on January 6, and does the fact that this is even a question give rise to any legal recourse? If there was no clemency decision-maker remaining to consider mercy in Lisa's case, was that even a constitutional problem that the courts would consider? If clemency is nothing more than an act of "executive grace," can you ever seek to judicially vindicate rights in or to clemency proceedings? These are the kinds of questions that courts have grappled with for decades, but I posit they were never so starkly framed as during the chaos of the final days of the Trump administration, when the "traditional fail-safe" of the U.S. justice system, executive clemency, was reduced to nothing more than the proverbial quixotic windmill.

The Importation of Clemency into the U.S. Federal Constitutional Scheme

The January 6th riot was an event that embroiled all of the actors central to the life-or-death decisions regarding the three remaining prisoners scheduled for execution in January 2021. In order to understand why the intervening chaos of the riot did not give rise to any obvious legal challenges, it is necessary to understand the role clemency plays in the U.S. legal system, and in particular in the death penalty scheme.

It is first important to note that in U.S. death penalty cases, *the vast majority of clemency actors are state governors and/or boards of pardon and parole,* not the president or the federal government. This is because the majority of death sentences come from the states and are handed down under state, not federal, law. In the federal system, as previously mentioned, the constitution grants the U.S. president ultimate (and nearly totally unfettered) clemency authority. In the remaining death penalty jurisdictions, clemency authority is divided among several distinct schemes: states in which the governor has sole decision-making authority (Alabama, Mississippi, Missouri, Montana, South Carolina, California,[16] South Dakota, North Carolina, Kentucky, Oregon, Tennessee, Wyoming); states in which governors retain the ultimate authority to deny clemency but require an affirmative recommendation from a reviewing body (typically, a parole board) in order to grant it (Arizona, Oklahoma, Louisiana, Florida, Idaho, Texas, Pennsylvania); states in which parole boards play an advisory role only but are required to issue a recommendation before clemency is ultimately decided on (Arkansas, Indiana, Ohio, Kansas); and states in which executive clemency boards retain total authority over state clemency decisions (Nevada, Nebraska, Georgia, Utah).

Clemency made its way into the U.S. legal system by way of the Founding Fathers, as they were contemplating which legal provisions from the English common law to import into the new republic. Alexander Hamilton was in fact one of the most vocal proponents of writing a clemency mechanism into the new constitution, in spite of criticisms that it would be unnecessary and even illogical to retain the capacity for clemency in a system operating without a monarch. William Blackstone, for example, asserted that clemency made little sense in a system without a king. Blackstone thought it made sense to retain a clemency power in a monarchy, as it would allow for the monarch to cultivate the love of his subjects through acts of mercy; but in a system governed only by law, what role would clemency serve? Would it not undercut the purely legal system into which it was integrated?[17]

Ultimately, the Founding Fathers were convinced by Alexander Hamilton's entreaty to retain the capacity for executive mercy in the new constitution. In *Federalist* No. 74, Hamilton famously wrote, "Humanity and good policy conspire to dictate, that the benign prerogative of pardoning should be as little as possible fettered or embarrassed. The criminal code of every country partakes so much of necessary severity, that without an easy access to exceptions in favor of unfortunate guilt, justice would wear a countenance too sanguinary and cruel."[18] Interestingly, the "necessary severity" of the criminal code was not something Hamilton seemed concerned about, so long as the system retained the "unfettered" ability to pardon. It would seem Hamilton saw reasons why a criminal code might need to be harsh, even excessive, provided there were opportunities along the way for the executive to consider whether guilt was in fact "unfortunate" and to act accordingly. The only constitutional limitations placed on presidential acts of clemency were in cases of treason and impeachment. These two limitations make clear that the Founders had some concern about framing the clemency power in such a way that it could be used to get around the foundational structure of government. Otherwise, the objective was to leave the clemency power as broad and "unfettered" as possible.

The Adoption of Clemency Regimes by the States

Nothing in the federal constitution requires the individual states to adopt mechanisms for granting executive clemency, whether in death penalty cases or otherwise. Nevertheless, a clemency function is found in every U.S. state constitution or code; as such, the possibility of executive clemency is available in every death penalty case. While states have different mechanisms for how this power is to be exercised and applied, the fact that every U.S. state chose to retain a clemency power in its own constitutional or criminal code underscores the perceived importance of this stage of review.

There is significant evidence to suggest that executive clemency in death penalty cases was exercised more frequently in the period prior to the brief abolition of the death penalty in 1972[19] than it was following its reinstatement in 1976. According to some studies, clemency was granted in nearly a quarter of death penalty cases in the lead-up to 1972.[20] In the period since 1976, however, the rate of individual clemency grants has hovered between 4 and 6 percent.[21] Reasons offered for this steep decline in the exercise of death row clemency differ. Some scholars and historians believe that the U.S. Supreme Court's reinstatement of the death penalty in 1976 with *Gregg v. Georgia*[22] sufficiently addressed the problem of arbitrariness in the application of the death penalty so as to make the more frequent grants of clemency that came before this time period unnecessary.[23] According to this argument, the need for clemency to reign in legal excess in death penalty cases was largely "solved" by adjustments made to the ways in which capital sentences were pursued and handed down.

Others argue—in my view, more persuasively—that the changing political situation in the United States in the 1980s and 1990s and the introduction of the "tough on crime era" of U.S. politics dealt the death blow, so to speak, to opportunities for mercy, particularly in cases of violent crimes, which all capital cases inherently are. Together with the "war on drugs," the "war on crime" saw a massive expansion of the prison industrial complex and the passage of numerous laws at both the state and federal levels aimed at heightening criminal penalties for all sorts of offenses and removing whatever sentencing discretion had existed for judges and other decision-makers up to that point. Clemency, the ultimate act of executive leniency, was simply not politically viable for the clemency decision-makers in the various death penalty jurisdictions. These decision-makers all were either directly elected (governors) or in some way dependent on elected officials' support (parole board members and others). Combined with the states' newfound enthusiasm for ramping up their death penalty efforts in light of this new era of maximalist punishment, the near disappearance of executive clemency meant that more than one thousand state executions were carried out between the late 1980s and early 2000s.[24] In this era, use of the death penalty and the corresponding absence of any form of mercy became as American as apple pie.

At the same time, however, courts were dealing with the consequences of this significant influx of criminal prosecutions—mainly, the need to adjudicate all of these cases, both at the trial level and throughout various stages of appeal. The criminal legal system was growing out of control, judges were overtaxed, and a curious thing kept happening: state death sentences (which accounted for, and still account for, most of the death sentences in the country) kept getting overturned by unelected, federal judges who found federal constitutional problems with the ways in which the cases had been resolved in the lower state courts. Indeed, in the period from 1973 and 1995, research shows that nearly two thirds of all state death sentences were being reversed by federal courts around the country.[25]

Contrary to the supposition of scholars who believed that *Gregg v. Georgia* had largely "fixed" the most glaring problems with states' application of the death penalty, thereby lessening the need for executive mercy and excusing the withering use of executive clemency in capital cases, federal judges were still finding issues with state death penalty prosecutions sufficient to overturn convictions and sentences. This reality was burdensome for everyone: not only did the frequent overturning of cases drain already overextended criminal legal systems, but the (largely southern) states from which those convictions and sentences emanated began to get very frustrated with federal interference in the disposition of their local death penalty cases.[26]

In response to these and other concerns, in 1996, Congress passed a sweeping criminal reform bill titled the Antiterrorism and Effective Death Penalty Act (AEDPA). In many ways, this bill was seen as an effort by Democrats to convince a largely skeptical electorate that they were just as capable as being "tough on crime" as their Republican counterparts. Signed off on by then president Bill Clinton and favorably voted on in the Senate by current U.S. president Joe Biden,[27] AEDPA neatly eviscerated the power of the federal courts to reign in state court excesses via federal habeas review. Professor James Liebman described the principles governing habeas review in the federal courts pre-AEDPA as follows: "Until 1996 the Court held firm to two principles. First, there were no time limits on federal habeas review. Second, a state court's prior adjudication of the legality of a state prisoner's conviction or sentence had no binding legal effect on the federal court's obligation to independently assess the legality of state action leading to incarceration, and to grant relief if the action was inconsistent with federal law in effect when the action occurred."[28] Before AEDPA took effect, the Supreme Court had begun to set some limits on the filing of federal habeas petitions (e.g., restricting the filing of multiple federal habeas petitions raising the same arguments on res judicata grounds),[29] but for the most part, the federal courts had been unfettered in their ability to take a "fresh look" at state death penalty convictions. AEDPA took direct aim at this potential for federal court oversight, significantly narrowing the grounds on which claims could be brought, creating a one-year time frame for filing a federal habeas petition subsequent to the termination of state court proceedings, and, even if these conditions were met, allowing a federal court to grant relief only if the decision of the state court was found to be "contrary to clearly established federal law" or an "unreasonable determination of the facts in light of the evidence."[30]

AEDPA was designed to limit the availability of federal habeas corpus relief to state prisoners, and in this respect it was immensely successful. Scholarship shows that the rates of habeas relief in the federal courts now stand somewhere around 12 percent and sinking,[31] as compared to relief being granted in capital cases between 66 and 75 percent of the time in the period prior.[32] Thus, around the same time that the use of executive clemency had been largely forgotten as an available means of reigning in the states' death penalty fervor, another major tool for ensuring fairness in death penalty cases—the ability of the federal courts to grant habeas relief pursuant to their review of the established facts and governing law in a given case—was virtually eliminated.

AEDPA and *Herrera v. Collins*

Although AEDPA's legislative proponents loudly decried the "ease" with which state death row prisoners could access relief in the federal courts, there were already existing judicial limitations that restricted prisoners' ability to raise new claims and present new evidence in federal habeas corpus proceedings. In 1992, the Supreme Court was asked to confront a somewhat confounding question in a death penalty case out of Texas, *Herrera v. Collins*.[33] The question presented was, "Do the Eighth and Fourteenth Amendments permit a state to execute an individual who is innocent of the crime for which he or she was convicted and sentenced to death?" Put another way, is there a constitutional problem with the execution of a person who is actually innocent?

Petitioner Leon Herrera's case arrived at the high court after the Fifth Circuit Court of Appeals denied Herrera's motion to file a successive petition for federal habeas corpus relief after the discovery of new evidence pointing to his innocence. The courts below had held that regardless of whether the new evidence presented tended to show his innocence, innocence alone was not sufficient grounds to reopen a federal habeas proceeding absent additional evidence of a constitutional problem with the state court adjudication. Thus, the U.S. Supreme Court agreed to address whether the execution of a person who has been afforded due process but is actually innocent of the crime for which he has been convicted and sentenced to death would amount to a constitutional violation.

Writing for the Court, Chief Justice Rehnquist concluded that no— there is nothing in the Constitution that says the execution of an "actually innocent" person is itself unconstitutional, assuming that the individual was afforded all the substantive and procedural protections guaranteed him throughout the judicial process up until that point. In other words, so long as the trial was fair and the prisoner had access to counsel and the opportunity to pursue other available forms of relief, the fact that new evidence of innocence emerged subsequent to his already having lost in the federal courts did not itself constitute a new ground on which to reopen his federal habeas corpus proceedings. The Court wrote, "Claims of actual innocence based on newly discovered evidence have *never been held* to state a ground for federal habeas relief absent an independent constitutional violation occurring in the underlying state criminal proceeding."[34]

Despite the confidence with which it issued this pronouncement, the Court also seemed to understand that this holding would be shocking to some people and thus took pains to explain why such a legal conclusion was warranted, and also why it was not inherently unjust. To the first point, the Court explained that "once a defendant has been afforded a fair trial and convicted of the offense for which he was charged, the presumption of innocence disappears. . . . Thus, in the eyes of the law, [despite presenting new evidence of innocence, this] petitioner does not come before the Court as one who is 'innocent,' but, on the contrary, as one who has been convicted by due process of law."[35] Second, the Court emphasized that "[Herrera was not] without a forum to raise his actual innocence claim. For under Texas law, petitioner may file a request for executive clemency. . . . Clemency is deeply rooted in our Anglo-American tradition of law, and is the historic remedy for preventing miscarriages of justice where judicial process has been exhausted."[36] Because clemency exists, the Court reasoned, such "necessary severity" was acceptable—even if it meant that the legal system could otherwise condone the execution of an innocent person.

As such, the possibility of clemency became a critical component of the Court's reasoning as to why highly restrictive standards for federal habeas corpus review were permissible, even in death penalty cases. By pointing to the availability of executive clemency, the Court in *Herrera* seemed to acknowledge that it might be a constitutional fairness problem were Herrera left without "a forum in which to press his actual innocence claim," but luckily, the possibility of clemency here meant that the Court did not have to address this concern. The Texas clemency process, such as it was, was available to Herrera to ventilate his actual innocence claim.

I would argue that in justifying its decision in these terms, the Court has elevated clemency review in capital cases to occupy a critical space in the U.S. death penalty scheme—to serve as a bulwark against the rapidly narrowing avenues for judicial relief available to state and federal death row prisoners. If clemency were not, in fact, "available" to death row prisoners in the way in which the Court reasoned cushioned its holding in *Herrera*, then the Court is left without adequate justification for narrowing capital prisoners' access to federal habeas relief so dramatically.[37]

The "Availability" of Clemency Today

It should come as no surprise that even as Mr. Herrera's case was before the Supreme Court, clemency existed as little more than a formal right in Texas. In Texas, the so-called death penalty capital of the United States, there have been only three individual grants of clemency in the modern era of the death penalty. This is due in part to structural constraints on the governor's clemency power in Texas, where the board of pardons and paroles must issue a majority vote in favor of clemency before the governor can commute a death row sentence, as well as the long-standing cultural support for the death penalty in the Lonestar State. Returning to the issue of needing political "cover" for granting clemency, in Texas it is all but a foregone conclusion that decision-makers will not face blowback for not showing mercy. As the nearly nonexistent record of clemency grants in the state shows, the converse is far less certain.

Much has changed since the U.S. Supreme Court decided *Herrera*, however, making its reliance on the availability of clemency to death row prisoners even more significant. First, AEDPA severely curtailed the federal courts' already limited ability to grant relief in state death penalty cases. Second, in 1998, the Supreme Court decided another case touching on executive clemency—finding that "although clemency was an act of grace," "some *minimal* procedural safeguards" must exist in these proceedings, because a person retains an interest in his life up until his death.[38] Third, in 2007, the Court held in *Harbison v. Bell* that the federal statute governing the provision of attorneys to state death row prisoners in pressing their rights in federal court, 18 U.S.C. section 3599(e), extended to the provision of federal funding for these federal attorneys to continue representing state death row prisoners in state death penalty decisions. These three developments, taken together, further confirm that clemency occupies a specific and significant place in ensuring fairness in the way the death penalty operates in our country today. At the same time, the significant weight of lower court jurisprudence around clemency still treats clemency as a facet of our legal system that can be wholly unpredictable, arbitrary, and subject to whim. These two things cannot both be true.

At the start of this chapter, I pointed out that every U.S. death penalty jurisdiction provides for the possibility of executive clemency in death penalty cases. In states where governors have sole decision-making authority over clemency, the "rules" governing the submission of executive clemency petitions tend to be fairly open and dependent on the gubernatorial administration in power at the time. But most death penalty states have hybrid schemes for capital clemency review, typically involving a state board of pardons and paroles. These clemency schemes tend to be governed by various state statutes and regulations that provide detailed and often complex instructions to applicants for consideration of this executive grace.[39] What was considered to be nothing more than an "act of grace"[40] during the first hundred or so years of this republic has become increasingly legalized by the importation of procedural rules and regulations to govern its administration.

What's more, the U.S. Supreme Court further formalized the significance of this part of death penalty review by relying on its availability in *Herrera* to support its holding that there is nothing inherently unconstitutional about the execution of an actually innocent petitioner who has not otherwise identified constitutional problems in his conviction or sentence. By then allowing for the provision of federally appointed attorneys to represent state prisoners in clemency in *Harbison v. Bell* and acknowledging that "some" minimal due process protections govern capital clemency proceedings in *Ohio Adult Parole Authority*, the Court further established clemency as a necessary fail-safe in our ongoing administration of the death penalty.

Grace Demands Protection

Perhaps more than anything else, the Supreme Court's opinion in *Harbison v. Bell* that state death row prisoners may be represented by federal public defenders has significantly increased the chances that death-sentenced individuals will be represented robustly in clemency proceedings. This expanded access to counsel may help to account for the small uptick in the number of individual clemency grants across death penalty jurisdictions. (Slowly shifting public attitudes toward the death penalty and the frequency of botched executions probably play some role in this change, too.) Between 1983 and 2009, the rate of "individual" clemency grants (measured by looking at the number of cases in which an individual person has been spared execution by a grant of clemency, over the total number of executions in that time period) hovered around 4 percent;[41] between 2009 and 2024, that rate rose to about 6 percent (twenty-eight individual grants of clemency over 448 executions).[42] Dogged defense attorneys are identifying jurors in their clients' cases who state they would have voted differently if they knew then what they know now, and those attorneys are launching large, public campaigns for clemency that sometimes even garner international support. Governors seem to be remembering the "mercy function," and the political climate is once again becoming more favorable to acts of mercy, particularly in terms of reigning in the now acknowledged excesses of the criminal justice system.

Against all this, Lisa Montgomery's case—and indeed, the cases of all thirteen prisoners executed under Trump—was an aberration. At the same time that more states were turning toward mercy and death sentences were declining around the country, the federal government set off on the bloodiest and most unexpected spree of executions in the modern era.

What are the lessons we can learn from these aberrant executions? One is that we can no longer be satisfied with the explanation that it is never possible to challenge clemency proceedings simply because clemency is an "act of grace." Grace requires protection. Clemency may have originated in governance by kings, but it has been transformed to occupy a wholly different space in our criminal legal systems. A second lesson is that it is not acceptable to condition applications for clemency on successfully surmounting considerable procedural obstacles (filing petitions by a certain deadline, limiting witnesses to a certain number, printing and distributing certain numbers of petition copies, etc.) and then say there is no judicial recourse when the state or federal government fails to play its part in the procedural process.

Lisa Montgomery's clemency application contained *hundreds* of pages of supplementary documents, letters in support, and other evidence tending to show that her death sentence was disproportionate, cruel, and based on an insufficient understanding of her life up until the time of her crime. And yet, a decision on her clemency petition was never communicated; she was executed in silence. Eleven of the other twelve prisoners put to death during the federal execution spree presented similarly robust petitions, all complying with the Department of Justice's labyrinthine rules for seeking federal clemency in a capital case. For three of these prisoners, the Department of Justice's consideration of their clemency applications came at the same time as the most egregious attack on our democracy in recent times—the January 6th Capitol riot. There is no question that the White House's attention, and the Department of Justice's attention, and really the entire country's attention, was not on these clemency requests. And yet, because of the paper-thin law surrounding rights in clemency, there was nowhere for these prisoners to go to vindicate their rights to such consideration. If the United States continues to pursue and apply the death penalty in certain cases, justice demands more.

Notes

1   In addition to Lisa, federal death row prisoners Dustin Higgs and Corey Johnson were also scheduled for execution in the early days of 2021 prior to the presidential transition. Like so much else about this time, the decision to hold executions just days prior to the inauguration of a presidential successor who had come out against the death penalty was wholly unprecedented. While this chapter focuses on Lisa's story for clemency to make broader points about the issues inherent with the operation of capital clemency in the United States today, this is not to discount the incredibly strong arguments for mercy that Dustin Higgs and Corey Johnson also presented. Indeed, all thirteen prisoners executed under Trump had substantial arguments for why they should be spared from execution (not least of which was that it was wholly cruel and unusual to schedule these executions at a time when the United States was deeply in the grips of the COVID-19 pandemic). Remarkably, nearly every prisoner scheduled for execution under Trump had received a stay of execution from either a federal district or appellate court— something that is by no means a given, and a reflection of the serious questions jurists identified about the fairness or constitutionality of each of the thirteen federal prisoners' convictions or sentences. Every one of these stays was vacated by the U.S. Supreme Court, which offered *no written opinion* in any of these cases to explain why it was vacating the reasoned stays from the courts below. *See* David Cole, "A Rush to Execute," *New York Review*, February 25, 2021. For more information on the thirteen prisoners executed under Trump and the compelling reasons why each of them deserved executive grace, please also visit "Federal Executions Updates," Death Penalty Information Center, https://deathpenaltyinfo.org/.
2   "Tell President Trump to Stop the Execution of Lisa Montgomery," petition created by Cornell Center on the Death Penalty Worldwide, MoveOn, https://sign .moveon.org/.
3   "UN experts call for clemency for Lisa Montgomery, as US reschedules planned execution," *UN News*, December 3, 2020, https://news.un.org/.
4   Jackie Fielding, "'The Most Broken of the Broken,'" Brennan Center for Justice, January 12, 2021, https://www.brennancenter.org/.
5   *See* Kent Faulk, "Why Did Fob James Commute Judith Ann Neelley's Death Sentence in 1999?," *AL.com*, January 29, 2017, https://www.al.com/. *See also* "Alabama," ABA Capital Clemency Resource Initiative Clearinghouse, https:// www.capitalclemency.org.

6 Petition for Executive Clemency on Behalf of Lisa Marie Montgomery, Presented to Donald J. Trump, December 24, 2020, at 14. Document on file with author.

7 *Id.* at 14.

8 Petition for Executive Clemency, *supra* note 6 at 1.

9 "Frequently Asked Questions" (response to "If the President denies a clemency request, is the applicant told why?"), Office of the Pardon Attorney, U.S. Department of Justice, https://www.justice.gov/pardon/.

10 "Federal Capital Clemency Memorandum," ABA Capital Clemency Resource Initiative Clearinghouse, https://www.capitalclemency.org/.

11 Remarkably, Bobbi Jo Stinnett's daughter survived her mother's murder.

12 Petition for Executive Clemency, *supra* note 6 at 9.

13 "Prior to trial, Mrs. Montgomery was represented by four different defense teams employing a series of mitigation specialists and investigators. Mrs. Montgomery's multiple trial defense teams lacked the training and experience necessary to deal with a client with serious mental health issues. Moreover, the fourth and final defense team made the mistake of focusing solely on the crime, hastily zeroing in on the defense of pseudocyesis, rather than their client and her complex biopsychosocial history. Mot. for Collateral Relief to Vacate, Set Aside, or Correct Sentence and for a New Trial, 11, Case 4:12-cv-08001-GAF, 60.

14 Petition for Executive Clemency, *supra* note 6 at 10. "Data collected by researchers at Cornell law school (*sic*) verifies that Mrs. Montgomery is the only person on death row (state or federal) for such a crime. The data supporting the research is attached. The reason for this is apparent. As Garnett and Zimmerman explain 'these crimes are inevitably the product of serious mental illness. Women who commit such crimes also are likely to have been victimized themselves.'"

15 It is important to note that Lisa actually received not one, but *two* stays of execution from federal courts in the days and weeks leading up to her execution. This in spite of the fact that stays of execution are becoming increasingly hard to come by under current Supreme Court precedent. One such stay was based on significant evidence that Lisa's mental state in the time leading to her execution had diminished so significantly that she was no longer in touch with reality and no longer able to understand the government's plans to put her to death. The Supreme Court, in *Ford v. Wainwright*, 477 U.S. 399 (1986), ruled that it would violate the Eighth Amendment to execute a person so mentally ill they could no longer understand why they were being executed. A federal court in Indiana found that significant evidence showed that Lisa was precisely so disassociated that her execution would likely violate this core constitutional protection. The Supreme Court, continuing to act as the enforcement arm of Trump's federal execution efforts, vacated this stay with no written explanation. *See* Cole, "Rush to Execute."

16 California is included in this group even though there is one limitation on the governor's clemency power—namely, the ability to commute a death sentence of

a "twice convicted felon." In such cases, the governor would have to seek approval of a majority of the California Supreme Court in order to grant commutations. *See* "California," ABA Capital Clemency Resource Initiative Clearinghouse, https://www.capitalclemency.org/. Because this scheme is not replicated elsewhere, however, and because California otherwise gives the governor full discretion over capital clemency decisions, it is included in this group.

17 *See* William Blackstone, *Commentaries*, 4:397–402. "This is indeed one of the great advantages of monarchy in general, above any other form of government; that there is a magistrate, who has it in his power to extend mercy, wherever he thinks it is deserved: holding a court of equity in his own breast, to soften the rigour of the general law, in such criminal cases as merit an exemption from punishment. . . . In democracies, however, this power of pardon can never subsist; for there nothing higher is acknowledged than the magistrate who administers the laws: and it would be impolitic for the power of judging and of pardoning to center in one and the same person. This (as the president Montesquieu observes) would oblige him very often to contradict himself, to make and to unmake his decisions: it would tend to confound all ideas of right among the mass of the people; as they would find it difficult to tell, whether a prisoner were discharged by his innocence, or obtained a pardon through favour. . . . But in monarchies the king acts in a superior sphere; and, though he regulates the whole government as the first mover, yet he does not appear in any of the disagreeable or invidious parts of it. . . . To him therefore the people look up as the fountain of nothing but bounty and grace; and these repeated acts of goodness, coming immediately from his own hand, endear the sovereign to his subjects, and contribute more than any thing to root in their hearts that filial affection, and personal loyalty, which are the sure establishment of a prince."

18 Alexander Hamilton, *Federalist* No. 74, March 25, 1788, https://avalon.law.yale.edu.

19 *Furman v. Georgia*, 408 U.S. 238 (1972).

20 Adam M. Gershowitz, "Rethinking the Timing of Capital Clemency," *Michigan Law Review* 113 (2014): 1, 4.

21 I use the term *individual* clemency grants to distinguish from *mass* grants of clemency, where a governor uses the clemency power to effectively "clear" death row in a given state by commuting all death sentences. The most famous example of this was in Illinois, where Governor George Ryan commuted more than a hundred death sentences after first instituting an executive moratorium, citing concerns about innocence. Governors in New Mexico, New Jersey, and Maryland have also conducted mass clemency grants, typically around the same time or immediately following the state's adoption of prospective death penalty abolition. I define individual clemency grants as those grants where a decision is made to a commute a death sentence after individualized consideration of a particular prisoner's death penalty case, typically in the days or weeks prior to a scheduled execution. The rates of individual grants I am citing here is based on my own analysis of the number of clemencies granted out of the number of scheduled

executions in the same time period, excluding those clemencies that fall into the "mass grant" category.

22 428 U.S. 153 (1976). In *Gregg*, the Supreme Court held that states could reinstate the death penalty so long as they enacted legislative schemes for its application that sufficiently narrowed the criteria for determining which sorts of crimes would give rise to a death sentence.

23 "The sentencing stage of capital prosecutions now eliminates almost all of the people who would have received clemency in days gone by. . . . The small number of commutations seen today is a testament to that success." Paul J. Larkin Jr., "The Demise of Capital Clemency," *Washington and Lee Law Review* 73 (November 2016): 1295, 1312.

24 According to the Death Penalty Information Center, 1,182 executions were carried out between January 1, 1983 and December 31, 2009. In that same time period, there were forty-eight individual grants of clemency across all remaining death penalty jurisdictions, resulting in a clemency over execution rate of about 4%. *See* Execution Database, and "List of Clemencies since 1976," Death Penalty Information Center, https://deathpenaltyinfo.org/.

25 "Nationally, during the 23-year study period, the overall rate of prejudicial error in the American capital punishment system was 68%. In other words, courts found serious, reversible error in nearly 7 of every 10 of the thousands of capital sentences that were fully reviewed during the period." James S. Liebman, Jeffrey Fagan, and Valerie West, "A Broken System: Error Rates in Capital Cases, 1973–1995" (Columbia Law School, Public Law Research Paper No. 15, Columbia University, New York, June 2000), https://scholarship.law.columbia.edu/.

26 Here, it is important to remember that the death penalty today is a largely geographically limited phenomenon. For example, only 2% of U.S. counties are responsible for more than 50% of death sentences in the United States. "The 2% Death Penalty: The Geographic Arbitrariness of Capital Punishment in the United States," Death Penalty Information Center, https://deathpenaltyinfo .org/. There is also no denying that the death penalty remains a largely southern phenomenon—with only a few exceptions, the states that retain the death penalty are geographically southern. In the lead-up to President Bill Clinton's 1996 reelection campaign, it was critical for the Democratic Party to retain voters in southern states. The country had become "tough on crime," and the national leadership needed to follow suit—meaning, the national leadership needed to show people in the states, and in the southern states in particular, that it would support their autonomy in addressing criminal justice problems.

27 To give some credit where credit is due, President Biden was troubled by AEDPA's constriction of federal habeas corpus and warned that including the language that eventually passed in the bill—limiting federal courts' ability to grant habeas relief in state cases—could have significant consequences for fairness, particularly in cases of actual innocence. Radley Balko, "Joe Biden Fought This Destructive Law. 25 Years Later, He Can Help Repeal It," *Washington Post*,

April 27, 2021; "Roll Call Vote 104th Congress—1st Session," United States Senate, https://www.senate.gov/.

28 James S. Liebman, "An 'Effective Death Penalty'? AEDPA and Error Detection in Capital Cases," *Brooklyn Law Review* 67 (2001): 411, 415.

29 *Id.*

30 18 U.S.C. §§ 2254(d)(1) and 2254(d)(2).

31 *See* David R. Dow and Eric M. Freedman, "The Effects of AEDPA on Justice," in *The Future of America's Death Penalty*, ed. Charles S. Lanier, William J. Bowers, and James R. Acker (Durham, NC: Carolina Academic Press, 2009), 261.

32 *See* Gershowitz, *supra* note 20.

33 506 U.S. 390 (1993).

34 *Herrera* at 400 (emphasis added).

35 *Id.* at 399.

36 *Id.* at 411.

37 In addition to AEDPA significantly limiting the ability of state death row prisoners to access federal habeas relief, the Supreme Court in recent years has continued to issue opinions further burdening death row prisoners' ability to receive stays of execution. *See Bucklew v. Precythe*, 139 S. Ct. 1112 (2019).

38 *Ohio Adult Parole Authority v. Woodard*, 523 U.S. 272 (1998), 285, 289 (emphasis in original).

39 *See generally* "State Information," ABA Capital Clemency Resource Initiative, www.capitalclemency.org/.

40 *United States v. Wilson*, 32 U.S. (7 Pet.) 150 (1833) ("a pardon is an act of grace . . .").

41 List of Clemencies since 1976," Death Penalty Information Center, https://deathpenaltyinfo.org/.

42 According to the Death Penalty Information Center (DPIC), 448 executions were carried out between January 1, 2009 and February 2, 2024. *See* Execution Database, Death Penalty Information Center, https://deathpenaltyinfo.org/. In that same time period, this author used the DPIC database to calculate that twenty-eight individual grants of clemency (excluding "mass" clemency grants and commutations pursuant to abolition of the death penalty in the jurisdiction) were carried out during that same time period. *See* "List of Clemencies since 1976."

PART IV

Methods of Execution and Rationale

12

The Fate of Lethal Injection

Decomposition of the Paradigm and Its Consequences

AUSTIN SARAT, MATTEA DENNEY,
NICOLAS GRABER-MITCHELL, GREENE KO,
ROSE MROCZKA, AND LAUREN PELOSI

This chapter examines the use of lethal injection from 2010 to 2020. The decade marks the "decomposition" of the standard three-drug protocol and the proliferating use of new drugs or drug combinations in U.S. executions, a development that is associated with an increase in the number of mishaps encountered during lethal injections. We describe and analyze these mishaps as well as the ways that death penalty jurisdictions responded and adapted to them. The recent history of lethal injection echoes the longer history of the death penalty. When states encountered problems with their previous methods of execution, they first attempted to address these problems by tinkering with their existing methods. When their tinkering failed, they adopted allegedly more humane execution methods. And when they ran into difficulties with the new methods, states scrambled to hide executions from public view. New drug combinations may have allowed the machinery of death to keep running. New procedures may have given the lethal injection process a veneer of legitimacy. But as we show in this chapter, none of these recent changes has resolved the fate of the practice or repaired its vexing problems.

Lethal Injection in Arkansas

In April 2017, with its supply of lethal injection drugs about to expire, the state of Arkansas announced that it would perform eight executions over eleven days.[1] Though legal problems halted half of them, the other half were carried out as planned. It had been approximately twelve years since Arkansas's last execution in 2005. For that execution, Arkansas used the well-established, "traditional" three-drug lethal injection cocktail: sodium thiopental, pancuronium bromide, and potassium chloride.

Eight years later, in 2013, after failing to obtain new supplies of those drugs, Arkansas adopted a new execution protocol that called for the use of lorazepam and phenobarbital.[2] Critics noted that those drugs had never before been used in an execution and that they were unlikely to cause death quickly, if at all.[3] In 2015, the state retreated and once again changed its drug protocol. This time, it adopted a three-drug cocktail used by some other states. It began with midazolam, a sedative, and followed it with vecuronium bromide and potassium chloride.[4]

The first of Arkansas's 2017 executions, and its first using midazolam, was that of Ledell Lee, who was sentenced to death in 1995 for the rape and murder of his twenty-six-year-old neighbor, Debra Reese. Questions about factual innocence surrounded Lee's conviction, which led to the American Civil Liberties Union and the Innocence Project unsuccessfully appealing to have the DNA evidence tested. Despite these efforts, the execution took place on April 20, ten days before Arkansas's batch of new lethal injection drugs would expire.

After placing intravenous lines (IVs) in Lee's arms, Arkansas's execution team started the flow of midazolam at 11:44 p.m.[5] Slowly, Lee's eyes shut as he swallowed repeatedly. The coroner pronounced him dead twelve minutes after the execution began. Unlike some of the midazolam executions[6] in other states, Lee's appeared to go off without a hitch.

Emboldened by its apparent success, Arkansas went ahead with its plan to kill Jack Jones four days later—over twenty years after his conviction for the vicious rape and murder of Mary Jones and the rape and physical assault of her eleven-year-old daughter, Lacy. More than two decades after his sentencing, guards steered the wheelchair-bound Jones[7] into Arkansas's death chamber. When the witnesses arrived at 7:00 p.m., Jones was already strapped to a gurney, intravenous lines sticking out of his arms. At 7:06 p.m., the warden wiped a hand over his face, signaling the start of the execution.[8]

Throughout the fourteen-minute execution, correctional staff checked Jones's consciousness by sticking a tongue depressor in his mouth, "lifting his eyelids and rubbing his sternum."[9] According to his lawyer, Jones began to gasp and gulp for air four minutes into the execution—a sign that he was experiencing physical pain. Witnesses said that his mouth moved like a "fish . . . chomping on bait."[10] Soon, the movement slowed and the team declared Jones dead at 7:20 p.m.

His legal team and state officials interpreted the movement of the inmate's mouth in different ways. Jones's lawyers contended that he "was moving his lips and gulping for air [which is] evidence that the [midazolam] did not properly sedate him."[11] They called Jones's death "torturous." A Department of Corrections spokesperson disagreed, stating that "the inmate was apologizing to the department director, Wendy Kelley, and thanking her for the way she treated him."[12] During Jones's execution, the prison staff shut off the death chamber microphone before the lethal injection began, which was standard procedure in Arkansas.[13] Had the microphone been on, we might have a better understanding of Jones's final moments.

Witnesses also could not see the problems that occurred an hour earlier, when the state made several attempts to place an adequate IV. For forty-five minutes, guards could not find a suitable vein. In a detailed timeline of the execution, Arkansas officials claimed that it took only eight minutes to place Jones's IV. Yet the autopsy report notes that medical examiners "found five needle marks on Jones's neck and clavicle . . . area" that were covered up with makeup.[14]

The same day it executed Jones, Arkansas also put Marcel Williams to death. Williams had been convicted and sentenced to death for the 1997 kidnapping, rape, and murder of a twenty-two-year-old mother, Stacy Errickson.[15] The Williams execution lasted seventeen minutes. Witnesses reported that he moved "up until three minutes before he was declared dead."[16] According to Jacob Rosenberg, one of the media witnesses at the execution, "His eyes began to droop and eventually close. . . . His breaths became deep and heavy. His back arched off the gurney [countless times] as he sucked in air."[17] Throughout the execution, state officials conducted consciousness checks by feeling his pulse and touching his eyes. After one check, a member of the execution team could be seen whispering, "I'm not sure."[18] In a statement to the press, Williams's lawyer said that he was "gravely concerned" about the execution and feared that Williams was conscious and in pain during the procedure.[19]

The executions of Jack Jones and Marcel Williams were followed by an even more troubling execution three days later—the fourth and final killing of the week. On April 27, 2017, Kenneth Williams became the 200th person—and the 140th African American—to be executed in Arkansas since 1913. About three minutes after receiving a dose of midazolam, Williams began to thrash about and convulse on the gurney. One reporter said that he "lurched forward 15 times, then another five times, more slowly" before gasping and "taking labored breaths."[20] Witnesses could hear the inmate moaning and groaning.

Despite those widely reported details, state officials insisted that everything went as planned, calling the execution "flawless." A Department of Corrections spokesperson insisted that "Williams [only] coughed without sound—in direct contradiction of media witness testimony."[21] Governor Asa Hutchinson refused to heed calls for an investigation and reportedly "remained confident in the state's protocol."[22]

Yet, an independent autopsy confirmed that Williams's execution was anything but flawless. Joseph Cohen, the California-based pathologist who conducted it, concluded that Williams "experienced pain" and likely felt "a sensation of air hunger, fear, shortness of breath, respiratory distress, and dizziness."[23] The press and Williams's legal team described his execution as a "horrifying" botch.[24]

Even as it encountered mishaps in its rapid-paced executions, Arkansas did not slow down. Instead, it hid behind various provisions in its execution procedure—such as inserting the IV behind a curtain and switching off the microphone after an inmate's final words—that obscured key parts of the execution process from view. The state insisted, against considerable evidence to the contrary, that all went according to plan. More than three years later, a federal court cleared Arkansas to continue using midazolam in its executions, as long as it tweaked its procedures slightly.[25] This pattern of mishaps and responses now is paradigmatic of the practice of lethal injection across the United States.

Lethal Injection and the Modern Death Penalty

This single week in Arkansas provides a window into the fate of lethal injection and the consequences of the decomposition of the standard three-drug protocol. For every lethal injection during the more than thirty years between 1977 and 2009, all states had used the same lethal injection protocol. However, drug shortages beginning in 2009 forced

death penalty states to make a lethal choice. They could halt capital punishment, revive defunct methods of execution, or try new ways of carrying out lethal injection. Most chose the third option, turning to untested
drugs and drug combinations.

As a result, over the course of the last decade, the lethal injection paradigm decomposed. For many years, lethal injection meant the use of a
single drug; now it signifies an execution method that uses a wide variety
of drugs and procedures. In this section, we first recount the origins of
the once standard three-drug protocol before turning to the protocol's col-
lapse and the rise of new lethal injection techniques. Next, we discuss what
happened in the execution chamber during lethal injections carried out
between 2010 and 2020 and show that as states switched to new drug protocols, lethal injection became more prone to mishaps. Finally, we examine
state responses to the threat that mishaps pose to lethal injection. In the
face of criticism, they adopted secrecy statutes and adjusted their procedural documents to both prevent and obscure mishaps. In our conclusion,
we take up what lethal injection's decomposition means for the practice
itself and for the United States' continuing use of capital punishment.

In July 1976, the Supreme Court ended a four-year de facto moratorium
on the death penalty when it announced its decision in the landmark case
Gregg v. Georgia.[26] After *Gregg*, thirty-seven death penalty states reinstated
capital punishment, including Oklahoma. The same month the *Gregg*
decision was announced, Oklahoma governor David Boren convened a
special legislative session to swiftly restore capital punishment.[27] Although
Oklahoma law designated the electric chair as its method of execution, the
state's only electric chair was no longer in working condition.[28]

Responding to this situation, State Senator Bill Dawson and State
Representative Bill Wiseman proposed that the state adopt a new
method of execution: lethal injection. New York State had been the
first state to consider adopting lethal injection, in 1888, but the method
had never been used to execute an inmate in the United States or elsewhere.[29] Dawson and Wiseman argued that lethal injection had two
clear advantages over other methods. First, it was much cheaper than
other methods of execution, including electrocution, lethal gas, hanging,
and shooting.[30] They also claimed, without any sort of evidence, that it
would be more humane. Death could be accomplished with "no struggle, no stench, no pain."[31]

For advice about which drugs might be used, they reached out to the Oklahoma Medical Association, which refused to help for fear of violating medical ethics. The legislators had trouble enlisting help from other medical practitioners until they consulted A. Jay Chapman, Oklahoma's chief medical examiner. Later, Chapman described himself as "an expert in dead bodies but not an expert in getting them that way."[32]

Believing that lethal injection would be less violent and gruesome than the electric chair, Chapman offered a blueprint for Oklahoma's lethal injection law: "An intravenous saline drip shall be started in the prisoner's arm, into which shall be introduced a lethal injection consisting of an ultrashort-acting barbiturate in combination with a chemical paralytic."[33] This language would quickly become the model for many states' lethal injection laws.

The proposal to adopt lethal injection was very controversial among death penalty supporters. Some argued that making executions less gruesome and painful would weaken the death penalty's deterrent effect. Others said that it would prompt suicidal people to commit murders in hopes of dying painlessly via lethal injection.[34] Few disputed the premise that this new execution method was indeed more humane than other methods.

During Oklahoma's legislative debate, State Senator Gene Stipe offered an amendment to limit the duration of lethal injections.[35] He argued that if there was no such limit, the condemned might languish between life and death for hours or even days. Stipe proposed a five-minute limit, contending that the longest recorded hanging in U.S. history lasted four minutes and fifty-eight seconds and no electrocution exceeded five minutes. The amendment failed, but not before the bill's sponsors remarked that they expected most executions to take less than five minutes.

After extensive debate, the Oklahoma Senate passed the lethal injection bill by a 26–20 vote; the house soon followed suit, 74–18. On May 11, 1977, the governor signed legislation making Oklahoma the first state to adopt lethal injection as its method of execution.

Initially, the state's new execution protocol called for the use of only two drugs: sodium thiopental, the "ultrashort-acting barbiturate" that would anesthetize the inmate, and pancuronium bromide, the "chemical paralytic" that would asphyxiate the inmate. Potassium chloride, the final piece of the traditional three-drug protocol, which stops the heart, was added to the protocol four years later, before anyone was put to death by lethal injection, even though its lethal injection statute made no mention of a third drug.[36]

As Senator Dawson hoped, the new lethal injection law "put Oklahoma in one of those rare instances of being a pioneer."[37] However, at the same time that Oklahoma's bill was up for debate, the Texas legislature also considered a bill that would change the state's method of execution from electrocution to lethal injection. In Texas, lethal injection's proponents stressed that lethal injection would be a less violent alternative to electrocution. Texas Representative George Robert Close described electrocution as "a very scary thing to see. Blood squirts out of the nose. The eyeballs pop out. The body almost virtually catches fire. I voted for a more humane treatment because death is pretty final. That's enough of a penalty."[38] W. J. Estelle, the director of the Texas Department of Corrections, argued that "the lethal injection method suits our state of civilization more than electrocution."[39]

In Texas, death penalty supporters worried that lethal injection provided an easy way out for criminals. They claimed that its supposed lack of pain and violence defeated the primary purpose of the death penalty—to deter future crimes. Underlying their objection to lethal injection was a belief that vicious murderers did not deserve to die painlessly or more humanely than their victims did.

Death penalty opponents also objected to the Texas lethal injection bill, arguing that the death penalty itself is inhumane and cruel regardless of the method used.[40] Abolitionists were concerned that switching to lethal injection, which better masks signs of violence and pain, would "salve the public conscience" and open an execution floodgate.[41] Pointing to the fact that Black inmates were much more likely to get the death penalty for similar crimes than their white counterparts, critics added that the apparent humanity of lethal injection would not benefit the condemned but instead "the affluent white majority which kills blacks, browns and poor 'white n–' in the name of Texas."[42] Abolitionist groups packed House committee hearings hoping to pressure lawmakers to halt all state executions.[43]

Despite these efforts, Texas became the second state to adopt lethal injection, on May 12, 1977, one day after Oklahoma. Texas's statute was almost identical to Oklahoma's and did not name specific drugs.[44] After spending several months considering various drugs and drug combinations, the Texas Department of Corrections decided to use "sodium thiopental in lethal doses."[45] And, like Oklahoma, Texas added pancuronium bromide and potassium chloride before carrying out its first lethal injection in 1982.

Death penalty states across the United States quickly followed Oklahoma and Texas in adopting lethal injection. Between 1977 and 1982, Idaho, New Mexico, Washington, and Massachusetts switched to lethal injection.[46] Unlike Oklahoma and Texas, which executed a combined total of 681 inmates between 1976 and 2020, these four states have executed only nine inmates in total over the same time period.[47] Three of these early adopters—New Mexico, Washington, and Massachusetts—have since abolished the death penalty.

In December 1982, Texas used its three-drug lethal injection protocol for the first time, in the execution of Charles Brooks Jr.[48] Brooks's death did not live up to lethal injection's promise of a quick and humane death. Before the drugs began to flow, three technicians repeatedly failed in their efforts to insert an IV into a vein in Brooks's arm, spattering with blood the sheet covering him.[49] During the several minutes it took for the drugs to take effect, Brooks's eyes looked forward in terror. He wagged his head, his fingers trembled, he mouthed words, and let out a harsh rasp.[50] It took seven minutes for Brooks to die.

Despite these problems, states continued to adopt lethal injection. By the end of 1983, seven additional states—Arkansas, Illinois, Montana, Nevada, New Jersey, North Carolina, and Utah—had switched their execution method to lethal injection."[51] By 1988, a total of twenty-one states had passed lethal injection statutes. Strikingly, every one of them chose the traditional three-drug protocol. This was still true when Nebraska became the thirty-ninth state to adopt the method in 2009. From 1982 until the end of 2009, every execution by lethal injection was done in one way: sodium thiopental to anesthetize the inmate, pancuronium bromide to paralyze them, and potassium chloride to stop their heart.

The Collapse of the Original Lethal Injection Paradigm

The post-2009 period has witnessed the unravelling of the original lethal injection paradigm with its three-drug protocol. By 2016, no states were employing it. Instead, they were executing people with a variety of novel drug combinations. The shift from one dominant drug protocol to many was made possible by the advent of a new legal doctrine that granted states wide latitude to experiment with their drugs. This doctrine had its beginnings in the Supreme Court's *Baze v. Rees*[52] decision, its first on the constitutionality of lethal injection.

In 2004, Ralph Baze, who had been sentenced to death in Kentucky for the murder of a sheriff and deputy sheriff, and another Kentucky inmate on death row, Thomas Bowling, filed lawsuits challenging the constitutionality of their upcoming executions. They contended that lethal injection violated the Eighth Amendment because an improper administration of the traditional three-drug protocol could cause "excruciating pain." They argued that because other execution methods posed a "lower risk of causing pain or suffering," the lethal injection protocol could inflict "unnecessary and wanton . . . pain." Baze and Bowling proposed two alternative protocols in their suits. The first used only sodium thiopental to cause an overdose, eschewing the second and third drugs. The second alternative omitted the paralytic agent while retaining the first and third drugs.

After the Kentucky Supreme Court upheld the state's execution protocol, Baze and Bowling appealed to the Supreme Court. The Court later ruled 7–2 against Baze and Bowling. The plurality opinion, written by Chief Justice Roberts and joined by Justices Samuel Alito and Anthony Kennedy, found lethal injection to be constitutional. Furthermore, it introduced the requirement that any plaintiff mounting an Eighth Amendment challenge to a method of execution had to present a "feasible, readily implemented" alternative that would "significantly reduce a substantial risk of severe pain."[53] The Court also held that pancuronium bromide, the paralytic in the three-drug combination, served the valid purposes of "hastening death" and "preserving the dignity of the procedure, especially where convulsions or seizures could be misperceived as signs of consciousness or distress."[54]

Baze indicated that the Court would defer to the choices states made concerning their execution protocols. It assigned to plaintiffs the burden of proving that protocols created an unconstitutional risk, rather than requiring states to prove that they did not do so.[55] As a result, states were left with considerable latitude to experiment with new protocols or to stick with the traditional three-drug protocol.

Just after *Baze*, an Ohio court decided that the state could no longer use a three-drug execution protocol, because it contravened state law.[56] To continue executing people, Ohio instead implemented a new protocol: a single large dose of sodium thiopental.[57] Ohio's break from tradition was the first step in lethal injection's decomposition. Though its switch was the result of litigation in state court, other states quickly followed suit, adopting the one-drug protocol because of its relative simplicity.[58] By the end of 2013, thirteen states had switched to such a protocol.

Just as Ohio's one-drug execution method began to spread, states started to encounter difficulties in obtaining execution drugs. Bowing to pressure from abolitionist groups, many U.S. drug manufacturers decided to limit the distribution of drugs used for lethal injections. One producer, the U.S. pharmaceutical company Hospira, stopped producing sodium thiopental entirely.[59] In December 2010, after losing access to this drug, Oklahoma executed John Duty with pentobarbital, another short-acting barbiturate that had never before been used in an execution.[60] For its second drug, Oklahoma used vecuronium bromide, a common substitute for the original pancuronium bromide.[61] For its third drug, Oklahoma continued to use potassium chloride.

With U.S. supply chains cut off, some states turned to European drug companies.[62] In response, the British anti–death penalty group Reprieve launched its Stop the Lethal Injection Project. Manufacturers that had been selling drugs for executions found themselves on the receiving end of a shaming campaign.[63] Later, both the United Kingdom and the European Union banned the exportation of drugs for executions. As Gibson and Lain note, European governments, not the drug companies themselves, were the "true change agents." Those governments insisted that those companies confirm to the abolitionist norms of what Gibson and Cain label the international "moral marketplace."[64]

In response to these decisions, other states soon followed Oklahoma's lead and started to use drugs like pentobarbital. Thirteen states held pentobarbital executions in 2011 alone.[65] Some used a one-drug pentobarbital protocol. By 2013, the concurrent shifts from three drugs to one drug and from sodium thiopental to pentobarbital had combined to produce four distinct lethal injection protocols.[66] Table 12.1 shows the

Table 12.1: Drug Protocols Used between 2010 and 2013

	One-drug	Three-drug
Sodium thiopental	Ohio, Washington	Texas, Louisiana, Oklahoma, Florida, Mississippi, Virginia, Alabama, Georgia, Arizona
Pentobarbital	Ohio, Arizona, Idaho, Texas, South Dakota, Georgia, Missouri	Oklahoma, Texas, South Carolina, Mississippi, Alabama, Arizona, Texas, Georgia, Delaware, Virginia, Florida, Idaho

drug protocols used in executions from January 2010 through September 2013, by state (states that held executions with multiple protocols are listed twice). However, the switch to pentobarbital did not alleviate supply pressures.[67] Soon, the drug's only major producer began to restrict its sale to death penalty states.[68] As a result, states had to find other drugs to use in executions.

In 2013, Florida geared up to conduct the nation's first execution with midazolam hydrochloride in place of the first drug in its three-drug protocol.[69] Richard Dieter, executive director of the Death Penalty Information Center (DPIC), called it "an experiment on a living human being."[70] A lethal injection drug expert at the Death Penalty Clinic at the University of California, Berkeley, told National Public Radio (NPR) in 2013, "If [midazolam] does not in fact deeply anesthetize the prisoner, then he or she could be conscious and aware of being both paralyzed and able to experience pain and the experience of cardiac arrest."[71] Nevertheless, Florida's execution proceeded as planned. In 2014, Oklahoma, Arizona, and Ohio also conducted executions with midazolam.

Two of those states, Ohio and Arizona, did not just replace the first drug in the traditional three-drug protocol with midazolam, they also dropped the second and third drugs for hydromorphone, an opiate made from morphine.[72] In both states, the first executions using the new drug combination were botched, and no executions with that protocol have happened since.

However, states have continued to experiment with other drugs and drug combinations. Their forays beyond the well-trodden ground of barbiturates, the class of drugs to which sodium thiopental and pentobarbital belong, did not end with midazolam. In 2017, as drug manufacturers refused to provide Florida with that drug, the state chose to use a different sedative, etomidate, in its place. Etomidate is an ultra-short-acting sedative and anesthetic that has no analgesic (pain-blocking) abilities, and it had never before been used in an execution.[73]

Florida conducted seven executions with etomidate in combination with rocuronium bromide and potassium acetate between 2017 and 2019. In fact, that protocol's third drug was also a novel choice: Oklahoma inadvertently used potassium acetate instead of potassium chloride in a 2015 execution, but no state had used it intentionally when Florida adopted it in 2017.

Like Florida, Nebraska had trouble acquiring its lethal injection drugs in the latter part of the 2010s. After it failed for years to find drugs, the state allowed its corrections director to choose a new protocol. In 2018, Nebraska held the only U.S. execution conducted with a four-drug combination when it used diazepam, fentanyl, cisatracurium besylate, and potassium chloride.[74] The first three drugs, which tranquilized, knocked out, and paralyzed the inmate respectively, were all new to executions.

By the end of 2020, states had used at least ten distinct drug protocols in their executions.[75] Some protocols were used multiple times, and some were used just once. Even so, the traditional three-drug protocol was all but forgotten: its last use was in 2012. To better understand states' changing protocols over time, in table 12.2 we sort them into three different categories: barbiturate combinations, barbiturate overdoses, and sedative combinations. Figure 12.1 shows the dramatic changes in states' drug protocols. After years of experimentation, all that remains of

Table 12.2: Classification of Lethal Injection Drug Protocols

Classification	Characteristics	Examples
Barbiturate combination	Sodium thiopental or pentobarbital in combination with a paralytic and a heart-stopper	Sodium thiopental, pancuronium bromide, and potassium chloride (*traditional three-drug protocol*)
		Pentobarbital, rocuronium bromide, and potassium chloride
Barbiturate overdose	Sodium thiopental or pentobarbital on their own	Sodium thiopental alone
		Pentobarbital alone
Sedative combination	Midazolam, etomidate, or diazepam in combination with other drugs	Midazolam and hydromorphone
		Etomidate, vecuronium bromide, and potassium acetate

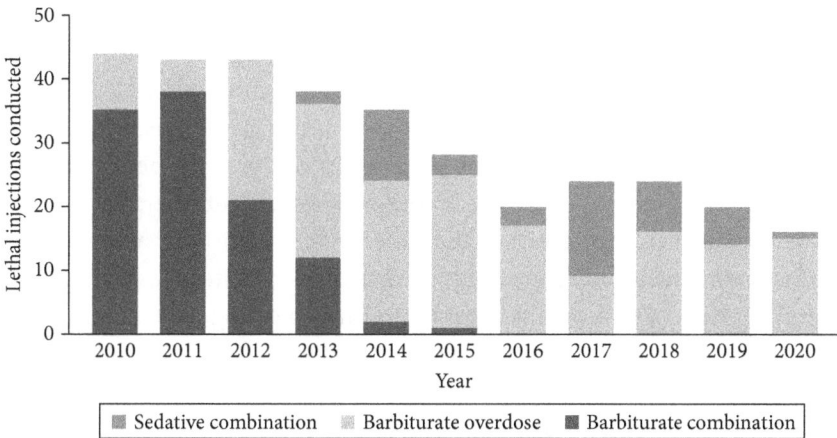

Figure 12.1: Protocol Type By Year of Use

the original paradigm is a needle in the inmate's arm and a declaration of death.[76]

Lethal Injection Mishaps, 2010–2020

From 2010 to the end of 2020, states and the federal government carried out 335 lethal injections, making up the overwhelming majority of executions in those eleven years.[77] As the executions of Jack Jones and Marcel Williams show, some of these executions went wrong. In what follows, we describe the ways in which the decade's mishaps occurred, the reasons they did, and how states, inmates, and others reacted when complications occurred.

Problems with U.S. executions are, of course, nothing new. For as long as the United States has used capital punishment, states have encountered such problems. Sarat et al. report that 3 percent of the executions carried out from 1890 to 2010 were botched in some way.[78] Hangings sometimes resulted in gruesome beheadings and slow asphyxiations. During electrocutions, inmates convulsed and occasionally burst into flames. Lethal gas, billed as yet another humane execution technology, caused its victims to cough, jerk, and writhe for several minutes before death. Lethal injection, too, as we have already noted, has not been free of mishaps.

To analyze lethal injection's problems over the last decade, we examined every execution for evidence of various mishaps—discrete, identifiable moments in an execution when lethal injection faltered. Mishaps include identifiable procedural errors committed by the execution team. For example, officials sometimes start the injection early, before the inmate can finish their last words. In other cases, executioners are unable to set intravenous lines or set them incorrectly. Mishaps also include unforeseen bodily reactions to lethal drugs, such as inmates crying out, claiming that the injections burn, coughing, gasping, or heaving their chests. These reactions signal that an inmate underwent unnecessary emotional or physical suffering, or otherwise responded to the execution in an unexpected way.

Such difficulties occurred in many lethal injections from 2010 through 2020.[79] For example, in twenty-seven of the lethal injections carried out during that period, or 8.1 percent, executioners struggled to set adequate IVs, as in the 2014 execution of Clayton Lockett in Oklahoma.[80]

In 1999, when he was twenty-three years old, Lockett beat and raped a group of young women before shooting and killing one of them.[81] At his trial, Lockett's counsel offered no defense. After three hours of deliberation, the jury found him guilty of "conspiracy, first-degree burglary, three counts of assault with a dangerous weapon, three counts of forcible oral sodomy, four counts of first-degree rape, four counts of kidnapping and two counts of robbery by force and fear."[82] He "was sentenced to death for first-degree murder, and more than 2,285 years in prison for his other convictions."[83]

Fifteen years later, after he had attempted suicide on the morning of his execution, guards dragged Lockett into Oklahoma's death chamber.[84] Once there, and after the inmate was strapped to a gurney, a paramedic tried to place an intravenous line in Lockett's arms and feet but failed to find an adequate vein. After three failed attempts, the paramedic asked for assistance from a doctor on hand, who ostensibly was there only to check for consciousness and to pronounce the time of death. Fifty-one minutes after starting to place the IV, the two successfully placed it in Lockett's groin in a painful and invasive procedure. They covered the IV with a sheet to hide Lockett's groin from the witnesses.

At 6:23 p.m., the executioners started the flow of midazolam. Lockett looked confused for several minutes as he waited for the drugs to take effect, then closed his eyes. During the first consciousness check, the doctor found that Lockett was still conscious, prompting a two-minute pause before a second check. The second time, the doctor determined that Lockett was unconscious. At this point, the executioners injected the paralytic, vecuronium bromide.

After the injection, Lockett moved his feet and head while mumbling, "Oh, man." He began to writhe and struggle against the restraints holding him down. On the electric heart monitor, his heart rate fell by two thirds. The doctor again entered the execution chamber and lifted the sheet, revealing a "protrusion the size of a tennis ball" where the IV had failed.[85] Instead of sending the drugs into his bloodstream, they had gone into the flesh of his groin. The warden closed the curtain between the witness room and the execution chamber as the doctor and paramedic scrambled to finish the execution. At 6:56 p.m., the director of the Oklahoma Department of Corrections, who had watched from the witness room, stopped the execution. Ten minutes later, and more than forty minutes after the lethal injection drugs began to flow, Clayton Lockett died. Many reports say he died from a heart attack, but an independent autopsy attributed his death to the lethal injection drugs themselves.[86]

Lockett's botched lethal injection was one of the most infamous in the death penalty's recent history. However, even when the execution team sets effective lines—or realizes that they cannot set an effective IV and stops the execution—the process is often painful. As executioners poke and prod inmates with needles, they fall back on a variety of techniques that inflict substantially more pain than simply placing an IV into an arm.[87]

Even if the IV is set correctly, the rest of the lethal injection process is not pain free. In 4.8 percent of the last decade's lethal injections, inmates cried out in pain at some point during their executions. One such inmate was Anthony Shore, who was executed for a series of murders that gave him the name the "Tourniquet Killer."[88]

On January 18, 2018, with IVs already set, Shore apologized to his victims, saying that "no amount of words or apology could ever undo what I've done. . . . I wish I could undo the past, but it is what it is." Soon after the injection of compounded pentobarbital began, Shore cried, "Oooh-ee, I can feel that it does burn. Burning!"[89] He then shook on the gurney and struggled to breathe before dying thirteen minutes later, according to a witness's sworn affidavit.

The burning sensation that Shore reported occurs with surprising frequency in lethal injections.[90] In fact, this problem may result from specific changes that states have made to their lethal injection protocols. Over time, they have generally increased the amount of each drug that they inject into inmates. For example, Virginia's 1995 drug protocol called for 120 mEq of potassium chloride as its final drug; by 2011, it had doubled the dose to 240 mEq. Similarly, Oklahoma's execution protocol used 100 mg of midazolam when it executed Clayton Lockett; soon after, it increased the amount fivefold. These massive doses push lethal injection far outside of the realm of standard pharmaceutical practice.[91]

In eighty-three lethal injections, the inmate spoke or made noise after the injection began—utterances that ranged from screams or sobs to slurred sentences.[92] Commonly, inmates exhibit unusual breathing patterns, body movements, and dramatic changes in skin color. On seventy-three occasions, efforts may have included coughing, snorting, and other sudden respirations. In 183 lethal injections, the inmate moved after the injection began. Many twitched or jerked, some heaved their chests, and others fluttered their eyes as the drugs took effect.

Some of these reactions may be inevitable consequences of death by lethal injection. Lethal injection works on a microscopic level inside the inmate, concealing its operation from view.[93] In fact, medical professionals disagree about how each of the drugs used in lethal injection actually kills.[94] Further complicating the effort to understand what happens during a lethal injection is the paralytic used in many protocols. If administered correctly, it prevents inmates from indicating any pain, even involuntarily, making it difficult for witnesses to determine if the condemned suffered.[95]

Though it is often impossible for inmates to register what is happening during a lethal injection, certain disturbing indications show that in practice, lethal injection often is far removed from the original promise that it would allow the condemned to die by peacefully falling asleep. In September 2020, an NPR investigation found signs of pulmonary edema—fluid filling the lungs—in 84 percent of the 216 post–lethal injection autopsies it reviewed.[96] Some autopsies reveal that inmates' lungs filled while they continued to breathe, which would cause them to feel as if they were drowning and suffocating.[97]

As states switched drug protocols, the frequency and the nature of mishaps shifted dramatically. Most striking was the increased frequency with which witnesses or newspapers said that executions were "botched." Between 2010 and 2020, newspapers and independent witnesses used this term to describe twenty-eight of the lethal injections, or 8.4 percent.[98] Newspapers or witnesses characterized 7.3 percent of barbiturate overdose executions as botched, about twice the rate as barbiturate combinations (3.7%). In sedative combination executions, the rate skyrocketed to 22.4 percent.

Another striking difference between barbiturate combination protocols and the bevy of novel cocktails is how long they take to work. Between 2010 and 2020, barbiturate overdose executions lasted 62 percent longer than barbiturate combination executions, including the traditional three-drug protocol.[99] Sedative combinations resulted in executions that lasted twice as long as their barbiturate combination counterparts.[100]

The average execution time in 2010 was just over nine minutes. In 2020, the average time was over twenty minutes. More than seventy-four of the executions we analyzed took longer than twenty minutes—four times longer than lethal injection's creators expected the method to take.[101] In fact, almost none of the lethal injections between 2010 and 2020 lasted for fewer than five minutes. In a few jarring cases, lethal injections took longer than an hour to cause death. Why do executions take longer? Sedative combination protocols, which were commonly used in the latter half of the last decade, take more than twice as long to kill as barbiturate combination protocols, which were used predominantly in the first half of the 2010s.

The Choreography: States Change and Hide Procedures

States responded to the problems we have described in two different ways. Some states modified their execution procedures to make mishaps less likely; changes included adding consciousness checks, mandating that the IV be clearly visible, and inserting backup lines in case the primary line fails. Other states chose to make it harder to identify or label any irregularity in the execution chamber as a departure from their protocols and procedures. They introduced greater ambiguity and discretion into their procedures, affording executioners greater flexibility when something goes wrong. Some states also attempted to keep their procedures and drug suppliers secret from inmates and the public. These two responses, specificity and obfuscation, are not mutually exclusive. In fact, as states made changes to prevent errors and complications, they often made other procedures less detailed.[102]

As the lethal injection paradigm decomposed, some death penalty states attempted to avert preventable errors with procedural adjustments. For example, they added steps to stages of the lethal injection process where preventable mistakes commonly occur, such as in the injection of the sedative or anesthetic. If the executioners inject the second or third drugs before the first drug anesthetizes the inmate, the condemned will suffer excruciating pain. Similarly, paralytics must have time to immobilize the inmate, or his pain will be apparent to witnesses as he jerks and squirms on the table. In the late 2000s and early 2010s, at least nine states[103] specified waiting periods between the injection of each drug in the lethal cocktail. One particularly instructive case is Virginia, which had made no mention of waiting periods in its October 2010 protocol. However, the state's July 2012 protocol called for a thirty-second waiting period after the first drug's injection, and by February 2014 its procedure called for a two-minute waiting period at the same juncture.[104]

After 2010, at least seven state procedures[105] required that officials conduct "consciousness checks" on the condemned inmate. Executioners must evaluate an inmate's consciousness with auditory and physical stimuli between injecting the first and second drugs. For example, in its December 2010 protocol, Pennsylvania instructed officials to close the curtain and call the inmate's name in a loud voice before "assess[ing] consciousness of the inmate by tactical stimulation . . . touching the inmate's shoulder and brushing the inmate's eyelashes."[106]

A few states also added specificity when it comes to the placement of IVs, especially after the botched execution of Clayton Lockett. Oklahoma, for example, required officials to record the number of IV insertion attempts, read the drug name out loud before its administration, leave the IV in the inmate after death for a medical examiner to see, and ensure that the IV insertion remains visible.

Ohio's 2004 protocol only briefly mentioned IV access. It recorded a preference for setting IVs into the inmate's arms but did not require anything of the execution team to ensure the IVs are working. In 2009, before Lockett's ill-fated execution, Ohio began to specify that execution- ers use a saline drip to test the IVs, perform vein assessments ahead of time, and ensure that the IV insertion points are visible throughout the execution.

Procedural specificity also occurs in protocols that identify deci- sional contingencies (if, then) in the lethal injection process. We call this "branching." From 2010 to 2020, many lethal injection protocols came to resemble decision trees with many branches, rather than a simple set of instructions. Figure 12.2 displays Ohio's protocol as a decision tree.

At least fourteen states[107] adopted one or more elements of branch- ing, providing additional instructions in case IV lines cannot be es- tablished, drugs do not cause unconsciousness or death, or an IV line fails. Three of these states—Arizona, Idaho, and Oklahoma—include a contingency procedure to revive the inmate if they go into cardiac arrest. These protocols provide executioners with specific methods to address various problems as they arise. Further, by acknowledging a wide range of potential complications, states ensure that fewer events fall outside the purview of lethal injection protocols, making even problematic le- thal injections more difficult to criticize.

Increases in specificity may help imbue lethal injection with legiti- macy after problematic executions. In making changes, states implic- itly signal that lethal injection can be improved by better procedures and that they are committed to such improvement. Legal scholar Jody Madeira notes that mistakes have been normalized in the lethal in- jection paradigm: "Corrections has long explored execution methods through a 'learning-by-doing' process, and may interpret each botched execution as a unique event instead of a patterned consequence of haphazard lethal injection reform."[108] By amending their procedures, states treat lethal injection mishaps as anomalies—wrongs that can be righted with procedural tweaks.

At the same time that they dealt with mishaps by adding checks to their procedures, death penalty states attempted to obscure the existing problems by hiding executions, and information related to executions, from public view. According to the DPIC, of the seventeen states that carried out executions between 2011 and 2018, fourteen prevented wit- nesses from seeing at least one part of the execution, fifteen prevented

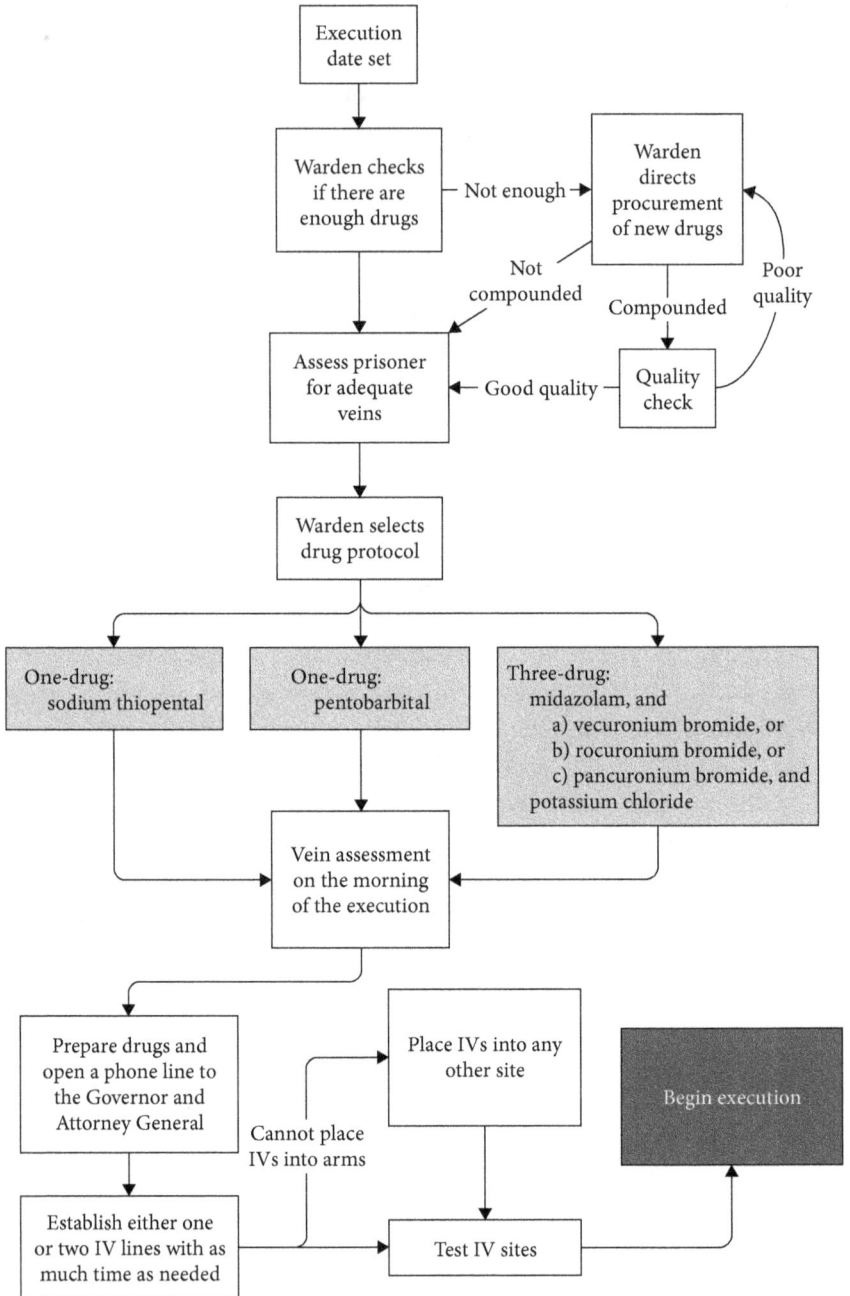

Figure 12.2: Branching in Ohio's Lethal Injection Procedure

witnesses from hearing the sounds of the execution, and sixteen concealed the source of the drugs used.[109] All seventeen states prevented witnesses from seeing when the lethal drugs were administered.[110] As states hide more of their procedures and executions, it becomes increasingly difficult to know if, or when, an execution went wrong.

Another way states have adapted to execution mishaps is by making their protocols *less specific* at certain points of the process. They have done this by introducing greater ambiguity in the language governing crucial parts of their protocols. For example, even as states have added more checks to ensure that IVs are working, they also have allowed executioners to attempt to set lines for longer periods of time and in more places on the inmates' bodies, requiring only that they act in a "reasonable" manner, without defining what counts as reasonable. Thus, Ohio's procedure, exemplifying the language used in many post-2010 death penalty protocols, allows its IV team to "make such a number of attempts to establish an IV site as *may be reasonable*" (italics added).

States also have added ambiguity to the process by removing language pertaining to the duration of executions. No state procedures now specify a maximum time that should pass between injection and death. As a result, lethal injection's critics cannot point to a specific regulation in order to hold states accountable for prolonged executions.

In fact, the refusal of courts and legislatures to impose time constraints on executions has been integral to the survival of lethal injection.[111] One exemplary case *West v. Schofield* (2017), before the Tennessee Supreme Court.[112] Several inmates challenged the constitutionality of the state's one-drug pentobarbital protocol, partially on the grounds that it creates a substantial risk of a lingering death. One of the defendants' expert witnesses reviewed thirty pentobarbital executions conducted in Georgia, Ohio, and Texas and found that all of these executions resulted in death within thirty minutes of the first pentobarbital injection. Because no procedural, legal, or judicial standard of "lingering death" had ever been established, the Tennessee court had to decide whether a half-hour death constituted cruel and unusual punishment. Without explicitly affirming a thirty-minute standard for lethal injections, it ruled in favor of the protocol's constitutionality.

By explicitly or implicitly authorizing officials to exercise discretion, states have made it hard to say when complications occur. For example, several states have set extremely broad expectations about how long the IV insertion should take. In 2017, Kentucky specified a one-hour window for the process before an execution must be stopped,[113] but in 2018 it revised its protocol and expanded that window to three hours. In 2016, Ohio made its lack of a standard explicit, writing in its protocol that the IV insertion team should take "as much time as necessary."

While protocols previously limited IV insertion site options to minimize pain, more recently they allow for a wider array of sites. In 2006, Missouri was the only death penalty state to allow for IV insertions anywhere, including painfully through the femoral vein, which runs from the upper thigh to the pelvic area. After 2010, eight states[114] provided lists of ordered preferences for a large number of insertion sites, and protocols from least thirteen states[115] indicated no preference for an IV site, leaving that decision for the IV team to make. Additionally, in the same period, four states[116] explicitly called for a "cutdown" procedure[117] in order to place a central venous line (in the chest) when necessary, and three of them currently call for it. Protocols in four more states[118] allow a central venous line placement without proscribing a cutdown.

Discretion is also frequently permitted in cases where the dosage prescribed by a protocol is insufficient to kill. At least nineteen states' protocols[119] have allowed officials overseeing an execution to inject additional doses as they see fit. Thirteen of those states[120] have left the length of the waiting period between rounds of injection completely up to prison officials' discretion. Among states that do specify a waiting period length, the periods are inconsistent.[121] Occasionally, permission for a second injection is accompanied by permission for a range of other actions. For example, Oklahoma's 2015 protocol allows the execution team to close the curtain, remove all of the witnesses, inject additional doses, and "determine how to proceed"—a generous grant of discretion that gives officials room to change the procedure on the fly.

Moreover, the choice of drugs for any particular execution is increasingly left to the warden overseeing the execution. At least fourteen death penalty states[122] no longer specify a particular drug protocol, as they did before 2009. Instead, they allow officials to choose from a menu of drugs and drug combinations if needed.[123] Idaho's 2012 protocol says that "which option is used is dependent on the availability of chemicals," making explicit that these menus serve to enable executions to proceed in the face of drug shortages.

Ambiguity and discretion provide executioners with a kind of blank check that brings lingering, fraught deaths into the fold of acceptable executions. Ambiguous language allows officials to elide details and avoid the specific provisions that once protected inmates from painful procedures and protracted executions. The discretion that protocols now allow means that executioners have wide latitude to modify execution procedures, allowing them to do what they decide is necessary to kill the inmate while acting within the authority granted by the state.

Conclusion: Failure, Reform, Failure in the United States' Death Penalty System

The recent history of lethal injection echoes the longer history of the death penalty. When states encountered problems with earlier methods of execution, they first attempted to address these problems by tinkering with their existing methods. When tinkering failed, they adopted allegedly more humane execution methods. When they ran into difficulties with the new methods, state actors scrambled to hide the death penalty from public view.[124] They have followed this same playbook during the era of lethal injection.

Since 2010, states have tinkered with procedures and implemented secrecy measures. Our glimpse into the death chamber—aided by newspaper articles, independent investigations, and court documents—reveals that procedural changes have done little to make lethal injection more humane.[125] According to Deborah Denno, "It is questionable whether any of the [changes to lethal injection procedures] . . . can fix [them] with a sufficient degree of reliability."[126] In fact, lethal injection became more prone to error as states switched from barbiturate combinations to other types of drug protocols.[127] As the original lethal injection paradigm has decomposed, its problems have grown.

Some states have responded to the problems with lethal injection by resurrecting older methods of execution as backups in case lethal injection becomes "unavailable" in the future. In 2014 and 2015, six states made the firing squad, electrocution, or lethal gas their backup method of execution, and the federal government joined them in 2020.[128] If lethal injection becomes "unavailable," Missouri, Utah, and Wyoming allow execution by firing squad; Tennessee will execute by electric chair; and Oklahoma will execute with nitrogen gas.[129]

The recent actions of Ohio governor Mike Dewine may shed particular light on the fate of lethal injection. On December 8, 2020, Dewine announced an "unofficial moratorium" on his state's death penalty.[130] The moratorium came almost three years after a federal judge compared Ohio's lethal injection procedure to "waterboarding, suffocation, and exposure to chemical fire." The judge found that lethal injection "will almost certainly subject prisoners to severe pain and needless suffering." Dewine responded that "Ohio is not going to execute someone under my watch when a federal judge has found it to be cruel and unusual punishment." [131] Ohio's subsequent efforts to keep lethal injection alive—by switching drug cocktails, adding checks to its procedure, and obscuring mishaps in its death chamber—have not solved its problems.

Some scholars argue that the evolution of the United States' methods of execution is a story of progress.[132] To them, the adoption of each new execution method marked the abandonment of more barbaric and gruesome methods.[133] But 2010 to 2020 was less a period of progress than one of deterioration and decline. New drugs and drug combinations may have allowed the machinery of death to keep running, and new procedures may have given the increasingly jerry-rigged lethal injection process a veneer of legitimacy, but none of these changes has resolved its fate or repaired its vexing problems. As Arkansas found out during its 2017 execution spree, there is little that can be done to save lethal injection from its status as the United States' least reliable and most problematic death penalty method.

Notes

An earlier version of this essay appeared in the *British Journal of American Legal Studies* 11 (2022): 81–111.

1 Mark Berman, "With Lethal Injection Drugs Expiring, Arkansas Plans Unprecedented Seven Executions in 11 Days," *Washington Post*, April 7, 2017.

2 Lethal Injection Procedure (Attachment C), Arkansas Department of Corrections, 2013.

3 Jeannie Nuss, "Arkansas Turns to Different Lethal Injection Drug," *AP News*, April 19, 2013.

4 Lethal Injection Procedure.

5 Eric Besson, John Moritz, and Aziza Musa, "State Carries Out 1 Execution," *Arkansas Democrat-Gazette* (Little Rock), April 21, 2017.

6 Previous midazolam executions had been botched and riddled with mishaps. "Witnessing Death: AP Reporters Describe Problem Executions," *AP News*, April 29, 2017.

7 He developed diabetes in prison and had a leg amputated.

8 Andrew DeMillo and Kelly P. Kissel, "Arkansas Executes Jones," *AP News*, April 25, 2017.

9 Ed Pilkington, Jamiles Lartey, and Jacob Rosenberg, "Arkansas Carries Out First Double Execution in the US for 16 Years," *The Guardian*, April 25, 2017.

10 Eric Besson, Lisa Hammersly, and John Moritz, "2 Killers Executed Hours Apart," *Arkansas Democrat-Gazette* (Little Rock), April 25, 2017.

11 Besson, Hammersly, and Moritz, "2 Killers Executed."

12 DeMillo and Kissel, "Arkansas Executes Jones."

13 Kelly P. Kissel, "New Issue in Executions: Should the Death Chamber Be Silent?," Associated Press, April 25, 2017.

14 John Moritz, "4 Arkansas Inmates Died of Injection, Recently Completed Reports Show," *Arkansas Democrat-Gazette* (Little Rock), June 8, 2017.

15 Frank E. Lockwood, "Arkansas Jurors Were Never Told of Marcel Williams' Life; Grave Error, Judge Said," *Arkansas Democrat-Gazette* (Little Rock), April 24, 2017.

16 Fiona Keating, "Judge Orders Blood and Tissue Samples from Botched Arkansas Execution Body for Autopsy," *International Business Times*, April 30, 2017.

17 Keating, "Judge Orders."

18 Kissel, "New Issue in Executions."

19 Keating, "Judge Orders."

20 Liliana Segura, "Arkansas Justice: Racism, Torture, and a Botched Execution," *The Intercept*, November 12, 2017.

21 Phil McCausland, "Arkansas Execution of Kenneth Williams 'Horrifying': Lawyer," *NBC News*, April 27, 2017.

22 McCausland, "Arkansas Execution."

23 Moritz, "4 Arkansas Inmates Died of Injection."

24 McCausland, "Arkansas Execution."

25 Andrew DeMillo, "Federal Judge Upholds Use of Sedative in Arkansas Executions," *AP News*, June 2, 2020.

26 428 U.S. 153 (1976).

27 Russell Von Creel, "Capital Punishment," in *The Encyclopedia of Oklahoma History and Culture*, ed. Dianna Everett et al. (Oklahoma City: Oklahoma Historical Society, 2008), 219.

28 *Third Reading of SB 10*, 1977.

29 Elbridge T. Gerry, Alfred P. Southwick, and Matthew Hale, *Report of the Commission to Investigate and Report the Most Humane and Practical Method of Carrying into Effect the Sentence of Death in Capital Cases* (Troy, NY: Troy Press, 1888).

30 *Third Reading of SB 10*, 1977.

31 Vince Beiser, "A Guilty Man," *Mother Jones*, September/October 2005.

32 Deborah W. Denno, "The Lethal Injection Quandary: How Medicine Has Dismantled the Death Penalty," *Fordham Law Review* 76, no. 1 (2007): 66.

33 Denno, 66–67.

34 *Motion to Reconsider Vote on SB 10*, 1977.

35 *Third Reading of SB 10*, 1977.

36 Denno, "Lethal Injection Quandary," 74.

37 *Motion to Reconsider Vote on SB 10*, 1977.

38 Jonathan R. Sorenson and Rocky LeAnn Pilgrim, *Lethal Injection: Capital Punishment in Texas during the Modern Era* (Austin: University of Texas Press, 2006), 9.

39 Sorenson and Pilgrim, 10.

40 Sorenson and Pilgrim, 9–11.

41 *House Study Group Bill Analysis of HB 945*, Texas House of Representatives Committee on Criminal Jurisprudence, 1977.

42 Sorenson and Pilgrim, *Lethal Injection*, 11.

43 "Execution Opponents Seek Moratorium," *Lubbock Avalanche-Journal*, February 28, 1977.

44 *An Act Relating to Criminal Procedure; Amending 22 O.S. 1971, Section 1014; Specifying the Manner of Inflicting Punishment of Death; and Making Provisions Severable 1977; An Act Relating to the Method of Execution of Convicts Sentenced to Death; Amending Articles 43.14 and 43.18 of the Code of Criminal Procedure, 1965, As Amended*, 1977.

45 James Welsh, "The Medical Technology of Execution: Lethal Injection," *International Review of Law, Computers and Technology* 12, no. 1 (1998): 75–98.

46 Idaho in 1978, New Mexico in 1979, Washington in 1981, and Massachusetts in 1982.

47 According to the Death Penalty Information Center's Execution Database (https://deathpenaltyinfo.org/), Idaho executed three inmates with lethal injection, New Mexico executed one, Washington executed five, and Massachusetts executed none.

48 Dick Reavis, "Charlie Brooks' Last Words," *Texas Monthly*, February 1, 1983.

49 Don Colburn, "Lethal Injection," *Washington Post*, December 11, 1990.

50 Reavis, "Charles Brooks' Last Words."

51 Denno, "Lethal Injection Quandary."

52 *Baze v. Rees*, 553 U.S. 35 (2008).

53 *Baze*, 553 U.S. at 52.

54 *Baze*, 553 U.S. at 57.

55 This standard, promulgated by the plurality of the Court in *Baze*, became the basis for the majority opinion in *Glossip v. Gross*, 135 S. Ct. 2726 (2015). In *Glossip*, petitioners challenged Oklahoma's midazolam lethal injection protocol. The Court held that the protocol was permissible for the same reasons that Kentucky's use of the traditional three-drug protocol was permissible in *Baze*. Nowadays,

the requirement that inmates present a readily available alternative method that significantly reduces a substantial risk of severe pain is known as the "*Glossip* doctrine."

56 Deborah Denno, "Lethal Injection Chaos Post-*Baze*," *Georgetown Law Journal* 102 (2013): 1354.

57 The new protocol was the same as the one that Ralph Baze and Thomas Bowling had suggested in *Baze v. Rees*.

58 Denno, "Lethal Injection Chaos," 1358–60.

59 Jeffrey E. Stern, "The Cruel and Unusual Execution of Clayton Lockett," *The Atlantic*, June 2015.

60 Sean Murphy, "Man Apologizes to Victim's Family," *The Oklahoman* (Oklahoma City), December 17, 2010.

61 In general, we do not distinguish drug protocols that switch their second and third drugs for close analogues that have the same intended effect when injected. For example, states sometimes substitute vecuronium bromide or rocuronium bromide for pancuronium bromide, as is the case here. With few exceptions, it is very difficult to determine exactly which second and third drugs a state used in a given execution, because newspapers commonly report the first drug but not the others. Furthermore, execution procedures often allow many choices between second and third drugs.

62 Raymond Bonner, "Drug Company in Cross Hairs of Death Penalty Opponents," *New York Times*, March 30, 2011.

63 "A Prolonged Stay: The Reasons Behind the Slow Pace of Executions." ProPublica. May 22, 2013. www/propublica.org/.

64 James Gibson and Corian Barrett Lain, "Death Penalty Drugs and the International Moral Marketplace," *Georgetown Law Journal* 100, no. 5 (2015): 1215.

65 The states were Oklahoma, Texas, South Carolina, Mississippi, Alabama, Arizona, Texas, Georgia, Delaware, Virginia, Florida, Idaho, and Ohio.

66 Administrative documents allowed for even more novel drug combinations, like midazolam and hydromorphone, as backups.

67 "Ohio Turns to Untried Execution Drug Mix Due to Shortage of Pentobarbital," *The Guardian*, October 28, 2013.

68 David Jolly, "Danish Company Blocks Sale of Drug for U.S. Executions," *New York Times*, July 1, 2011.

69 Morgan Watkins, "Happ Executed Using New Drug," *Gainesville Sun*, October 15, 2013. Just as we do not typically distinguish between protocols that use close analogues in the second or third drugs, we do not distinguish between protocols using midazolam and midazolam hydrochloride. Newspaper reports and administrative protocols are generally not specific enough to do so.

70 Bill Cottrell, "Florida Executes Man with New Lethal Injection Drug," Reuters, October 15, 2013.

71 "Lacking Lethal Injection Drugs, States Find Untested Backups," *NPR*, October 26, 2013.

72 Hydromorphone had never been used in a lethal injection. The federal court that approved the first execution with Ohio's new protocol wrote, "There is absolutely no question that Ohio's current protocol presents an experiment in lethal injection processes." *In re Ohio Execution Protocol Litigation*, 994 F. Supp. 2d 906 (2014).

73 Lesley M. Williams, Katharine L. Boyd, and Brian M. Fitzgerald, "Etomidate," in *StatPearls* (Treasure Island, FL: StatPearls, 2021).

74 Mitch Smith, "Fentanyl Used to Execute Nebraska Inmate, in a First for U.S.," *New York Times*, August 14, 2018.

75 The true number is likely higher due to untraceable differences in analogous second and third drugs.

76 Sometimes, as in the case of Romell Broom, not even death is guaranteed.

77 In that time, Virginia electrocuted two people, Utah shot one, and Tennessee electrocuted five, for a total of 343 executions.

78 Austin Sarat, Katherine Blumstein, Aubrey Jones, Heather Richard, and Madeline Sprung-Keyser, *Gruesome Spectacles: Botched Executions and America's Death Penalty* (Stanford, CA: Stanford University Press, 2014).

79 To find mishaps, we conducted a thorough examination of every execution attempt from 2010 to 2020. First, we used the DPIC's Execution Database (2021) to build a list of every execution in the United States over those eleven years. Then, we compiled multiple news articles with firsthand accounts of each execution. Since court filings often contain more detailed information about specific executions, we used state and federal court documents to augment our database. We then developed a coding system to standardize how we would classify events in each execution. For example, to identify "sudden respiration," we looked for the keywords *gasping, snorting, coughing, sputtering, grunting, blowing*, and *choking* in the documents. Another researcher did a blind recoding of every execution to ensure accuracy. We further augmented the DPIC's database with the drugs used in each execution.

80 Stern, "Cruel and Unusual Execution."

81 Ziva Branstetter, "Death Row Inmate Killed Teen Because She Wouldn't Back Down," *Tulsa World*, April 20, 2014.

82 Jaime Fuller, "Why Were the Two Inmates in Oklahoma on Death Row in the First Place?," *Washington Post*, April 30, 2014.

83 Fuller.

84 Guards had to use a Taser on Lockett to get him to leave his cell that morning.

85 Stern, "Cruel and Unusual Execution."

86 "Autopsy: Oklahoma Inmate Dies from Lethal Injection Drugs, Not Heart Attack after 'Botched' Execution," *KFOR-TV*, August 28, 2014.

87 This kind of mishap occurred, for instance, in the attempted execution of sixty-nine-year-old Alva Campbell. Campbell had been sentenced to death for killing a teenager during a carjacking twenty years prior to his execution. In November 2017, an Ohio medical team used an ultraviolet light to probe both of Alva Campbell's arms for a suitable vein. The team poked Campbell twice with a needle

in his right arm, then once in his left. But Campbell had lung cancer, chronic obstructive pulmonary disease, and pneumonia, and he relied on daily oxygen treatments; none of these veins could support the IV. When they tried his left leg, Campbell threw his head back and cried out in pain. The *Columbus Dispatch* reported that after the prison director called off the execution, "Campbell removed his glasses and appeared to rub tears from his withered face." Marty Schladen, "After Four Unsuccessful Needle Pokes, Columbus Killer's Execution Called Off," *Columbus Dispatch*, November 15, 2017.

88 Jolie McCullough, "Texas Executes Houston Serial Killer Anthony Shore," *Texas Tribune* (Austin), January 18, 2018; Ed Pilkington, "Texas to Execute Third Prisoner This Year amid Reports of Botched Killings," *The Guardian*, February 1, 2018.

89 Michael Graczyk, "'Tourniquet Killer' Executed in Texas for 1992 Strangling," *AP News*, January 19, 2018.

90 Lawyers have called on medical experts to explain the phenomenon in the courtroom. In Ohio's long-running lethal injection consolidated case, a federal district court received hundreds of pages of testimony from doctors and pharmacists about the effects of midazolam. As one doctor in that case remarked, "Midazolam itself is highly acidic, and while that is not problematic when the drug is used in therapeutic doses, at the dosage used in the protocol, it may cause severe burning pain upon injection." Another doctor, this time called by the state, disagreed and argued that midazolam could not cause a burning sensation, even in high doses. Ultimately, the court ruled that it was "certain or very likely that . . . midazolam cannot reduce consciousness to the level at which a condemned inmate will not experience severe pain." *Henness (In re Ohio Execution Protocol Litigation*, 2019 U.S. Dist. LEXIS 8200 (United States District Court for the Southern District of Ohio 2019). Though an appeals court later reversed the court's ruling, the mishap in Shore's execution—the inmate reporting pain during the execution—is central to today's legal challenges to lethal injection.

91 Even before increases, lethal injection protocols already used dosages far beyond what doctors had ever used therapeutically. Dosage increases have made it harder to evaluate and understand the effects of these drugs, introducing more uncertainty into lethal injection. Outside of the United States' execution chambers, no one has studied what happens when you inject someone with 500 mg of midazolam.

92 Often, witnesses cannot tell if an inmate is making sounds, because many states' execution chambers block any sounds from escaping. For example, in Arkansas's 2017 execution of Jack Jones, witnesses remarked that it looked as if Jones was making noise, but the state disputed that. States sometimes decide to turn off death chamber microphones soon after the final statement. For example, Oklahoma's September 2014 protocol required the execution team to turn off the microphone after the inmate's last words. In April 2014, before the execution of Clayton Lockett, Oklahoma's protocol did not mention the microphone at all. Microphone procedures are also the subject of death penalty litigation. The Ninth Circuit Court ruled

that Arizona had to keep its microphones on during executions to make sure that press witnesses could hear what happened, which would prevent the ambiguity seen in Jack Jones's execution. *First Amendment Coalition v. Ryan*, 938 F.3d 1069 (United States Court of Appeals for the Ninth Circuit 2019).

93 David R. Dow, "The Beginning of the End of America's Death-Penalty Experiment," *Politico*, July 25, 2014.

94 In many court cases that involve evaluating midazolam there is disagreement between medical experts. Examples include *Henness (In re Ohio Execution Protocol Litigation*, 2019 U.S. Dist. LEXIS 8200 (United States District Court for the Southern District of Ohio 2019) and *Glossip v. Gross*.

95 Sarat et al., *Gruesome Spectacles*.

96 Noah Caldwell, Alisa Chang, and Jolie Myers, "Gasping for Air: Autopsies Reveal Troubling Effects for Lethal Injection," NPR, September 21, 2020, https://www.npr .org/.

97 In our research, fifty-one executions we examined contained mishaps that suggest those inmates suffered from pulmonary edema, such as gurgling and gasping, two uncommon breathing changes that doctors identified as possible signs of pulmonary edema. Since the paralytics prevent some of these signs from being apparent to outside observers, our count includes only inmates who suffered pulmonary edema while they were still able to breathe, which accounts for the discrepancy between our count and NPR's.

98 Newspapers and witnesses rarely have access to the administrative documents that govern executions, but they often notice when something seems to have gone wrong. As such, we counted executions in this category when journalists mentioned that something was out of the ordinary as well as when they used the word *botch*. There was a slight increase in the rate from 1980 through 2010, when Sarat et al. found that 7.1% of lethal injections were botched. Sarat et al., *Gruesome Spectacles*, 177.

99 This difference is made even more remarkable by the fact that some states require a short waiting period between the first and next drugs in barbiturate and sedative combination executions. Despite that brief break, one-drug barbiturate overdose protocols took longer.

100 We found that executions between 2010 and 2020 that used a barbiturate combination lasted 10.4 minutes on average; barbiturate overdoses lasted 16.8 minutes; sedative combinations lasted 20.7 minutes.

101 As we remarked earlier in this chapter, the sponsor of Oklahoma's trailblazing lethal injection bill expected each execution to take less than five minutes.

102 We investigated protocol changes throughout the decade by collecting as many of the documents as we could. To do this, we filed Freedom of Information Act requests with the departments of corrections in all states that had the death penalty during the time period studied. Some states (including Delaware, Louisiana, South Carolina, and Wyoming) denied these requests, and most states provided information with information redacted. To supplement our protocol database,

we contacted Assistant Federal Public Defender Jennifer Moreno, who provided us with many protocols she was able to collect. Moreno formerly worked at the Berkeley Law School Lethal Injection Project. The claims we make are limited in scope because secrecy measures restrict our ability to create an exhaustive database.

103 These states are Arizona, Delaware, Idaho, Oklahoma, Pennsylvania, South Dakota, Tennessee, Utah, and Virginia.

104 In 2010, Virginia's first drug was sodium thiopental. In 2012, its first drug was pentobarbital. In 2014, Virginia permitted the first drug to be sodium thiopental, pentobarbital, or midazolam; regardless of the drug, the state prescribed a two-minute waiting period. Another example is Pennsylvania, which added a two-minute waiting period to its procedure in 2010.

105 These states are Alabama, California, Idaho, Oklahoma, Pennsylvania, South Dakota, and Virginia.

106 In August 2013, Missouri added a provision for medical personnel to "use standard clinical techniques to assess consciousness, such as checking for movement, opened eyes, eyelash reflex, [and] pupillary responses or diameters." Some states specify that officials should use an electroencephalogram, which monitors brain activity, or other medical technology to access inmates' consciousness.

107 These states are Alabama, Arizona, Arkansas, California, Florida, Georgia, Idaho, Kentucky, Missouri, Nebraska, Ohio, Oklahoma, Tennessee, and Virginia.

108 Jody Lyneé Madeira, "The Ghosts in the 'Machinery of Death': The Rhetoric of Mistake in Lethal Injection Reform," in *Law's Mistakes*, edited by Austin Sarat, Lawrence Douglas, and Martha Umphrey (Amherst: University of Massachusetts Press, 2016), 98.

109 In addition to using new drugs over the last decade, states also searched for new sources of drugs. With major manufacturers unwilling to provide lethal injection drugs, states turned to compounding pharmacies. Compounding pharmacies make drugs in small batches and are not subject to strict regulation. In 2018, at least ten states sourced their drugs from compounding pharmacies. On occasion, states have stopped all executions because pharmacies provided contaminated drugs, and state inspectors have found that compounding pharmacies often adopt unsafe and unsanitary practices. In order to shield compounding pharmacies from public pressure to stop supplying lethal injection drugs, many states have enacted secrecy statutes to conceal their identity. Barri Dean, "What Are Those Ingredients You Are Mixing Up behind Your Veil?," *Howard Law Journal* 62, no. 1 (2018).

110 Robin Konrad, *Behind the Curtain: Secrecy and the Death Penalty in the United States* (Washington, DC: Death Penalty Information Center, 2018).

111 In January 2014, a quarter-century after Dennis McGuire brutally raped and killed eight-months-pregnant Joy Stewart, it took roughly twenty-five minutes for Ohio to kill him. It was the longest of the fifty-three executions Ohio had conducted since it resumed lethal injection in 1999. For ten minutes, McGuire intermittently

gasped and snorted for air. Donald Morgan, the warden of Southern Ohio Correctional Facility, wrote, immediately after overseeing the execution, "The process worked very well." Later in the month, on reviewing the lethal injection as per standard procedure, Special Assistant Joseph Andrews found that everything in the execution went according to plan. Advocates called for a moratorium on the death penalty, in vain. Josh Sweigart, "Warden Says Execution Went as Planned," *Dayton Daily News*, February 5, 2014.

112 519 S.W.3d 550.

113 In 2011, Delaware also allowed one hour. In 2014, Louisiana allowed one hour.

114 These states are Arkansas, Delaware, Florida, Idaho, Kentucky, Louisiana, Oklahoma, and South Dakota.

115 Alabama, Arizona, Georgia, Indiana, Missouri, Nebraska, Nevada, North Carolina, Pennsylvania, Texas, Utah, Virginia, and Washington.

116 Alabama, Florida, Indiana, and Oklahoma.

117 The invasive surgery, in which officials place a central venous line by cutting away the inmate's flesh, has fallen out of favor in the medical community. Most central lines are placed today via the Seldinger technique, a safety enhancement over the previous "cutdown" technique. Ari D. Leib, Bryan S. England, and John Kiel, "Central Line," in *StatPearls* (Treasure Island, (FL: StatPearls, 2021. The cutdown procedure is so gruesome that Texas (as of 2005), Delaware (as of 2011), and Ohio and Oklahoma (both as of 2014) have explicitly forbidden it in their executions.

118 Idaho, Kentucky, Louisiana, and Mississippi.

119 The nineteen states are Alabama, Arkansas, California, Delaware, Florida, Georgia, Idaho, Kentucky, Missouri, Nebraska, North Carolina, Ohio, Oklahoma, South Dakota, Tennessee, Texas, Utah, Virginia, and Washington.

120 The thirteen states are Alabama, Arkansas, Florida, Georgia, Idaho, Missouri, Nebraska, North Carolina, Ohio, Tennessee, Texas, Virginia, and Washington.

121 Oklahoma has prescribed five minutes; California, Delaware, South Dakota, and Utah have prescribed ten minutes; Kentucky has prescribed twenty.

122 These states are Arizona, California, Delaware, Idaho, Indiana, Kentucky, Louisiana, Mississippi, Ohio, Oklahoma, Pennsylvania, South Dakota, Virginia, and Washington.

123 In January 2014, Ohio was unable to obtain pentobarbital for its preferred protocol and instead drew on its menu of options, selecting a novel combination of midazolam and another sedative, hydromorphone, to kill Dennis McGuire. In July, Arizona encountered a pentobarbital shortage, and for the execution of Joseph Wood it turned to midazolam and hydromorphone as well. McGuire's and Wood's executions lasted 24 and 117 minutes, respectively, and were widely recognized as botches.

124 In the eighteenth century, maintaining this secrecy took the form of placing hoods over the inmates' heads to hide their contortions. With the advent of the electric chair in 1890, it took the form of conducting midnight executions deep behind the walls of state prisons. Richard C. Dieter, "Methods of Execution and

Their Effect on the Use of the Death Penalty in the United States Symposium: The Lethal Injection Debate: Law and Science," *Fordham Urban Law Journal* 35, no. 4 (2008): 791.

125 According to Stephen E. Smith, states tend to implement "minor reforms" after botches. Stephen Eliot Smith, "Going through All These Things Twice: A Brief History of Botched Executions," *Otago Law Review* 12, no. 4 (2009): 777–828.

126 Denno, "Lethal Injection Quandary," 117.

127 This assertion is backed by scholars like Madeira. Madeira states that "rapid innovation also intensifies organizational stress, increasing the likelihood of the very mistakes that reforms purportedly reduce," and as a result, capital punishment by lethal injection is characterized by frequent reform and has become engulfed in a "culture of mistake." Madeira, "Ghosts," 83–84.

128 James C. Feldman, "Nothing Less Than the Dignity of Man: The Eighth Amendment and State Efforts to Reinstitute Traditional Methods of Execution," *Washington Law Review* 90, no. 3 (2015): 1313–48. Maurice Chammah, Andrew Cohen, and Eli Hagar, "After Lethal Injection," The Marshall Project, June 1, 2015, www.themarshallproject.org/.

129 Feldman, "Nothing Less," 1331–36.

130 Joseph Choi, "DeWine Says Lethal Injection 'Impossible' Option for Ohio Executions," *The Hill*, December 8, 2020.

131 "Ohio Governor Mike DeWine Calls Lethal Injection a Practical Impossibility, Says State Will Not Execute Anyone in 2021," Death Penalty Information Center, December 15, 2020, https://deathpenaltyinfo.org/.

132 Sarat et al., *Gruesome Spectacles*, 7; David Garland, *Peculiar Institution: America's Death Penalty in an Age of Abolition* (Cambridge, MA: Belknap Press of Harvard University Press, 2010): 183.

133 Dieter, "Methods of Execution," 798.

13

Deterrence and the Death Penalty

A False Promise

MICHAEL L. RADELET

Until the mid-1980s or so, general deterrence was the primary justification offered by proponents for retaining the death penalty in the United
States. General deterrence is the idea that *convicted* offenders should be
punished to discourage *potential* offenders from committing the same
sort of criminal offense.[1] It is part of a larger cost-benefit analysis that
potential murderers allegedly calculate: whatever potential benefits they
may derive from killing others are outweighed by the potential risks and
costs. The argument has also been applied to drug crimes (for which the
death penalty is authorized in thirty-three countries) and terrorism,[2] but
in this essay I will focus on the threat and/or use of the death penalty for
criminal homicide, which is the only crime for which inmates are sitting
on death row in the United States today.

In early 2020, after my home state of Colorado became the twenty-
second state (plus Washington, D.C.) to abolish the death penalty,[3]
death remained a possible punishment for the most aggravated forms of
murder in twenty-eight states and in cases under the jurisdictions of the
U.S. military and the U.S. government. In addition, all U.S. jurisdictions
(except Alaska)[4] have provisions for a sentence of life in prison without
parole (LWOP) for those convicted of the most aggravated murders.[5]
In the many hours of debate over the abolition bill in the Colorado legislature, the possibility of deterrence was barely mentioned, and even
when it was, the speakers almost always pointed to their "gut feelings"
rather than to empirical research.[6] With LWOP, regardless of whether
or not the death penalty stands as a legal punishment, the convicted
offender will die in prison, so the fuss about the death penalty is about
when and how.

Colorado is bordered by six states that retain the death penalty: Wyoming, Nebraska, Kansas, Oklahoma, Arizona, and Utah. Therefore, since in Colorado the mandatory penalty for first-degree murder is LWOP rather than execution, one would expect that people contemplating a capital murder in those six states would come to Colorado to commit their crimes. Yet, as least so far, no offenders from those six states have come to Colorado to commit their murders in order to escape their own state's execution gurney.

General Principles of Deterrence

According to the logic of general deterrence, an unknown number of people would commit a capital offense if the maximum punishment was a prison sentence, but they would not do it if they faced the death penalty. It is a difficult assertion to measure, since instead of modeling why people behave in certain ways, we are trying to understand why they do not. And the reasons that most people do not commit mass murders or rape murders, or murders of police officers or other aggravated murders, have little or nothing to do with the criminal law. In other words, even if murder was completely legal, most people would still *not* kill.

In a broad sense, deterrence theory argues that the deterrent effect of punishment is a function of three main elements: certainty, celerity, and severity. *Certainty* means that people do not violate laws if they think that they will be caught and punished. Regardless of the fine or punishment, drivers do not speed if they see a police officer in the rearview mirror and college students do not cheat on exams if they know that the professor is watching. The low probability of death (that is, low level of certainty) may explain why death as a punishment not only fails to deter at least some potential murderers, but also fails to deter workers who perform other dangerous jobs, or cigarette smokers, or skydivers. Logging workers have the highest death rates of any occupational class in the United States; those who work in the fishing industry or as pilots or navigators also have high death rates.[7] Clearly, the perceived benefits of the (legal) activity exceed the perceived risks. A rational bank robber who carries a gun might see the risks of death (ranging from being shot by the victim or by bystanders or by the police up to death on the gurney), low though they may be, as simply occupational hazards.[8]

Celerity refers to the elapsed time between the commission of an offense and the administration of punishment. In theory, the more quickly a punishment is carried out, the greater its deterrent effect. It does no good to punish a dog for fouling the carpet several hours after the act. Smokers are not deterred by the threat of illness or death because they may believe that such negative effects are not only uncertain but will not be felt for many years.

Most relevant to the possible deterrent effect of the death penalty is *severity*. Here one hypothesizes that perceived increases in the severity of punishment directly increase the punishment's deterrent effect. I am more likely to return library books in a timely fashion if I know the fine for overdue books is five dollars per day rather than fifty cents per day. Libraries would no doubt have lower rates of overdue library books if dilatory borrowers were sent to the gallows.

The question of the deterrent effect of executions is not straightforward. Obviously, we would all cease speeding if the police had the authority to shoot us through the back window of the car. But the deterrence question hinges on deterring homicides not deterred by prison sentences. Further, the deterrent effect of a punishment is not a consistent direct effect of its severity. Increases in the severity of punishment have decreasing incremental deterrent effects. For example, if a library fine is one dollar per day, increasing it to two dollars will have a greater deterrent effect than increasing the fine from five to six dollars or from twenty to twenty-one dollars. Eventually, further increases in the severity of a punishment will no longer add to any deterrent benefits.[9] Increasing the fine to twenty-one dollars per day for overdue library books will not deter anyone who is not deterred by a twenty dollars per day fine. More simply, *if one wishes to deter another from sitting on a stove, medium heat works just as well as high heat.* When applied to the death penalty, we are not interested in the deterrent effect per se, but in the *marginal deterrent effect*—the effect on homicide rates over and above the effects of less severe punishment (i.e., LWOP).

This point is especially relevant to understanding the changing role of the deterrence argument in death penalty debates. LWOP as an alternative to the death penalty was virtually unheard of when I was born, when those spared the execution chamber might be paroled in ten or fifteen years.[10] The crucial question today is whether the death penalty has marginal deterrent effects *over and above* the deterrent effects of LWOP.

Another point central to deterrence theory is that potential offenders must have some idea of the odds that they will get caught and the odds that they might be executed. Yet, no systematic interviews of death row inmates (or murderers in general) have been conducted that might reveal what they were thinking at the time of the crime. In my own observations, having spent time with roughly two hundred death row inmates, very few knew when they got out of bed on the day of the murder that sent them to death row that on that day, they would kill someone. If they had, more would have devised better methods to avoid arrest, much less avoid the use of lethal violence altogether. Many death row inmates are beset with different types of mental illnesses or are developmentally impaired, factors that might impede rational calculations. Deterrence theory would suggest that potential offenders are logical actors.

It is beyond question that at least some offenders would rather be dead than face a life term in prison. While precise figures are not available, some offenders facing the death penalty commit suicide (and more commit "suicide by cop" at the time of the crime), and others plead guilty at trial, waive mitigation, and even ask for the death penalty. Some on death row fire their attorneys and waive their appeals, effectively volunteering for death, preferring death to prison life. As of mid-2021, there have been 1,533 inmates put to death in the United States since 1976, of whom 149 (9.7%) forfeited their appeals.[11] Interestingly, 55.6 percent of those executed since 1976 were white (n=853), compared to 85.2 percent of those executed after dropping their appeals (n=127).[12]

In the past, the deterrence argument was the primary point made by death penalty supporters to justify their opinion. Writing in a special issue of the *Annals of the American Academy of Political and Social Science* devoted to the death penalty in 1952, criminologist Robert Caldwell asserted, "The most frequently advanced and widely accepted argument in favor of the death penalty is that the threat of its infliction deters people from committing capital offenses."[13] More recently, a 1986 Gallup poll "found 61% of the public saying the death penalty would deter people from committing murder."[14]

By October 2014, only about 6 percent of the death penalty's supporters offered deterrence as the rationale for their stand.[15] Clearly, a major
factor in the declining support for the death penalty over the past four
decades, measured in 2019 at 36 percent in support (in contrast to 60%
who support life imprisonment),[16] is the rapid plunging of support for
the deterrence argument.[17]

It is also theoretically possible that instead of deterrence, executions
have the opposite effect and actually tend to (slightly) increase homicide rates. This possibility, called the "brutalization hypothesis," suggests that by taking a life, the state is sending a message to all citizens
that killing people under some circumstances can be justified. The state
is saying that some people "deserve" to die. As Cesare Beccaria wrote in
1794, "The example of atrocity that the death penalty presents . . . does
not make it useful . . . laws designed to temper human conduct should
not enhance a savage example which is all the more baneful when the
legally sanctioned death is inflicted deliberately and ceremoniously. To
me it is an absurdity that the law which expresses the common will
and detests and punishes homicide should itself commit one."[18] The
support for this hypothesis is modest, but like with studies investigat-
ing any deterrence effects, it is abundant.[19] To overstate just a bit, the
executioners' deterrent message, "Respect life or we will kill you," may
be misunderstood.

Some Examples of Research on General Deterrence

Scores of researchers, including such eminent criminologists as Edward
Sutherland[20] and Thorsten Sellin,[21] have examined the possibility that
the death penalty has a greater deterrent effect on homicide rates than
alternative punishments.[22] These studies typically look at homicide rates
over time to see if they vary with the number of executions, or compare
homicide rates in similar jurisdictions with and without the death penalty. Overall, the vast majority of deterrence studies have failed to support the hypothesis that the death penalty is a more effective deterrent
to criminal homicides than imprisonment. As two of this country's most
experienced deterrence researchers concluded after their review of the
scholarship, "The empirical evidence does not support the belief that
capital punishment was an effective deterrent for murder in years past.

Nor is there any indication that returning to our past execution practices would have any deterrent impact on the current homicide problem."[23]

On the other hand, some econometric studies have claimed to find deterrent effects,[24] but these studies have been sharply criticized and, most criminologists would say, discredited. In the first decade of the twenty-first century, there was a resurgence of econometric studies that purported to find deterrent effects.[25] To give a bit of the flavor of some of the problems with these studies, consider three.

One example of these recent studies was published by Dale Cloninger and Roberto Marchesini.[26] Cloninger is no stranger to deterrence debates. In 1977 he published a study using 1960 data from forty-eight states and concluded that each execution deterred 560 murders (an assertion that many scholars would find preposterous on its face).[27] Later, his research was thoroughly discredited,[28] but to this day, Professor Cloninger has never retracted his conclusions.

Cloninger and Marchesini began their 2001 paper by observing that appellate courts permitted only three executions in Texas in 1996 (in the prior three years, Texas averaged seventeen executions per year). In 1997, after judicial questions were settled, Texas executed thirty-seven inmates. Their calculations led the authors to conclude that the paucity of executions in 1996 caused some 249 more homicides in the state than would have occurred had executions continued unabated. Exactly how the deterrence process supposedly works is not specified; readers were left to assume that executions deter not only capital murders but also all other types of criminal homicide. These results were challenged by Jonathan Sorensen, who obtained the original data set from Professor Cloninger and reanalyzed it. He found that "Cloninger and Marchesini's erroneous findings stem from three sources: failure to consider historical trends in the relationship between U.S. and Texas homicide rates, failure to account for reporting bias in the U.S. homicide data, and failure to utilize a localized composite crime index as the portfolio against which to measure changes in Texas homicides."[29]

A second group of researchers purporting to find a deterrent effect includes Paul Rubin and Hashem Dezhbakhsh at Emory University in Atlanta, and their former student Joanna Shepherd. Their studies conclude that each execution deters eighteen murders,[30] or three murders in a second study;[31] that one less murder is committed for every 2.75 years' reduction in the length of stay on death row;[32] and that the moratorium on executions in the United States between 1967 and 1976 led to substantially higher homicide rates.[33] This body of scholarship is curious not only because the number of homicides deterred varies widely from study to study, but also in its finding of the *types* of homicides that are deterred.

Joanna Shepherd found that the homicides deterred by executions are not the premeditated or felony murders that are most likely to send people to the execution chamber, but domestic homicides that most often occur at moments of passion.[34] This finding is in direct contradiction to a basic tenet of deterrence theory that holds that the homicides that are easiest to deter are the most premeditated. Again, like many of the studies done by other econometricians, no theoretical explanation is offered that might explain these strange patterns.

A third econometric study purporting to find a deterrent effect was published by Naci Mocan and his student, Kaj Gittings. This paper is worth special study not only because of its widespread circulation by death penalty proponents, but also because of its lack of theoretical content and blatant errors in measurement and analysis. The authors conclude,

> This paper uses a data set that consists of the entire history of 6,143 death sentences between 1977 and 1997 in the United States to investigate the impact of capital punishment on homicide. We merge this data set with state panels that include crime and deterrence measures as well as state characteristics. Our data set allows us not only to analyze the impact of executions, but also for the first time in the literature, the impact of commutations as well as total removals from death row on criminal activity. . . . We find a significant relationship between the execution, removal and commutation rates and the rate of homicide. Each additional execution decreases homicides by about 5, and each additional commutation increases homicides by the same amount, while one additional removal from death row generates one additional homicide. . . . Executions, commutations and removals have no impact on robberies, burglaries, assaults or motor-vehicle thefts.[35]

This study first came to light in an article in the *Washington Post*.[36] Titled "Murderous Pardons?," the article stated that Mocan and Gittings had examined the effects of executions and the "pardons" of 123 death row inmates from 1977 to 1997. They concluded that each execution leads to five or six fewer homicides and every three "pardons" lead to 1.5 additional homicides.

In reality, no death row inmates were "pardoned" over this time period, and as of mid-2021, only one death row inmate had been pardoned in the previous forty years.[37] Yet, the initial draft of the Mocan and Gittings paper was titled "Pardons, Executions, and Homicide." The theoretical link between the grant of a "pardon" (or commutation) and the decision to kill is not developed by Mocan, perhaps because his use of the term *pardon* indicates some lack of understanding about criminal behavior and the criminal justice system. It is totally unclear, for example, why a member of the general public is going to go out and kill someone if a governor commutes a death sentence because of doubts about a prisoner's sanity or guilt. This is particularly true in the bulk of commutation cases that rarely attract more than a short article in the back pages of the local newspaper. How many potential murders know the odds that a death sentence will be commuted?

The confusion is in part caused by Mocan's misinterpretation of commutation data gathered by the Bureau of Justice Statistics (BJS),[38] and his use of the terms *pardon* and *commutation* as synonymous.[39] BJS collects commutation data from states, but those reporting it often confuse judicial commutations with gubernatorial commutations. Even after I alerted Mocan to this issue and gave him the name of the person at the Bureau of Justice Statistics who collects the data and could educate him about their flaws, he declined to investigate the issue.

UCLA statistics professor Richard Berk reexamined the data used in this study and concluded,

A number of papers have recently appeared claiming to show that in the United States executions deter serious crimes. There are many statistical problems with the data analyses reported. This paper addresses the problem of "influence," which occurs when a very small and atypical fraction of the data dominate the statistical results. The number of executions by state and year is the key explanatory variable, and most states in most years execute no one. A very few states in particular years execute more than 5 individuals. Such values represent about 1% of the available observations. Re-analysis of the existing data are presented showing that claims of deterrence are a statistical artifact of this anomalous 1%.[40]

This critique has been available since early 2004, but Professor Mocan has not responded to it, suggesting that he has not found error in Professor Berk's work. Unfortunately, Professor Mocan has also been silent as various pro–death penalty groups circulate his work.[41]

In a more recent paper, Mocan and one of his students, Laura Argys, examined death sentences between 1973 and 1997, "including 113 cases in which the governor commuted the sentence."[42] In this paper he continued to use the same flawed clemency data; in reality, there were only thirty-five commutations during this time period. Mocan reports that "if the governor was a woman, the probability that an inmate's death sentence would be commuted increased by 34 percentage points."[43] In fact, no female governor has ever commuted a post-*Furman* death sentence.[44]

Evaluations by Groups of Experts

Studying the deterrence issue can be challenging. Some methodologies are relatively simple, such as comparing homicide rates in states with the death penalty to those where it has been banned.[45] Here the data are clear and are easy to interpret, and they have consistently shown that states without the death penalty, in general, have lower homicide rates than states that allow or use it. However, there are many other differences between the two categories of states, so while this body of research supports the assertion that the death penalty does not have deterrent effects stronger than imprisonment, it does not definitively prove it.

An alternative methodology, pioneered by Isaac Ehrlich in the 1970s, uses sophisticated econometric methods to compare homicide rates in abolitionist and retentionist jurisdictions, or in one jurisdiction before and after the death penalty has been permissible within its borders.[46] This study was subjected to numerous criticisms,[47] although both the original paper and the criticisms are highly technical, statistically sophisticated, and difficult or impossible for nonexperts to understand. One option is to look at what various groups of "experts" have concluded about the body of deterrence studies.[48] I will review four such groups; the last is the most important by far.

Police Chiefs

A 2009 study by the Death Penalty Information Center surveyed five hundred randomly selected police chiefs from around the United States to ascertain what they thought about the death penalty (and other issues). The report found that "the nation's police chiefs rank the death penalty last in their priorities for effective crime reduction. The officers do not believe the death penalty acts as a deterrent to murder, and they rate it as one of most inefficient uses of taxpayer dollars in fighting crime." Only 37 percent of the respondents agreed that "the death penalty significantly reduces the number of homicides," while 32 percent agreed that "the death penalty is one of the most important law enforcement tools." Only 24 percent agreed with a key assumption of deterrence theorists: "Murderers think about the range of possible punishments before committing homicides."[49]

Radelet and Akers

In 1996, Radelet and Akers surveyed some of the top criminologists in the United States: sixty-seven current and former presidents of the top three criminology professional organizations—the American Society of Criminology, the Academy of Criminal Justice Sciences, and the Law and Society Association.[50] The respondents were not asked to disclose their personal opinions about the wisdom of the death penalty, but instead, "on the basis of their knowledge of the literature and research in criminology," to share their evaluations of the research on deterrence. Eleven questions were used, and with all the measures, the overwhelming majority (roughly 85–90%) of the experts rejected the idea that the death penalty offered significant marginal deterrent effects. For example, only 4.5 percent of the respondents agreed with the statement "Overall, over the last 20 years, the threat or use of the death penalty in the United States has been a stronger deterrent to homicide than the threat or use of long (or life) prison sentences."[51]

Radelet and Laycock

Given the importance of the deterrence question, in 2009 Radelet and Traci Laycock conducted a similar study to see if the results could be replicated with a slightly different group of respondents.[52] The study was

conducted by sending questionnaires to the most eminent criminologists in the country, including fellows of the American Society of Criminology, winners of the American Society of Criminology's prestigious
Sutherland Award, and presidents of the American Society of Criminology who were not surveyed in the 1996 project. A total of seventy-nine
questionnaires were returned, for a response rate of 84 percent. Again,
we used a dozen questions to measure their thoughts on the deterrence
research, all of which were identical or quite similar to the questions
used in the 1996 study.

The results were quite consistent with the earlier study. Here, just
over 90 percent of the respondents disagreed or strongly disagreed with
the assertion that the threat or use of the death penalty in the United
States has been a stronger deterrent to homicide than the threat or use
of long (or life) prison sentences. Other questions found very weak, if
any, support for the deterrence hypothesis. "In short," the authors conclude, "the consensus among criminologists is that the death penalty
does not add any significant deterrent effect above that of long-term
imprisonment."[53]

The National Academy of Sciences: The Final(?) Word on the Deterrence Issue

Perhaps the final word on the deterrence question was delivered in
two reports by the National Academy of Sciences, the premier body of
scholars in the United States, if not the world.[54] The lead author on the
first report, released in 1978, was Lawrence R. Klein, who had just completed a term as president of the American Economic Association and
would go on to win a Nobel Prize in Economic Science in 1980.[55] The
authors focused on the work of Isaac Ehrlich, whose 1975 study purporting to find that each execution deterred eight homicides had been
widely circulated and used as a justification for the reintroduction of the
death penalty after it had been invalidated by the U.S. Supreme Court
in 1972.[56] The panel found a number of errors in the Ehrlich study, concluding that they found it "unthinkable" to base policy decisions about
the death penalty on this work. "In short, we see too many plausible
explanations for his finding a deterrent effect other than the theory that
capital punishment deters murder."[57]

A second and more comprehensive review of the deterrence literature was issued by another panel of the National Academy of Sciences
in 2012.[58] Their 123-page report reviews different methodologies and
studies that have been employed to study deterrence, and the limits and
challenges of each approach. They determined: "The committee con-
cludes that research to date on the effect of capital punishment on homicide is *not informative* about whether capital punishment decreases,
increases, or has no effect on homicide rates. Therefore, the committee
recommends that these studies not be used to inform deliberations requiring judgments about the effect of the death penalty on homicide.
Consequently, claims that research demonstrates that capital punishment decreases or increases the homicide rate by a specified amount or
has no effect on the homicide rate should not influence policy judgments
about capital punishment."[59] In short, there is no credible evidence that
the death penalty deters more homicides than alternative punishments
of long prison sentences.

Conclusion

Those who continue to believe that the death penalty exerts significantly
more deterrent effects than prison terms are not alone in retaining beliefs that are counter to empirical evidence. For example, some continue
to believe that there is no climate change, that ex-president Trump
won the 2020 election, that vaccines for COVID-19 are more dangerous
than the disease itself, and/or that President Obama was born in Kenya.
Justifying the death penalty on deterrence grounds is more polite than
justifying it on retributive grounds. Saying we do not like to execute
people but we simply *have to* so we can lower the homicide rate is more
polite than saying that we need to execute prisoners solely because of
our unadulterated hatred for them, and LWOP does not make them suffer enough.

We must leave it to our descendants to determine when the arguments over the alleged deterrent effect of the death penalty ended, but
we can at least say that a "crushing blow" to the adherents of the argument was delivered by the National Academy of Sciences in their 2012
report.[60] Since that study was published there have been very few new
deterrence studies published, and none (at least in major outlets) that

have offered data that allegedly show that executing offenders has a positive deterrent effect. In criminology, the question of the deterrent effect of the death penalty has become, at least for now, a nonissue.

Notes

1 On the other hand, specific deterrence, which holds that an offender does not repeat the criminal act because he or she does not want to be punished again, is not relevant to the death penalty debate. Specific deterrence requires a cognitive calculation by the potential offender, and none of us can accomplish this after death. Executed offenders do not commit new crimes because they are incapacitated, not because they have been deterred.

2 Jeffrey Fagan, "Deterrence and the Death Penalty in International Perspective," in *Moving Away from the Death Penalty: Arguments, Trends, and Perspectives*, ed. Roger Hood and Carolyn Hoyle (New York: United Nations, 2015), 84–99.

3 In March 2022, Virginia became the twenty-third. Hailey Fuchs, "Virginia Becomes the First Southern State to Abolish the Death Penalty," *New York Times*, March 25, 2021, A20.

4 The maximum prison term in Alaska is ninety-nine years, which, in effect, is LWOP.

5 "LWOP is a sentencing alternative in all 28 states that practice the death penalty, in addition to the federal government and U.S. Military. Of the 22 states that do not practice the death penalty, Alaska is the only state that does not permit life without parole as a possible sentence." "Life without Parole," Death Penalty Information Center, https://deathpenaltyinfo.org/. The only way to reduce a LWOP sentence is through the power of executive clemency. In some jurisdictions, those convicted of first-degree murder face a *mandatory* sentence of LWOP; the trial judge does not have the discretion to impose any lesser punishment.

6 I attended all these hearings; this assertion is based on my observations.

7 Andy Kiersz and Madison Huff, "The 34 Deadliest Jobs in America," *Business Insider*, June 2, 2020. https://www.businessinsider.com/.

8 "In 2008, 64% of all homicides were cleared, compared to 72% in 1980." Alexia Cooper and Erica L. Smith, *Homicide Trends in the United States, 1980–2008*, NCJ 236018 (Washington, DC: Bureau of Justice Statistics, November 2011), 31, https://bjs.ojp.gov/. Arguably, the best way to reduce the homicide rate would be to increase the certainty of apprehension, such as by employing more cold-case detectives to investigate unsolved homicides. This would have the added benefit of rendering some peace to more of the families of victims.

9 In general, the certainty of punishment is a more effective deterrent than severity. As two leading researchers conclude, "In particular, there is little evidence that increases in the severity of punishment yield strong marginal deterrent effects; further, credible arguments can be advanced that current levels of severity cannot be

justified by their social and economic costs and benefits." Steven N. Durlauf and Daniel S. Nagin, "The Deterrent Effect of Imprisonment," in *Controlling Crime: Statistics and Tradeoffs*, ed. Philip J. Cook, Jens Ludwig, and Justin McCrary (Chicago: University of Chicago Press, 2011), 43. *See also* "Half of Murder Cases Were Unsolved in 2020," *Crime Report*, October 8, 2021, https://thecrimereport .org/; "Trends in Homicide": What You Need to Know," Council on Criminal Justice, December 2023, https://counciloncj.org.

10 G. I. Giarini and R. G. Farrow, "The Paroling of Capital Offenders," *Annals of the American Academy of Political and Social Science* 284 (1952): 84–95; "Year that States Adopted Life without Parole (LWOP) Sentencing," Death Penalty Information Center, https://deathpenaltyinfo.org.

11 Execution Database, Death Penalty Information Center, https://deathpenaltyinfo .org/.

12 These numbers are as of 2021. To my knowledge, no researchers have explored the question of why white prisoners are more likely than Black prisoners to give up their appeals.

13 Robert G. Caldwell, "Why Is the Death Penalty Retained?," *Annual Review of the American Academy of Political and Social Science* 284 (1952): 50–51.

14 Jeffrey M. Jones, "The Death Penalty," Gallup, August 30, 2002, https://news.gallup .com/.

15 "Death Penalty," Gallup, https://news.gallup.com/.

16 *Id.*

17 According to the Pew Research Center, in 2021 only 35% of those polled believed that the death penalty had a deterrent effect.

18 Cesare Beccaria, "On the Penalty of Death," in *Capital Punishment*, ed. Thorsten Sellin (New York: Harper and Row, 1967), 43.

19 *See, e.g.*, William Bailey, "Deterrence, Brutalization, and the Death Penalty: Another Examination of Oklahoma's Return to Capital Punishment," *Criminology* 36 (1998): 717–33; William G. Bowers, Glenn Pierce, and John F. McDevitt, *Legal Homicide: Death as Punishment in America, 1864–1982* (Boston: Northeastern University Press, 1984), 271–336; John K. Cochran, Mitchell B. Chamlin, and Mark Seth, "Deterrence or Brutalization? An Impact Assessment of Oklahoma's Return to Capital Punishment," *Criminology* 32 (1994): 107–34.

20 Edwin H. Sutherland, "Murder and the Death Penalty," *Journal of Criminal Law and Criminology* (1925): 522–29.

21 Thorsten Sellin, *The Death Penalty* (Philadelphia: American Law Institute, 1959).

22 For an overview of these studies, *see* Robert Angel, Samuel E. DeWitt, and Rose Bellandi, "Is Capital Punishment an Effective Deterrent for Murder? An Updated Review of Research and Theory," in *America's Experiment with Capital Punishment*, ed. James R. Acker, Robert M. Bohm, and Charles S. Lanier, 3rd ed. (Durham, NC: Carolina Academic Press, 2014), 271–88; Roger Hood and Carolyn Hoyle, *The Death Penalty: A Worldwide Perspective* (Oxford: Oxford University Press, 2015), 389–425; Raymond Paternoster, *Capital Punishment in America* (New

York: Lexington Books, 1991), 217–45; Ruth D. Peterson and William C. Bailey, "Is Capital Punishment an Effective Deterrent for Murder? An Examination of Social Science Research," in Acker, Bohm, and Lanier, *America's Experiment*, 243–70; Franklin E. Zimring and Gordon Hawkins, *Capital Punishment and the American Agenda* (New York: Cambridge University Press, 1986), 176–86.

23 Peterson and Bailey, "Is Capital Punishment an Effective Deterrent," 265.

24 The most widely circulated of these studies is Isaac Ehrlich, "The Deterrent Effect of Capital Punishment: A Question of Life and Death," *American Economic Review* 65 (1975): 397–417.

25 Some of these studies are reviewed and critiqued in Jeffrey Fagan, *Deterrence and the Death Penalty: A Critical Review of New Evidence* (Testimony to the New York State Assembly Standing Committee on Codes Assembly Standing Committee on the Judiciary and Assembly Standing Committee on Correction, January 21, 2005), https://files.deathpenaltyinfo.org/. Among both criminologists and economists, since 2000 there has been a noticeable decline in research that examines the deterrent effect of the death penalty.

26 Dale O. Cloninger and Roberto Marchesini, "Execution and Deterrence: A Quasi-Controlled Group Experiment," *Applied Economics* 33 (2001): 569–76.

27 Dale O. Cloninger, "Deterrence and the Death Penalty: A Cross Sectional Analysis," *Journal of Behavioral Economics* 6 (1977): 87–105.

28 Richard M. McGahey, "Dr. Ehrlich's Magic Bullet: Econometric Theory, Econometrics, and the Death Penalty," *Crime and Delinquency* 26 (1980): 485–502.

29 Jon Sorensen, "Execution and Deterrence? A Re-analysis of Cloninger and Marchesini Study," in *Lethal Injection: Capital Punishment in Texas during the Modern Era*, ed. Jon Sorenson and Rocky Leann Pilgrim (Austin: University of Texas Press, 2006).

30 Hashem Dezhbakhsh, Paul H. Rubin, and Joanna M. Shepherd, "Does Capital Punishment Have a Deterrent Effect? New Evidence from Post-moratorium Panel Data," *American Law and Economics Review* 5 (2003): 344–76.

31 Joanna M. Shepherd, "Murders of Passion, Execution Delays and the Deterrence of Capital Punishment," *Journal of Legal Studies* 33 (2004): 283–321.

32 *Id.*

33 Hashem Dezhbakhsh and Joanna M. Shepherd, "The Deterrent Effect of Capital Punishment: Evidence from a 'Judicial Experiment,'" *Economic Inquiry* 44 (2006): 512–35.

34 Shepherd, "Murders of Passion."

35 H. Naci Mocan and R. Kaj Gittings, "Getting Off Death Row: Commuted Sentences and the Deterrent Effect of Capital Punishment," *Journal of Law and Economics* 46 (2003): 474.

36 "Murderous Pardons?," *Washington Post*, January 20, 2002, B5. Later, one of the editors from the *Post* used this article to illustrate how newspapers sometimes publish "nonsense." George Lardner, "The Role of the Press in the Clemency Process," *Capital University Law Review* 31 (2002): 179–84.

37 That man is Earl Washington, whose death sentence was commuted in 1994, and who was eventually pardoned in 2000, well after the years studied by Mocan and Gittings. This glaring error is a good example of why academics need to take more care before circulating first (unrefereed) drafts of their work to newspapers.

38 For accurate data on commutations, *see* Michael L. Radelet and Barbara A. Zsembik, "Executive Clemency in Post-*Furman* Capital Cases," *University of Richmond Law Review* 27 (1993): 289–314, updated at "List of Clemencies since 1976," Death Penalty Information Center, https://deathpenaltyinfo.org/.

39 In the published version of the paper, Mocan changed the term *pardon* to *commutation*, with no explanation. No theoretical explanation is given for why either a pardon or commutation might affect homicide rates—only the term was changed. The published version continued to use the erroneous commutation data, and the authors failed to even acknowledge that the validity of the data had been challenged.

40 Richard Berk, "New Claims about Executions and General Deterrence: Déjà Vu All Over Again," *Journal of Empirical Legal Studies* 2 (2005): 303–30.

41 Other scholars, after more comprehensive reanalysis, have found more serious errors that further discredited the Mocan and Gittings work. John Donohue and Justin Wolfers, "Uses and Abuses of Empirical Evidence in the Death Penalty Debate," *Stanford Law Review* 58 (2005): 791–856; Jeffrey Fagan, "Death and Deterrence Redux: Science, Law, and Causal Reasoning on Capital Punishment," *Ohio State Journal of Criminal Law* 4 (2006): 255–320.

42 Laura M. Argys and H. Naci Mocan, "Who Shall Live and Who Shall Die? An Analysis of Prisoners on Death Row in the United States," *Journal of Legal Studies* 33 (2004): 255–82; Richard Morin, "Lame Ducks and the Death Penalty," *Washington Post* (Outlook section), December 15, 2002, B5.

43 *See* "List of Clemencies since 1976."

44 This conclusion comes from examining files I have collected of every case in which the death penalty was commuted in the United States since 1972, and the list of 294 death sentences that have been commuted since 1976. *See* Radelet and Zsembik, "Executive Clemency"; "List of Clemencies since 1976."

45 "Murder Rate of Death Penalty States Compared to Non-Death Penalty States," Death Penalty Information Center, https://deathpenaltyinfo.org/.

46 Isaac Ehrlich, "The Deterrent Effect of Capital Punishment: A Question of Life and Death," *American Economic Review* 65 (1975): 397–417.

47 *See, e.g.,* William J. Bowers and Glenn L. Pierce, "The Illusion of Deterrence in Isaac Ehrlich's Research on Capital Punishment," *Yale Law Journal* 85 (1975): 187–208.

48 For example, in 1990.

49 Death Penalty Information Center, *Smart on Crime: Reconsidering the Death Penalty in a Time of Economic Crisis* (Washington, DC: Death Penalty Information Center, October 2009), https://deathpenaltyinfo.org/.

50 Michael L. Radelet and Ronald L. Akers, "Deterrence and the Death Penalty: The Views of the Experts," *Journal of Criminal Law and Criminology* 87 (1996): 1–16. In 1984, eleven criminologists at the University of Florida (led by Radelet, who was then a member of the faculty) signed a statement stating, "As criminologists at the state's leading university, we feel a professional and ethical obligation to report that there is no credible scientific research that supports the contention that the threat or use of the death penalty is or has been a deterrent to homicide. Other justifications of capital punishment are possible. However, whether or not the death penalty reduces the homicide rate is an empirical question which cannot be answered on moral or political grounds. This question has been clearly answered by numerous research projects conducted over the last 50 years. This deterrence research does not provide a legitimate basis for our state's death penalty policy." The statement was published by several Florida newspapers and elicited a modest amount of hate mail. One newspaper published a long editorial responding to what they saw as our erroneous conclusion. "There Are Facts to Bolster View that Death Penalty Is Deterrent," *Florida Times Union*, September 7, 1984.

51 This is consistent with a 1989 policy position adopted by the American Society of Criminology, one of only two policy positions ever adopted in the history of that organization. "Be it resolved that because social science research has demonstrated the death penalty to be racist in application and social science research has found no consistent evidence of crime deterrence through execution, the American Society of Criminology publicly condemns this form of punishment, and urges its members to use their professional skills in legislatures and courts to seek a speedy abolition of this form of punishment." *See* "Policy Page," American Society of Criminology, https://asc41.com.

52 Michael L. Radelet and Traci L. Laycock, "Do Executions Lower Homicide Rates? The Views of Leading Criminologists," *Journal of Criminal Law and Criminology* 99 (2009):489–508.

53 *Id.* at 504.

54 "The National Academy of Sciences is a private, non-profit society of distinguished scholars. Established by an Act of Congress, signed by President Abraham Lincoln in 1863, the NAS is charged with providing independent, objective advice to the nation on matters related to science and technology. Scientists are elected by their peers to membership in the NAS for outstanding contributions to research. The NAS is committed to furthering science in America, and its members are active contributors to the international scientific community. Approximately 500 current and deceased members of the NAS have won Nobel Prizes." *See* "Mission," National Academy of Sciences, link no longer available.

55 Lawrence R. Klein, Brian Forst, and Victor Filatov, "The Deterrent Effect of Capital Punishment: An Assessment of the Evidence," in *Deterrence and Incapacitation: Estimating the Effects of Criminal Sanctions on Crime Rates* (Report of the Panel on Research and Deterrence), ed. Alfred Blumstein, Jacqueline Cohen, and Daniel Nagin (Washington, DC: National Academy of Sciences, 1978), 336–60.

56 *Furman v. Georgia*, 408 U.S. 238 (1972).

57 Klein, Forst, and Filatov, 358.

58 Daniel Nagin and John V. Pepper, eds., *Deterrence and the Death Penalty* (Washington, DC: Committee on Law and Justice, National Research Council of the National Academies, 2012).

59 *Id.* at 2 (my emphasis).

60 *Id.*

ACKNOWLEDGMENTS

The editors thank our essayists for sharing their keen insights regarding the inherent flaws in capital punishment. We are grateful to the staff of New York University Press for helping us turn a rough manuscript into a polished book, with a special thanks to assistant editor in chief Ilene Kalish and editorial assistant Priyanka Ray. Finally, we would like to thank our families for allowing us to devote our time and energy to yet another death penalty project.

MAYA PAGNI BARAK is Associate Professor of Criminology and Criminal Justice at the University of Michigan–Dearborn. She is co-author of *Defense: Inside the Lives of America's Death Penalty Lawyers*.

FRANK R. BAUMGARTNER is the Richard J. Richardson Distinguished Professorship in the Department of Political Science at UNC–Chapel Hill. He is the co-author of *Deadly Justice: A Statistical Portrait of the Death Penalty* and *The Decline of the Death Penalty and the Discovery of Innocence*.

JOHN D. BESSLER is a law professor at the University of Baltimore. He is the author of multiple books on the death penalty and the Eighth Amendment, including *The Death Penalty as Torture: From the Dark Ages to Abolition*; *Cruel and Unusual: The American Death Penalty and the Founders' Eighth Amendment*; *Kiss of Death: America's Love Affair with the Death Penalty*; *Legacy of Violence: Lynch Mobs and Executions in Minnesota*; and *Death in the Dark: Midnight Executions in America*. Bessler also served as the editor of Justice Stephen Breyer's 2016 book *Against the Death Penalty*.

RICHARD J. BONNIE is the Harrison Foundation Professor of Medicine and Law and Director of the Institute of Law, Psychiatry and Public Policy at the University of Virginia. He is widely considered to be one of the nation's leading scholars on the death penalty and mental illness.

MATTEA DENNEY is a 2022 graduate of Amherst College.

RICHARD C. DIETER is the former Executive Director of the Death Penalty Information Center. He has written over forty reports and articles on the death penalty. His most recent publication is *Battle Scars: Military*

Veterans and the Death Penalty: A Report by the Death Penalty Information Center.

JON B. GOULD is Dean of the School of Social Ecology at the University of California, Irvine. He is the co-author of *Defense: Inside the Lives of America's Death Penalty Lawyers*. Gould is also the author of *How to Succeed in College (While Really Trying): A Professor's Inside Advice; The Innocence Commission: Preventing Wrongful Convictions and Restoring the Criminal Justice System*; and *Speak No Evil: The Triumph of Hate Speech Regulation*.

NICOLAS GRABER-MITCHELL is a 2022 graduate of Amherst College.

GREENE KO is a 2022 graduate of Amherst College.

BHARAT MALKANI is a senior lecturer and Director of Teaching and Learning at the School of Law and Politics at Cardiff University. Prior to that, he was a legal researcher at the American Bar Association Juvenile Justice Center and was involved in appellate litigation against the juvenile death penalty. Malkani is the author of the recently published book *Slavery and the Death Penalty: A Study in Abolition*.

ROSE MROCZKA is a 2021 graduate of Amherst College.

NGOZI NDULUE clerked for the Honorable Eric L. Clay of the United States Court of Appeals for the Sixth Circuit before working as an assistant federal public defender, as a staff member at the Ohio Justice and Policy Center, and as Senior Director of Criminal Justice Programs at the NAACP. She presently serves as Director of Research and Special Projects at the Death Penalty Information Center. Ndulue was the lead author of *Enduring Justice: The Persistence of Racial Discrimination in the U.S. Death Penalty*, a report issued by the Death Penalty Information Center in 2020.

LAUREN PELOSI is a 2022 graduate of Amherst College.

MICHAEL L. RADELET is a professor in the Department of Sociology at the University of Colorado and a faculty affiliate at the University's

Institute of Behavioral Science. His research and writing touches on multiple issues involving capital punishment, including the question of whether the death penalty has a deterrent effect. His books include *The History of the Death Penalty in Colorado*; *In Spite of Innocence: Erroneous Convictions in Capital Cases* (with Hugo Adam Bedau and Constance E. Putnam); and *Executing the Mentally Ill: The Criminal Justice System and the Case of Alvin Ford* (with Kent S. Miller). He also served as the editor of *Facing the Death Penalty: Essays on a Cruel and Unusual Punishment* and was first author on two seminal articles on the death penalty and deterrence.

AUSTIN SARAT is the William Nelson Cromwell Professor of Jurisprudence and Political Science at Amherst College in Amherst, Massachusetts. He has written, co-written, or edited more than fifty books in the fields of law and political science, including *Gruesome Spectacles: Botched Executions and America's Death Penalty*.

LAURA SCHAEFER is a deputy federal public defender in the capital habeas unit of the Office of the Federal Public Defender for the Central District of California. Prior to that, she was a staff attorney and capital clemency counsel at the American Bar Association Death Penalty Representation Project. She previously worked as a post-conviction fellow with the Office of Capital Writs in Austin, Texas, where she represented condemned prisoners in their post-conviction appeals. Schaefer is the co-author of the book *Representing Death-Sentenced Prisoners in Clemency: A Guide for Practitioners* and the book chapter "Defense Lawyering and Wrongful Convictions" in *Examining Wrongful Convictions: Stepping Back, Moving Forward*.

RUSSELL STETLER served as the National Mitigation Coordinator in the Office of the Federal Public Defender in Oakland, California. He is the author of many articles on mitigation in capital murder cases, including "The Past, Present, and Future of the Mitigation Profession," "*Lockett v. Ohio* and the Rise of the Mitigation Specialists," and "The Mystery of Mitigation: What Jurors Need to Make a Reasoned Moral Response in Capital Sentencing."

SCOTT E. SUNDBY is a professor at the University of Miami School of Law. He is the author of *A Life and Death Decision: A Jury Weighs the Death Penalty* and multiple articles on the death penalty, including "War and Peace in the Jury Room: How Capital Juries Reach Unanimity" and "The Capital Jury and Empathy: The Problem of Worthy and Unworthy Victims."

ABOUT THE EDITORS

Todd C. Peppers is a political science professor in the Department of Public Affairs at Roanoke College as well as a visiting professor of law at the Washington and Lee School of Law. He is the co-author of *Crossing the River Styx: Memoir of a Death Row Chaplain, A Courageous Fool: Marie Deans and Her Struggle against the Death Penalty*, and *Anatomy of an Execution: The Life and Death of Douglas Christopher Thomas*.

Mary Welek Atwell is professor emeritus of Criminal Justice at Radford University. She is the author of multiple books and articles on capital punishment, including *An American Dilemma: International Law, Capital Punishment, and Federalism, Wretched Sisters: Gender and Capital Punishment, Evolving Standards of Decency: Popular Culture and Capital Punishment*, and *Equal Protection of the Law? Gender and Justice in the United States*.

Jamie Almallen is an assistant public defender in the Richmond Public Defender's Office.

abolition: 14, 130; juvenile death penalty, 46, 55–61, 63, 68; public opinion and, 16–18; state action, 74, 93, 130, 227, 263, 290
abuse, in defendants' lives, 55, 96, 97, 101, 103–106, 107–108, 112, 184, 233–234
addiction, 80, 96, 97, 103, 112–113, 181, 184, 225
African Americans. *See* race: discrimination and
aggravating circumstances, 75–76, 193; in cases against women, 95–96; mental illness, 105–106
Ake v. Oklahoma, 220
Alito, Samuel, 152
Allen, Wanda Jean, 101–102
American Bar Association (ABA): guidelines for capital defense, 181, 184; opposition to juvenile death penalty, 49; policy on mental illness, 77, 85
Antiterrorism and Effective Death Penalty Act (AEDPA), 204, 242–243, 246
arbitrariness, *See* death penalty: arbitrariness
Atkins v. Virginia, 57–58, 76
attorneys. *See* defense lawyers; prosecutors

Baldus Study, 157–158, 203–204
Barfield, Velma, 97–98
Barrett, Amy Coney, 154
Batson v. Kentucky, 222–223
Baze v. Reese, 265–266
Beccaria, Cesare, 294
Black, Hugo, 139–141

Blackmun, Harry, 148, 151
Brady Rule, 220
Brennan, William, 141, 149, 151
Breyer, Stephen, 141, 153, 158

Callins v. Collins, 151
Capital defense offices, 29, 201
capital juries: community conscience, 213–214, 227–228; death qualification, 223–226; diversity on, 221–223; non-unanimous jury, 228
Capital Jury Project, 193
capital punishment. *See* death penalty
capital trials: 27, 32, 183, 215, 227; expert witnesses, 220; guilt phase, 14; juveniles, 48; mitigation specialists, 219; penalty phase, 217, 219
childhood trauma. *See* abuse, in defendants' lives
clemency, 13, 111, 245; founders' intentions, 240; political factors, 241; president's role, 234, 238, 240; state authorities, 239–241, 246, 293
Cloninger, Dale, 295
Coker v. Georgia, 123, 150
Coleman, Lisa, 100–101
costs, 26, 39

death penalty: arbitrariness, 19, 30, 39, 57, 66, 74, 75, 101, 114, 129, 151, 158, 159, 161, 163, 191, 193, 197, 241; cost, 26, 39; decline in use of, viii, 2, 19–22, 200; geographical disparities, 19, 23, 30, 154, 201; mandatory, 13, 47, 73, 150, 159;

death penalty (cont.)
  moral arguments, 215; public support, 2, 17, 18, 19, 201, 227, 293; torture, 159, 161–162, 164; unconstitutional, 7, 45–48, 93, 95, 114, 122, 141, 154
Death Penalty Information Center, 192, 194, 299
defense lawyers, 2, 29, 73, 84, 179–188, 194, 200, 215–217, 226; competence, 28, 29, 109, 113, 180, 217–218, 238; post-conviction, 110–111
deterrence, 290, 291–292; arguments, vii, 27, 293–294, 301; studies, 294–297, 299–300
Dezhbakhsh, Hashem, 295
discretion, 47; in charging, 29; in execution process, 278–279; *Furman* and, 46, 192
Douglas, William O., 141–149

Eddings v. Oklahoma, 48–49, 197
Eighth Amendment (cruel and unusual punishment), 61, 74, 86, 122, 141, 144, 150, 155–156, 160, 162, 191, 214, 265
Erhlich, Isaac, 298
evolving standards of decency, 147–148, 156
execution: costs, 31, 34, 38; federal, 36, 233; methods, 3, 257, 279; numbers and rates, 200. *See also* lethal injection
exoneration, 14, 15, 160, 201, 215, 218

feminist criminological theory, 96–97
Ford v. Wainwright, 163
Fourteenth Amendment (equal protection of the law), 141–144, 155–156, 160, 162
Frankfurter, Felix, 142, 146
Furman v. Georgia, 7, 45–48, 114, 122, 141, 150, 191, 193, 214
future dangerousness, 205, 207; racial bias, 102–103

gender, 93–94, 112; gender bias, 97, 113, 114; gendered expectations for defendants, 95–97, 99, 106; for lawyers, 185

Giarratano, Joe, 79–84
Ginsburg, Ruth Bader, 65, 141
Gittings, Kaj, 295–298
Glossip v. Gross, 141, 152
Goldburg, Arthur, 149
Gorsuch, Neil, 159
Graham v Florida, 64
Gregg v. Georgia, 12, 32, 47, 93, 95, 122, 141, 150, 193, 214, 241, 242, 261

Hall v Florida, 148
Harbison v. Bell, 246, 247
Herrera v. Collins, 244–245, 247
Homicide rate, 295, 296, 301

innocence, 4, 7, 10, 28, 29, 220, 244–245, 258; media and, 16, 18; public opinion and, 8, 16–17, 23
intellectual disability, 55, 73, 76, 94, 98–99, 102, 113, 149, 198, 206, 293
International Covenant on Civil and Political Rights, 50
international law: juveniles and, 52, 58–59, 61–62; Supreme Court and, 53

Juvenile Death Penalty Initiative, 56
juveniles: arbitrary death penalty, 46, 55; death sentences, 142–144, 194; evolving standards of decency, 56, 60; exonerations, 54; racism, 53, 67–68, 126–127, 142–143; United States as outlier, 58–59

Kagan, Elena, 64
Kennedy, Anthony, 60, 148, 198
Kennedy v. Louisiana, 198

Leopold, Nathan, and Loeb, Richard, 205–206
lethal injection, 257–258, 277–278; drug protocol, 260, 261–264, 267, 268–269; history of, 262–264; problems, 257–260, 261, 266, 269–273, 275–276, 279
Lewis, Teresa, 98–99

life without parole (LWOP), 31, 33, 201, 205, 219, 290, 291; juveniles, 62–65, 67, 207
Lockett v. Ohio, 48, 148, 196–197, 206, 216–217
Lockett, Clayton, 270–271
lynching, 122, 125

Malvo, Lee Boyd, 59
Marchesini, Roberto, 295
Marshall, Thurgood, 141, 151
Marshall Hypothesis, 8
McGautha v. California, 150
McKleskey v. Kemp, 75, 123–124, 157–158
mental illness, 55, 99–100, 105–106, 107, 109–110, 157, 184, 233, 235, 293; competency, 79–82, 88–90; mitigating circumstance, 75–78, 216, 225, 227, 237–238
midazolam, 152, 258, 267
Mills v. Maryland, 148
mitigation, 77, 78, 101, 109, 181–183, 191–192, 198, 219, 221, 228, 293; evidence, 75–76, 184, 185, 204, 217, 218; factors, 193–195; funding, 201–202, 219; juveniles, 48
Mocan, Naci, 296–298
Model Penal Code, 78, 158, 193–195
Montgomery, Lisa, 93, 107–112, 233–234, 236–238, 248
Montgomery v. Louisiana, 64, 66, 207
Moore, Bobby, 206
Morgan v. Illinois, 223–225

Northam, Ralph, 1, 129

O'Connor, Sandra Day, 51, 62
originalism, 152

Panetti v. Quarterman, 87–89
Panetti v. Scott, 87–90
peremptory challenges, 222–223
Plantz, Marilyn, 98–99
plea bargains, 27, 35, 183

post-conviction proceedings, 84–86
Powell, Lewis, 49, 74, 158
Prejean, Sister Helen, 7
Proffitt v. Florida, 141
prosecutors, 96, 110; discretion, 124, 207; misconduct, 28, 160

race: discrimination and, 1, 18, 29–30, 120,202, 222; disparities, 123–125, 128, 129; gender and, 100, 101–103, 125; juvenile death penalty, 46, 53; Latinx, 121; Native American, 121; statistical evidence, 123–124, 158; Supreme Court and, 123
racial justice acts, 128–129
rehabilitation, 192, 196, 204, 207
Rehnquist, William, 51, 244
retribution, 27, 122
Rideau, Walter, 206–207
Riggs, Christina, 99–100
Roberts v. North Carolina, 12
Rompilla v. Beard, 199
Roper v. Simmons, 46, 52, 60–64, 68, 76, 161
Rubin, Paul, 295

Scalia, Antonin, 51, 62, 152
Sellin, Thorsten, 294
sentencing, 12–13, 75, 87, 90, 91, 113, 123, 125, 157–158, 183, 195, 215, 216–217, 223–226; aggravating and mitigating factors, 74, 78, 193, 201, 228, 237–238; future dangerousness, 102–103; juveniles, 64, 65, 68, 126–127; sentences overturned, 10, 128, 242; and sexual orientation, 100–101, 102
Shepherd, Joanna, 296
Shore, Anthony, 271–272
Sorenson, Jonathan, 295
Sotomayor, Sonia, 65, 111, 153
Stanford v. Kentucky, 51, 53, 56, 58
state court supervision of capital punishment, 75, 90–91

Stevens, John Paul, 51
Stevenson, Bryan, 208
Stewart, Potter, 150
Streib, Victor, 50–51
Sutherland, Edward, 294

Thompson v. Oklahoma, 50, 56
torture, 145–148; death penalty as, 8, 155, 159, 161–164
Trop v. Dulles, 147–148
Trump, Donald J., 93, 107, 111, 208, 233–235, 238, 248
Tucker, Karla Faye, 94, 103–104

United Nations Convention on the Rights of the Child, 52

Virginia death penalty, 1, 128, 227
voir dire, 225–226

Washington, Earl Jr., 1
White, Byron, 51
Wiggins v. Smith, 181, 199
Williams v. Taylor, 199
Witherspoon v. Illinois, 214
women: characteristics of offenders, 94, 96, 112–113, 125; gender bias, 93; number of executions, 94–95; theories of criminality, 96–97. *See also* gender
Woodson v. North Carolina, 12, 195
wrongful convictions, 1, 8, 16, 28, 36–37, 39, 54, 153, 160, 180, 201–202, 207
Wuornos, Aileen, 94, 103–106